ACCOUNTANTS'

HANDBOOK

ELEVENTH EDITION
2009 CUMULATIVE SUPPLEMENT

Update Service

BECOME A SUBSCRIBER!
Did you purchase this product from a bookstore?

If you did, it's important for you to become a subscriber. John Wiley & Sons, Inc. may publish, on a periodic basis, supplements and new editions to reflect the latest changes in the subject matter that you *need to know* in order to stay competitive in this ever-changing industry. By contacting the Wiley office nearest you, you'll receive any current update at no additional charge. In addition, you'll receive future updates and revised or related volumes on a 30-day examination review.

If you purchased this product directly from John Wiley & Sons, Inc., we have already recorded your subscription for this update service.

To become a subscriber, please call **1-877-762-2974** or send your name, company name (if applicable), address, and the title of the product to:

mailing address:	**Supplement Department**
	John Wiley & Sons, Inc.
	One Wiley Drive
	Somerset, NJ 08875
e-mail:	**subscriber@wiley.com**
fax:	**1-732-302-2300**

For customers outside the United States, please contact the Wiley office nearest you:

Professional & Reference Division
John Wiley & Sons Canada, Ltd.
22 Worcester Road
Etobicoke, Ontario M9W 1L1
CANADA
Phone: 416-236-4433
Phone: 1-800-567-4797
Fax: 416-236-4447
Email: canada@wiley.com

John Wiley & Sons, Ltd.
The Atrium
Southern Gate, Chichester
West Sussex PO 19 8SQ
ENGLAND
Phone: 44-1243-779777
Fax: 44-1243-775878
Email: customer@wiley.co.uk

John Wiley & Sons Australia, Ltd.
33 Park Road
P.O. Box 1226
Milton, Queensland 4064
AUSTRALIA
Phone: 61-7-3859-9755
Fax: 61-7-3859-9715
Email: brisbane@johnwiley.com.au

John Wiley & Sons (Asia) Pte., Ltd.
2 Clementi Loop #02-01
SINGAPORE 129809
Phone: 65-64632400
Fax: 65-64634604/5/6
Customer Service: 65-64604280
Email: enquiry@wiley.com.sg

ACCOUNTANTS' HANDBOOK

ELEVENTH EDITION
2009 CUMULATIVE SUPPLEMENT

LYNFORD GRAHAM

WILEY

John Wiley & Sons, Inc.

ABOUT THE EDITOR

Lynford Graham, CPA, PhD, CFE, is a Certified Public Accountant with more than 25 years of public accounting experience in audit practice and national policy development groups. He is currently Visiting Professor of Accountancy and Executive in Residence at Bentley University in Waltham, Massachusetts. He was a Partner and the Director of Audit Policy for BDO Seidman, LLP, and was a National Accounting & SEC Consulting Partner for Coopers & Lybrand, responsible for the technical issues research function and database, auditing research, audit automation, and audit sampling techniques. Prior to joining BDO Seidman LLP, Dr. Graham was an Associate Professor of Accounting and Information Systems and a Graduate Faculty Fellow at Rutgers University in Newark, New Jersey, where he taught primarily financial accounting courses. Dr. Graham is a member of the American Institute of Certified Public Accountants and a recent past member of the AICPA Auditing Standards Board. He is a Certified Fraud Examiner and a member of the Association of Certified Fraud Examiners. Throughout his career he has maintained an active profile in the academic as well as the business community. In 2002 he received the Distinguished Service Award of the Auditing Section of the AAA. His numerous academic and business publications span a variety of topical areas including information systems, internal controls, expert systems, audit risk, audit planning, fraud, sampling, analytical procedures, audit judgment, and international accounting and auditing. Dr. Graham holds an MBA in Industrial Management and PhD in Business and Applied Economics from the University of Pennsylvania (Wharton School).

ABOUT THE CONTRIBUTORS

Antonetti, Michael A., CPA, CMA, is a partner with Crowe Horwath LLP. Mr. Antonetti has over 20 years of experience providing assurance and business advisory services to clients in many industries including manufacturing, distribution, banking, professional services, transportation and hospitality. Mr. Antonetti's experience also includes assisting clients with merger, acquisition, and divestiture transactions and application of the related accounting standards. Mr. Antonetti also serves clients with international operations in Europe, Asia and North and South America.

Bahl, Yogash is a partner in our Deloitte Financial Advisory Services LLP practice and is the Northeast leader of the Antifraud Programs and Controls practice. Mr. Bahl has more than 14 years of experience in performing forensic investigations and providing dispute consulting services. He also provides advisory services to companies in various industries with respect to structuring collaboration, distribution, co-promotion, and licensing agreements. Mr. Bahl earned his MBA in Finance and Statistics and BS in Accounting and International Business from New York University's Stern School of Business.

Beaton, Neil J., CPA/ABV, CFA, ASA, is the partner in charge of Grant Thornton LLP's national valuation services group. He has over 25 years of experience analyzing both closely held and publicly traded companies. Mr. Beaton has appeared as an expert witness in numerous courts across the country, lectures at local universities, is an instructor for the AICPA's business valuation courses, and speaks nationally on business valuation topics with a special emphasis on early-stage and high-technology companies. He has served on the AICPA's National Accreditation Commission and the FASB's Valuation Resource Group. He has a Bachelor of Arts degree in Economics from Stanford University and a Masters of Business Administration in Finance from National University. In addition to his formal education, Mr. Beaton is a Certified Public Accountant, accredited in Business Valuation, a Chartered Financial Analyst, and an Accredited Senior Appraiser in business valuation from the American Society of Appraisers.

Grant Thornton LLP is the U.S. member firm of Grant Thornton International, one of the six global accounting, tax, and business advisory organizations. Through member firms in 112 countries, including 51 offices in the United States, the partners and employees of Grant Thornton member firms provide personalized attention and the highest quality service to public and private clients around the globe. Visit Grant Thornton LLP at www.GrantThornton.com.

Epstein, Barry Jay, PhD, CPA, is a partner at Russell Novak & Company, LLP. With almost 40 years' experience in the public accounting profession as auditor and technical director/partner for several national and local firms, Dr. Epstein's current practice is concentrated on providing technical consultations to CPA firms and corporations on U.S. GAAP and IFRS accounting and financial reporting matters; U.S. and international auditing standards; financial analysis; forensic accounting investigations; and corporate governance. A widely published authority on accounting and auditing, his current publications include *Wiley GAAP*, now in its 22nd edition, and *Wiley IFRS*, for both of which he is the lead coauthor. He previously chaired the Audit Committee of the AICPA's Board of Examiners, responsible for the Uniform CPA Examination, and has served on other professional panels at state and national levels. Dr. Epstein holds degrees from DePaul University (Chicago—BSC, accounting and finance, 1967), University of Chicago (MBA, Economics and Industrial Relations, 1969), and University of Pittsburgh (PhD Information Systems and Finance, 1979).

Gini, Ernest J., CPA, CGFM, is a partner with Macias Gini & O'Connell LLP (MGO) with 33 years of experience as a CPA. An expert in the field of governmental and nonprofit accounting, Mr. Gini was appointed to the 2006–2007 AICPA Virtual Grassroots Panel, formerly known as the Group of 100. He is a Certified Government Financial Manager with the Association of Government Accountants and has conducted seminars for public finance officials on the New Financial Reporting Model (GASB 34), Changes to OMB Circular A-133, Accounting for Redevelopment Agencies, Single Audit Applications, Changes in Government Auditing Standards, GASB Statement Updates, Program-Specific Audits, and other topics. He also served on the GASB Advisory Committee on the *User Guide to Local Government Financial Statements* and was a contributor to *What You Should Know about Your Local Government's Finances: A Guide to Financial Statements*.

Hydoski, Frank is a director in the New York Forensics & Dispute Services practice of Deloitte Financial Advisory Services LLP. He is responsible for developing new products and approaches in forensic accounting and investigations for clients in both the private and public sector. Mr. Hydoski is internationally recognized for his work in complex investigations, especially those requiring information technologies to facilitate forensic analysis. He was the chief investigator examining the United Nations Oil-for-Food Programme, and he also led a crucial part of the massive forensic effort in the investigation of Holocaust-era accounts held by Swiss banks.

The authors wish to acknowledge the contributions of Donald F. Andersen, Daniel L. Collins, Stephen Doka, Daniel Krittman, Satish Lalchand, and Michael Shepard, all part of Deloitte FAS LLP.

Leisner, Christopher J., CPA, CMC, is founder of Creative IP Solutions, LLC, an intellectual property consulting firm that specializes in managing and monetizing intellectual property for a diverse domestic and international client base, from Fortune 100 companies to privately held companies. A speaker at several IP management and patent securitization conferences, Mr. Leisner has authored several articles and white papers on IP value extraction techniques and has served as an expert witness on accounting malpractice, fraud, and damages. He was previously Midwest Partner in Charge of Litigation Consulting Services and Regional Business Line Leader for Specialty Consulting Services at BDO Seidman, LLP. A certified management consultant, Mr. Leisner has assisted clients in resolving various business issues relating to strategic planning, equity and debt financing, mergers and acquisitions support, management reporting systems, and internal control procedures.

O'Connell, Kevin J., CPA, is the managing partner of Macias Gini & O'Connell LLP (MGO), a leading California certified public accounting and consulting firm. He has over 15 years of experience in federal, state, and local financial compliance auditing at all levels of government, including California's largest cities and counties and governmental component organizations in the airport, mass transit, utilities, and healthcare industries. Mr. O'Connell has served on the AICPA State and Local Government Expert Panel and contributed to the AICPA guide *Audits of State and Local Governments (GASB 34 Edition)*. In 2007, he was recognized by *CPA Technology Advisor* magazine as one of the nation's top 40 tax and accounting professionals under the age of 40 who will help lead the professions of public accounting and professional tax preparation into the future.

Pon Cynthia, CPA, has over 15 years of professional experience providing auditing, accounting, and consulting services to the private and public sectors. She leads the San Francisco Bay Area public sector assurance practice of Macias Gini & O'Connell LLP (MGO), bringing extensive experience in federal, state, and local financial and compliance auditing. Ms. Pon is an expert in the application of governmental GAAP and has been recognized by the Governmental Accounting Standards Board for her leadership in assisting large California governments with early implementation of its standards. She also serves on the Government Finance Officers Association Special Review Committee for Comprehensive Annual Financial Report awards and has instructed numerous governmental clients on a variety of audit issues and challenges.

Shim, Jae K., PhD, is a professor of accounting and finance at California State University, Long Beach, and CEO of Delta Consulting Company, a financial consulting and training firm. Dr. Shim received his MBA and PhD degrees from the University of California at Berkeley (Haas School of Business). He has been a consultant to commercial and nonprofit organizations for over 30 years. Dr. Shim has also published numerous articles in professional and academic journals and has over 50 college and professional books to his credit.

Victor, George I., is a partner of Quality Control at Holtz Rubenstein Reminick LLP, responsible for the development and maintenance of quality control, staff training, technical research, consulting, and review of completed engagements. Mr. Victor has extensive experience in providing accounting and advisory services to both privately held and SEC reporting companies, including audits of financial statements, SEC filings for public offerings and periodic reporting, private placements and complex business combinations. He provides consulting services in the areas of quality control and technical matters to other CPA firms, traveling domestically as well as to Latin America, India, and the United Kingdom. He is a member of the American Institute of CPAs (AICPA) the New York State Society of CPAs (NYSSCPA), and has chaired the NYSSCPA's Accounting and Auditing Oversight Committee and SEC Practice Committee. He is also a member of the editorial board of the *CPA Journal*. A frequent author and lecturer, Mr. Victor has been published or quoted in various international and national publications and professional journals, and lectures on SEC, accounting, and auditing related topics.

CONTENTS

Note to the Reader: Sections not in the main bound volume, *Accountants' Handbook Eleventh Edition* (978-0-471-79041-9), are indicated by "(New)" after the title. Material from the main bound volume that has been updated for *this* supplement is indicated by "(Revised)" after the title. Material new to or modified in *this* supplement is indicated by an asterisk (*) in the left margin in the contents and throughout the supplement.

PREFACE

This is the second supplement to the 11th edition of the *Accountant's Handbook*. Annual updates to this work provide important revisions and new topics that update the *Handbook* between editions. In addition, feedback suggests additional topical areas that are of interest to our readers. We are pleased to expand the *Handbook* to include those topical areas of significant interest. This supplement provides significantly revised and enhanced chapters by new authors. Of special note is the revised chapter on valuations. Fair value accounting is growing in importance as an accounting principle with wider financial accounting applicability. However, there remains controversy regarding the recognition of gains and losses based on market values when those values are determined by appraisals and estimates, and not necessarily by actual transaction values. This revised chapter provides insight on the process of valuations.

Chapter 18, "Cash, Loans, and Investments," and Chapter 18A, "Transfers of Financial Assets," significantly reorganize and update the *Handbook*. As a result of the financial liquidity crisis in 2008 and the new fair value options for accounting for many more assets, the principles of accounting for financial asset transfers and the complexities of valuing investments and transfers will be a focus of contemporary study and debate.

Chapter 21, "Property, Plant, Equipment, and Depreciation," is a revised chapter providing updates and enhanced examples of important issues regarding a topic relevant to most business entities.

Chapter 44, "Valuation of Assets, Liabilities, and Nonpublic Companies," is a replacement of an existing chapter on this subject and includes a discussion of the issues involved in valuation of assets for purposes either of determining fair value or for tests of impairment. Fair values and appraisals, while providing relevant information for financial statement users, are also based on estimates and sometimes imprecise methods of valuation. The tension between the more subjective fair value measurement approach and the more objective historical cost accounting approach for asset and liability measurement will play out in future years, but the techniques used in valuation are important today to those charged with business governance, management, auditors, and financial information users.

Chapter 46, "Forensic Accounting in Litigation Consulting Services," Investigations, and Compliance Matters is a fresh look at the contemporary scene of litigation support and forensic accounting practice. Several other chapters in the *Handbook* discuss forensic procedures and issues of fraud, and this chapter serves as a keystone to the discussions in those other chapters.

ACCOUNTANTS' HANDBOOK

ELEVENTH EDITION

FINANCIAL ACCOUNTING AND GENERAL TOPICS

CASH, LOANS, AND INVESTMENTS (REVISED)

Michael A. Antonetti, CPA, CMA
Crowe Horwath LLP[†]

---

†   The information contained in this chapter does not necessarily represent the views of Crowe Horwath LLP.

18.1 INTRODUCTION TO CASH

(a) NATURE AND IMPORTANCE OF CASH   Cash is both the beginning and the end of the operating cycle (cash–inventory–sales–receivables–cash) in the typical business enterprise, and almost all transactions affect cash either directly or indirectly. Cash transactions are probably the most frequently recurring type entered into by a business because (except for barter transactions) every sale leads to a cash receipt and every expense to a cash disbursement. Cash is recognized as the most liquid of assets, and thus has prominence for users who are focusing on issues of liquidity.

Cash derives its primary importance from its dual role as a medium of exchange and a unit of measure. As a medium of exchange, it has a part in the majority of transactions entered into by an enterprise. Assets are acquired and realized, and liabilities are incurred and liquidated, in terms of cash. Thus, cash is generally the most active asset possessed by a company. As a unit of measure, it sets the terms in which all properties and claims against the company are stated in its financial statements. Price-change reporting, which addresses disclosures for fluctuations in value as general and specific price levels rise and fall, is discussed in another chapter in the *Accountants' Handbook.*

(b) CASH ACCOUNTING AND CONTROL   The major challenge in accounting for cash is maintaining adequate control over the great variety and quantity of cash transactions. Cash receipts may come from such diverse sources as cash sales, cash on delivery (COD) transactions, collections on accounts and notes receivable, loans, security issues, income from investments, and sales of such properties as retired assets, scrap, and investments. Disbursements may be made for a variety of expense items, for cash purchases and in payment of various liabilities, for dividends and for taxes. Thus, the variety of cash transactions in itself presents inherent problems.

The quantity of cash transactions constitutes another source of difficulty. To handle expeditiously the volume of cash transactions calls for appropriate equipment, careful organization and segregation of duties, planning of procedures, and design of appropriate forms. Information as to available cash balances is of daily interest to the management of every company, and this information must be accurate and prompt if it is to be useful.

(c) MISREPRESENTED CASH BALANCES   Companies sometimes misrepresent their cash balance to improve the appearance of their financial liquidity. This practice is sometimes called *window dressing.* Smith and Skousen describe this practice as follows:

> Certain practices designed to present a more favorable financial condition than is actually the case may be encountered. For example, cash records may be held open for a few days after the close of a fiscal period and cash received from customers during this period reported as receipts of the preceding period. An improved cash position is thus reported. If this balance is then used as a basis for drawing predated checks in payment of accounts payable, the ratio of current assets to current liabilities is improved. The current ratio may also be improved by writing checks in payment of obligations and entering these on the books even though checks are not to be mailed until the following period.[1]

---

1.   Jay M. Smith, Jr. and K. Fred Skonsen, *Intermediate Accounting, Tenth Edition* (Cincinnati: South-Western Publishing, 1990).

18.2 ACCOUNTING FOR AND REPORTING CASH

(a) CLASSIFICATION AND PRESENTATION   The presentation of cash in the balance sheet is largely an issue of appropriate classification and description. Because of its importance in evaluating an entity's financial condition, cash must be stated as accurately as possible. This calls for careful analysis of each component of cash so that no items will improperly be included in, or excluded from, current assets. In this connection, paragraphs 4–6 of Chapter 3 of Accounting Research Bulletin (ARB) No. 43, *Restatement and Revision of Accounting Research Bulletins*, state, in part:

> For accounting purposes, the term current assets is used to designate cash and other assets or resources commonly identified as those which are reasonably expected to be realized in cash or sold or consumed during the normal operating cycle of the business. Thus the term comprehends in general such resources as (a) cash available for current operations and items which are the equivalent of cash. . . .
>
> The ordinary operations of a business involve a circulation of capital within the current asset group. Cash is expended for materials, finished parts, operating supplies, labor, and other factory services, and such expenditures are accumulated as inventory cost. Inventory costs, upon sale of the products to which such costs attach, are converted into trade receivables and ultimately into cash again. The average time intervening between the acquisition of materials or services entering this process and the final cash realization constitutes an operating cycle. . . .
>
> This concept of the nature of current assets contemplates the exclusion from that classification of such resources as: (a) cash and claims to cash which are restricted as to withdrawal or use for other than current operations, are designated for expenditure in the acquisition or construction of noncurrent assets, or are segregated for the liquidation of long-term debts. . . .

As the one asset that is liquid, that is, expendable with no intermediary transactions or conversions, cash assumes the position of prime importance in the balance sheet and is generally presented as the first item among the assets of the enterprise. Four examples of presentation are:

1. Cash and cash equivalents
2. Cash
3. Cash and equivalents
4. Cash combined with marketable securities

Generally, the form shown in example 1 above is widely used, but the important point is that cash subject to withdrawal restrictions should not be combined with cash of immediate availability. In this regard, O'Reilly et al. state in *Montgomery's Auditing*: "The cash caption on the balance sheet should include cash on hand and balances with financial institutions that are immediately available for any purpose and cash equivalents."

Paragraph 8 of FASB Statement No. 95, *Statement of Cash Flows*, states that cash equivalents are short-term highly liquid investments that are both:

- Readily convertible to known amounts of cash
- So near their maturity that they present insignificant risk of changes in value because of changes in interest rates

Paragraph 8 also states that "generally only investments with original maturities of three months or less qualify under that definition." Original maturity is further defined as maturity to the entity holding the investment. Statement 95 clarifies that the maturity date must be three months from the date of its acquisition by the entity. Thus, a Treasury note purchased three years ago and held does not become a cash equivalent when its remaining maturity is three months. Cash equivalents include Treasury bills, commercial paper, and money market funds.

(b) DEFINITION OF *CASH*   Cash exists both in physical and book entry forms: physical in the form of coin and paper currency as well as other negotiable instruments of various kinds, and book entry in various forms such as commercial bank deposits and savings deposits. In addition to coin and paper currency, other kinds of physical cash instruments that are commonly reported as cash for financial accounting purposes include certificates of deposit, bank checks, demand bills of exchange (in some cases), travelers' checks, post office or other money orders, bank drafts, cashiers' checks, certain short-term Treasury bills, and money market funds.

All these forms of cash involve credit and depend for their ready acceptance on the integrity and liquidity of some person or institution other than those offering or accepting them as cash. This is true even for coin and paper currency, which is ultimately dependent on the credit of the government issuing it. Given this integrity and liquidity, the book entry forms and other physical instruments are properly viewed as cash because of their immediate convertibility into cash in its currency form at the will of the holder. Convertibility in the case of savings accounts, certificates of deposit, and other time deposits may be something less than immediate depending on stipulated conditions imposed by the depository, but the assurance of such convertibility makes these items a generally accepted form of cash. However, only investments with original maturities of three months or less qualify for presentation as cash equivalents, as described above.

(c) RESTRICTED *CASH*   Cash restricted as to use by agreement, such as amounts deposited in escrow or for a specified purpose subject to release only at the order of a person other than the depositor, should not be classified in the balance sheet as cash and, unless deposited to meet an existing current liability, should presumably be excluded from current assets. Cash is sometimes received from customers in advance payment for work being performed under contract or under similar circumstances. Such cash is properly designated as cash in the balance sheet, but may be properly classified as a current asset only if the resulting customer's deposit is classified as a current liability. Cash restricted as to withdrawal because of inability of the depository to meet demands for withdrawal (such as deposits in banks in receivership) is not a current asset and should not be designated in the balance sheet as cash without an appropriate qualifying caption.

In regard to cash awaiting use for construction or other capital purposes or held for the payment of long-term debt, O'Reilly et al. state:

> Cash sometimes includes balances with trustees, such as sinking funds or other amounts not immediately available, for example, those restricted to uses other than current operations, designated for acquisition or construction of noncurrent assets, or segregated for the liquidation of long-term debt. Restrictions are considered effective if the company clearly intends to observe them, even though the funds are not actually set aside in special bank accounts. The facts pertaining to

those balances should be adequately disclosed, and the amounts should be properly classified as current or noncurrent.[2]

(d) BANK OVERDRAFTS Overdrafts may be of two kinds: (1) an actual bank overdraft, resulting from payment by the bank of checks in an amount exceeding the balance available to cover such checks; (2) a book overdraft, arising from issuance of checks in an amount in excess of the balance in the account on which drawn, although such checks have not cleared through the bank in an amount sufficient to exhaust the account.

Actual bank overdrafts represent the total of checks honored by the bank without sufficient funds in the account to cover them; such an overdraft is the bank's way of temporarily loaning funds to its customer. Accordingly, bank overdrafts (other than those that arise in connection with a "zero-balance" or similar arrangement with a bank) represent short-term loans and should be classified as liabilities if the right of offset does not exist.

Book overdrafts representing outstanding checks in excess of funds on deposit should generally be classified as liabilities and cash reinstated at the balance sheet date. Such credit book balances should not be viewed as offsets to other cash accounts except where the legal right of setoff exists within the same bank due to the existence of other positive balances in that bank.

FASB Interpretation (FIN) No. 39, *Offsetting of Amounts Related to Certain Contracts (An Interpretation of APB Opinion No. 10 and FASB Statement No. 105)*, provides guidance on whether the right of offset has been met. Where right of offset does not exist, the credit balance can be viewed as a reinstatement of the liabilities that were cleared in the bookkeeping process. When outstanding checks in excess of funds on deposit are reclassified, it is preferable that they be separately classified; if they are included in accounts payable, the amounts so included should be disclosed, if material. Reclassifying as a liability all outstanding checks (including those covered by funds on deposit in the bank account concerned) is generally not considered acceptable.

(e) FOREIGN BALANCES Cash in foreign countries may properly be included in the balance sheet as cash if stated at its equivalent in U.S. currency at the prevailing rate of exchange and if no exchange restrictions exist to prevent the transfer of such monies to the domicile of the owner. Depending on circumstances and the extent to which such cash balances may be subject to exchange control or other restrictions, the amount of cash so included should be considered for disclosure, by being stated either separately, parenthetically, or otherwise. The question of exchange restrictions (or economic conditions) preventing transfer of cash across national boundaries is of prime importance, and cash in foreign countries should be classified as a current asset only if appropriate review establishes that no significant restrictions or conditions exist with respect to the amounts involved. If restrictions exist but ultimate transfer seems probable, the cash may be included in the balance sheet in a noncurrent classification.

Difficulty in stating foreign cash balances at their equivalent in U.S. currency occurs when more than one rate of exchange exists. In this situation, the use of an exchange rate related to earnings received from the foreign subsidiary for the purpose of translating foreign currency accounts is recommended. Paragraphs 26–28 of FASB Statement No. 52, *Foreign Currency Translation*, provide guidance on the selection of exchange rates.

---

2. Vincent M. O'Reilly et al., *Montgomery's Auditing, Twelfth Edition* (New York: John Wiley & Sons, 1998), Section 17.17.

(f) COMPENSATING CASH BALANCES   It is not uncommon for banks to require that a current or prospective borrower maintain a compensating balance on deposit with the bank. Frequently, the required compensating balance is based on the average outstanding loan balance. A compensating deposit balance may also be required to assure future credit availability (including maintenance of an unused line of credit). The compensating balance requirement may be (1) written into a loan or line of credit agreement, (2) the subject of a supplementary written agreement, or (3) based on an oral understanding. In some instances, a fee is paid on an unused line of credit (or commitment) to ensure credit availability.

The Securities and Exchange Commission (SEC) originally defined compensating balances in Accounting Series Release (ASR) No. 148 as follows:

> A compensating balance is defined as that portion of any demand deposit (or any time deposit or certificate of deposit) maintained by a corporation (or by any other person on behalf of the corporation) which constitutes support for existing borrowing arrangements of the corporation (or any other person) with a lending institution. Such arrangements would include both outstanding borrowings and the assurance of future credit availability.

For SEC registrants, requirements for the disclosure of restrictions on the withdrawal or use of cash and cash items, such as compensating balance arrangements, are set forth in Rule 5-02.1 of Regulation S-X as follows:

> CASH AND CASH ITEMS.
> Separate disclosure shall be made of the cash and cash items which are restricted as to withdrawal or usage. The provisions of any restrictions shall be described in a note to the financial statements. Restrictions may include legally restricted deposits held as compensating balances against short-term borrowing arrangements, contracts entered into with others, or company statements of intention with regard to particular deposits; however, time deposits and short-term certificates of deposit are not generally included in legally restricted deposits. In cases where compensating balance arrangements exist but are not agreements which legally restrict the use of cash amounts shown on the balance sheet, describe in the notes to the financial statements these arrangements and the amount involved, if determinable, for the most recent audited balance sheet required and for any subsequent unaudited balance sheet required in the notes to the financial statements. Compensating balances that are maintained under an agreement to assure future credit availability shall be disclosed in the notes to the financial statements along with the amount and terms of such agreement.

Guidelines and interpretations for disclosure of compensating balance arrangements are described within SEC Financial Reporting Release (FRR) No. 203 and SEC Staff Accounting Bulletin (SAB) Topic 6H. These provide useful information in evaluating the need for segregation and disclosure of compensating balance arrangements, including determination of the amount to be disclosed. Cash float and other factors should be considered.

Although no other authoritative literature requires compensating balance disclosures in the financial statements of non-SEC registrants, disclosure of material compensating balances will usually be necessary for fair presentation of the financial statements in accordance with generally accepted accounting principles (GAAP). Consequently, the disclosure of material compensating balance arrangements in financial statements of non-SEC reporting companies, whether maintained under a written agreement or under an informal agreement confirmed by the bank, is usually considered necessary as an "informative disclosure" under the third standard of reporting. It should be noted that compensating balances may also relate to an agreement or an understanding relative to future credit availability (including unused lines of credit). Compensating balances related to future credit availability should be disclosed as well as those related to outstanding borrowings.

(i) Disclosure   In circumstances where compensating balances relative to outstanding loans and future credit availability are not legally restricted as to withdrawal, note disclosure is appropriate.

(ii) Segregation in the Balance Sheet   Cash that is not subject to withdrawal should be classified as a noncurrent asset to the extent such cash relates to the noncurrent portion of the debt that causes its restriction. To the extent legally restricted cash relates to short-term borrowings, it may be included with unrestricted amounts on one line in financial statements of non-SEC reporting companies, provided the caption is appropriate and there is disclosure of the restricted amounts in the notes, for example, "Cash and restricted cash (Note 3)." Rule 5-02.1 of Regulation S-X requires SEC-reporting companies to disclose separately funds legally restricted as to withdrawal, but FRR No. 203.02.b is more specific in its requirement to segregate all legally restricted cash in the balance sheet.

No single example is appropriate for the disclosure of all compensating balance arrangements and future credit availability (including unused lines of credit) because the terms of loan agreements vary greatly. However, the following hypothetical examples illustrate methods of disclosing the details of compensating balance agreements and future credit availability.

The following is an example of disclosure where withdrawal of the compensating balance was legally restricted at the date of the balance sheet.

CASH ITEMS DISCLOSED ON BALANCE SHEET
SEC-Reporting Companies
Current assets

Cash	$3,500,000
Restricted cash compensating balances (Note X)	$6,000,000

Non-SEC Reporting Companies

Current assets	$9,500,000
Cash and restricted cash (Note X)	

Note X. Compensating Balances

A maximum of $100,000,000 is available to the company under a revolving credit agreement. Under the terms of the agreement, the company is required to maintain on deposit with the bank a compensating balance, restricted as to use, of 10 percent of the outstanding loan balance. At December 31, 20XX, $6,000,000 of the cash balance shown in the balance sheet was so restricted after adjusting for differences of "float" between the balance shown by the books of the company and the records of the bank.

For SEC-reporting companies, the following disclosure should be added to the above note:

This "float" amount consisted of $3,000,000 of unpresented checks less $500,000 of deposits of delayed availability at the agreed-upon schedule of 1.5 days' deposits.

The following is an example of disclosure for both SEC and non-SEC reporting companies where withdrawal of the compensating balance was not legally restricted at the date of the balance sheet.

Current assets
    Cash (Note X) $10,000,000
Note X. Compensating Balances

Under an informal agreement with a lending bank, the company maintains on deposit with the bank a compensating balance of 5 percent of an unused line of credit and 10 percent of the outstanding loan balance. At December 31, 20XX, approximately $5,800,000 of the cash balance shown in the balance sheet represented a compensating balance.

(g) UNUSED LINES OF CREDIT   Rules 5-02.19 and 22 of Regulation S-X require that the amount and terms (including commitment fees and the conditions under which commitments may be withdrawn) of unused lines of credit or unused commitments for financing arrangements be disclosed. The term *unused lines of credit* is used for short-term financing arrangements; the term *unused commitments* refers to long-term financing arrangements. The requirements of Regulation S-X are as follows:

5.02.19 ACCOUNTS AND NOTES PAYABLE. (b) The amount and terms (including commitment fees and the conditions under which lines may be withdrawn) of unused lines of credit for short-term financing shall be disclosed, if significant, in the notes to the financial statements. The weighted average interest rate on short-term borrowings outstanding as of the date of each balance sheet presented shall be furnished in a note. The amount of these lines of credit which support a commercial paper borrowing arrangement or similar arrangements shall be separately identified.

5.02.22 BONDS, MORTGAGES, AND OTHER LONG-TERM DEBT, INCLUDING CAPITALIZED LEASES. (b) The amount and terms (including commitment fees and the conditions under which commitments may be withdrawn) of unused commitments for long-term financing arrangements that would be disclosed under this rule if used shall be disclosed in the notes to the financial statements if significant.

Many future credit arrangements are informal. Even formal arrangements may be withdrawn by lending institutions on very short notice, usually resulting from an adverse change in the financial position of a company. Therefore, limitations relating to the subsequent use of such lines of credit make it particularly difficult to provide informative and adequate disclosure so that the reader does not get a more favorable picture than is warranted. Because of the uncertainty of the duration of some lines of credit, disclosure of these types of lines of credit in financial statements requires the exercise of individual judgment based on the facts of the particular situation, and disclosures should include the limitations and conditions of subsequent use. Unused lines of credit or commitments that may be withdrawn at the mere option of the lender need not be disclosed but, if disclosed, the nature of the arrangement should be disclosed as well.

(i) Fee Paid for Future Credit Availability   A commitment fee has an effect on the cost of borrowing that is similar to that of a compensating balance. If a fee is paid to a lending bank for an unused line of credit or commitment, such fee should be disclosed if significant (Rule 502.19b of Regulation S-X).

(ii) Disclosure   The following is an example of disclosure of binding bank credit arrangements. Information of this nature may be combined with note disclosure of indebtedness.

> NOTE X. UNUSED LINES OF CREDIT
> Bank lines of credit under which notes payable of $105,000,000 were outstanding at December 31, 20XX, aggregated $152,500,000. The use of these lines generally is restricted to the extent that the Company is required periodically to liquidate its indebtedness to individual banks for 30 to 60 days each year. Borrowings under such agreements are at interest rates ranging from $\frac{1}{4}$ to $\frac{1}{2}$ of 1% above the prime rate, plus a commitment fee of $\frac{1}{4}$ to $\frac{1}{2}$ of 1% on the unused available credit. Commitments by the banks generally expire one year from the date of the agreement and are generally renewed.

For SEC-reporting companies, the following disclosure should be added to the above note:

> Total commitment fees paid on the unused lines of credit amounted to $175,000 for 20XX, $195,000 for 20XX, and $180,000 for 20XX.

(h) CONCENTRATION OF CREDIT RISK   Disclosures related to cash balances should include the existence of uninsured cash balances that represent a significant concentration of credit risk. American Institute of Certified Public Accountants (AICPA) Technical Practice Aid No. 2110.06, *Disclosure of Cash Balances in Excess of Federally Insured Amounts*, provides the following guidance:

> **Inquiry.** Should the existence of cash on deposit with banks in excess of Federal Deposit Insurance Corporation (FDIC)–insured limits be disclosed in the financial statements?
> **Reply.** The existence of uninsured cash balances should be disclosed if the uninsured balances represent a significant concentration of credit risk. Credit risk is defined in FASB Statement No. 105, *Disclosure of Information about Financial Instruments with Off-Balance-Sheet Risk and Financial Instruments with Concentrations of Credit Risk*, Paragraph 7 (AC F25.107), as "the possibility that a loss may occur from the failure of another party to perform according to the terms of the contract." As a result, bank statement balances in excess of FDIC-insured amounts represent credit risk.
>   An example of disclosure for this circumstance might be:
>   The Company maintains its cash in bank deposit accounts which, at times, may exceed federally insured limits. The Company has not experienced any losses in such account. The Company believes it is not exposed to any significant credit risk on cash and cash equivalents.

(i) Fair Value Disclosures   FASB Statement No. 107, *Disclosures about Fair Value of Financial Instruments*, requires disclosure of fair values of all financial instruments. The disclosure should include the method and significant assumptions used to estimate fair value. Due to the short-term maturity of cash and cash equivalents, this requirement is often met by the following sample disclosure:

> *Cash and Cash Equivalents.* The carrying amount approximates fair value because of the short-term maturity of those instruments.

18.3   LOANS

(a) INTRODUCTION   Although not the primary focus of their business, manufacturers, wholesalers, retailers, and service companies may nevertheless originate loans in connection with their revenue-generating activities. FASB Statement No. 114, *Accounting by Creditors for Impairment of a Loan*, applies to all creditors and defines a loan, in paragraph 4, as:

> a contractual right to receive money on demand or on fixed or determinable dates that is recognized as an asset in the creditor's statement of financial position. Examples include but are not limited to accounts receivable (with terms exceeding one year) and notes receivable.

However, there are certain requirements, as discussed below, for any type of credit arrangement, including trade receivables. In contrast, one of the most significant activities for financial institutions is the origination and acquisition of loans in order to generate interest revenue. Chapter 31 discusses matters of interest to financial institutions and entities involved in lending and deposit taking activities.

(b) INITIAL RECOGNITION AND MEASUREMENT   Paragraph 8a of Statement of Position (SOP) 01-6, *Accounting by Certain Entities (Including Entities with Trade Receivables) That Lend to or Finance the Activities of Others*, states that:

> Loans and trade receivables that management has the intent and ability to hold for the foreseeable future or until maturity or payoff should be reported in the balance sheet at outstanding principal adjusted for any chargeoffs, the allowance for loan losses (or the allowance for doubtful accounts), any deferred fees or costs on originated loans, and any unamortized premiums or discounts on purchased loans.

Generally, interest income on loans is accrued at the contractual rate, and premiums and discounts are amortized using the interest method in accordance with FASB Statement No. 91, *Accounting for Nonrefundable Fees and Costs Associated with Originating or Acquiring Loans and Initial Direct Costs of Leases.*

Accounting Principles Board (APB) Opinion No. 21, *Interest on Receivables and Payables*, discusses the appropriate accounting when the face amount of a note does not reasonably represent the present value of the consideration given or received in the exchange. APB 21 (par. 3) excludes from its scope "receivables and payables arising from transactions with customers or suppliers in the normal course of business which are due in customary trade terms not exceeding approximately one year" and "transactions between parent and subsidiary companies and between subsidiaries of a common parent."

Non-interest-bearing loans, loans with unrealistic interest rates, and loans obtained in exchange for property, goods, or services with fair values materially different from the principal amount of the loan lead to the recognition of premiums and discounts. APB 21 (par. 16) requires discounts and premiums to be reported "as a direct deduction from or addition to the face amount of the [loan]." Appendix A of APB 21 provides illustrations of the appropriate balance sheet presentation.

Nonrefundable fees and costs associated with an entity's lending activities are discussed in Statement 91. Such considerations are most prevalent for financial institutions, and the accounting for these fees and costs is discussed in Chapter 31.

Some acquired loans may have experienced a decline in credit quality. SOP 03-3, *Accounting for Certain Loans or Debt Securities Acquired in a Transfer*, addresses the accounting and reporting for those loans. Loans that have been acquired should be evaluated to determine whether the provisions of SOP 03-3 should be applied.

(c) LOAN IMPAIRMENT AND INCOME RECOGNITION FASB Concepts Statement No. 6, *Elements of Financial Statements* (par. 25), defines assets as "probable future economic benefits obtained or controlled by a particular entity as a result of past transactions or events." FASB Statement No. 5, *Accounting for Contingencies*, and Statement 114 address the accounting by creditors for impairment of certain loans. These Statements indicate that "a loan is impaired when, based on current information and events, it is probable that a creditor will be unable to collect all amounts due according to the contractual terms of the loan agreement." It applies to all creditors. While both Statements address loan impairment, Statement 5 generally addresses smaller-balance homogeneous loans while Statement 114 addresses all loans except those specifically excluded (par. 6):

- Large groups of smaller-balance homogeneous loans that are collectively evaluated for impairment. Those loans may include but are not limited to credit card, residential mortgage, and consumer installment loans.
- Loans that are measured at fair value or at the lower of cost or fair value, for example, in accordance with FASB Statement No. 65, *Accounting for Certain Mortgage Banking Activities*, or other specialized industry practice.
- Leases as defined in FASB Statement No. 13, *Accounting for Leases*.
- Debt securities as defined in FASB Statement No. 115, *Accounting for Certain Investments in Debt and Equity Securities*.

Statement 114 does not specify how a creditor should identify loans that are to be evaluated for impairment. However, in practice, a number of different mechanisms are employed to identify loans for impairment evaluation. These mechanisms include but are not limited to past-due reports, reports from regulatory examiners, reviews of incomplete loan files of financial institutions, identification of those borrowers facing financial difficulties or operating in industries facing such difficulties, and loss statistics pertaining to certain categories of loans.

(i) Impairment Measurement Guidelines The measurement of impairment should take into account both contractual interest payments and contractual principal payments consistent with the original payment terms of the loan agreement. For loans within the scope of Statement 114, the creditor should measure impairment based on the present value of expected future cash flows discounted at the loan's effective interest rate. A loan's effective interest rate is defined as "the rate of return implicit in the loan (i.e., the contractual interest rate adjusted

for any net deferred loan fees or costs, premium, or discount existing at the origination or acquisition of the loan)" (par. 14).

Statement 114 provides that, as a practical expedient, creditors may alternatively measure impairment based on a loan's observable market price or the fair value of the collateral if the loan is collateral dependent. If the latter approach is used, the measurement of impairment should take into account estimated costs to sell the collateral, on a discounted basis. Furthermore, when a creditor determines that foreclosure is probable, impairment must be measured based on the fair value of the collateral.

When valuations are based on appraisals, particular attention should be given to the objectivity and competence of the specialist providing the appraisal and the methods and assumptions used to develop the appraised fair value. Additionally, the appraisal should be assessed as to its suitability for the purpose. For example, "appraisals" are sometimes obtained to assess the feasibility of a commercial development project (e.g., a golf course and condominium complex) and assume the existence of the completed project. Such an "appraisal" might not be useful in assessing the *as-is* fair value of a property comprised mostly of raw land in foreclosure. While companies are not precluded from internally appraising collateral, the increased objectivity of third-party appraisals may provide more objective valuations to assist management in decision making and also permit auditors to rely on the work of a specialist performing the appraisal. Valuations are the subject of a separate chapter in the *Accountants' Handbook*.

In any event, a valuation allowance should be established if the recorded investment in the loan (including accrued interest, net deferred loan fees or costs, and unamortized discount or premium) exceeds the impaired measure. The recognition of such an allowance is accompanied by a corresponding charge to bad debt expense.

(ii) Income Recognition   Once a loan has been impaired, some entities, particularly financial institutions, suspend the accrual of interest because such accruals do not in those circumstances reflect economic reality.

The recognition of interest income on impaired loans was initially addressed by Statement 114 (pars. 17–19). Subsequent to its issuance, however, a number of commentators requested an extension of the effective date of the Statement due to the difficulty of applying the new guidelines. As a result, the FASB issued Statement No. 118, *Accounting by Creditors for Impairment of a Loan—Income Recognition and Disclosures*, to "allow a creditor to use existing methods for recognizing interest income on impaired loans" (par. 3). Statement 118 eliminated the original income recognition provisions of paragraphs 17–19 of Statement 114. However, Statement 114 (par. 17), as amended, recognizes that accounting methods for the recognition of interest income include using "a cost-recovery method, a cash-basis method, or some combination of those methods." While the decision to recognize interest income on impaired or defaulted loans requires judgment and consideration of the facts and circumstances, oftentimes companies do not recognize as income the interest on loans defaulted more than 90 days.

(d) TROUBLED DEBT RESTRUCTURINGS   Occasionally, a loan may be restructured to meet a borrower's changing circumstances, and a new loan is recognized. However, if "the creditor for economic or legal reasons related to the debtor's financial difficulties grants a concession to the debtor that it would not otherwise consider" (par. 2 of Statement 15), the transaction should be accounted for in accordance with FASB Statement No. 15, *Accounting* *by Debtors and Creditors for Troubled Debt Restructurings.* The following types of restructuring arrangements are discussed in Statement 15:

- Transfers of assets of the debtor or an equity interest in the debtor to fully or partially satisfy the debt
- Modification of debt terms, including reduction of one or more of the following: (1) interest rates with or without extension of maturity date(s), (2) face or maturity amounts, and (3) accrued interest

Creditors that receive assets or an equity interest in the debtor in full satisfaction of the loan should account for the restructuring at the fair value of the assets or equity interest received or the fair value of the loan, whichever is more clearly determinable. In the case of a partial satisfaction of the loan, the fair value of the loan may not be used (Statement 15, par. 28, fn. 16).

Statement 114 amended Statement 15 to require that a creditor account for a troubled debt restructuring involving a modification of terms in accordance with Statement 114. However, the effective interest rate to be used in these situations is the original contractual rate and not the rate specified in the restructuring agreement. Furthermore, creditors must disclose "the amount of commitments, if any, to lend additional funds to debtors owing receivables whose terms have been modified in troubled debt restructurings" (Statement 15, par. 40b).

(e) NOTES RECEIVED FOR CAPITAL STOCK   An entity may sometimes receive a note from the sale of capital stock or as a contribution to paid-in capital. The Emerging Issues Task Force (EITF), in EITF 85-1, *Classifying Notes Received for Capital Stock*, addressed the issue of whether an entity should report the note receivable as a reduction of shareholders' equity or as an asset. The EITF "reached a consensus that reporting the note as an asset is generally not appropriate, except in very limited circumstances when there is substantial evidence of ability and intent to pay within a reasonably short period of time." One situation where such a note receivable may be reported as an asset is the payment of the note prior to issuance of the financial statements.

(f) DISCLOSURES   There are a number of standards that require disclosures related to loans as follows:

- APB Opinion No. 22, *Disclosure of Accounting Policies,* paragraphs 8 and 12
- SOP 01-6, paragraphs 13–17
- APB Opinion No. 12, *Omnibus Opinion—1967—Classification and Disclosure of Allowances; Disclosure of Depreciable Assets and Depreciation; Deferred Compensation Contracts; Capital Changes; Convertible Debt and Debt Issued with Stock Warrants; Amortization of Debt Discount and Expense or Premium,* paragraphs 2 and 3
- Statement 5, paragraphs 9–11
- SOP 94-6, *Disclosure of Certain Significant Risks and Uncertainties*, paragraphs 13 and 14
- FSP-SOP 94-6-1, *Terms of Loan Products That May Give Rise to a Concentration of Credit Risk*
- Statement 114 as amended by Statement 118, paragraph 20A
- SOP 03-3, paragraphs 14–16
- Statement 107

18.4   DEBT SECURITIES

(a) INTRODUCTION   An entity may invest in debt securities (e.g., bonds) to generate interest revenue and/or to realize gains from their sale at increased market prices. Statement 115 is the primary standard applicable to investments in debt securities. The FASB has also issued a special report entitled, *A Guide to Implementation of Statement 115 on Accounting for Certain Investments in Debt and Equity Securities*, which contains a series of questions and answers (herein referred to by question number as FASB Q&A) useful in understanding and implementing the Statement. Paragraph 137 of Statement 115 defines, in part, debt securities as those securities that represent "a creditor relationship with an enterprise." These securities include:

- U.S. Treasury securities; U.S. government agency securities; municipal securities; corporate bonds; convertible debt; commercial paper; all securitized debt instruments, such as collateralized mortgage obligations (CMOs) and real estate mortgage investment conduits (REMICs); and interest-only and principal-only strips
- A CMO (or other instrument) that is issued in equity form but is required to be accounted for as a nonequity instrument regardless of how that instrument is classified (i.e., whether equity or debt) in the issuer's statement of financial position
- Preferred stock that by its terms either must be redeemed by the issuing enterprise or is redeemable at the option of the investor

Except as mentioned below, Statement 115 "applies to all debt securities, including securities that have been grouped with loans in the statement of financial position" (EITF Topic No. D-39, *Questions Related to the Implementation of FASB Statement No. 115*). These include (1) a bank's originated and securitized mortgage loans that continue to be reported as loans in the Call Report, (2) bank investments in unrated industrial development bonds classified as loans in the Call Report, and (3) "Brady Bonds." In addition, FASB Technical Bulletin No. 94-1, *Application of Statement 115 to Debt Securities Restructured in a Troubled Debt Restructuring*, indicates that "Statement 115 applies to all loans that meet the definition of a security in that Statement. Thus, any loan that was restructured in a troubled debt restructuring involving a modification of terms, including those restructured before the effective date of Statement 114, would be subject to the provisions of Statement 115 if the debt instrument meets the definition of a security" (par. 3).

Excluded from the definition of debt securities are unsecuritized loans, options on debt securities, accounts receivable, option contracts, financial futures contracts, forward contracts, and lease contracts. In addition, since Statement 115 generally requires that investments in debt securities be presented at fair value, enterprises that already use similar measurement guidelines in accounting for these investments—for example, brokers and dealers in securities, defined benefit pension plans, and investment companies—need not apply the requirements of the Statement. In this regard, Statement 115 (par. 4) states, in part, "This Statement does not apply to enterprises whose specialized accounting practices include accounting for substantially all investments in debt and equity securities at market value or fair value, with changes in value recognized in earnings (income) or in the change in net assets. . . ."

Not-for-profit organizations are also excluded from the Statement's provisions. However, the Statement applies "to cooperatives and mutual enterprises, including credit unions and mutual insurance companies" (par. 4).

As discussed in Chapter 18A in this supplement, "Transfers of Financial Assets," certain financial assets subject to prepayment are measured like investment in debt securities. Those assets include interest-only strips, retained interests in securitizations, loans, other receivables, or other financial assets that can contractually be prepaid or otherwise settled in such a way that the holder would not recover substantially all of its recorded investment, except for instruments that are within the scope of FASB Statement No. 133, *Accounting for Derivative Instruments and Hedging Activities*.

EITF 99-20, *Recognition of Interest Income and Impairment on Purchased and Retained Beneficial Interests in Securitized Financial Assets*, provides interest income recognition and measurement guidance for interests retained in a securitization transaction accounted for as a sale. The scope of EITF 99-20 includes retained beneficial interests in securitization transactions that are accounted for as sales under Statement 140 and certain purchased beneficial interests in securitized financial assets. The scope includes beneficial interests that (par. 5):

- Are either debt securities under Statement 115 or required to be accounted for like debt securities under Statement 115 pursuant to paragraph 14 of Statement 140.
- Involve securitized financial assets that have contractual cash flows (e.g., loans, receivables, debt securities, and guaranteed lease residuals, among other items). Thus, the consensus in this issue does not apply to securitized financial assets that do not involve contractual cash flows (e.g., common stock equity securities, among other items). The Task Force observed that the guidance in EITF Issue No. 96-12, *Recognition of Interest Income and Balance Sheet Classification of Structured Notes*, may be applied to those beneficial interests involving securitized financial assets that do not involve contractual cash flows.
- Do not result in consolidation of the entity issuing the beneficial interest by the holder of the beneficial interests.

Under EITF 99-20, when an adverse change in the expected cash flows (principal or interest) to be received occurs and the fair value of the beneficial interest is less than its carrying amount, an other-than-temporary impairment has occurred. In determining whether an adverse change in cash flows has occurred, the present value of the remaining cash flows, as estimated at the initial transaction date (or the last date previously revised), which will be the book value if there is no premium or discount, should be compared to the present value of the expected cash flows at the current reporting date. The estimated cash flows should be reflective of those a market participant would use and should be discounted at a rate equal to the current effective yield. If an other-than-temporary impairment is recognized as a result of this analysis, the yield is changed to the market rate. The last revised estimated cash flows would be used for future impairment analysis purposes.

Under EITF 99-20, when an adverse change in the expected cash flows to be received occurs, but the fair value of the beneficial interest is still greater than the carrying value, then the investor should recalculate the amount of accretable yield for the beneficial interest on the date of evaluation as the excess of estimated cash flows over the beneficial interest's reference amount (the reference amount is equal to (1) the initial investment less (2) cash received to date less (3) other than temporary impairments recognized to date plus (4) the yield accreted to date). The adjustment should be accounted for prospectively as a change in estimate in conformity with APB Opinion No. 20, *Accounting Changes*, with the amount of periodic accretion adjusted over the remaining life of the beneficial interest.

(b) INITIAL RECOGNITION AND MEASUREMENT   Upon acquisition, debt securities are classified into one of three categories: (1) held-to-maturity, (2) trading, or (3) available-for-sale. Generally, these securities are initially recorded at cost with appropriate identification of premium or discounts. EITF Issue No. 94-8, *Accounting for Conversion of a Loan into a Debt Security in a Debt Restructuring*, states that "the initial cost basis of a debt security of the original debtor received as part of a debt restructuring should be the security's fair value at the date of the restructuring."

(i) Held-to-Maturity   An entity that has the positive intent and ability to hold a debt security to maturity should classify such security as a held-to-maturity security. Otherwise, the security should be classified as trading or available-for-sale. A positive intent and ability to hold a security to maturity does not exist if management's intent to hold the security to maturity is uncertain, if the intent is "to hold the security for only an indefinite period" (par. 9), or if there is a "mere absence of an intent to sell" (par. 59). FASB Q&A No. 18 states that "given the unique opportunities for profit embedded in a convertible security, it generally would be contradictory to assert the positive intent and ability to hold a convertible debt security to maturity and forego [*sic*] the opportunity to exercise the conversion feature." In determining positive intent and ability, the following additional guidance is available:

- Statement 115 (par. 9) states that "a debt security should not, for example, be classified as held-to-maturity if the enterprise anticipates that the security would be available to be sold in response to . . . needs for liquidity (e.g., due to the withdrawal of deposits, increased demands for loans, surrender of insurance policies, or payment of insurance claims)," or changes in (1) "market interest rates and related changes in the security's prepayment risk," (2) "the availability of and the yield on alternative investments," (3) "funding sources and terms," or (4) "foreign currency risk."
- Statement 115 (par. 7), as amended, provides that "a security may not be classified as held-to-maturity if that security can contractually be prepaid or otherwise settled in such a way that the holder of the security would not recover substantially all of its recorded investment."
- FASB Statement No. 140, *Accounting for Transfers and Servicing of Financial Assets and Extinguishments of Liabilities—A Replacement of FASB Statement 125* (par. 14), also requires that "interest-only strips, other interests that continue to be held by a transferor in securitizations, loans, other receivables, or other financial assets that can contractually be prepaid or otherwise settled in such a way that the holder would not recover substantially all of its recorded investment, except for instruments within the scope of Statement 133, shall be subsequently measured like investments in debt securities classified as available-for-sale or trading under Statement 115, as amended."

(ii) Trading   Debt securities classified as trading securities are those that are "bought and held principally for the purpose of selling them in the near term (thus held for only a short period of time)" (par. 12a). These include mortgage-backed securities held for sale in conjunction with mortgage banking activities.

(iii) Available-for-Sale   Debt securities that are not classified as held-to-maturity or trading securities are classified as available-for-sale securities.

(c) ACCOUNTING AFTER ACQUISITION   Gains and losses realized upon the sale of debt securities are included in earnings. As discussed in Chapter 18A of this supplement, "Transfers of Financial Assets," sale accounting is appropriate only for transfers of financial assets in which the transferor surrenders control over those financial assets pursuant to the provisions of Statement 140, paragraph 9. Otherwise, the transferor should account for the transfer as a secured borrowing with pledge of collateral pursuant to Statement 140, paragraph 15.

Generally, interest income is recognized at the contractual rate and premiums and discounts are amortized using the interest method. As discussed above, certain beneficial interests should follow the guidance in EITF 99-20. In addition, the retrospective interest method should be used for recognizing income on structured note securities that are classified as available-for-sale or held-to-maturity and that meet one or more of the conditions set forth in EITF 96-12. Structured notes are debt instruments whose cash flows are linked to the movement in one or more indexes, interest rates, foreign exchange rates, commodities prices, prepayment rates, or other market variables.

The amount at which a debt security is presented in the statement of financial position depends on its classification, as discussed below. This will require a determination of fair value: "the amount at which a financial instrument could be exchanged in a current transaction between willing parties, other than in a forced or liquidation sale. If a quoted market price is available for an instrument, the fair value to be used in applying [the] Statement is the product of the number of trading units of the instrument times its market price" (par. 137). If a quoted market price is not available for a debt security, pricing techniques such as "discounted cash flow analysis, matrix pricing, option-adjusted spread models, and fundamental analysis" (par. 111) can be used to obtain an estimate of fair value.

The appropriateness of a security's classification must be reassessed at each reporting date. In making this assessment, prior sales and transfers should be considered. Transfers to another category are discussed below.

(i) Held-to-Maturity   Debt securities classified as held-to-maturity are carried at amortized cost. As with loans, premiums and discounts pertaining to these securities are generally amortized using the interest method in accordance with Statement 91.

In assessing the appropriateness of the held-to-maturity designation at each reporting date, Statement 115 (par. 8) provides that transfers or sales due to the following changes in circumstances do not refute the held-to-maturity classification of other debt securities:

- Evidence of a significant deterioration in the issuer's creditworthiness
- A change in tax law that eliminates or reduces the tax-exempt status of interest on the debt security (but not a change in tax law that revises the marginal tax rates applicable to interest income)
- A major business combination or major disposition (such as sale of a components of an entity) that necessitates the sale or transfer of held-to-maturity securities to maintain the enterprise's existing interest rate risk position or credit risk policy
- A change in statutory or regulatory requirements significantly modifying either what constitutes a permissible investment or the maximum level of investments in certain kinds of securities, thereby causing an enterprise to dispose of a held-to-maturity security
- A significant increase by the regulator in the industry's capital requirements that causes the enterprise to downsize by selling held-to-maturity securities

- A significant increase in the risk weights of debt securities used for regulatory risk-based capital purposes

It is not appropriate to apply these exceptions to situations that are similar, but not the same as, those listed above. However, the Statement indicates that "in addition to the foregoing changes in circumstances, other events that are isolated, nonrecurring, and unusual for the reporting enterprise that could not have been reasonably anticipated may cause the enterprise to sell or transfer a held-to-maturity security without necessarily calling into question its intent to hold other debt securities to maturity" (par. 8).

FASB Q&A No. 29 indicates that "the sale of a held-to-maturity security in response to a tender offer will call into question an investor's intent to hold other debt securities to maturity in the future." In addition, FASB Q&A No. 24 notes that "sales of held-to-maturity securities to fund an acquisition (or a disposition, for example, if deposit liabilities are being assumed by the other party) are inconsistent with [Statement 115] paragraph 8."

(ii) Trading   Debt securities classified as trading securities are carried at fair value. The resulting unrealized gain or loss is reflected in earnings.

(iii) Available-for-Sale   Debt securities classified as available-for-sale are, like debt securities classified as trading, carried at fair value. Unrealized holding gains and losses for available-for-sale securities (including those classified as current assets) are excluded from earnings and reported in Other Comprehensive Income (OCI), net of related deferred income taxes. These unrealized gains and losses should include the entire change in the fair value of foreign currency–denominated available-for-sale debt securities, and not just the portion attributable to changes in exchange rates.

The FASB staff has announced that "when an entity has decided to sell an available-for-sale security whose fair value is less than its cost and the entity does not expect the fair value of the security to recover prior to the expected time of sale, a write-down for other-than-temporary impairment should be recognized in earnings in the period in which the decision to sell is made" (EITF Topic No. D-44, *Recognition of Other-Than-Temporary Impairment upon the Planned Sale of a Security Whose Cost Exceeds Fair Value*, which was superseded with the issuance of FSP FAS 115-1 and FAS 124-1, *The Meaning of Other-Than-Temporary Impairment and Its Application to Certain Investments*).

(iv) Transfers between Categories   Changes in the classification of investments in debt securities are accounted for at fair value. The following table summarizes the proper accounting for transfers:

Transfer From	Transfer To	Accounting Principles
Trading	Available-for-Sale	The unrealized holding gain or loss at the date of the transfer will have already been recognized in earnings and shall not be reversed.
	Held-to-Maturity	The unrealized holding gain or loss at the date of the transfer will have already been recognized in earnings and shall not be reversed.

Transfer From	Transfer To	Accounting Principles
Available-for-Sale	Trading	The portion of the unrealized holding gain or loss at the date of the transfer that has not been previously recognized in earnings shall be recognized in earnings immediately.
	Held-to-Maturity	The unrealized holding gain or loss at the date of the transfer shall continue to be reported in a separate component of shareholders' equity, such as accumulated other comprehensive income, but shall be amortized over the remaining life of the security as an adjustment of yield in a manner consistent with the amortization of any premium or discount.
Held-to-Maturity	Trading	The portion of the unrealized holding gain or loss at the date of the transfer that has not been previously recognized in earnings shall be recognized in earnings immediately.
	Available-for-Sale	The unrealized holding gain or loss at the date of the transfer shall be reported in other comprehensive income.

(d) IMPAIRMENT   Temporary declines in the fair value of securities below amortized cost are not recognized since it is generally held that such declines will ultimately reverse. However, the evaluation of whether an impairment is considered other-than-temporary has been a long-standing practice issue. In order to provide some guidance on evaluating other-than-temporary impairment, the FASB issued FSP FAS 115-1 and FAS 124-1 in November 2005. While the FSP clarifies the accounting in a few areas, it largely refers to existing accounting literature and incorporates the existing guidance from the SEC. The FSP refers to a basic three-step model:

Step 1: Determine whether an investment is impaired (i.e., fair value is less than cost). Generally, cost equals amortized cost less any previous write-downs.

Step 2: Determine whether the impairment is other-than-temporary. Other-than-temporary does not mean permanent, and an investment does not have to be deemed permanently impaired in order to require a write-down.

Step 3: If the impairment is deemed to be other-than-temporary, recognize an impairment loss equal to the difference between the carrying amount and its fair value, measured as of the balance sheet date. Further, the fair value becomes the new cost basis of the investment and should not be adjusted for subsequent recoveries in fair value.

Step 1: Determine Whether an Investment Is Impaired
Paragraphs 7 to 12 of FSP FAS 115-1 and FAS 124-1 state the following:

Impairment shall be assessed at the individual security level (herein referred to as "an investment"). An investment is impaired if the fair value of the investment is less than its cost. Except as provided in paragraph 10, an investor shall assess whether an investment is impaired in each reporting period. For entities that issue interim financial statements, each interim period is a reporting period.

An investor shall not combine separate contracts (a debt security and a guarantee or other credit enhancement) for purposes of determining whether a debt security is impaired or can contractually be prepaid or otherwise settled in such a way that the investor would not recover substantially all of its cost.

For investments other than cost-method investments (see paragraph 4(c)), if the fair value of the investment is less than its cost, proceed to Step 2.

Because the fair value of cost-method investments is not readily determinable, the evaluation of whether an investment is impaired shall be determined as follows:

(a) If an investor has estimated the fair value of a cost-method investment (for example, for disclosure under FASB Statement No. 107, *Disclosures about Fair Value of Financial Instruments*), that estimate shall be used to determine if the investment is impaired for the reporting periods in which the investor estimates fair value. If the fair value of the investment is less than its cost, proceed to Step 2.

(b) For reporting periods in which an investor has not estimated the fair value of a cost-method investment, the investor shall evaluate whether an event or change in circumstances has occurred in that period that may have a significant adverse effect on the fair value of the investment (an "impairment indicator"). Impairment indicators include, but are not limited to:

1. A significant deterioration in the earnings performance, credit rating, asset quality, or business prospects of the investee
2. A significant adverse change in the regulatory, economic, or technological environment of the investee
3. A significant adverse change in the general market condition of either the geographic area or the industry in which the investee operates
4. A bona fide offer to purchase (whether solicited or unsolicited), an offer by the investee to sell, or a completed auction process for the same or similar security for an amount less than the cost of the investment
5. Factors that raise significant concerns about the investee's ability to continue as a going concern, such as negative cash flows from operations, working capital deficiencies, or noncompliance with statutory capital requirements or debt covenants.

In addition, if an investment was previously tested for impairment under Step 2 and the investor concluded that the investment was not other-than-temporarily impaired, the investor shall continue to evaluate whether the investment is impaired (that is, shall estimate the fair value of the investment) in each subsequent reporting period until either (a) the investment experiences a recovery of fair value up to (or beyond) its cost or (b) the investor recognizes an other-than-temporary impairment loss.

If an impairment indicator is present, the investor shall estimate the fair value of the investment. If the fair value of the investment is less than its cost, proceed to Step 2.

Step 2:   Evaluate Whether an Impairment Is Other Than Temporary

Paragraphs 13 and 14 of FSP FAS 115-1 and FAS 124-1 state the following:

> When the fair value of an investment is less than its cost at the balance sheet date of the reporting period for which impairment is assessed, the impairment is either temporary or other than temporary. An investor shall apply other guidance that is pertinent to the determination of whether an impairment is other than temporary, such as paragraph 16 of Statement 115 (which references SEC Staff Accounting Bulletin Topic 5M, Other Than Temporary Impairment of Certain Investments in Debt and Equity Securities), paragraph 6 of APB Opinion No. 18, The Equity Method of Accounting for Investments in Common Stock, and EITF 99-20.
>
> In applying that guidance, questions sometimes arise about whether an investor shall recognize an other-than-temporary impairment only when it intends to sell a specifically identified available-for-sale debt or equity security at a loss shortly after the balance sheet date. When an investor has decided to sell an impaired available-for-sale security and the investor does not expect the fair value of the security to fully recover prior to the expected time of sale, the security shall be deemed other-than-temporarily impaired in the period in which the decision to sell is made. However, an investor shall recognize an impairment loss when the impairment is deemed other than temporary even if a decision to sell has not been made.

Step 3:   If the Impairment Is Other Than Temporary, Recognize an Impairment Loss Equal to the Difference between the Investment's Cost and Its Fair Value

Paragraph 15 of FSP FAS 115-1 and FAS 124-1 states the following:

> If it is determined in Step 2 that the impairment is other than temporary, then an impairment loss shall be recognized in earnings equal to the entire difference between the investment's cost and its fair value at the balance sheet date of the reporting period for which the assessment is made. The measurement of the impairment shall not include partial recoveries subsequent to the balance sheet date. The fair value of the investment would then become the new cost basis of the investment and shall not be adjusted for subsequent recoveries in fair value.

FSP FAS 115-1 refers to Paragraph 16 of Statement 115 for determining whether an impairment is other than temporary:

> For individual securities classified as either available-for-sale or held-to-maturity, an enterprise shall determine whether a decline in fair value below the amortized cost basis is other than temporary. (If a security has been the hedged item in a fair value hedge, the security's "amortized cost basis" shall reflect the effect of the adjustments of its carrying amount made pursuant to paragraph 22(b) of Statement 133.) For example, if it is probable that the investor will be unable to collect all amounts due according to the contractual terms of a debt security not impaired at acquisition, an other-than-temporary impairment shall be considered to have occurred. [Footnote 4] If the decline in fair value is judged to be other than temporary, the cost basis of the individual security shall be written down to fair value as a new cost basis and the amount of the write-down shall be included

in earnings (that is, accounted for as a realized loss). The new cost basis shall not be changed for subsequent recoveries in fair value. Subsequent increases in the fair value of available-for-sale securities shall be included in other comprehensive income pursuant to paragraph 13; subsequent decreases in fair value, if not an other-than-temporary impairment, also shall be included in other comprehensive income.

Footnote 4: A decline in the value of a security that is other than temporary is also discussed in FSP FAS 115-1 and FAS 124-1, AICPA Statement on Auditing Standards No. 92, *Auditing Derivative Instruments, Hedging Activities, and Investments in Securities*, and in SEC Staff Accounting Bulletin No. 59, *Accounting for Noncurrent Marketable Equity Securities*.

As referenced in Statement 115, paragraph 47 of SAS 92 provides the following guidance:

Impairment Losses. Regardless of the valuation method used, generally accepted accounting principles might require recognizing in earnings an impairment loss for a decline in fair value that is other than temporary. Determinations of whether losses are other than temporary often involve estimating the outcome of future events. Accordingly, judgment is required in determining whether factors exist that indicate that an impairment loss has been incurred at the end of the reporting period. These judgments are based on subjective as well as objective factors, including knowledge and experience about past and current events and assumptions about future events. The following are examples of such factors.

(a) Fair value is significantly below cost and

- The decline is attributable to adverse conditions specifically related to the security or to specific conditions in an industry or in a geographic area.
- The decline has existed for an extended period of time.
- Management does not possess both the intent and the ability to hold the security for a period of time sufficient to allow for any anticipated recovery in fair value.

(b) The security has been downgraded by a rating agency.
(c) The financial condition of the issuer has deteriorated.
(d) Dividends have been reduced or eliminated, or scheduled interest payments have not been made.
(e) The entity recorded losses from the security subsequent to the end of the reporting period.

As referenced in Statement 115, SAB 59 (as amended by SAB No. 103, *Update of Codification of Staff Accounting Bulletins*) provides the following guidance as Topic 5: "Miscellaneous Accounting, Other Than Temporary Impairment of Certain Investments in Debt and Equity Securities":

M. Other Than Temporary Impairment of Certain Investments in Debt and Equity Securities
Facts: Paragraph 16 of Statement 115 specifies that "[f]or individual securities classified as either available-for-sale or held-to-maturity, an enterprise shall

determine whether a decline in fair value below the amortized cost basis is other than temporary. . . . If the decline in fair value is judged to be other than temporary, the cost basis of the individual security shall be written down to fair value as a new cost basis and the amount of the write-down shall be included in earnings (that is, accounted for as a realized loss)."

Statement 115 does not define the phrase "other than temporary." In applying this guidance to its own situation, Company A has interpreted "other than temporary" to mean permanent impairment. Therefore, because Company A's management has not been able to determine that its investment in Company B is permanently impaired, no realized loss has been recognized even though the market price of B's shares is currently less than one-third of A's average acquisition price.

Question: Does the staff believe that the phrase "other than temporary" should be interpreted to mean "permanent"?

Interpretive Response: No. The staff believes that the FASB consciously chose the phrase "other than temporary" because it did not intend that the test be "permanent impairment," as has been used elsewhere in accounting practice. [Footnote 12]

Footnote 12: Footnote 4 to Statement 115 refers to this SAB for a discussion of considerations applicable to a determination as to whether a decline in market value below cost, at a particular point in time, is other than temporary. FASB's implementation guide, *A Guide to Implementation of Statement 115 on Accounting for Certain Investments in Debt and Equity Securities*, SAS 92, *Auditing Derivative Instruments, Hedging Activities, and Investments in Securities*, AICPA Audit Guide, *Auditing Derivative Instruments, Hedging Activities, and Investments in Securities*, and EITF Topic D-44 also address issues related to the determination of whether a decline in fair value of a investment security is other than temporary.

The value of investments in marketable securities classified as either available-for-sale or held-to-maturity may decline for various reasons. The market price may be affected by general market conditions which reflect prospects for the economy as a whole or by specific information pertaining to an industry or an individual company. Such declines require further investigation by management. Acting upon the premise that a write-down may be required, management should consider all available evidence to evaluate the realizable value of its investment.

There are numerous factors to be considered in such an evaluation, and their relative significance will vary from case to case. The staff believes that the following are only a few examples of the factors which, individually or in combination, indicate that a decline is other than temporary and that a write-down of the carrying value is required:

(a) The length of the time and the extent to which the market value has been less than cost;

(b) The financial condition and near-term prospects of the issuer, including any specific events which may influence the operations of the issuer, such as changes in technology that may impair the earnings potential of the investment or the discontinuance of a segment of the business that may affect the future earnings potential; or

(c) The intent and ability of the holder to retain its investment in the issuer for a period of time sufficient to allow for any anticipated recovery in market value.

Unless evidence exists to support a realizable value equal to or greater than the carrying value of the investment, a write-down to fair value accounted for as a realized loss should be recorded. In accordance with the guidance of paragraph 16 of Statement 115, such loss should be recognized in the determination of net income of the period in which it occurs and the written-down value of the investment in the company becomes the new cost basis of the investment.

In addition to retaining the disclosure requirements of the superseded EITF 03-1, *The Meaning of Other-Than-Temporary Impairment and Its Application to Certain Investments*, and referring to existing GAAP and SEC guidance, FSP FAS 115-1 and FAS 124-1 also clarifies the following:

- If the impairment is considered other-than-temporary, then the impairment should be measured as the difference between fair value and cost basis at the balance sheet date. (paragraph 15 of the FSP FAS 115-1 and FAS 124-1)
- For post-impairment income recognition, income must be recognized on expected, not contractual, cash flows. (paragraph 16 of the FSP FAS 115-1 and FAS 124-1)
- If the decision is made to sell an investment in a loss position, the loss should be recorded in the period the decision is made rather than when the actual sale occurs, incorporating existing guidance in EITF Topic 0-44. (paragraph 14 of the FSP FAS 115-1 and FAS 124-1)

(e) DISCLOSURES   The references applicable to disclosure requirements are:

- Statement 105, paragraph 20
- Statement 115, paragraphs 19–22
- SOP 03-3, paragraphs 14–16
- FSP FAS 115-1 and FAS 124-1, paragraph 17

18.5   EQUITY SECURITIES

(a) INTRODUCTION   Equity securities are often purchased to generate dividend income, to realize gains from their sale to other parties, and/or to achieve control over another enterprise. Except as discussed below, Statement 115, as amended, is the primary standard applicable to investments in equity securities that have readily determinable fair values. As mentioned earlier, the FASB has also issued a special report entitled *A Guide to Implementation of Statement 115 on Accounting for Certain Investments in Debt and Equity Securities*, which contains a series of questions and answers useful in understanding and implementing the Statement.

Statement 115 (par. 137) defines an equity security as "any security representing an ownership interest in an enterprise (e.g., common, preferred, or other capital stock) or the right to acquire (e.g., warrants, rights, and call options) or dispose of (e.g., put options) an ownership interest in an enterprise at fixed or determinable prices." This definition excludes "convertible debt or preferred stock that by its terms either must be redeemed by the issuing enterprise or is redeemable at the option of the investor." FASB Q&A No. 3 indicates that this "definition does not include written equity options because they represent *obligations* of the writer, not investments. Is also does not include cash-settled options on equity securities or options on equity-based indexes, because those instruments do not represent ownership interests in an enterprise. Options on debt securities are not within the scope of the Statement." In addition, the Statement does not apply to:

- "Enterprises whose specialized accounting practices include accounting for substantially all investments in debt and equity securities at market value or fair value, with changes in value recognized in earnings (income) or in the change in net assets" (par. 4).
- Not-for-profit organizations. However, the Statement applies "to cooperatives and mutual enterprises, including credit unions and mutual insurance companies" (par. 4).
- "Investments in equity securities accounted for under the equity method nor to investments in consolidated subsidiaries" (par. 4). Consolidation and the equity method of accounting are discussed in Chapter 11 of this *Handbook*.
- Equity securities that do not have readily determinable fair values (e.g., restricted stock).

FASB Q&A No. 4 notes that "APB Opinion No. 18, *The Equity Method of Accounting for Investments in Common Stock*, describes the cost method and the equity method of accounting for investments in common stock and specifies the criteria for determining when to use the equity method. Equity securities that do not have readily determinable fair values that are not required to be accounted for by the equity method are typically carried at cost, as described in paragraph 6 of Opinion 18, adjusted for other-than-temporary impairment."

(b) INITIAL RECOGNITION AND MEASUREMENT   Upon acquisition, equity securities are generally recorded at cost, presumably fair value at acquisition, and classified into one of two categories: (1) available-for-sale or (2) trading. FASB Q&A No. 38 provides that the initial basis under Statement 115 of a marketable equity security that should no longer be accounted for under the equity method would be the previous carrying amount of the investment. The Q&A notes that "paragraph 19(1) of APB Opinion No. 18, *The Equity Method of Accounting for Investments in Common Stock*, states that the earnings or losses that relate to the stock retained should remain as a part of the carrying amount of the investment and that the investment account should not be adjusted retroactively."

(c) ACCOUNTING AFTER ACQUISITION   Gains and losses realized on the sale of equity securities are included in earnings and dividend income is recognized upon declaration. As previously discussed in the section, sale accounting is appropriate only for transfers of financial assets in which the transferor surrenders control over those financial assets pursuant to the provisions of Statement 140, paragraph 9. Otherwise, the transferor should account for the transfer as a secured borrowing with pledge of collateral pursuant to Statement 140, paragraph 15.

Equity securities are carried at fair value. As with debt securities, the accounting for the resulting unrealized gain or loss depends on the equity security's classification. Changes in the fair value of equity securities classified as trading are reflected in earnings while changes in the fair value of equity securities classified as available-for-sale are reflected in a separate component of shareholder's equity (or other comprehensive income), net of the related deferred income tax effects.

(d) IMPAIRMENT   Declines in fair value that are deemed to be "other-than-temporary" should be accounted for as realized losses, resulting in a new cost basis for the security. Impairment is discussed above. For equity securities with readily determinable market values, the impairment guidance in paragraph 16 of Statement 115 (see above) should be followed. For investments in equity securities that are carried on the cost method, FSP FAS 115-1 and FAS 124-1 refers to Paragraph 6 of APB 18 for determining whether an impairment is other than temporary:

> a. THE COST METHOD. An investor records an investment in the stock of an investee at cost, and recognizes as income dividends received that are distributed from net accumulated earnings of the investee since the date of acquisition by the investor. The net accumulated earnings of an investee subsequent to the date of investment are recognized by the investor only to the extent distributed by the investee as dividends. Dividends received in excess of earnings subsequent to the date of investment are considered a return of investment and are recorded as reductions of cost of the investment. A series of operating losses of an investee or other factors may indicate that a decrease in value of the investment has occurred which is other than temporary and should accordingly be recognized. [Footnote 3a]
>
> Footnote 3a: FSP FAS 115-1 and FAS 124-1 discusses the methodology for determining impairment and evaluating whether the impairment is other than temporary.

Paragraph 10 of FSP FAS 115-1 and FAS 124-1 discusses the impairment considerations for cost-method investments for which the fair value is not readily determinable.

(e) TRANSFERS BETWEEN CATEGORIES   The transfer of equity securities between categories is accounted for in the same manner as the transfer of debt securities discussed above. Of course, transfers to or from the held-to-maturity category do not apply.

(f) DISCLOSURES   The references applicable to disclosure requirements are:

- Statement 105, paragraph 20
- Statement 115, paragraphs 19, 21–22
- FSP FAS 115-1 and FAS 124-1, paragraph 18

18.6   SOURCES AND SUGGESTED REFERENCES

American Institute of CPAs, "Accounting by Certain Entities (Including Entities with Trade Receivables) That Lend to or Finance the Activities of Others," Statement of Position 01-6, AICPA, New York.

American Institute of CPAs, "Accounting for Certain Purchased Loans and Debt Securities Acquired in a Transfer," Statement of Position 03-3, AICPA, New York.

American Institute of CPAs, "Disclosure of Certain Significant Risks and Uncertainties," Statement of Position 94-6, AICPA, New York.

Bort, Richard, *Corporate Cash Management Handbook*, Warren, Gorham & Lamont, Boston, 1989.

Committee on Accounting Procedure, "Restatement and Revision of Accounting Research Bulletins," Accounting Research Bulletin No. 43, AICPA, New York, 1953.

Financial Accounting Standards Board, "A Guide to Implementation of Statement 115 on Accounting for Certain Investments in Debt and Equity Securities," Special Report FASB, Norwalk, CT, 1995.

Financial Accounting Standards Board, "Accounting for Changes That Result in a Transferor Regaining Control of Financial Assets Sold," EITF Issue No. 02-9, FASB, Norwalk, CT.

Financial Accounting Standards Board, "Accounting for Contingencies," Statement of Financial Accounting Standards No. 5, FASB, Stamford, CT, 1975.

Financial Accounting Standards Board, "Accounting for Conversion of a Loan into a Debt Security in a Debt Restructuring," EITF Issue No. 94-8, FASB, Norwalk, CT, 1997.

Financial Accounting Standards Board, "Accounting for Nonrefundable Fees and Costs Associated with Originating or Acquiring Loans and Initial Direct Costs of Leases," Statement of Financial Accounting Standards No. 91, FASB, Norwalk, CT.

Financial Accounting Standards Board, "Accounting for Transfers and Servicing of Financial Assets and Extinguishments of Liabilities," Statement of Financial Accounting Standards No. 140, FASB, Norwalk, CT, 2000.

Financial Accounting Standards Board, "Accounting by Debtors and Creditors for Troubled Debt Restructurings," Statement of Financial Accounting Standards No. 15, FASB, Stamford, CT, 1977.

Financial Accounting Standards Board, "Accounting by Creditors for Impairment of a Loan," Statement of Financial Accounting Standards No. 114, FASB, Norwalk, CT, 1993.

Financial Accounting Standards Board, "Accounting by Creditors for Impairment of a Loan—Income Recognition and Disclosures," Statement of Financial Accounting Standards No. 118, FASB, Norwalk, CT, 1994.

Financial Accounting Standards Board, "Accounting for Certain Investment in Debt and Equity Securities," Statement of Financial Accounting Standards No. 115, FASB, Norwalk, CT, 1993.

Financial Accounting Standards Board, "Accounting for Transfers and Servicing of Financial Assets and Extinguishment of Liabilities," Statement of Financial Accounting Standards No. 140, FASB, Norwalk, CT, 2001.

Financial Accounting Standards Board, "Balance Sheet Treatment of a Sale of Mortgage Servicing Rights with a Sub servicing Agreement," EITF Issue 90-21, FASB, Norwalk, CT.

Financial Accounting Standards Board, "Classifying Notes Receivable for Capital Stock," EITF Issue 85-1, FASB, Norwalk, CT.

Financial Accounting Standards Board, "Consolidation of All Majority-Owned Subsidiaries," Statement of Financial Accounting Standards No. 94, FASB, Stamford, CT, 1987.

Financial Accounting Standards Board, "Determination of What Risks and Rewards, If Any, Can Be Retained and Whether Any Unresolved Contingencies May Exist in a Sale of Mortgage Loan Servicing Rights," EITF Issue 95-5, FASB, Norwalk, CT.

Financial Accounting Standards Board, "Financial Reporting and Changing Prices," Statement of Financial Accounting Standards No. 89, FASB, Stamford, CT, 1986.

Financial Accounting Standards Board, "Foreign Currency Translation," Statement of Financial Accounting Standards No. 52, FASB, Stamford, CT, 1981.

Financial Accounting Standards Board, "Questions and Answers Related to Servicing Activities in a Qualifying Special-Purpose Entity under FASB Statement No. 140," Topic D-99, FASB, Norwalk, CT.

Financial Accounting Standards Board, "Questions Related to the Implementation of FASB Statement No. 115," EITF Topic No. D-39, FASB, Norwalk, CT.

Financial Accounting Standards Board, "Recognition of Interest Income and Impairment on Purchased and Retained Beneficial Interests in Securitized Financial Assets," EITF Issue No. 99-20, FASB, Norwalk, CT.

Financial Accounting Standards Board, "Reporting Comprehensive Income," Statement of Financial Accounting Standards No. 130, FASB, Norwalk, CT, 1997.

Financial Accounting Standards Board, "Terms of Loan Products That May Give Rise to a Concentration of Credit Risk," FASB Staff Position-SOP 94-6-1.

Financial Accounting Standards Board, "The Applicability of FASB Statement No. 115 to Desecuritizations of Financial Assets," EITF Topic No. D-51, FASB, Norwalk, CT.

Financial Accounting Standards Board, "The Meaning of Other-Than-Temporary Impairment and Its Application to Certain Investments," EITF Issue 03-1, FASB, Norwalk, CT.

Keiso, Donald E., Weygandt, Jerry D., and Warfield, Terry D., *Intermediate Accounting, Twelfth Edition,* John Wiley & Sons, Hoboken, NJ, 2006.

Meigs, Walter B., Larsen, E. John, and Meigs, Robert F., *Principles of Auditing, Ninth Edition,* Irwin, Homewood, IL, 1988.

O'Reilly, Vincent M., McDonnell, Patrick J., Winograd, Barry N., Gerson, James, S., and Jaenicke, Henry R., *Montgomery's Auditing, Twelfth Edition,* John Wiley & Sons, New York, 1998.

Securities and Exchange Commission, "Notice of Adoption of Amendments to Regulation S-X and Related Interpretations and Guidelines Regarding Disclosure of Compensating Balances and Short-Term Borrowing Arrangements," Accounting Series Release No. 148, SEC, Washington, DC, November 1973.

Smith, Jay M., Jr., and Skousen, K. Fred, *Intermediate Accounting, Tenth Edition,* South-Western Publishing, Cincinnati, OH, 1990.

*CHAPTER **18A**

TRANSFERS OF FINANCIAL ASSETS (NEW)

Michael A. Antonetti, CPA, CMA
Crowe Horwath LLP†

† The information contained in this chapter does not necessarily represent the views of Crowe Horwath LLP.

18A.1 INTRODUCTION

Transfers of financial assets take many forms. Accounting for transfers in which the transferor has no continuing involvement with the transferred assets or with the transferee has not been controversial. However, transfers of financial assets often occur in which the transferor has some continuing involvement either with the assets transferred or with the transferee. Examples of continuing involvement are recourse, servicing, agreements to reacquire, options written or held, and pledges of collateral. Transfers of financial assets with continuing involvement raise issues about the circumstances under which the transfers should be considered as sales of all or part of the assets or as secured borrowings and about how transferors and transferees should account for sales and secured borrowings.[1] During September 2000, the Financial Accounting Standards Board (FASB) issued Statement No. 140, *Accounting for Transfers and Servicing of Financial Assets and Extinguishments of Liabilities—A Replacement of FASB Statement 125*, to address the accounting for transfers of financial assets.

As discussed further below, Statement 140 provides accounting and reporting standards for transfers and servicing of financial assets and extinguishment of liabilities. Those standards are based on consistent application of a financial-components approach that focuses on control. Under that approach, after a transfer of financial assets, an entity recognizes the financial and servicing assets it controls and the liabilities it has incurred, derecognizes financial assets when control has been surrendered, and derecognizes liabilities when extinguished. Statement 140 provides consistent standards for distinguishing transfers of financial assets that are sales from transfers that are secured borrowings.[2] Statement 140 was effective for most transfers and servicing of financial assets and extinguishments of liabilities occurring after March 31, 2001.

In recent years, additional guidance has been issued to clarify or amend some of the provisions contained within Statement 140, such as the following:

- FASB Statement No. 155, *Accounting for Certain Hybrid Financial Instruments—An Amendment of FASB Statements No. 133 and 140*, issued in February 2006 and effective for all financial instruments acquired or issued after the beginning of an entity's first fiscal year that begins after September 15, 2006
- FASB Statement No. 156, *Accounting for Servicing of Financial Assets—An Amendment of FASB Statement No. 140*, issued in March 2006 and effective as of the beginning of an entity's first fiscal year that begins after September 15, 2006
- FASB Statement No. 157, *Fair Value Measurements*, issued in September 2006 and effective for financial statements issued for fiscal years beginning after November 15, 2007, and interim periods within those fiscal years
- FASB Staff Position No. 140-1, *Accounting for Accrued Interest Receivable Related to Securitized and Sold Receivables under Statement 140*, issued on April 14, 2003, and effective for fiscal quarters beginning after March 31, 2003
- FASB Staff Position No. 140-2, *Clarification of the Application of Paragraphs 40(b) and 40(c) of FASB Statement No. 140*, issued on November 9, 2005, and effective immediately

---

1. FASB Statement No. 140, *Accounting for Transfers and Servicing of Financial Assets and Extinguishments of Liabilities—A Replacement of FASB Statement 125*, September 2000 (from Summary page).
2. Statement 140 (from Summary page).

- FASB Staff Position No. 140-3, *Accounting for Transfers of Financial Assets and Repurchase Financing Transactions*, issued on February 20, 2008, and effective for financial statements issued for fiscal years beginning after November 15, 2008 and interim periods within those fiscal years

The information contained within this chapter includes the effects of the additional guidance that has amended Statement 140.

18A.2   WHAT ARE FINANCIAL ASSETS?

Statement 140 defines a **financial asset** as "cash, evidence of an ownership interest in an entity, or a contract that conveys to [one] entity a right (a) to receive cash or another financial instrument from a [second] entity or (b) to exchange other financial instruments on potentially favorable terms with the [second] entity."[3] Some common financial assets include trade receivables, credit card receivables, residential mortgage receivables, government bonds, and corporate bonds. Transfers of financial assets are discussed further below.

18A.3   WHAT ARE BENEFICIAL INTERESTS?

As discussed further below, many financial asset transfers utilize a qualifying special-purpose entity. A qualifying special-purpose entity issues to third parties interests in the cash flows generated by the financial assets that it holds. These interests are often referred to as *beneficial interests*. Statement 140 defines **beneficial interests** as "rights to receive all or portions of specified cash inflows to a trust or other entity, including senior and subordinated shares of interest, principal, or other cash inflows to be 'passed-through' or 'paid-through,' premiums due to guarantors, commercial paper obligations, and residual interests, whether in the form of debt or equity."[4] Common investors in beneficial interests include banks, insurance companies, brokers and dealers, hedge funds, and pension funds.

18A.4   WHAT IS A FINANCIAL ASSET TRANSFER?

Statement 140 defines a **transfer** as "the conveyance of a noncash financial asset by and to someone other than the issuer of that financial asset. Thus, a transfer includes selling a receivable, putting it into a securitization trust, or posting it as collateral but excludes the origination of that receivable, the settlement of that receivable, or the restructuring of that receivable into a security in a troubled debt restructuring."[5] A **transferor** is "an entity that transfers a financial asset, a portion of a financial asset, or a group of financial assets that it controls to another entity,"[6] while a **transferee** is "an entity that receives a financial asset, a portion of a financial asset, or a group of financial assets from a transferor."[7]

Companies wish to transfer and derecognize financial assets for a variety of reasons. Most importantly, a transfer of financial assets improves a company's liquidity. Other benefits from

---

3.   Statement 140 (Appendix E).
4.   Ibid.
5.   Ibid.
6.   Ibid.
7.   Ibid.

transferring financial assets include improved balance sheet ratios, increased return on assets and equity, and an ability to manage interest rate and credit risks.

18A.5 WHAT ARE THE CONTROL CRITERIA THAT MUST BE MET FOR A TRANSFER OF FINANCIAL ASSETS TO BE RECORDED AS A SALE?

Paragraph 9 of Statement 140 states,

> A transfer of financial assets (or all or a portion of a financial asset) in which the transferor surrenders control over those financial assets shall be accounted for as a sale to the extent that consideration other than beneficial interests in the transferred assets is received in exchange. The transferor has surrendered control over transferred assets if and only if *all of the following conditions* are met:
>
> a. The transferred assets have been isolated from the transferor—put presumptively beyond the reach of the transferor and its creditors, even in bankruptcy or other receivership.
> b. Each transferee (or if the transferee is a qualifying special purpose entity, each holder of its beneficial interests) has the right to pledge or exchange the assets (or beneficial interests) it received, and no condition both constrains the transferee (or holder) from taking advantage of its right to pledge or exchange and provides more than a trivial benefit to the transferor.
> c. The transferor does not maintain effective control over the transferred assets through either (1) an agreement that both entitles and obligates the transferor to repurchase or redeem them before their maturity or (2) the ability to unilaterally cause the holder to return specific assets, other than through a cleanup call.[8]

If the transferor maintains control of the financial assets after the transfer, then the transfer is considered a secured borrowing arrangement.

In recent years, many mortgage stakeholders such as banks and government-sponsored entities have had to restate their financial statements. Often, one company will discover an accounting issue related to Statement 140 and, when the details become public, another company will find that they, too, have the same issue. Below are excerpts from restatements discussed in annual reports on Form 10-K as filed with the Securities and Exchange Commission:

> **Doral Financial Corporation Annual Report on Form 10-K/A for the year ended December 31, 2004 as filed with the SEC on February 27, 2006:**
>
> In October 2005, new information came to the attention of the Audit Committee regarding the possible existence of certain recourse provisions in the Company's mortgage loan sales to local financial institutions that were not captured by the Company's financial reporting process. The Audit Committee promptly asked Latham to investigate this issue. On December 14, 2005, Latham informed the Audit Committee that, based on its investigation, it is likely that there were oral agreements or understandings between the former treasurer and the former director emeritus of the Company and FirstBank Puerto Rico, a wholly-owned banking

---

8.   Statement 140 (paragraph 9).

subsidiary of First BanCorp ("FirstBank"), providing recourse beyond the limited recourse established in the written contracts. Based on an analysis of these findings and other evidence reviewed by the Company, the Company concluded that the mortgage loan sales to FirstBank did not qualify as sales under Statement of Financial Accounting Standard ("SFAS") 140, "Accounting for Transfers and Servicing of Financial Assets and Extinguishments of Liabilities" ("SFAS 140"), because these sales did not satisfy the "reasonable assurance" standard of SFAS 140 regarding the isolation of assets in bankruptcy. In addition, the former treasurer entered into side letters guaranteeing the yield to an investor in connection with certain sales of IOs. Neither the oral recourse agreements or understandings nor the side letters were captured by the Company's financial reporting process or communicated to the Audit Committee, PwC or the Company's internal and external counsel. This resulted in the misapplication of generally accepted accounting principles in the United States of America ("GAAP") to several transactions and had a material impact on the Company's consolidated financial statements.

In addition, on December 14, 2005, based on the results of the independent investigation, the Audit Committee concluded that it was necessary to reverse a number of transactions, including a transaction occurring during the fourth quarter of 2004, involving generally contemporaneous purchases and sales of mortgage loans from and to local financial institutions where the amounts purchased and sold, and other terms of the transactions, were similar. The decision followed a determination that there was insufficient contemporaneous documentation to substantiate the business purpose for these transactions in light of the timing and similarity of the purchase and sale amounts and other terms of the transactions. For some periods, the gains on sale previously recorded in connection with such transactions had a material impact on the Company's consolidated financial statements.

Bluegreen Corp. Annual Report on Form 10-K for the year ended December 31, 2005 as filed with the SEC on March 16, 2006:

In connection with the securitization of certain of its receivables in December 2005, the Company undertook a review of the prior accounting treatment for certain of its existing and prior notes receivable purchase facilities (together the "Purchase Facilities"). As a result of that review, on December 15, 2005, the Company determined that it would restate its consolidated financial statements for the first three quarters of fiscal 2005 and the fiscal years ended December 31, 2003 and 2004 due to certain misapplications of GAAP in the accounting for sales of the Company's vacation ownership notes receivable and other related matters. The following sections describe the restatement matters in more detail.

The restatement reflects the sales of notes receivable under three separate Purchase Facilities as on-balance-sheet financing transactions as opposed to off-balance-sheet sales transactions as the Company had originally accounted for these transactions pursuant to Statement of Financial Accounting Standards No. 140, "Accounting for Transfers and Servicing of Financial Assets and Extinguishments of Liabilities" ("SFAS 140"). Accordingly, the consolidated financial statements have been restated to (1) remove the gain on sale of notes receivable and retained interest in notes receivable sold previously recognized, (2) re-recognize the original notes receivable sold and the related interest income for the periods outstanding, (3) and recognize debt for the cash proceeds received from the Purchase Facilities and the related interest expense for the periods outstanding.

The Company consummated two term securitization transactions, one in December 2002 and one in July 2004, which included substantially all of the notes receivable that had been previously accounted for as having been sold under the Purchase Facilities. Both of these term securitization transactions have been accounted for as sales pursuant to SFAS 140, and therefore the notes receivable financed under the Purchase Facilities are considered to be sold in the term securitization transactions, with resulting gains on sale recognized at that time.

In connection with the sales of notes receivable, we retain servicing rights. Receivables servicing includes processing payments from borrowers, accounting for principal and interest on such receivables, making advances when required, performing collections efforts with delinquent borrowers, processing defaults, reporting to investors and lenders on portfolio activity, and performing other administrative duties. During the review of our accounting policies related to the sales of notes receivables, the Company determined that the servicing fees earned for servicing the sold notes receivable reflected fair value (i.e., adequate compensation) at the time of the transaction. Pursuant to SFAS 140, a servicing asset exists when the benefits of servicing are more than adequate compensation. Accordingly, the consolidated financial statements have been restated to remove the original values recognized as servicing assets as well as the related servicing asset amortization expense.

Also, as a part of its re-evaluation of these transactions, the Company determined that the computation of the gains on sales of receivables in the December 2002 and July 2004 term securitization transactions did not take into account the fair value allocation of financial components methodology for recording its retained interest as prescribed by SFAS 140. The impact of the fair value allocation of financial components methodology is to reduce the gain on sale, but once the retained interest is marked to market value immediately thereafter, the impact will be to increase other comprehensive income in the balance sheet.

As part of the restatement, the company recorded, as of the beginning of fiscal 2004, a cumulative charge of $7.8 million to retained earnings and a $4.0 million increase to beginning other comprehensive income reflecting the impact of the change in accounting for the above mentioned transactions originating in prior periods. Also, the restatement resulted in a reduction of net income of $6.0 million for fiscal 2003 and an increase of $6.1 million for fiscal 2004.

(a) THE TRANSFERRED ASSETS HAVE BEEN ISOLATED FROM THE TRANSFEROR
Generally, a transfer of financial assets directly to third parties with no continuing involvement by the transferor will qualify for sale accounting provided the other Statement 140 criteria are met; however, a transfer can still qualify for sale accounting even though the transferor may have some continuing involvement (e.g., providing recourse for credit risk, servicing the financial assets, etc.) with the financial assets. Sale accounting is not based on whether the transferor has continuing involvement with the financial assets, but rather whether the transferor has given up effective control of the financial assets to the transferee. See the discussion

below regarding the use of qualifying special-purpose entities to legally isolate the financial assets from the transferor.

(b) EACH TRANSFEREE HAS THE RIGHT TO PLEDGE OR EXCHANGE THE ASSETS IT RECEIVED

"Sale accounting is allowed . . . only if each transferee has the right to pledge, or the right to exchange, the transferred assets or beneficial interests it received, but constraints on that right also matter. Many transferor-imposed or other conditions on a transferee's right to pledge or exchange a transferred asset both constrain a transferee from pledging or exchanging the transferred assets and, through that constraint, provide more than a trivial benefit to the transferor."[9] Some conditions that constrain a transferee's ability to control a financial asset include (1) a transferor prohibiting a subsequent sale of the financial assets by the transferee, (2) a call option held by the transferor on the financial assets, and (3) other transferor-imposed terms that limit a transferee's ability to exchange, sell, or pledge the financial assets. Generally, most restrictions imposed by a transferor would prevent sale accounting because they would be deemed to provide "more than a trivial benefit" to the transferor.

"Some conditions do not constrain a transferee from pledging or exchanging the asset and therefore do not preclude a transfer subject to such a condition from being accounted for as a sale. For example, a transferor's right of first refusal on the occurrence of a bona fide offer to the transferee from a third party presumptively would not constrain a transferee, because that right in itself does not enable the transferor to compel the transferee to sell the assets and the transferee would be in a position to receive the sum offered by exchanging the asset, albeit possibly from the transferor rather than the third party."[10]

(c) THE TRANSFEROR DOES NOT MAINTAIN EFFECTIVE CONTROL OVER THE TRANSFERRED ASSETS THROUGH EITHER A REPURCHASE AGREEMENT OR THE ABILITY TO UNILATERALLY CAUSE THE HOLDER TO RETURN SPECIFIC ASSETS

Financial asset transfers that include a right for the transferor to repurchase, redeem, or require the transferee to return the financial assets to the transferor prior to maturity would not qualify for sale accounting because the transferor never gave up effective control of the financial assets. Whether or not a transferor exercises one of these rights is irrelevant in the determination of sale accounting. The mere existence of these rights creates effective control over the transferred financial assets. As such, the transferor would have to account for the transfer as a secured borrowing.

If the transferor's right to reclaim transferred assets is contingent on an event that is outside of the transferor's control, then this right would not preclude sale accounting as long as the other conditions within paragraph 9 of Statement 140 are met. If such an outside event were to occur, then the transferor would have to again recognize the transferred financial assets as it would once again have effective control.

As noted within paragraph 9 of Statement 140, a cleanup call does not preclude sale accounting. Statement 140 defines a *cleanup call* as "an option held by the servicer or its affiliate, which may be the transferor, to purchase the remaining transferred financial assets, or the remaining beneficial interests not held by the transferor, its affiliates, or its agents in a qualifying SPE [special-purpose entity] (or in a series of beneficial interests in transferred assets within a qualifying SPE), if the amount of outstanding assets or beneficial interests falls

---

9.   Statement 140 (paragraph 29).
10.   Statement 140 (paragraph 30).

to a level at which the cost of servicing those assets or beneficial interests becomes burden-some in relation to the benefits of servicing."[11]

The right of a servicer, which may also be the transferor, to initiate a cleanup call would not cause the servicer to maintain effective control over the transferred assets, provided the servicer may only call a *de minimis* level of outstanding financial assets or beneficial interests.

18A.6   WHAT IS A QUALIFYING SPECIAL-PURPOSE ENTITY?

Many companies create *special-purpose entities* to facilitate the sale accounting treatment for a transfer of financial assets because such entities help isolate the financial assets from the transferor and its creditors. Paragraph 35 of Statement 140 describes the conditions under which a company may transfer financial assets to a trust or other legal vehicle that is deemed to be a qualifying special-purpose entity (SPE). A qualifying SPE is significantly limited in the activities it may perform, the types of assets it may own, and the situations in which it may dispose of assets. If a transfer of financial assets to a qualifying SPE meets the sale criteria specified in paragraph 9 of Statement 140, then the qualifying SPE does not have to be consolidated by the transferor.

Paragraph 35 of Statement 140 states,

> A qualifying SPE is a trust or other legal vehicle that meets *all* of the following conditions:
>
> a.   It is demonstrably distinct from the transferor.
> b.   Its permitted activities (1) are significantly limited, (2) were entirely specified in the legal documents that established the SPE or created the beneficial interests in the transferred assets that it holds, and (3) may be significantly changed only with the approval of the holders of at least a majority of the beneficial interests held by entities other than any transferor, its affiliates, and its agents.
> c.   It may hold only:
>
> (i)   Financial assets transferred to it that are passive in nature
> (ii)   Passive derivative financial instruments that pertain to beneficial interests issued or sold to parties other than the transferor, its affiliates, or its agents
> (iii) Financial assets (for example, guarantees or rights to collateral) that would reimburse it if others were to fail to adequately service financial assets transferred to it or to timely pay obligations due to it and that it entered into when it was established, when assets were transferred to it, or when beneficial interests (other than derivative financial instruments) were issued by the SPE
> (iv)   Servicing rights related to financial assets that it holds
> (v)   Temporarily, nonfinancial assets obtained in connection with the collection of financial assets that it holds
> (vi)   Cash collected from assets that it holds and investments purchased with that cash pending distribution to holders of beneficial interests that are appropriate for that purpose (that is, money-market or other relatively risk-free instruments without options and with maturities no later than the expected distribution date).

---

11.   Statement 140 (Appendix E).

d. If it can sell or otherwise dispose of noncash financial assets, it can do so only in automatic response to one of the following conditions:

(i) Occurrence of an event or circumstance that (a) is specified in the legal documents that established the SPE or created the beneficial interests in the transferred assets that it holds; (b) is outside the control of the transferor, its affiliates, or its agents; and (c) causes, or is expected at the date of transfer to cause, the fair value of those financial assets to decline by a specified degree below the fair value of those assets when the SPE obtained them

(ii) Exercise by a BIH ("beneficial interest holder") (other than the transferor, its affiliates, or its agents) of a right to put that holder's beneficial interest back to the SPE

(iii) Exercise by the transferor of a call or ROAP ("removal-of-accounts provision") specified in the legal documents that established the SPE, transferred assets to the SPE, or created the beneficial interests in the transferred assets that it holds

(iv) Termination of the SPE or maturity of the beneficial interests in those financial assets on a fixed or determinable date that is specified at inception

(a) IT IS DEMONSTRABLY DISTINCT FROM THE TRANSFEROR   A qualifying SPE is demonstrably distinct from the transferor only if it cannot be unilaterally dissolved by any transferor, its affiliates, or its agents and either (1) at least 10 percent of the fair value of its beneficial interests is held by parties other than any transferor, its affiliates, or its agents or (2) the transfer is a guaranteed mortgage securitization.[12] If a transferor retains more than 90 percent of the fair value of beneficial interests of the qualifying SPE, the transferor is deemed to have control of the transferred financial assets and, therefore, sale accounting would be precluded. "An ability to unilaterally dissolve an SPE can take many forms, including but not limited to holding sufficient beneficial interests to demand that the trustee dissolve the SPE, the right to call all the assets transferred to the SPE, and a right to call or a prepayment privilege on the beneficial interests held by other parties."[13]

A guaranteed mortgage securitization is a securitization of a mortgage loan that includes a substantive guarantee by a third party. Guaranteed mortgage securitizations are exempt from the 10 percent holding threshold described above. Mortgage-backed securities that continue to be held by a transferor in a guaranteed mortgage securitization in which the SPE meets all conditions for being a qualifying SPE are classified in the financial statements of the transferor as securities that are subsequently measured under FASB Statement No. 115, *Accounting for Certain Investments in Debt and Equity Securities.*

(b) ITS PERMITTED ACTIVITIES ARE SIGNIFICANTLY LIMITED, WERE ENTIRELY SPECIFIED IN THE LEGAL DOCUMENTS THAT CREATED IT, AND MAY BE SIGNIFICANTLY CHANGED ONLY WITH THE APPROVAL OF A MAJORITY OF THE HOLDERS OTHER THAN THE TRANSFEROR   The powers of the SPE must be limited to those activities allowed by paragraph 35 of Statement 140 for it to be a qualifying SPE. In addition, the qualifying SPE's activities must be entirely specified in the legal documents that created it.

---

12.   Statement 140 (paragraph 36).
13.   Ibid.

The beneficial interest holders other than any transferor, its affiliates, or its agents may have the ability to change the powers of a qualifying SPE (QSPE). If a QSPE's activities change such that it no longer meets the conditions specified in paragraph 35 of Statement 140, then the QSPE would lose its qualifying status and the transferred financial assets would no longer qualify for sale accounting. In these instances, paragraph 55 of Statement 140 requires the transferor to re-recognize the transferred assets on the date in which the QSPE became disqualified. The transferor initially measures the financial assets and any liabilities at fair value on the date of the change, as if the transferor purchased the assets and assumed the liabilities on that date.

(c) IT MAY HOLD PASSIVE FINANCIAL INSTRUMENTS   A qualifying SPE may hold passive financial instruments, including passive derivative financial instruments. Financial instruments are passive only if holding the instrument does not involve its holder in making decisions other than the decisions inherent in servicing.

Typical passive financial instruments transferred to a QSPE include residential mortgage loans, credit card receivables, and trade receivables. A QSPE can only hold financial assets that were transferred to it by the transferor. A QSPE cannot create financial assets, such as loans, nor can it actively purchase financial assets or manage an asset portfolio.

(d) IT MAY SELL OR DISPOSE OF NONCASH FINANCIAL ASSETS ONLY IN RESPONSE TO CERTAIN CONDITIONS   If a sale of assets from a qualifying SPE occurs, it must be an automatic response to one of the conditions described in paragraph 35(d) of Statement 140. The QSPE cannot have discretion to choose which assets to be disposed of or when the disposal may occur because such discretion would make the SPE an active rather than a passive entity and, thereby, jeopardize its qualifying status.

Examples of requirements to sell, exchange, put, or distribute (hereinafter referred to collectively as *dispose of*) noncash financial assets that *are* **permitted** activities of a QSPE include requirements to dispose of transferred assets in response to:

1. A failure to properly service transferred assets that could result in the loss of a substantial third-party credit guarantee
2. A default by the obligor
3. A downgrade by a major rating agency of the transferred assets or of the underlying obligor to a rating below a specified minimum rating
4. The involuntary insolvency of the transferor
5. A decline in the fair value of the transferred assets to a specified value less than their fair value at the time they were transferred to the SPE

The following are examples of powers or requirements to dispose of noncash financial assets that *are not* **permitted** activities of a QSPE, because they do not respond automatically to the occurrence of a specified event or circumstance outside the control of the transferor, its affiliates, or its agents that causes, or is expected to cause, the fair value of those transferred assets to decline by a specified degree below the fair value of those assets when the SPE obtained them:

1. A power that allows an SPE to choose to either dispose of transferred assets or hold them in response to a default, a downgrade, a decline in fair value, or a servicing failure

2. A requirement to dispose of marketable equity securities upon a specified decline from their "highest fair value" if that power could result in disposing of the asset in exchange for an amount that is more than the fair value of those assets at the time they were transferred to the SPE

3. A requirement to dispose of transferred assets in response to the violation of a non-substantive contractual provision (i.e., a provision for which there is not a sufficiently large disincentive to ensure performance)[14]

18A.7   WHAT ARE SECURITIZATIONS?

Securitization is "the process by which financial assets are transformed into securities."[15] "Financial assets such as mortgage loans, automobile loans, trade receivables, credit card receivables, and other revolving charge accounts are assets commonly transferred in securitizations."[16]

Securitization often begins with the creation of a legal entity (e.g., a corporation or trust) to own the portfolio of financial assets. The legal entity's capital structure (used to fund the purchase of the portfolio) is designed in ways to attract investors to the repackaged cash flows. Credit enhancement (e.g., a guarantee by the transferor or a third party) is added and the resulting securities often are rated by a third-party rating agency (e.g., Moody's). Proceeds from the sale of the resulting securities are used to acquire the portfolio of financial assets. The transferor may continue in the role of servicer, collecting and remitting payments from obligors on the transferred assets, or may have other continuing involvement with the transaction.

"A securitization carried out in one transfer or a series of transfers may or may not isolate the transferred assets beyond the reach of the transferor and its creditors. Whether it does depends on the structure of the securitization transaction taken as a whole, considering such factors as the type and extent of further involvement in arrangements to protect investors from credit and interest rate risks, the availability of other assets, and the powers of bankruptcy courts or other receivers."[17] Securitizations that meet the criteria in paragraph 9 of Statement 140 qualify for sale accounting.

Many securitizations use two transfers intended to isolate transferred assets beyond the reach of the transferor and its creditors, even in bankruptcy. In those "two-step" structures:

1. The corporation transfers financial assets to a special-purpose corporation that, although wholly owned, is so designed that the possibility that the transferor or its creditors could reclaim the assets is remote. This first transfer is designed to be judged to be a true sale at law, in part because the transferor does not provide "excessive" credit or yield protection to the special-purpose corporation. Additionally, the transferred assets are likely to be judged beyond the reach of the transferor or the transferor's creditors even in bankruptcy.

2. The special-purpose corporation transfers the assets to a trust or other legal vehicle with a sufficient increase in the credit or yield protection on the second transfer (provided by a junior beneficial interest that continues to be held by the transferor or other means) to merit the high credit rating sought by third-party investors who

---

14.   Statement 140 (paragraphs 42–43).
15.   Statement 140 (Appendix E).
16.   Statement 140 (paragraph 73).
17.   Statement 140 (paragraph 80).

buy senior beneficial interests in the trust. Because of that aspect of its design, that second transfer might not be judged to be a true sale at law and, thus, the transferred assets could at least in theory be reached by a bankruptcy trustee for the special-purpose corporation.

However, the special-purpose corporation is designed to make remote the possibility that it would enter bankruptcy, either by itself or by substantive consolidation into a bankruptcy of its parent, should that occur. For example, its charter forbids it from undertaking any other business or incurring any liabilities, so that there can be no creditors to petition to place it in bankruptcy. Furthermore, its dedication to a single purpose is intended to make it extremely unlikely, even if it somehow entered bankruptcy, that a receiver under the U.S. Bankruptcy Code could reclaim the transferred assets because it has no other assets to substitute for the transferred assets.[18]

18A.8 WHAT IS A REMOVAL-OF-ACCOUNTS PROVISION IN A SECURITIZATION?[19]

Many transfers of financial assets in securitizations empower the transferor to reclaim assets subject to certain restrictions. Such a power is sometimes called a *removal-of-accounts provision* (ROAP). Whether a ROAP precludes sale accounting depends on whether the ROAP results in the transferor's maintaining effective control over specific transferred assets.

The following are examples of ROAPs that preclude transfers from being accounted for as sales:

1. An unconditional ROAP or repurchase agreement that allows the transferor to specify the assets that may be removed, because such a provision allows the transferor unilaterally to remove specific assets
2. A ROAP conditioned on a transferor's decision to exit some portion of its business, because whether it can be triggered by canceling an affinity relationship, spinning off a business segment, or accepting a third party's bid to purchase a specified (e.g., geographic) portion of the transferor's business, such a provision allows the transferor unilaterally to remove specific assets

The following are examples of ROAPs that *do not* preclude transfers from being accounted for as sales:

1. A ROAP for random removal of excess assets, if the ROAP is sufficiently limited so that the transferor cannot remove specific transferred assets, for example, by limiting removals to the amount of the interests that continue to be held by the transferor and to one removal per month
2. A ROAP for defaulted receivables, because the removal would be allowed only after a third party's action (default) and could not be caused unilaterally by the transferor
3. A ROAP conditioned on a third-party cancellation, or expiration without renewal, of an affinity or private-label arrangement, because the removal would be allowed only after a third party's action (cancellation) or decision not to act (expiration) and could not be caused unilaterally by the transferor

---

18.   Statement 140 (paragraph 83).
19.   Section taken from Statement 140 (paragraphs 85–88).

A ROAP that can be exercised only in response to a third party's action that has not yet occurred does not maintain the transferor's effective control over assets potentially subject to that ROAP. However, when a third party's action (such as default or cancellation) or decision not to act (expiration) occurs that allows removal of assets to be initiated solely by the transferor, the transferor must recognize any assets subject to the ROAP, whether the ROAP is exercised or not. If the ROAP is exercised, the assets are recognized because the transferor has reclaimed the assets. If the ROAP is not exercised, the assets are recognized because the transferor now can unilaterally cause the qualifying SPE to return those specific assets and, therefore, the transferor once again has effective control over those transferred assets.

18A.9   HOW SHOULD A TRANSFEROR ACCOUNT FOR A TRANSFER OF FINANCIAL ASSETS THAT QUALIFIES FOR SALE ACCOUNTING?

Paragraphs 10 and 11 of Statement 140 (as amended by Statement 157) summarize the accounting that a transferor must follow related to a sale of financial assets.

Upon completion of any transfer of financial assets, the transferor shall:

- Initially recognize and measure at fair value, if practicable, servicing assets and servicing liabilities that require recognition under the provisions of paragraph 13 of Statement 140 (discussed further below).
- Allocate the previous carrying amount between the assets sold, if any, and the interests that continue to be held by the transferor, if any, based on their relative fair values at the date of transfer.
- Continue to carry in its statement of financial position any interest it continues to hold in the transferred assets, including, if applicable, beneficial interest in assets transferred to a qualifying SPE in a securitization, and any undivided interests.

Upon completion of a transfer of financial assets that satisfies the conditions to be accounted for as a sale, the transferor (seller) shall:

- Derecognize all assets sold.
- Recognize all assets obtained and liabilities incurred in consideration as proceeds of the sale, including cash, put or call options held or written (e.g., guarantee or recourse obligations), forward commitments (e.g., commitments to deliver additional receivables during the revolving periods of some securitizations), swaps (e.g., provisions that convert interest rates from fixed to variable), and servicing assets and servicing liabilities, if applicable.
- Initially measure at fair value assets obtained and liabilities incurred in a sale or, if it is not practicable to estimate the fair value of an asset or a liability, apply alternative measures.
- Recognize in earnings any gain or loss on the sale.

A gain or loss on the transfer of financial assets is calculated as the difference between the net proceeds received from the sale and the carrying value of the assets transferred. Paragraph 56 of Statement 140 states,

> The proceeds from a sale of financial assets consist of the cash and any other assets obtained, including separately recognized servicing assets, in the transfer less any liabilities incurred, including separately recognized servicing liabilities. Any asset obtained that is not an interest in the transferred asset is part of the proceeds from the sale. Any liability incurred, even if it is related to the transferred

assets, is a reduction of the proceeds. Any derivative financial instrument entered into concurrently with a transfer of financial assets is either an asset obtained or a liability incurred and part of the proceeds received in the transfer. All proceeds and reductions of proceeds from a sale shall be initially measured at fair value, if practicable.

For transfers of financial assets recorded as sales, the transferee should recognize all assets obtained and any liabilities incurred and initially measure them at fair value.

"If a transfer of financial assets in exchange for cash or other consideration (other than beneficial interests in the transferred assets) does not meet the criteria for a sale in paragraph 9, the transferor and transferee shall account for the transfer as a secured borrowing with pledge of collateral." [20] See below for further discussion regarding secured borrowings.

18A.10   HOW SHOULD A TRANSFEROR SUBSEQUENTLY ACCOUNT FOR FINANCIAL INSTRUMENTS OBTAINED OR CREATED AS PART OF A SALE OF FINANCIAL ASSETS?

Statement 140 does not address how assets and liabilities should be accounted for subsequent to a sale transaction. Those assets and liabilities should be accounted for using the accounting guidance that would otherwise be applicable, regardless of the method of acquisition. For instance, derivatives and forward sales agreements should be accounted for in accordance with SFAS 133, *Accounting for Derivative Instruments and Hedging Activities*.

Statement 156 was issued in March 2006 and amended Statement 140 with respect to the accounting for separately recognized servicing assets and servicing liabilities. See below for further discussion regarding the accounting for servicing rights.

18A.11   HOW SHOULD A TRANSFEROR ACCOUNT FOR THE RE-RECOGNITION OF PREVIOUSLY SOLD ASSETS?

Certain events may occur that result in a transferor reacquiring control of previously derecognized financial assets. For instance, a QSPE might lose its qualifying status if at least 90 percent of the fair value of the beneficial interests issued by the QSPE is no longer held by third parties. Paragraph 55 of Statement 140 states,

A change in law, status of the transferee as a qualifying SPE, or other circumstance may result in the transferor's regaining control of assets previously accounted for appropriately as having been sold, because one or more of the conditions in paragraph 9 are no longer met. Such a change, unless it arises solely from either the initial application of this Statement or a change in market prices (for example, an increase in price that moves into-the-money a freestanding call that was originally sufficiently out-of-the money that it was judged not to constrain the transferee), is accounted for in the same manner as a purchase of the assets from the former transferee(s) in exchange for liabilities assumed (paragraph 11). After that change, the transferor recognizes in its financial statements those assets together with liabilities to the former transferee(s) or beneficial interest holders (BIHs) in those assets (paragraph 38). The transferor initially

20.   Statement 140 (paragraph 12).

measures those assets and liabilities at fair value on the date of the change, as if the transferor purchased the assets and assumed the liabilities on that date. The former transferee would derecognize the assets on that date, as if it had sold the assets in exchange for a receivable from the transferor.

(a) EXAMPLE OF FINANCIAL ASSET TRANSFER RECORDED AS A SALE The following example illustrates the accounting for a financial asset transfer recorded as a sale that includes cash proceeds, derivatives, and other liabilities.

(i) Facts[21] Company A sells loans with a fair value of $1,100 and a carrying amount of $1,000. Company A undertakes no servicing responsibilities but obtains an option to purchase from the transferee loans similar to the loans sold (which are readily obtainable in the marketplace) and assumes a limited recourse obligation to repurchase delinquent loans. Company

Fair Values		
Cash proceeds	$1,050	
Interest rate swap	40	
Call option	70	
Recourse obligation	60	
Net Proceeds		
Cash received	$1,050	
Plus: Call option	70	
Plus: Interest rate swap	40	
Less: Recourse obligation	(60)	
Net proceeds	$1,100	
Gain on Sale		
Net proceeds	$1,100	
Carrying amount of loans sold	1,000	
Gain on sale	$ 100	
Journal Entry to Record Transfer		
Cash	$1,050	
Interest rate swap	40	
Call option	70	
Loans		$1,000
Recourse obligation		60
Gain on sale		100

---

21. Example taken from Statement 140 (paragraph 57).

A agrees to provide the transferee a return at a floating rate of interest even though the contractual terms of the loan are fixed in nature (that provision is effectively an interest rate swap).

18A.12   WHAT ARE SERVICING ASSETS AND LIABILITIES?

"Servicing of mortgage loans, credit card receivables, or other financial assets commonly includes, but is not limited to, collecting principal, interest, and escrow payments from borrowers; paying taxes and insurance from escrowed funds; monitoring delinquencies; executing foreclosure if necessary; temporarily investing funds pending distribution; remitting fees to guarantors, trustees, and others providing services; and accounting for and remitting principal and interest payments to the holders of beneficial interests in the financial assets. Servicing is inherent in all financial assets."[22]

Paragraph 13 of Statement 140 states,

> An entity shall recognize and initially measure at fair value, if practicable, a servicing asset or servicing liability each time it undertakes an obligation to service a financial asset by entering into a servicing contract in any of the following situations:
>
> **a.**   A transfer of the servicer's financial assets that meets the requirements for sale accounting
>
> **b.**   A transfer of the servicer's financial assets to a qualifying SPE in a guaranteed mortgage securitization in which the transferor retains all of the resulting securities and classifies them as either available-for-sale securities or trading securities in accordance with FASB Statement No. 115, *Accounting for Certain Investments in Debt and Equity Securities*
>
> **c.**   An acquisition or assumption of a servicing obligation that does not relate to financial assets of the servicer or its consolidated affiliates.
>
> An entity that transfers its financial assets to a qualifying SPE in a guaranteed mortgage securitization in which the transferor retains all of the resulting securities and classifies them as debt securities held-to-maturity in accordance with Statement 115 may either separately recognize its servicing assets or servicing liabilities or report those servicing assets or servicing liabilities together with the asset being serviced.

"A servicer of financial assets commonly receives the benefits of servicing—revenues from contractually specified servicing fees, a portion of the interest from the financial assets, late charges, and other ancillary sources, including 'float' (income earned on balances held in trust by servicers from the date a loan payment is received from the borrower to the date funds are forwarded to investors), all of which it is entitled to receive only if it performs the servicing—and incurs the costs of servicing the assets. Typically, the benefits of servicing are expected to be more than adequate compensation to a servicer for performing the servicing, and the contract results in a servicing asset. However, if the benefits of servicing are not expected to adequately compensate a servicer for performing the servicing, the contract results in a servicing liability. (A servicing asset may become a servicing liability, or vice versa, if circumstances change, and the initial measure for servicing may be zero if the benefits of servicing are just adequate to compensate the servicer for its servicing responsibilities.) A servicer

---

22.   Statement 140 (paragraph 61).

would account for its servicing contract that qualifies for separate recognition as a servicing asset or a servicing liability initially measured at its fair value regardless of whether explicit consideration was exchanged."[23]

Statement 140 defines *adequate compensation* as "The amount of benefits of servicing that would fairly compensate a substitute servicer should one be required, which includes the profit that would be demanded in the marketplace."[24] The determination of adequate compensation should be made independent of a servicer's internal cost structure.

"A servicer that transfers or securitizes financial assets in a transaction that does not meet the requirements for sale accounting and is accounted for as a secured borrowing with the underlying assets remaining on the transferor's balance sheet shall not recognize a servicing asset or a servicing liability. However, if a transferor enters into a servicing contract when the transferor transfers mortgage loans in a guaranteed mortgage securitization, retains all the resulting securities, and classifies those securities as either available-for-sale securities or trading securities in accordance with Statement 115, the transferor shall separately recognize a servicing asset or a servicing liability."[25]

18A.13   HOW SHOULD SERVICING ASSETS AND SERVICING LIABILITIES BE ACCOUNTED FOR UNDER STATEMENT 156?

Statement 156 was issued in March 2006 and amended Statement 140 with respect to the accounting for separately recognized servicing assets and servicing liabilities. Specifically, Statement 156:

1. Requires an entity to recognize a servicing asset or servicing liability each time it undertakes an obligation to service a financial asset by entering into a servicing contract in any of the following situations:

   a. A transfer of the servicer's financial assets that meets the requirements for sale accounting
   b. A transfer of the servicer's financial assets to a qualifying special-purpose entity in a guaranteed mortgage securitization in which the transferor retains all of the resulting securities and classifies them as either available-for-sale securities or trading securities in accordance with Statement 115
   c. An acquisition or assumption of an obligation to service a financial asset that does not relate to financial assets of the servicer or its consolidated affiliates

2. Requires all separately recognized servicing assets and servicing liabilities to be initially measured at fair value, if practicable.

---

23.   Statement 140 (paragraph 62).
24.   Statement 140 (Appendix E).
25.   Statement 140 (paragraph 62A).

3. Permits an entity to choose either of the following subsequent measurement methods for each class of separately recognized servicing assets and servicing liabilities:

   a. *Amortization method*—Amortize servicing assets or servicing liabilities in proportion to and over the period of estimated net servicing income or net servicing loss and assess servicing assets or servicing liabilities for impairment or increased obligation based on fair value at each reporting date.

   b. *Fair value measurement method*—Measure servicing assets or servicing liabilities at fair value at each reporting date and report changes in fair value in earnings in the period in which the changes occur.

4. At its initial adoption, permits a one-time reclassification of available-for-sale securities to trading securities by entities with recognized servicing rights, without calling into question the treatment of other available-for-sale securities under Statement 115, provided that the available-for-sale securities are identified in some manner as offsetting the entity's exposure to changes in fair value of servicing assets or servicing liabilities that a servicer elects to subsequently measure at fair value.

5. Requires separate presentation of servicing assets and servicing liabilities subsequently measured at fair value in the statement of financial position and additional disclosures for all separately recognized servicing assets and servicing liabilities.[26]

"The election shall be made separately for each class of servicing assets and servicing liabilities. An entity shall apply the same subsequent measurement method to each servicing asset and servicing liability in a class. Classes of servicing assets and servicing liabilities shall be identified based on (a) the availability of market inputs used in determining the fair value of servicing assets or servicing liabilities, (b) an entity's method for managing the risks of its servicing assets or servicing liabilities, or (c) both. Once an entity elects the fair value measurement method for a class of servicing assets and servicing liabilities, that election shall not be reversed."[27]

(a) EXAMPLE OF A FINANCIAL ASSET TRANSFER RECORDED AS A SALE WITH A SERVICING RIGHT   The following example illustrates the accounting for a financial asset transfer recorded as a sale that includes cash proceeds and a servicing asset.

(i) Facts[28]   Company C originates $1,000 of loans that yield 10 percent interest income for their estimated lives of 9 years. Company C sells the $1,000 principal plus the right to receive interest income of 8 percent to another entity for $1,000. Company C will continue to service the loans, and the contract stipulates that its compensation for performing the servicing is the right to receive half of the interest income not sold. The remaining half of the interest income

26. FASB Statement No. 156, *Accounting for Servicing of Financial Assets—An Amendment of FASB Statement No. 140*, March 2006 (from Summary page).
27. Statement 140 (paragraph 13A).
28. Example taken from Statement 140 (paragraph 65).

not sold is considered an interest-only strip receivable that Company C classifies as an available-for-sale security. At the date of the transfer, the fair value of the loans is $1,100. The fair values of the servicing asset and the interest-only strip receivable are $40 and $60, respectively.

Fair Values

Cash proceeds	$1,000
Servicing asset	40
Interest-only strip receivable	60

Net Proceeds

Cash received	$1,000
Plus: Servicing asset	40
Net proceeds	$1,040

Carrying Amount Based on Relative Fair Values

	Fair Value	Percentage of Total Fair Value	Allocated Carrying Amount
Loans sold	$1,040.00	$ 94.55	$ 945.50
Interest-only strip receivable	60.00	5.45	54.50
Total	$1,100.00	$100.00	$1,000.00

Gain on Sale

Net proceeds	$1,040.00
Less: Carrying amount of loans sold	(945.50)
Gain on sale	$ 94.50

Journal Entry to Record Transfer and Recognize Interest-Only Strip Receivable and Servicing Asset

Cash	$1,000.00	
Interest-only strip receivable	$54.50	
Servicing asset	$40.00	
Loans		$1,000.00
Gain on sale		$94.50

Journal Entry to Begin to Subsequently Measure Interest-Only Strip Receivable Like an Available-for-Sale Security

Interest-only strip receivable	$5.50	
Other comprehensive income		$5.50

18A.14   WHEN SHOULD A TRANSFER OF FINANCIAL ASSETS BE RECORDED AS A SECURED BORROWING?

A transfer should be accounted for as a secured borrowing if the transfer does not meet the sale criteria specified by paragraph 9 of Statement 140.

> An agreement that both entitles and obligates the transferor to repurchase or redeem transferred assets from the transferee maintains the transferor's effective control over those assets under paragraph 9(c)(1), and the transfer is therefore to be accounted for as a secured borrowing, if and only if all of the following conditions are met:
>
> - The assets to be repurchased or redeemed are the same or substantially the same as those transferred.
> - The transferor is able to repurchase or redeem them on substantially the agreed terms, even in the event of default by the transferee.
> - The agreement is to repurchase or redeem them before maturity, at a fixed or determinable price.
> - The agreement is entered into concurrently with the transfer.[29]

Generally, secured borrowings result in the transferor recognizing cash from the borrowing and a liability to return the cash to the transferee.

(a) THE ASSETS TO BE REPURCHASED OR REDEEMED ARE THE SAME OR SUBSTANTIALLY THE SAME AS THOSE TRANSFERRED[30]   Assets to be repurchased or redeemed are considered the same or substantially the same as those transferred if they have the same primary obligator, identical form and type, the same maturity, identical contractual interest rates, similar assets as collateral, and the same aggregate unpaid principal amount.

(b) THE TRANSFEROR IS ABLE TO REPURCHASE OR REDEEM THEM ON SUBSTANTIALLY THE AGREED TERMS, EVEN IN THE EVENT OF DEFAULT BY THE TRANSFEREE[31]   To be able to repurchase or redeem assets on substantially the agreed terms, even in the event of default by the transferee, a transferor must at all times during the contract term have obtained cash or other collateral sufficient to fund substantially all of the cost of purchasing replacement assets from others.

(c) THE AGREEMENT IS TO REPURCHASE OR REDEEM THEM BEFORE MATURITY, AT A FIXED OR DETERMINABLE PRICE   The agreement must require the transferor to repurchase or redeem the transferred assets before the maturity of the transferred assets at a fixed or determinable price. If the term of the repurchase agreement extends to the maturity date of the transferred asset, this condition would not be met.

---

29.   Statement 140 (paragraph 47).
30.   Section taken from Statement 140 (paragraph 48).
31.   Section taken from Statement 140 (paragraph 49).

(d) THE AGREEMENT IS ENTERED INTO CONCURRENTLY WITH THE TRANSFER

The agreement to repurchase or redeem the transferred assets must be entered into at the same time that the transferor transfers the financial assets. If the right or obligation to repurchase the transferred assets is not entered into concurrently with the initial transfer, the transferor would not effectively maintain control over the transferred assets at the time of transfer.

18A.15   HOW SHOULD COLLATERAL BE ACCOUNTED FOR WITHIN A SECURED BORROWING?[32]

A debtor may grant a security interest in certain assets to a lender (the secured party) to serve as collateral for its obligation under a borrowing, with or without recourse to other assets of the debtor. If collateral is transferred to the secured party, the custodial arrangement is commonly referred to as a pledge. Secured parties sometimes are permitted to sell or repledge (or otherwise transfer) collateral held under a pledge. The accounting for noncash collateral by the debtor (or obligor) and the secured party depends on whether the secured party has the right to sell or repledge the collateral and on whether the debtor has defaulted.

- If the secured party (transferee) has the right by contract or custom to sell or repledge the collateral, then the debtor (transferor) shall reclassify that asset and report that asset in its statement of financial position separately (e.g., as security pledged to creditors) from other assets not so encumbered.
- If the secured party (transferee) sells collateral pledged to it, it shall recognize the proceeds from the sale and its obligation to return the collateral. The sale of the collateral is a transfer subject to the provisions of Statement 140.
- If the debtor (transferor) defaults under the terms of the secured contract and is no longer entitled to redeem the pledged asset, it shall derecognize the pledged asset, and the security party (transferee) shall recognize the collateral as its asset initially measured at fair value or, if it has already sold the collateral, derecognize its obligation to return the collateral.
- Except as provided in paragraph 15(c), the debtor (transferor) shall continue to carry the collateral as its asset, and the secured party (transferee) shall not recognize the pledged asset.

18A.16   WHAT ARE SECURITIES LENDING TRANSACTIONS?[33]

"Securities lending transactions are initiated by broker-dealers and other financial institutions that need specific securities to cover a short sale or a customer's failure to deliver securities sold. Transferees ('borrowers') of securities generally are required to provide collateral to the transferor ('lender') of securities, commonly cash but sometimes other securities or standby letters of credit, with a value slightly higher than that of the securities borrowed. If the collateral is cash, the transferor typically earns a return by investing that cash at rates higher than the rate paid or rebated to the transferee. [. . .] If the 'collateral' is other than cash, the transferor typically receives a fee. Securities custodians or other agents commonly carry out securities lending activities on behalf of clients."

---

32.   Statement 140 (paragraph 15).
33.   Statement 140 (paragraph 91).

The accounting for a securities lending transaction is based on whether the transaction meets the criteria for sale accounting in paragraph 9 of Statement 140.

(a) EXAMPLE OF A SECURITIES LENDING TRANSACTION ACCOUNTED FOR AS A SECURED BORROWING   The following example illustrates the accounting for a securities lending transaction treated as a secured borrowing, in which the securities borrower (transferee) sells the securities upon receipt and later buys similar securities to return to the securities lender (transferor).

Facts[34]

Transferor's carrying amount and fair value of security loaned	$1,000
Cash collateral	$1,020
Transferor's return from investing cash collateral at a 5 percent annual rate	$ 5
Transferor's rebate to the securities borrower at a 4 percent annual rate	$ 4

For simplicity, the fair value of the security is assumed not to change during the 35-day term of the transaction.

Journal Entries for the Transferor

At inception:

Journal entry to record the receipt
of cash collateral

Cash		$1,020	
	Payable under securities loan agreements		$1,020

Journal entry to reclassify loaned
securities that the secured party has the
right to sell or repledge

Securities pledged to creditors		$1,000	
	Securities		$1,000

Journal entry to record investment of
cash collateral

Money market instrument		$1,020	
	Cash		$1,020

(*Continued*)

---

34.   Example taken from Statement 140 (paragraph 95).

Journal Entries for the Transferor *(Continued)*

At conclusion:

Journal entry to record results of
investment

Cash		$1,025	
	Interest		$5
	Money market instrument		$1,020

Journal entry to record return of
security

Securities		$1,000	
	Securities pledged to creditors		$1,000

Journal entry to record repayment of
cash collateral plus interest

Payable under securities loan agreements		$1,020	
Interest		$4	
	Cash		$1,024

Journal Entries for the Transferee

At inception:

Journal entry to record transfer of cash
collateral

Receivable under securities loan agreements		$1,020	
	Cash		$1,020

Journal entry to record sale of borrowed
securities to a third party and the resulting obligation to return securities that it
no longer holds

Cash		$1,000	
	Obligation to return bor-rowed securities		$1,000

At conclusion:

Journal entry to record the repurchase
of securities borrowed

Obligation to return borrowed securities		$1,000	
	Cash		$1,000

Journal Entries for the Transferee

Journal entry to record the receipt of cash
collateral and rebate interest

Cash	$1,024	
Receivable under securities loan agreements	$1,200	
Interest revenue		$4

18A.17   WHAT ARE REPURCHASE AGREEMENTS AND "WASH SALES"?

Government securities dealers, banks, other financial institutions, and corporate investors commonly use repurchase agreements to obtain or use short-term funds. Under those agreements, the transferor ("repo party") transfers a security to a transferee ("repo counterparty" or "reverse party") in exchange for cash and concurrently agrees to reacquire that security at a future date for an amount equal to the cash exchanged plus a stipulated "interest" factor.[35]

"Repurchase agreements can be effected in a variety of ways. Some repurchase agreements are similar to securities lending transactions in that the transferee has the right to sell or repledge the securities to a third party during the term of the repurchase agreement. In other repurchase agreements, the transferee does not have the right to sell or repledge the securities during the term of the repurchase agreement."[36]

"If the criteria in paragraph 9 of Statement 140 are met, including the criterion in paragraph 9(c)(1), the transferor shall account for the repurchase agreement as a sale of financial assets and a forward repurchase commitment, and the transferee shall account for the agreement as a purchase of financial assets and a forward resale commitment. Other transfers that are accompanied by an agreement to repurchase the transferred assets that shall be accounted for as sales include transfers with agreements to repurchase at maturity and transfers with repurchase agreements in which the transferee has not obtained collateral sufficient to fund substantially all of the cost of purchasing replacement assets."[37]

"As with securities lending transactions, under many agreements to repurchase transferred assets before their maturity the transferor maintains effective control over those assets. Repurchase agreements that do not meet all the criteria in paragraph 9 shall be treated as secured borrowings."[38]

A *wash sale* transaction is one in which a transferor both sells and repurchases the same or similar securities over a short period of time (generally less than 30 days). If the wash sale transaction did not involve a concurrent contract to repurchase or redeem the transferred financial assets from the transferee, then the transfer of financial assets should be recorded as a sale, provided all other criteria within paragraph 9 are met.

---

35.   Statement 140 (paragraph 96).
36.   Statement 140 (paragraph 97).
37.   Statement 140 (paragraph 98).
38.   Statement 140 (paragraph 100).

18A.18   WHAT ARE LOAN SYNDICATIONS AND LOAN PARTICIPATIONS?[39]

Borrowers often borrow amounts greater than any one lender is willing to lend. Therefore, it is common for groups of lenders to jointly fund those loans. That may be accomplished by a syndication under which several lenders share in lending to a single borrower, but each lender loans a specific amount to the borrower and has the right to repayment from the borrower.

A loan syndication is not a transfer of financial assets. Each lender in the syndication shall account for the amounts it is owed by the borrower. Repayments by the borrower may be made to a lead lender that then distributes the collections to the other lenders of the syndicate. In those circumstances, the lead lender is simply functioning as a servicer and, therefore, shall not recognize the aggregate loan as an asset.

Groups of banks or other entities also may jointly fund large borrowings through loan participations in which a single lender makes a large loan to a borrower and subsequently transfers undivided interests in the loan to other entities.

Transfers by the originating lender may take the legal form of either assignments or participations. The transfers are usually on a nonrecourse basis, and the transferor ("originating lender") continues to service the loan. The transferee ("participating entity") may or may not have the right to sell or transfer its participation during the term of the loan, depending on the terms of the participation agreement.

If the loan participation agreement gives the transferee the right to pledge or exchange those participations and the other criteria in paragraph 9 are met, the transfers to the transferee shall be accounted for by the transferor as sales of financial assets. A transferor's right of first refusal on a bona fide offer from a third party, a requirement to obtain the transferor's permission that shall not be unreasonably withheld, or a prohibition on sale to the transferor's competitor if other potential willing buyers exist is a limitation on the transferee's rights but presumptively does not constrain a transferee from exercising its right to pledge or exchange. However, if the loan participation agreement constrains the transferees from pledging or exchanging their participations, the transferor presumptively receives a more than trivial benefit, has not relinquished control over the loan, and shall account for the transfers as secured borrowings.

18A.19   WHAT ARE BANKER'S ACCEPTANCES AND RISK PARTICIPATIONS IN THEM?[40]

Banker's acceptances provide a way for a bank to finance a customer's purchase of goods from a vendor for periods usually not exceeding six months. Under an agreement between the bank, the customer, and the vendor, the bank agrees to pay the customer's liability to the vendor upon presentation of specified documents that provide evidence of delivery and acceptance of the purchased goods. The principal document is a draft or bill of exchange drawn by the customer that the bank stamps to signify its "acceptance" of the liability to make payment on the draft on its due date.

Once the bank accepts a draft, the customer is liable to repay the bank at the time the draft matures. The bank recognizes a receivable from the customer and a liability for the acceptance it has issued to the vendor. The accepted draft becomes a negotiable financial instrument. The

---

39.   Statement 140 (paragraphs 102–106).
40.   Section taken from Statement 140 (paragraphs 107–110).

vendor typically sells the accepted draft at a discount either to the accepting bank or in the marketplace.

A risk participation is a contract between the accepting bank and a participating bank in which the participating bank agrees, in exchange for a fee, to reimburse the accepting bank in the event that the accepting bank's customer fails to honor its liability to the accepting bank in connection with the banker's acceptance. The participating bank becomes a guarantor of the credit of the accepting bank's customer.

An accepting bank that obtains a risk participation shall not derecognize the liability for the banker's acceptance, because the accepting bank is still primarily liable to the holder of the banker's acceptance even though it benefits from a guarantee of reimbursement by a participating bank. The accepting bank shall not derecognize the receivable from the customer because it has not transferred the receivable: It controls the benefits inherent in that receivable and it is still entitled to receive payment from the customer. The accepting bank shall, however, record the guarantee purchased, and the participating bank shall record a liability for the guarantee issued.

(a) EXAMPLE OF A BANKER'S ACCEPTANCE WITH A RISK PARTICIPATION TRANSACTION ACCOUNTED FOR AS A SECURED BORROWING   The following example illustrates the accounting for a transaction in which an accepting bank assumes a liability to pay a customer's vendor and obtains a participation from another bank. The details of the banker's acceptance are provided below:

Facts[41]

Face value of the draft provided to vendor	$1,000
Term of the draft provided to vendor	90 days
Commission with an annual rate of 10 percent	$ 25
Fee paid for risk participation	$ 10

The following journal entries show the accounting treatment for this arrangement:

Journal Entries for Accepting Bank

At issuance of acceptance:

Receivable from customer	$1,000	
Cash	$ 25	
Time draft payable to vendor		$1,000
Deferred acceptance commission revenue		$ 25

(Continued)

---

41.   Example taken from Statement 140 (paragraph 111).

At purchase of risk participation from a participating bank: *(Continued)*

Guarantee purchased	$10	
Cash		$10

Upon presentation of the accepted time draft:

Time draft payable to vendor	$1,000	
Deferred acceptance commission revenue	$ 25	
Cash		$1,000
Acceptance commission revenue		$ 25

Upon collection from the customer (or the participating bank, if the customer defaults):

Cash	$1,000	
Guarantee expense	$ 10	
Receivable from customer		$1,000
Guarantee purchased		$ 10

Journal Entries for Participating Bank

Upon issuing the risk participation:

Cash	$10	
Guarantee liability		$10

Upon payment by the customer to the accepting bank:

Guarantee liability	$10	
Guarantee revenue		$10

OR:

In the event of total default by the customer:

Guarantee loss	$990	
Guarantee liability	$ 10	
Cash (paid to accepting bank)		$1,000

18A.20   WHAT ARE FACTORING ARRANGEMENTS AND TRANSFERS OF RECEIVABLES WITH RECOURSE?[42]

Factoring arrangements are a means of discounting accounts receivable on a nonrecourse, notification basis. Accounts receivable are sold outright, usually to a transferee (the factor) that assumes the full risk of collection, without recourse to the transferor in the event of a loss. Debtors are directed to send payments to the transferee. Factoring arrangements that meet the criteria in paragraph 9 of Statement 140 shall be accounted for as sales of financial assets because the transferor surrenders control over the receivables to the factor.

In a transfer of receivables with recourse, the transferor provides the transferee with full or limited recourse. The transferor is obligated under the terms of the recourse provision to make payments to the transferee or to repurchase receivables sold under certain circumstances, typically for defaults up to a specified percentage. The effect of a recourse provision on the application of paragraph 9 of Statement 140 may vary by jurisdiction. In some jurisdictions, transfers with full recourse may not place transferred assets beyond the reach of the transferor and its creditors, but transfers with limited recourse may. A transfer of receivables with recourse shall be accounted for as a sale, with the proceeds of the sale reduced by the fair value of the recourse obligation, if the criteria in paragraph 9 of Statement 140 are met. Otherwise, a transfer of receivables with recourse shall be accounted for as a secured borrowing.

18A.21   HOW SHOULD TRANSFERS OF FINANCIAL ASSETS BE MEASURED AT FAIR VALUE UNDER STATEMENT 157?

Statement 157 was issued in September 2006 and defines fair value, establishes a framework for measuring fair value in generally accepted accounting principles, and expands disclosures about fair value measurements. As noted above, Statement 157 is effective for financial statements issued for fiscal years beginning after November 15, 2007, and interim periods within those fiscal years.

(a) MEASUREMENT[43]   *Fair value* is the price that would be received to sell an asset or paid to transfer a liability in an orderly transaction between market participants at the measurement date.

A fair value measurement is for a particular asset or liability. Therefore, the measurement should consider attributes specific to the asset or liability, for example, the condition and/or location of the asset or liability and restrictions, if any, on the sale or use of the asset at the measurement date. The asset or liability might be a standalone asset or liability (for example, a financial instrument or an operating asset) or a group of assets and/or liabilities (for example, an asset group, a reporting unit, or a business). Whether the asset or liability is a standalone asset or liability or a group of assets and/or liabilities depends on its unit of account. The unit of account determines what is being measured by reference to the level at which the asset or liability is aggregated (or disaggregated) for purposes of applying other accounting pronouncements. The unit of account for the asset or liability should be determined in accordance with the provisions of other accounting pronouncements, except as provided in paragraph 27 of Statement 157.

---

42.   Section taken from Statement 140 (paragraphs 112–113).
43.   Section taken from FASB Statement No. 157, *Fair Value Measurements*, September 2007 (paragraphs 5–7).

A fair value measurement assumes that the asset or liability is exchanged in an orderly transaction between market participants to sell the asset or transfer the liability at the measurement date. An orderly transaction is a transaction that assumes exposure to the market for a period prior to the measurement date to allow for marketing activities that are usual and customary for transactions involving such assets or liabilities; it is not a forced transaction (for example, a forced liquidation or distress sale). The transaction to sell the asset or transfer the liability is a hypothetical transaction at the measurement date, considered from the perspective of a market participant that holds the asset or owes the liability. Therefore, the objective of a fair value measurement is to determine the price that would be received to sell the asset or paid to transfer the liability at the measurement date (an exit price).

A fair value measurement assumes that the transaction to sell the asset or transfer the liability occurs in the principal market for the asset or liability or, in the absence of a principal market, the most advantageous market for the asset or liability. The principal market is the market in which the reporting entity would sell the asset or transfer the liability with the greatest volume and level of activity for the asset or liability. The most advantageous market is the market in which the reporting entity would sell the asset or transfer the liability with the price that maximizes the amount that would be received for the asset or minimizes the amount that would be paid to transfer the liability, considering transaction costs in the respective market(s). In either case, the principal (or most advantageous) market (and thus, market participants) should be considered from the perspective of the reporting entity, thereby allowing for differences between and among entities with different activities. If there is a principal market for the asset or liability, the fair value measurement shall represent the price in that market (whether that price is directly observable or otherwise determined using a valuation technique), even if the price in a different market is potentially more advantageous at the measurement date.

The price in the principal (or most advantageous) market used to measure the fair value of the asset or liability shall not be adjusted for transaction costs. Transaction costs represent the incremental direct costs to sell the asset or transfer the liability in the principal (or most advantageous) market for the asset or liability. Transaction costs are not an attribute of the asset or liability; rather, they are specific to the transaction and will differ depending on how the reporting entity transacts. However, transaction costs do not include the costs that would be incurred to transport the asset or liability to (or from) its principal (or most advantageous) market. If location is an attribute of the asset or liability (as might be the case for a commodity), the price in the principal (or most advantageous) market used to measure the fair value of the asset or liability shall be adjusted for the costs, if any, that would be incurred to transport the asset or liability to (or from) its principal (or most advantageous) market.

(b) STATEMENT 157 APPLICATION TO ASSETS[44]   A fair value measurement for an asset assumes the highest and best use of the asset by market participants, considering the use of the asset that is physically possible, legally permissible, and financially feasible at the measurement date. In broad terms, *highest and best use* refers to the use of an asset by market participants that would maximize the value of the asset or the group of assets within which

---

44.   Section taken from Statement 157 (paragraph 12).

the asset would be used. Highest and best use is determined based on the use of the asset by market participants, even if the intended use of the asset by the reporting entity is different.

(c) STATEMENT 157 APPLICATION TO LIABILITIES[45]   A fair value measurement for a liability assumes that the liability is transferred to a market participant at the measurement date (the liability to the counterparty continues; it is not settled) and that the nonperformance risk relating to that liability is the same before and after its transfer. Nonperformance risk refers to the risk that the obligation will not be fulfilled and affects the value at which the liability is transferred. Therefore, the fair value of the liability shall reflect the nonperformance risk relating to that liability. Nonperformance risk includes but may not be limited to the reporting entity's own credit risk. The reporting entity shall consider the effect of its credit risk (credit standing) on the fair value of the liability in all periods in which the liability is measured at fair value. That effect may differ depending on the liability, for example, whether the liability is an obligation to deliver cash (a financial liability) or an obligation to deliver goods or services (a nonfinancial liability), and the terms of credit enhancements related to the liability, if any.

18A.22   WHAT ARE APPROPRIATE VALUATION TECHNIQUES UNDER STATEMENT 157?[46]

Valuation techniques consistent with the market approach, income approach, and/or cost approach shall be used to measure fair value. Key aspects of those approaches are summarized below:

- *Market approach.* The market approach uses prices and other relevant information generated by market transactions involving identical or comparable assets or liabilities (including a business). For example, valuation techniques consistent with the market approach often use market multiples derived from a set of comparables. Multiples might lie in ranges with a different multiple for each comparable. The selection of where within the range the appropriate multiple falls requires judgment, considering factors specific to the measurement (qualitative and quantitative). Valuation techniques consistent with the market approach include matrix pricing. Matrix pricing is a mathematical technique used principally to value debt securities without relying exclusively on quoted prices for the specific securities, but rather relying on the securities' relationship to other benchmark quoted securities.
- *Income approach.* The income approach uses valuation techniques to convert future amounts (for example, cash flows or earnings) to a single present amount (discounted). The measurement is based on the value indicated by current market expectations about those future amounts. Those valuation techniques include present value techniques; option-pricing models, such as the Black-Scholes-Merton formula (a closed-form model) and a binomial model (a lattice model), which incorporate present value techniques; and the multiperiod excess earnings method, which is used to measure the fair value of certain intangible assets.

---

45.   Section taken from Statement 157 (paragraph 15).
46.   Section taken from Statement 157 (paragraph 18).

- *Cost approach.* The cost approach is based on the amount that currently would be required to replace the service capacity of an asset (often referred to as *current replacement cost*). From the perspective of a market participant (seller), the price that would be received for the asset is determined based on the cost to a market participant (buyer) to acquire or construct a substitute asset of comparable utility, adjusted for obsolescence. Obsolescence encompasses physical deterioration, functional (technological) obsolescence, and economic (external) obsolescence and is broader than depreciation for financial reporting purposes (an allocation of historical cost) or tax purposes (based on specified service lives).

18A.23   WHAT ARE VALUATION INPUTS, AND HOW ARE THEY PRIORITIZED?

Valuation inputs are the assumptions that market participants use to price assets and liabilities. Valuation inputs maybe observable or unobservable. *Observable* inputs are inputs that reflect the assumptions that market participants would use in pricing the asset or liability developed based on market data obtained from sources independent of the reporting entity. *Unobservable* inputs are inputs that reflect the reporting entity's own assumptions about the assumptions market participants would use in pricing the asset or liability developed based on the best information available in the circumstances. Valuation techniques used to measure fair value should attempt to maximize the use of observable inputs and minimize the use of unobservable inputs.[47]

Statement 157 establishes a fair value hierarchy that gives the highest priority to quoted prices in active markets for identical assets or liabilities and the lowest priority to unobservable inputs. The levels of valuation inputs in the fair-value hierarchy are as follows:

> Level 1 inputs are quoted prices (unadjusted) in active markets for identical assets or liabilities that the reporting entity has the ability to access at the measurement date. An active market for the asset or liability is a market in which transactions for the asset or liability occur with sufficient frequency and volume to provide pricing information on an ongoing basis.
>
> Level 2 inputs are inputs other than quoted prices included within Level 1 that are observable for the asset or liability, either directly or indirectly. If the asset or liability has a specified (contractual) term, a Level 2 input must be observable for substantially the full term of the asset or liability. Level 2 inputs include the following:
>
> **a.** Quoted prices for similar assets or liabilities in active markets
> **b.** Quoted prices for identical or similar assets or liabilities in markets that are not active, that is, markets in which there are few transactions for the asset or liability, the prices are not current, or price quotations vary substantially either over time or among market makers (for example, some brokered markets), or in which little information is released publicly (for example, a principal-to-principal market)
> **c.** Inputs other than quoted prices that are observable for the asset or liability (for example, interest rates and yield curves observable at commonly quoted

---

47.   Statement 157 (paragraph 21).

intervals, volatilities, prepayment speeds, loss severities, credit risks, and default rates)

d. Inputs that are derived principally from or corroborated by observable market data by correlation or other means (market-corroborated inputs).

Level 3 inputs are unobservable inputs for the asset or liability. Unobservable inputs shall be used to measure fair value to the extent that observable inputs are not available, thereby allowing for situations in which there is little, if any, market activity for the asset or liability at the measurement date.[48]

18A.24   WHAT ARE THE FINANCIAL STATEMENT DISCLOSURE REQUIREMENTS OF STATEMENT 140, AS AMENDED?[49]

Paragraph 17 of Statement 140, as amended by Statement 156, lists the disclosures that companies are required to make in their financial statements. These disclosures are as follows:

a. For collateral:

    (1) If the entity has entered into repurchase agreements or securities lending transactions, its policy for requiring collateral or other security.

    (2) If the entity has pledged any of its assets as collateral that are not reclassified and separately reported in the statement of financial position pursuant to paragraph 15(a), the carrying amount and classification of those assets as of the date of the latest statement of financial position presented.

    (3) If the entity has accepted collateral that it is permitted by contract or custom to sell or repledge, the fair value as of the date of each statement of financial position presented of that collateral and of the portion of that collateral that it has sold or repledged, and information about the sources and uses of that collateral.

b. If debt was considered to be extinguished by in-substance defeasance under the provisions of FASB Statement No. 76, *Extinguishment of Debt,* prior to the effective date of Statement 125, a general description of the transaction and the amount of debt that is considered extinguished at the end of the period so long as that debt remains outstanding.

c. If assets are set aside after the effective date of Statement 125 solely for satisfying scheduled payments of a specific obligation, a description of the nature of restrictions placed on those assets.

d. If it is not practicable to estimate the fair value of certain assets obtained or liabilities incurred in transfers of financial assets during the period, a description of those items and the reasons why it is not practicable to estimate their fair value.

e. For all servicing assets and servicing liabilities:

    (1) Management's basis for determining its classes of servicing assets and servicing liabilities (paragraph 13A).

    (2) A description of the risks inherent in servicing assets and servicing liabilities and, if applicable, the instruments used to mitigate the income statement

---

48.   Statement 157 (summarized from paragraphs 22–30).

49.   Statement 140 (paragraph 17).

effect of changes in fair value of the servicing assets and servicing liabilities. (Disclosure of quantitative information about the instruments used to manage the risks inherent in servicing assets and servicing liabilities, including the fair value of those instruments at the beginning and end of the period, is encouraged but not required.)

(3) The amount of contractually specified servicing fees (as defined in the glossary), late fees, and ancillary fees earned for each period for which results of operations are presented, including a description of where each amount is reported in the statement of income.

f. For servicing assets and servicing liabilities subsequently measured at fair value:

(1) For each class of servicing assets and servicing liabilities, the activity in the balance of servicing assets and the activity in the balance of servicing liabilities (including a description of where changes in fair value are reported in the statement of income for each period for which results of operations are presented), including, but not limited to, the following:

(a) The beginning and ending balances.

(b) Additions (through purchases of servicing assets, assumptions of servicing obligations, and servicing obligations that result from transfers of financial assets).

(c) Disposals.

(d) Changes in fair value during the period resulting from:

(i) Changes in valuation inputs or assumptions used in the valuation model.

(ii) Other changes in fair value and a description of those changes.

(e) Other changes that affect the balance and a description of those changes

(2) A description of the valuation techniques or other methods used to estimate the fair value of servicing assets and servicing liabilities. If a valuation model is used, the description shall include the methodology and model validation procedures, as well as quantitative and qualitative information about the assumptions used in the valuation model (e.g., discount rates and prepayment speeds). (An entity that provides quantitative information about the instruments used to manage the risks inherent in the servicing assets and servicing liabilities, as encouraged by paragraph 17(e)(2), is also encouraged, but not required, to disclose a description of the valuation techniques, as well as quantitative and qualitative information about the assumptions used to estimate the fair value of those instruments.)

g. For servicing assets and servicing liabilities subsequently amortized in proportion to and over the period of estimated net servicing income or loss and assessed for impairment or increased obligation:

(1) For each class of servicing assets and servicing liabilities, the activity in the balance of servicing assets and the activity in the balance of servicing liabilities (including a description of where changes in the carrying amount are reported

in the statement of income for each period for which results of operations are presented), including, but not limited to, the following:

- **(a)** The beginning and ending balances.
- **(b)** Additions (through purchases of servicing assets, assumption of servicing obligations, and servicing obligations that result from transfers of financial assets).
- **(c)** Disposals.
- **(d)** Amortization.
- **(e)** Application of valuation allowance to adjust carrying value of servicing assets.
- **(f)** Other-than-temporary impairments.
- **(g)** Other changes that affect the balance and a description of those changes.

(2) For each class of servicing assets and servicing liabilities, the fair value of recognized servicing assets and servicing liabilities at the beginning and end of the period if it is practicable to estimate the value.

(3) A description of the valuation techniques or other methods used to estimate fair value of the servicing assets and servicing liabilities. If a valuation model is used, the description shall include the methodology and model validation procedures, as well as quantitative and qualitative information about the assumptions used in the valuation model (e.g., discount rates and prepayment speeds). (An entity that provides quantitative information about the instruments used to manage the risks inherent in the servicing assets and servicing liabilities, as encouraged by paragraph 17(e)(2), is also encouraged, but not required, to disclose a description of the valuation techniques as well as quantitative and qualitative information about the assumptions used to estimate the fair value of those instruments.)

(4) The risk characteristics of the underlying financial assets used to stratify recognized servicing assets for purposes of measuring impairment in accordance with paragraph 63.

(5) The activity by class in any valuation allowance for impairment of recognized servicing assets—including beginning and ending balances, aggregate additions charged and recoveries credited to operations, and aggregate write-downs charged against the allowance—for each period for which results of operations are presented.

(h) If the entity has securitized financial assets during any period presented and accounts for that transfer as a sale, for each major asset type (e.g., mortgage loans, credit card receivables, and automobile loans):

(1) Its accounting policies for initially measuring the interests that continue to be held by the transferor, if any, and servicing assets and servicing liabilities, if any, including the methodology (whether quoted market price, prices based on sales of similar assets and liabilities, or prices based on valuation techniques) used in determining their fair value.

(2) The characteristics of securitizations (a description of the transferor's continuing involvement with the transferred assets, including, but not limited to, servicing, recourse, and restrictions on interests that continue to be held by the transferor) and the gain or loss from sale of financial assets in securitizations.

(3)   The key assumptions used in measuring the fair value of interests that continue to be held by the transferor and servicing assets or servicing liabilities, if any, at the time of securitization (including, at a minimum, quantitative information about discount rates, expected prepayments including the expected weighted-average life of prepayable financial assets, and anticipated credit losses, if applicable).

(4)   Cash flows between the securitization SPE and the transferor, unless reported separately elsewhere in the financial statements or notes (including proceeds from new securitizations, proceeds from collections reinvested in revolving-period securitizations, purchases of delinquent or foreclosed loans, servicing fees, and cash flows received on interests that continue to be held by the transferor).

(i)   If the entity has interests that continue to be held by the transferor in financial assets that it has securitized or servicing assets or servicing liabilities relating to assets that it has securitized, at the date of the latest statement of financial position presented, for each major asset type (e.g., mortgage loans, credit card receivables, and automobile loans):

(1)   Its accounting policies for subsequently measuring those interests, including the methodology (whether quoted market price, prices based on sales of similar assets and liabilities, or prices based on valuation techniques) used in determining their fair value.

(2)   The key assumptions used in subsequently measuring the fair value of those interests (including, at a minimum, quantitative information about discount rates, expected prepayments including the expected weighted-average life of prepayable financial assets, and anticipated credit losses, including expected static pool losses, if applicable).

(3)   A sensitivity analysis or stress test showing the hypothetical effect on the fair value of those interests (including any servicing assets or servicing liabilities) of two or more unfavorable variations from the expected levels for each key assumption that is reported under (2) above independently from any change in another key assumption, and a description of the objectives, methodology, and limitations of the sensitivity analysis or stress test.

(4)   For the securitized assets and any other financial assets that it manages together with them:

(a)   The total principal amount outstanding, the portion that has been derecognized, and the portion that continues to be recognized in each category reported in the statement of financial position, at the end of the period.

(b)   Delinquencies at the end of the period.

(c)   Credit losses, net of recoveries, during the period.

18A.25 WHAT ARE THE FASB'S PROPOSED AMENDMENTS TO STATEMENT 140?[50]

(a) SUMMARY OF DECISIONS REACHED TO DATE The FASB staff has redeliberated topics related to Statement 140 several times in recent years. On June 18, 2008, the FASB staff prepared a summary of Board decisions for informational purposes only. The following six Board decisions are tentative and do not change current accounting:

1. *Redeliberations of 2005 Exposure Draft and Project Plan.* Recently, the Board deliberated several topics, including the unit of account for derecognition, the isolation criterion, and permitted activities of a qualifying SPE. The remaining issues for the Board to deliberate on are a proposal for a linked presentation model, disclosure requirements, the measurement of transferor-held beneficial interests, servicing, and the effective date and transition provisions for all proposed amendments.

2. *Qualifying SPE.* The Board decided to remove the concept of a qualifying SPE from Statement 140 and to remove the scope exception for QSPEs from Interpretation 46(R). This will require that variable-interest entities, previously accounted for as qualifying SPEs in Statement 140, will need to be analyzed for consolidation according to Interpretation 46(R). It will eliminate the provision in paragraph 9(b) that allowed entities to "look-through" to the rights of beneficial interest holders when analyzing control.

3. *Derecognition.*

   (a) Participating Interest Definition—The Board decided that only an entire financial asset or a portion of a financial asset that meets the definition of a participating interest will be eligible for derecognition. The participating interest may not be an interest in an equity instrument, a derivative financial instrument, or a hybrid financial instrument with an embedded derivative not clearly and closely related to the original financial asset. Additionally, a participating interest requires that (1) the cash flows received from the assets are divided among the interests in proportion to the share of ownership represented by each, (2) the participating interest holders have no recourse, other than standard representations and warranties, to the transferor or to each other, (3) no interest holder is subordinated to another, and (4) neither the transferor nor any participating interest holder has the right to pledge or exchange the entire financial asset in which it owns a participating interest.

   (b) Paragraph 9 Requirements—The Board also decided to amend the derecognition criteria in Statement 140 to improve financial reporting in the short term. Specifically, the Board voted to amend paragraphs 9(a) and 9(c) and to remove paragraph 9(b). Paragraph 9(a) will be clarified to require that the transferred

---

50. Section derived from www.fasb.org/project/transfers_of_financial_assets.shtml.

financial assets must be beyond the reach of the transferor or any of its consolidated affiliates. Additionally, the isolation analysis must consider all arrangements made in connection with the transfer. Paragraph 9(c) will be amended to (1) state that the transferor and its consolidated affiliates cannot maintain effective control over the financial assets and (2) include an additional criterion that states that if the transferor or its consolidated affiliates constrain the transferee and benefit from that constraint, the transferor maintains effective control over the transferred assets. This change incorporates similar requirements currently in paragraph 9(b).

(c) Minimum Threshold—The Board decided not to add a specific minimum requirement for the amount of beneficial interests that must be held by parties other than the transferor and its consolidated affiliates for a transferor to meet the sale accounting conditions for transfers of financial assets.

4. *Initial and Subsequent Measurement.* The Board decided that beneficial interests received by a transferor, in connection with a sale of an entire financial asset to an entity that is not consolidated by the transferor, should be considered proceeds of the sale and initially measured at fair value. Additionally, the Board decided that a participating interest in a financial asset that continues to be held by a transferor should be initially measured at its allocated carrying amount in accordance with the existing measurement guidance in paragraph 10 of Statement 140.

5. *Guaranteed Mortgage Securitization (GMS).* The Board decided to delete the exception that requires a transferor to reclassify interests received in a GMS securitization to securities under Statement 115 if the transfer does not qualify as a sale. The Board also decided to remove the exception for GMS transactions that requires a transferor to recognize a servicing asset or liability if the transfer does not qualify as a sale.

6. *Disclosures.* Subject to drafting changes, the Board decided on the following disclosure amendments in Statement 140:

(a) To provide an overall objective for the disclosure requirements.

(b) To include aggregation guidance for similar transfers.

(c) To require additional information about a transferor's calculation of gains and losses when that transfer involves an SPE, a transferor's continuing involvement in transferred financial assets, and liquidity, guarantee, and other commitments provide by third parties, and other amendments.

(d) To provide a definition of continuing involvement in the glossary.

(e) To require that paragraph 17(c) disclosure apply to all transfers within the scope of Statement 140.

(f) To eliminate explicit references to the methodology used in determining fair value as described in paragraphs 17(h)(1) and 17(i)(1).

(g) To eliminate footnote 10, which provides an exception for the disclosures required by paragraph 17(i)(4) if the transferor's only continuing involvement is servicing.

(b) PROPOSED EFFECTIVE DATE The Board decided that the proposed amendments to Statement 140 should be applied in fiscal years beginning after November 15, 2008 (effective date), on a prospective basis (e.g., a calendar year-end entity would apply the proposed amendments to Statement 140 for new transactions completed after January 1, 2009). However, qualifying SPEs that existed prior to the effective date would be subject to the consolidation guidance in fiscal years beginning after November 15, 2009. Transition disclosures would be provided for existing QSPEs during the one-year deferral period.

(c) NEXT STEPS The Board authorized the staff to proceed to draft the proposed amendments to Interpretation 46(R) and Statement 140 for vote by written ballot. The Board expects to issue a proposed Exposure Draft in the third quarter of 2008.

GOODWILL AND OTHER INTANGIBLE ASSETS: AN UPDATE[1] (NEW)

BARRY JAY EPSTEIN, PHD, CPA
Russell Novak & Company LLP
CHRISTOPHER J. LEISNER, CPA, CMC
Creative IP Solutions LLC

---

1. Portions of this chapter originally appeared in Chapter 20, "Goodwill and Other Intangible Assets," written by Lailani Moody, CPA, MBA, of Grant Thornton LLP. This entire chapter also appeared in the 2006 Cumulative Supplement to the *Accountants' Handbook*, Tenth Edition.

20A.1 CHARACTERIZATION OF INTANGIBLE ASSETS

Intangible assets are assets—other than financial assets—that lack physical substance yet do have utility and value in the hands of the reporting entity. Examples include patents, copyrights, trade names, customer lists, royalty agreements, databases, and computer software. They also include the assets called leasehold improvements, which are frequently but mistakenly viewed as being tangible assets.

The range of intangibles is quite broad, and this fact is perhaps more clearly understood now than during earlier years, since changing business and economic conditions have brought intellectual property and certain other intangible assets to much greater prominence than had formerly been the case. While for many mostly traditional (e.g., manufacturing) businesses the value of intangibles may still be underappreciated, for high-technology and other so-called knowledge-based companies, the primary assets may be intangible ones such as patents and copyrights. Even for professional services firms, the key assets may be "soft" resources such as knowledge bases and client relationships.

There are several possible taxonomies of intangible assets. First, intangible assets can be classified either as *identifiable*—for example, trademarks and most other intangibles—or as *unidentifiable*, which generally implies goodwill. A second way to classify intangible assets is based on how they are acquired. They can be internally developed or acquired from external sources, which include both simple purchases of one or more intangibles (e.g., groups of related patents) or those that are part of business combinations. Intangible assets acquired in a business combination may be recognized as assets separate from goodwill or as part of goodwill, depending on whether the intangible assets satisfy certain criteria. As discussed in this chapter, the applicable accounting pronouncements and accounting requirements differ significantly, depending on whether the intangible asset is identifiable, whether it is internally developed or acquired externally, and, if acquired externally, whether it was acquired in a business combination.

Yet other classification schemes for intangible assets were first offered by the now superseded Accounting Principles Board (APB) Opinion No. 17, which indicated that intangible assets could also be categorized based on either

1. Expected period of benefit—whether limited by law or contract, related to human or economic factors, or indefinite or indeterminate duration; or
2. Separability from an entire enterprise—rights transferable without title, salable, or inseparable from the enterprise or a substantial part of it.

While all of the foregoing taxonomies assist one in thinking about intangibles and are to a greater or lesser extent incorporated into current generally accepted accounting principles (GAAP) (primarily SFAS No. 142), perhaps the most important distinctions are between intangibles acquired in business combinations accounted for under SFAS No. 141 or otherwise; between those having finite lives and those having indefinite lives; and between those that are severable from the reporting entity and those that are not. All of these matters are addressed in this chapter.

20A.2   ACCOUNTING AND FINANCIAL MANAGEMENT OVERVIEW
Numerous pronouncements provide guidance on the accounting for intangibles. This section provides an overview of those pronouncements.

(a) INTANGIBLE ASSETS INCLUDING GOODWILL ACQUIRED IN A BUSINESS COMBINATION   Under SFAS No. 141, "Business Combinations," all business combinations must now be accounted for as purchases; pooling accounting is no longer permitted. This necessitates purchase-price allocation. It provides initial measurement and recognition guidance for intangible assets and goodwill acquired in a business combination, including mandates as to the recognition of intangible assets apart from goodwill.

Subsequent accounting for intangible assets, including goodwill, is provided in SFAS No. 142, "Goodwill and Other Intangible Assets." SFAS No. 142 provides that goodwill should not be amortized; it mandates that impairment tests of goodwill be conducted annually or, in some circumstances, more frequently; and it provides guidance on recognizing impairments. In contrast with earlier GAAP, which required amortization of all intangibles, SFAS No. 142 addresses whether intangible assets other than goodwill have *indefinite* useful lives and therefore should not be amortized but instead tested at least annually for impairment, or *finite* useful lives and therefore should be amortized over their estimated useful lives.

Intangible assets with finite useful lives are tested for impairment under SFAS No. 144, "Accounting for the Impairment or Disposal of Long-Lived Assets." Intangibles that have finite lives and thus are amortized must also be reviewed for recoverability of carrying amounts in a process similar to that under SFAS No. 144, and useful lives must be reassessed and altered when warranted by circumstances (e.g., technological obsolescence making the useful life of a patent much shorter than the legal term).

(b) INTANGIBLE ASSETS ACQUIRED SEPARATELY OR WITH OTHER ASSETS   SFAS No. 142 provides initial recognition and measurement guidance for intangible assets acquired other than in a business combination—that is, intangible assets acquired individually or together

with a group of other assets that do not constitute a business. SFAS No. 142 also provides guidance to the subsequent accounting for intangible assets, including determining whether they have finite or indeterminate useful lives and therefore whether they should be amortized or not. Finally, it addresses accounting for impairments of intangible assets with indeterminate lives. A separate standard, SFAS No. 144, provides guidance on impairment of intangible assets with finite useful lives.

(c) INTERNALLY DEVELOPED INTANGIBLE ASSETS   SFAS No. 142 addresses the initial and subsequent accounting for internally developed intangible assets. It carries forward the requirement set forth by the predecessor standard, APB No. 17, that the costs of internally developing, maintaining, or restoring intangibles that cannot be identified specifically, have indeterminate lives, or are inherent in an ongoing business and pertain to the entity as a whole cannot be capitalized. Such costs must be expensed currently as incurred.

(d) INTANGIBLE ASSETS RECOGNIZED ON ACQUISITION OF A NONCONTROLL-ING INTEREST IN A SUBSIDIARY   SFAS No. 142 provides guidance on the initial and subsequent accounting for goodwill and other intangible assets recognized on acquisition of noncontrolling interests in a subsidiary. Under current GAAP, goodwill associated with minority (i.e., noncontrolling) interests is not recognized. Note, however, that the Financial Accounting Standards Board (FASB) is currently considering a major change in purchase-business combination accounting that will, if adopted, result in the recognition of goodwill associated with minority interests.

(e) GOODWILL RECOGNIZED WHEN APPLYING THE EQUITY METHOD   SFAS No. 142 provides that amounts recognized as corresponding to goodwill in applying the equity method accounting to investments should not be amortized. Equity method goodwill is tested for impairment under APB Opinion No. 18, "The Equity Method of Accounting for Investments in Common Stock."

(f) SPECIFIC GUIDANCE ON CERTAIN INTANGIBLES   Accounting pronouncements, such as Statements of Position issued by the Accounting Standards Executive Committee of the American Institute of Certified Public Accountants (AICPA), provide guidance on the accounting for specific intangible assets, such as start-up costs, internally developed software, and advertising. These matters are addressed subsequently.

(g) INTANGIBLE ASSETS IN SPECIALIZED INDUSTRIES   Certain FASB Statements and Interpretations provide guidance on accounting for certain intangibles of specialized industries, such as airlines and computer software development. Impairment testing for intangible assets in many specialized industries is performed under the general requirements (SFAS No. 144), but for certain industries or assets, such as broadcasters' program rights, guidance under particular AICPA Industry Audit and Accounting Guides must be followed instead.

(h) THE NEW EMPHASIS ON MANAGEMENT OF INTANGIBLE ASSETS
(i) Sarbanes-Oxley Act of 2002—Implications for the Financial Reporting of Intangible Assets   Sound financial and operating management of reporting entities has always been a critical concern, of course, but developments in the early 2000s have caused renewed emphasis on managements' and directors' fiduciary duties, including the duty to maximize the value of all assets under management. The widely reported corporate management and financial

reporting scandals of the late 1990s, in particular, created a groundswell of demand for reforms in corporate governance practices. Among other things, this led to the hurried passage by Congress of the Sarbanes-Oxley Act of 2002 ("Sarbanes" or "the Act"), the ramifications of which are still being comprehended.

Sarbanes has generated a considerable amount of interest in, and focus on, the quality of financial reporting and the reliability of internal control systems. The widely publicized and sometimes controversial Section 404 requirements for reporting on the effectiveness of internal controls, certified by both management and the entity's independent accountants, has been a costly and demanding undertaking for many companies, including some whose quality of controls and financial management were previously unquestioned by investors.

Sarbanes has also highlighted the historically troublesome disparity between corporate managers and shareholders regarding many entities' true financial condition, which is sometimes referred to as the "transparency" issue. GAAP-basis financial reporting is based on a "mixed-attribute" model that combines historical costs and current fair values, with some costs subject to amortization and others only sporadically tested for impairment, making financial statements often unsuited for directly assessing the reporting entity's value. Because intangible assets now account for the majority of many publicly traded companies' stock values (by some estimates, as much as two-thirds), and because accounting for intangibles has been largely overlooked in the accounting pronouncements and literature, this area is now overdue for much greater attention. The demand for greater transparency has increased the pressure on accountants to develop the means to more fully report the value of intangible assets of the companies they manage, report, and/or opine on.

When the 2002 Sarbanes requirements are evaluated in conjunction with the 2001 FASB pronouncements regarding goodwill, intangibles, and business combinations (SFAS Nos. 141 and 142), it is clear that today's accountants (both internal staff and outside auditors) must increase their awareness of the intangible assets a company possesses and the value those assets bring to the company, which may in part be driven by the potential value those assets may hold for other entities. Even the SEC now recognizes that the way in which intangible assets are accounted for, as well as which valuation method is employed, can have a material effect on investors' decisions (see discussion by SEC staff on "market participation" valuation requirements in Section 20A.3(a)(ii)).

For example, when the accountant considers how off–balance-sheet transactions may impact (either negatively or positively) the financial condition of a company, intangible assets will be, in many instances, a likely asset class to inspect and analyze. Section 401(a) of the Act directed the SEC to enact rules so that

> [E]ach annual and quarterly report required to be filed with the Commission shall disclose all material off–balance-sheet transactions, arrangements, obligations (including contingent obligations), and other relationships of the issuer with unconsolidated entities or other persons, that may have a material current or future effect on financial condition, changes in financial condition, results of operations, liquidity, capital expenditures, capital resources, or significant components of revenues or expenses.

In its rules (Final Rule: Disclosure in Management's Discussion and Analysis about Off–Balance-Sheet Arrangements and Aggregate Contractual Obligations, effective April 7, 2003), the SEC mandated that registrants provide explanations of off–balance-sheet arrangements in separately captioned subsections of the so-called Management Discussion and Analysis (MD&A)

section of their periodic filings with the Commission. While certain of these disclosures were already required under MD&A rules, the new requirements are somewhat more comprehensive. These rules do not, however, alter underlying accounting for or disclosures about owned intangible assets, nor do they alter the accounting, under GAAP, for transfers or sales of such assets.

The SEC rule does require that executory contracts, such as purchase obligations for goods or services, be included in a new tabular presentation of off–balance-sheet obligations, which is at variance with GAAP requirements but deemed to be important because of liquidity implications. In the case of a license arrangement (e.g., for patent rights previously sold), disclosure in the MD&A under this rule would be appropriate, even though the obligation is not a liability under GAAP definitions.

(ii) Improved Internal Controls over Intangible Assets under Sarbanes In Section 404(a), the Act addresses a new requirement for management to prepare an internal control report that shall

(1) state the responsibility of management for establishing and maintaining an adequate internal control structure and procedures for financial reporting and

(2) contain an assessment, as of the end of the most recent fiscal year of the issuer, of the effectiveness of the internal control structure and procedures of the issuer for financial reporting.

As discussed previously, SFAS Nos. 141 and 142 require revised accounting for intangibles and goodwill arising from business combinations. Similarly, as a company generates new intellectual property through innovation, invention, or operational insights, it may be necessary to establish new accounting procedures to measure the carrying value and fair value of an acquired reporting unit (and perhaps existing reporting units), including the value of intangibles.

Both the cost to create and the cost to protect intangibles are measured and reported in the financial statements, either as an expense (if properly considered research and development costs under GAAP) or as capital assets. In general, due to SFAS No. 2's strict requirements, most of the cost of patent or other intellectual property development, if internally accomplished, will be expensed—one reason that GAAP-compliant financial reporting sometimes underserves entities that rely on intellectual property for their operations and valuation.

An important concern, then, is that if these assets are largely missing from the financial statements, how can these entities ensure that fiduciary responsibilities relative to these hidden assets are properly discharged? There are at least two aspects to this concern: first, developing and implementing internal controls over these assets such that the requirements of Sarbanes will be met; and second, that the value of these assets is recognized for the benefit of the shareholders.

An axiom in management is that what is not measured is not managed; a corollary to that is that what is not in plain sight is also likely not to be well managed. The relatively trivial carrying values of intellectual property often can result in undermanagement, meaning a failure to manage these assets for the benefit of shareholders, whether by using them more effectively internally or by seeking external sources of income from these intangible assets.

As part of a comprehensive effort to establish meaningful controls over their intangible assets, entities should consider developing metrics that would raise the profile of both the holdings of intangibles and of the productivity derived therefrom. Productivity measures would address (as appropriate) both internal usage and external revenue generation. When such internal control procedures are devised and monitored, compliance with this section of Sarbanes would seem to have been accomplished.

(iii) Practical Approaches to Internal Control Structures for Intangible Assets   The authors propose the following approach to the fabrication of an internal control structure used to capture, measure, and report the presence and value of intangible assets. This can be accomplished by assisting personnel in the legal, research, and/or technology transfer departments to establish the appropriate record-keeping and asset-control procedures. Those procedures would relate to documenting the creation, acquisition, and disposal of intellectual assets. Such documentation could include data about the specific identity of the asset; correspondence with appropriate patent, trademark, or copyright offices; ownership and/or assignments; estimated useful lives; associated costs to acquire or create; and, when appropriate, market values.

It is potentially the case that in-house and/or outside counsel may be aware of existing third-party claims that could be asserted against the company, as well as claims the company may be able to assert against third parties. Such analyses may already be in process by the tech-transfer and/or legal staff as part of their normal process of selecting what technologies to outlicense or protect through an infringement action. They may also be in possession of demand letters from other entities that are asserting claims based on their intellectual assets.

Accounting for such claims may also suggest that a review of the company's various insurance policies, vendor and customer contracts, and licensing agreements might be warranted. Because the accountant is typically required under SFAS No. 5 to assess the likelihood that a loss event will occur and whether the estimated loss amounts can be reasonably determined, this should be a routine procedure. Under SFAS No. 5, however, indemnification and insurance provisions may give rise to a recovery claim, but this cannot be offset.

As part of an assessment of the company's disclosure controls, it may be helpful to prepare documentation procedures throughout the life cycle of the intangible asset. If the company is International Organization for Standardization (ISO) compliant, much of the key information regarding intangibles may already be documented relating to

1. Creation and acquisition identification of the intangible asset
2. Applicable filings and prosecution of applications to obtain a formal or registered intellectual property right for the intangible asset
3. Encumbrances to ownership rights, including licensing and assignments that may narrow or eliminate rights for the intangible asset
4. Maintenance of the asset, such as repair and upkeep or the payment of appropriate registration fees
5. Outlicensing and/or cross-licensing agreements
6. Infringement claims against and/or by third parties regarding the intangible asset
7. Disposal, retirement, or expiration of the asset

An additional reference to assist accountants to structure internal control procedures is the guidance presented in the AICPA toolkit, *The Fair Value Measurement Valuation Toolkit for Financial Accounting Standards Board Statements of Financial Accounting Standards No. 141, Business Combinations, and No. 142, Goodwill and Other Intangible Assets.*

Much of the foregoing is directed toward maintaining a current record of the existence of intangible assets and various agreements, such as licensing arrangements. Another aspect, and one vital to the goal of maximizing shareholder wealth, is to address those actions that are not currently being taken but that could be valuable for the enterprise and its various stakeholders. Doing this requires that external data sources be incorporated into the entity's information system. Without external references, poor performance may be misread as good simply because of an improvement over prior periods.

One cited statistic, for example, is that each patent in existence (circa 2000) was producing an average of $60,000 in licensing revenues per year, or about $1,000,000 over its economic life. Information about the average licensing revenue per patent is an external metric that can be used to evaluate the entity's own licensing portfolio. Over time, such analyses can be used to gauge portfolio trends, to show whether the licensing revenue of the patent portfolio is acceptable versus expected licensing revenues, based on statistical averages. If not, an investigation can be focused to determine why not. This control mechanism is fully consistent with the explicit requirements and implicit objectives of Sarbanes.

This type of information also sets out a framework for an internal metric. The licensing revenue per patent can be determined for a company patent portfolio. An average licensing revenue can be determined and tracked over time. Patents that are underperforming can be reviewed to ascertain whether these should be preserved for commercial purposes other than licensing, or whether they should be sold or abandoned. Trend data can be accumulated over time to report on whether the portfolio is underperforming based on internally set expectations.

Some examples of metrics that can be used to evaluate an intellectual property (IP) program include the number of patents or patent applications owned by type (utility or design), by country, by the royalty income received from each patent, and by an average royalty for each type of patent or type of technology. Patents owned should include all patents to which the company has unimpaired title. (Title would be deemed impaired if the reporting entity is not the sole assignee.) The dollar value of sales for products covered by the patents is another metric that permits such evaluations of a patent portfolio or IP program.

20A.3 INITIAL RECOGNITION AND MEASUREMENT OF INTANGIBLE ASSETS

(a) ACQUIRED INTANGIBLE ASSETS   SFAS No. 142, "Goodwill and Other Intangible Assets," issued in June 2001, superseded the former standard, APB Opinion No. 17, "Intangible Assets." It uses the term *intangible assets* to refer to intangible assets other than goodwill. While amortization is no longer universally required, as it had been for more than 30 years under APB No. 17, SFAS No. 142 did carry forward certain of the requirements of that former standard.

(i) Cost Allocation and Other Valuation Issues   An intangible asset acquired either individually or with a group of other assets—other than as part of a business combination—is initially recognized and measured based on its fair value. The cost of a group of assets acquired in a transaction other than a business combination is allocated to the individual assets acquired based on their relative fair values and cannot result in the recognition of goodwill.

Intangible assets acquired in a business combination are initially recognized and measured in conformity with SFAS No. 141—that is, via the purchase price allocation process, which is based on fair values or—for goodwill only—represents the residual cost of the acquisition. Goodwill can arise only in connection with purchase accounting for business combinations. So-called *negative goodwill* is not included in the definition of goodwill as discussed in this chapter. (Under SFAS No. 141, any excess of fair value of net assets acquired over the cost of a business combination is recognized in earnings immediately.)

(ii) SEC/PCAOB Valuation Issues for Intangible Assets—More Changes, Greater Confusion on the Horizon   In unofficial remarks before the December 2004 AICPA National Conference on Current SEC and PCAOB Developments, a staff member of the SEC's Office of the Chief Accountant explained why fair value, determined by using the actual amounts negotiated by the buyer and seller (referred to below as "entity specific") would be superseded by an "estimated" fair value based on an analysis from a "marketplace participant" perspective. In these remarks, it was stated that

> An underpinning to the determination of fair value of an acquired intangible asset under SFAS No. 141 is that it is determined from the perspective of a market-place participant.

This is clear in SFAS No. 141, paragraph B174, which indicates that the fair value estimate

> should incorporate assumptions that marketplace participants would use in making estimates of fair value, such as assumptions about future contract renewals and other benefits such as those that might result from acquisition-related synergies. . . .

In contrast, the useful life concept in SFAS No. 142 is not necessarily viewed from that of a marketplace participant. Rather the useful life of an intangible asset is inherently related to the expectations of the particular entity and therefore would incorporate entity-specific assumptions.

In this context, the entity may believe that the fair value determination should therefore be entirely consistent with the useful life then assigned to the intangible asset as in this case, both were developed based on entity-specific assumptions.

I would point out, however, that the utilization of entity-specific assumptions to determine fair value in this case is just a proxy for those assumptions that may be developed by a marketplace participant.

Subsequent to these remarks, the FASB issued an Exposure Draft of SFAS No. 141(R) (June 2005), which in many particulars is based on an analysis of international accounting standards. At paragraph 20, proposed SFAS No. 141(R) seeks to clarify the definition of fair value for a business combination when it states:

> Business combinations are usually arm's-length exchange transactions in which knowledgeable, unrelated willing parties exchange equal values. Therefore, in the absence of evidence to the contrary, the exchange price (referred to as the consideration transferred in this Statement) paid by the acquirer on the acquisition date is presumed to be the best evidence of the acquisition date fair value of the acquirer's interest in the acquiree.

The SEC remarks and the FASB exposure draft provisions are indicative of a changing landscape of the acceptable valuation methodologies and technical experts to whom the accountant can turn for support when computing an intangible's fair value.

FASB Concept Statement No. 7 was identified in SFAS No. 142, issued in 2002, as guidance for valuation methodologies, principally citing the comparables and income method approaches. However, intangible asset values measured in actual business transactions are often based more on expected and potential benefits rather than on historical and/or actual revenues. Therefore, the application of the income approach requires a stacking or layering of assumptions. As the number of those assumptions increases, compliance with Rule 201 of the AICPA *Code of Professional Conduct* (specifically concerning the reliance on sufficient relevant data in support of any professional opinion) becomes more and more difficult.

There are real-world situations in which technical experts from other disciplines have addressed the situation of determining the fair value of intangibles where historical cash flows do not exist. One of those situations arises during the dispute resolution process, and a second is seen in the technology-transfer industry.

(iii) Valuation Approaches Supported by Court Opinions   In the federal courts, a jury is frequently asked to estimate the damages attributable to a violation of intellectual property rights. Several cases, including *Georgia Pacific v. United States Plywood Corp.* and *Panduit Corp. v. Stahlin Bros. Fibre Works, Inc.*, have compiled a technical body of knowledge regarding methodologies to determine the fair value of intangible assets. For example, *Panduit* sets forth these four tests:

1. Is there demand for the patented product?
2. Are there acceptable noninfringing alternatives to the infringing product?
3. Does the patent holder have the manufacturing and marketing capacity to make and sell more of the product?
4. Can the damages consultant quantify the lost profits to a reasonable degree of certainty?

In the earlier *Georgia-Pacific* case, the court considered 15 factors as a means to compute damages arising from a dispute over intangible assets:

1. The royalties received by Georgia-Pacific for licensing the patent, proving or tending to prove an established royalty
2. The rates paid by the licensee for the use of other similar patents
3. The nature and scope of the license, such as whether it is exclusive or nonexclusive, restricted or nonrestricted in terms of territory or customers
4. Georgia-Pacific's policy of maintaining its patent monopoly by licensing the use of the invention only under special conditions designed to preserve the monopoly
5. The commercial relationship between Georgia-Pacific and licensees, such as whether they are competitors in the same territory in the same line of business or whether they are inventor and promoter
6. The effect of selling the patented specialty in promoting sales of other Georgia-Pacific products; the existing value of the invention to Georgia-Pacific as a generator of sales of nonpatented items; and the extent of such derivative or "convoyed" sales
7. The duration of the patent and the term of the license
8. The established profitability of the patented product, its commercial success, and its current popularity
9. The utility and advantages of the patent property over any old modes or devices that had been used
10. The nature of the patented invention, its character in the commercial embodiment owned and produced by the licensor, and the benefits to those who have used it

11. The extent to which the infringer used the invention and any evidence probative of the value of that use

12. The portion of the profit or selling price that is customary in the particular business or in comparable businesses

13. The portion of the realizable profit that should be credited to the invention as distinguished from any nonpatented elements, manufacturing process, business risks, or significant features or improvements added by the infringer

14. The opinion testimony of qualified experts

15. The amount that Georgia-Pacific and a licensee would have agreed upon at the time the infringement began if they had reasonably and voluntarily tried to reach an agreement

In a subsequent case based in part on the *Panduit* findings, the courts have held that damages based on a loss of market share can be used to compute damages (*State Industries, Inc. v. Mor-Flo Industries, Inc.*). In *State Industries,* the Federal Circuit accepted evidence of the patentee's market share to prove that the patentee would have made at least a percentage of the infringer's sales had there been no infringement. Quantifying market share allows the patentee to measure lost profits in the ratio of their original market share to their diluted market share after the infringement.

In these cases and several others, the courts have held that intellectual property owners may be entitled to lost profits that can never be realized (hence the claim for "lost" profits), but were nonetheless measured to "a reasonable degree of accounting certainty."

(iv) Valuation Approaches Used by Tech-Transfer Practitioners   Taking a page from the dispute resolution practitioners, several technology-transfer specialists (also referred to as licensing professionals) have adopted market-based measures of value. Here, however, rather than measure the amount of damages, the computation is made for the purpose of measuring the amount of benefits that would be recognized by the adoption of the licensor's technology by the licensee. In 2002 Ted Hagelin analyzed different concepts and methods of valuation, including the cost, market, and income methods.[2] Other valuation methods developed especially for intellectual property law were also examined, including the "25 percent" rule, industry standards, ranking, surrogate measures, disaggregation, Monte Carlo, and option methods. In his article, Professor Hagelin presents a newly devised tech-transfer valuation model labeled "Competitive Advantage Valuation" and suggests that

> The . . . premise of the CAV [Competitive Advantage Valuation] method is that the value of a given intellectual property asset can best be measured by the competitive advantage which that asset contributes.

When one incorporates this tech-transfer CAV approach with the previously cited assertion by SEC staff that "market-participant" value drivers must be considered under SFAS Nos. 141 and 142, it becomes obvious that there are multiple, well-established, fully vetted intangible

---

2.   Ted Hagelin, "A New Method to Value Intellectual Property," *American Intellectual Property Law Association Quarterly Journal,* Vol. 30 (2000), p. 33.

asset valuation approaches that accounting practitioners can employ when answering the question, "What are the values of these intangible assets?"

(v) Valuation Approaches Seen in Wall Street Transactions   An additional market validation of the alignment of these various intangible asset valuation approaches is found in the emergence of numerous intellectual asset-based transactions on Wall Street. One of the most familiar transactions seen in the entertainment and garment industries is the securitization of anticipated intangible asset-based revenues, as reflected in the Bowie Bond (David Bowie) and Bill Blass securitizations.

Another example is the adaptation of the traditional lending structure known as a sale lease-back (used for tangible assets) that has been deployed using intangible assets and has been referred to as a sale/license-back. In a presentation to the National Knowledge and Intellectual Property Management Taskforce's annual executive briefing in September 2002, Mitchell Fillet, of Riderwood Group, Inc., stated that

> We are in the midst of a paradigm shift that is so economically powerful that it ranks with the other two that have defined our economic history. . . .
>
> I am suggesting that intellectual property, primarily patents and derivative products from those patents, as well as licenses to use that intellectual property, is emerging as an important asset class both on corporate balance sheets and off them, as collateral for loans and legally separate securitizations.

As a result of the sale/license-back structure, intangible assets are now being acquired by large investment banking firms, much as mortgage portfolios were acquired starting in the 1970s, thus giving birth to a highly liquid market for what had previously been difficult-to-trade assets. As such, the value drivers associated with intangible assets now reflect several of the financial modeling aspects found in commercial paper and various asset-backed securitizations.

As evidence of the importance such intangible assets have, and the market-based impact they can make, we can review the Federal Reserve Chairman's October 2005 comments on this market built on intangibles, citing the significant economic benefits to the U.S. economy of the secondary market launched in the mid-1970s:

> These increasingly complex financial instruments have contributed to the development of a far more flexible, efficient, and hence resilient financial system than the one that existed just a quarter-century ago. After the bursting of the stock market bubble in 2000, unlike previous periods following large financial shocks, no major financial institution defaulted, and the economy held up far better than many had anticipated.[3]

To gain an understanding about how intangible assets account for such significant market values, the accounting of a sale/license-back transaction can be reviewed; both the buyer and the seller in this transaction recognize distinct benefits.

---

3.   Alan Greenspan, speech on economic flexibility, presented before the National Italian American Foundation, Washington, D.C., October 12, 2005.

From the seller's position, the closing would generate significant pretax earnings, as the only significant offset to sales price paid for internally generated intangibles would be the transaction fees (attorneys, financial consultants, valuation experts) and any unamortized capitalized cost of the underlying assets. In the sale/license-back structure, the attributes of the intangible assets permit the transaction to unleash earnings (unlike the sale/lease-back that was treated as a financing), principally because title to the intangible asset is transferred to the buyer.

Additionally, any license-back provision would qualify as a fully deductible expense for tax purposes. Unlike the sale/lease-back of a tangible asset, which is governed by SFAS No. 13, the "license" in a sale/license-back is a period expense and not debt; the license is consumed in the period in which the expense is incurred. Such accounting treatment suggests that the seller's cost of capital would be reduced to the extent that the proceeds from the sale are used to reduce bank or other outstanding debt, thereby deleveraging the balance sheet.

From the buyer's perspective, intangible assets with measurable, market-based value (presumably from outlicensing potential) can be selectively acquired, without incurring all of the fixed and sunk costs attributed to a research and development facility. Generally speaking, the licensing activity of a large corporation enjoys a greater contribution margin than the company taken as a whole. Additionally, the operating costs would be partially offset by the license granted to the seller, and the intangible assets acquired would be treated as an amortizable asset.

(vi) Identifiable Intangibles Distinguishable from Goodwill   SFAS No. 141 provides that intangible assets acquired in a business combination are to be recognized as an asset *apart from goodwill*, but only if they meet the asset recognition criteria in the FASB's Statement of Financial Accounting Concept No. 5 (CON 5), *and* if either (1) control over the future economic benefits of the assets results from contractual or other legal rights (the "legal/ contractual" criterion) or (2) the intangible assets are capable of being separated or divided and sold, transferred, licensed, rented, or exchanged (referred to as the separability criterion). Even if the intangible assets cannot be sold, transferred, licensed, rented, or exchanged individually, the assets would still meet the separability criterion if they could be sold, transferred, licensed, rented, or exchanged along with a related contract, asset, or liability.

Examples of intangible assets that meet the "legal/contractual" criterion include trademarks, newspaper mastheads, Internet domain names, order backlog, books, magazines, musical works, license agreements, construction permits, broadcast rights, mortgage servicing contracts, patented technology, and computer software. Examples of assets that meet the separability criterion include customer lists, noncontractual customer relationships, unpatented technology, and databases such as title plants. Note that it is not necessary for the acquiring entity to actually intend to dispose of, sell, or rent the separable intangible in order to satisfy this criterion.

SFAS No. 141 presents a lengthy listing of intangibles that are to be separately recognized, along with the useful lives relevant for amortization purposes. Certain exceptions are identified, such as for those intangibles having indefinite lives, as is the case for perpetually renewable broadcast licenses, which are maintained at cost (subject to potential impairment write-downs) until a finite life can be ascertained, if ever. These intangibles generally can be categorized as being (i) customer- or market-based assets (e.g., customer lists, newspaper mastheads, and trademarked brand names); (ii) contract-based assets (e.g., covenants not to compete, broadcast rights); (iii) artistic-based assets (e.g., plays, other literary works, musical compositions); and (iv) technology-based assets (e.g., title plant, databases, computer software). With the exception of indefinite-life intangibles, all identifiable intangibles are to be amortized over their estimated useful lives, defined as the period over which the intangible asset is expected to directly or indirectly generate cash flows for the entity.

Appendix A to SFAS No. 141 identifies intangible assets that have characteristics that meet one of the two criteria (legal/contractual or separability). However, depending on the facts and circumstances, a specific acquired intangible asset might not meet the criteria. A good approach would be to first consider whether the acquired intangibles are among those specifically described by the FASB, and then to consider whether other intangibles also meeting the two criteria for separate capitalization might also be present.

Identified intangibles can be aggregated into permits, intellectual property, technology tools, procurement rights, competitor arrangements, and customer arrangements. *Permits* include:

- *Broadcast rights:* a license to transmit over certain bandwidths in the radio frequency spectrum, granted by the operation of communication laws
- *Certification marks:* the right to be able to assert that a product or service meets certain standards of quality or origin, such as "ISO 14000 Certified"
- *Collective marks:* rights to signify membership in an association
- *Construction permits:* rights to build a specified structure at a specified location
- *Franchise rights:* permits to engage in a trade-named business, to sell a trademarked good, or to sell a service-marked service in a particular geographic area
- *Internet domain names:* domain names using alphabetical characters such as www.samplecompany.com in lieu of using numeric addresses provide more memorable internet addresses
- *Operating rights:* permits to operate in a certain manner, such as that granted to a carrier to transport specified commodities
- *Use rights:* permits to use specified land, property, or air space in a particular manner, such as the right to cut timber, expel emissions, or land airplanes

Intellectual property includes, inter alia, the following:

- *Copyrights:* the rights to reproduce, distribute, and so on an original work of literature, music, art, photography, or film
- *Newspaper mastheads:* the rights to use the information that is displayed on the top of the first pages of newspapers
- *Patents:* the rights to make, use, or sell an invention for a specified period
- *Service marks:* the rights to use the name or symbol that distinguishes a service
- *Trade dress:* access to the overall appearance and image (unique color, shape, or package design) of a product
- *Trademarks:* rights to use the word, logo, or symbol that distinguishes a product
- *Trade names:* the right to use the name or symbol that distinguishes a business
- *Trade secrets:* information, such as a formula, process, or recipe, that is kept confidential
- *Unpatented technology:* access to the knowledge about the manner of accomplishing a task

Technology tools may consist of computer software, including programs, procedures, and documentation associated with computer hardware, as well as databases, which are collections of a particular type of information, such as scientific data or credit information.

Procurement rights include the following:

- *Construction contracts:* rights to acquire the subject of the contract in exchange for taking over the remaining obligations (including any payments)
- *Employment contracts:* rights to take the seller's place as the employer under the contract and thus obtain the employee's services in exchange for fulfilling the employer's remaining duties, such as payment of salaries and benefits, under the contract
- *Lease agreements:* if assignable, rights to step into the shoes of the lessee and thus obtain the rights to use assets that are the subject of the agreement, in exchange for making the remaining lease payments
- *License agreements:* rights to access or use properties that are the subjects of licenses in exchange for making any remaining license payments and adhering to other responsibilities as licensee
- *Royalty agreements:* rights to take the place of payors and thus assume the payors' remaining rights and duties under the agreements
- *Service or supply contracts:* rights to become the customer of particular contracts and thus purchase the specified products or services for the prices specified in those contracts

Competitor arrangements may include

- *Noncompete agreements:* rights to assurances that companies or individuals will refrain from conducting similar businesses or selling to specific customers for an agreed-upon period
- *Standstill agreements,* which convey rights to assurances that companies or individuals will refrain from engaging in certain activities for specified periods

Customer arrangements are items such as

- *Customer lists:* information about companies' customers, including names, contact information, and order histories that a third party, such as a competitor or a telemarketing firm, would want to use in its own business
- *Customer relationships:* the relationships between entities and their customers for which
  - The entities have information about the customers and have regular contacts with the customers and
  - The customers have the ability to make direct contact with the entity
- *Contracts and related customer relationships:* relationships that arise through contracts and are of value to buyers who can "step into the shoes" of the sellers and assume their remaining rights and duties under the contracts, and that hold the promise that the customers will place future orders with the entity
- *Noncontractual customer relationships:* relationships that arise through means such as regular contacts by sales or service representatives, the value of which are derived from the prospect of the customers placing future orders with the entities
- *Order or production backlogs:* providing buyers rights to step into the shoes of sellers on unfilled sales orders for services and for goods in amounts that exceed the quantity of finished goods and work-in-process on hand for filling the orders

(b) INTERNALLY DEVELOPED INTANGIBLE ASSETS   Costs of internally developing, maintaining, or restoring intangible assets including goodwill that are not specifically identifiable, that have indeterminate lives, or that are inherent in a continuing business and related to a reporting entity as a whole are recognized as an expense when incurred. This rule was grounded, in part, on the traditional aversion to recognition of self-developed goodwill, which is a prohibition nominally still in effect (although the prescribed procedures for the impairment testing of goodwill under SFAS No. 142 implicitly allow for recognition of self-created goodwill, to the extent that it replaces acquired goodwill).

As a practical matter, capitalization of internally developed intangibles is generally obviated by the requirements of SFAS No. 2, which requires that all research and development costs be expensed as incurred. This rule, which is controversial (e.g., the corresponding international financial reporting standard requires expensing of research costs but capitalization of development expenditures) and likely to become more so (as general awareness of the importance of intangibles increases and as the move toward the "knowledge-based economy" continues and even accelerates), would probably preclude most costs incurred in connection with internal generation of intangibles from being recognized as assets in any event.

20A.4 ACCOUNTING FOR INTANGIBLE ASSETS

(a) DETERMINING THE USEFUL LIFE OF AN INTANGIBLE ASSET   The accounting for recognized intangible assets is based on their useful lives *to the reporting entity*. Note that these may well differ from the legal or contractual lives, and could also easily diverge from the useful lives in the hands of *other* reporting entities holding similar or even identical assets. The amounts of intangible assets with finite useful lives are amortized, whereas the amounts assigned to intangible assets with indefinite useful lives are not amortized. The useful lives of intangible assets to a reporting entity are the respective periods over which the assets are expected to contribute directly or indirectly to the future cash flows of the reporting entity. The estimates of the useful lives of intangible assets to the reporting entity are based on analyses of all pertinent factors. Particular attention is to be given to the following:

- Expected use of the assets by the reporting entity
- Expected useful lives of other assets or groups of assets to which the useful lives of the intangible assets may relate, such as mineral rights to depleting assets
- Any legal, regulatory, or contractual provisions that may limit the useful lives
- Any legal, regulatory, or contractual provisions that enable renewals or extensions of the assets' legal or contractual lives without substantial cost, provided that there is evidence to support renewals or extensions, and renewals or extensions can be accomplished without material modifications of the respective existing terms and conditions
- Effects of obsolescence, demand, competition, and other economic factors, such as the stability of the industry, known technological advances, legislative action that results in an uncertain or changing regulatory environment, and expected changes in distribution channels
- Levels of maintenance expenditures required to obtain the expected future cash flows from the assets—for example, a material level of required maintenance in relation to the carrying amount of an asset may suggest a very limited useful life

If no legal, regulatory, contractual, competitive, economic, or other factors limit the useful lives of the intangible assets to the reporting entity, those useful lives are considered to be indefinite, which does not mean *infinite*.

(b) INTANGIBLE ASSETS SUBJECT TO AMORTIZATION   The amounts of recognized intangible assets recognized are to be amortized over the useful lives of the respective assets to the reporting entity, unless those lives are determined to be indefinite. SFAS No. 142 requires that the recorded amounts of intangible assets with finite lives, but without precisely known lives, be amortized over the best estimates of the useful lives. The methods of amortization should reflect the patterns by which the economic benefits of the intangible assets are consumed or otherwise used up. If the patterns cannot be reliably determined, the straight-line amortization method is to be used. Intangible assets are not written down or off in the period of acquisition unless impairments occur during that initial period, which is unlikely but not impossible.

Under SFAS No. 142, the amount of an intangible asset subject to amortization is the value initially assigned to the asset less any residual value. However, the residual value of an intangible asset must be presumed to be zero unless at the end of the useful life to the reporting entity the asset is expected to continue to have a useful life to another entity *and* either (a) the reporting entity has a commitment from a third party to purchase the asset at the end of its useful life to the reporting entity or (b) the residual value can be determined by reference to an exchange transaction in an existing market for that asset and that market is expected to exist at the end of the asset's useful life. In practice, residual values are rarely justified for intangibles subject to amortization.

Reporting entities must evaluate the remaining useful lives of intangible assets that are being amortized each reporting period to determine whether events and circumstances warrant a revision to the remaining periods of amortization. If estimates of intangible assets' useful lives are changed, the remaining carrying amounts of the intangible assets are to be amortized prospectively over their revised remaining useful lives.

If any of the intangible assets being amortized are subsequently determined to have indefinite useful lives, these assets are to be tested for impairment, as is discussed subsequently. These intangible assets are then no longer amortized and are instead accounted for the same way as other intangible assets not subject to amortization.

Intangible assets subject to amortization are to be reviewed for impairments in conformity with SFAS No. 144. After an impairment loss is recognized, the adjusted carrying amount of that intangible asset is its new accounting basis. A previously recognized impairment loss is not subsequently reversed, despite evidence of value recovery.

(c) INTANGIBLE ASSETS NOT SUBJECT TO AMORTIZATION   Intangible assets that were determined to have indefinite useful lives are not amortized until their respective useful lives are determined no longer to be indefinite. The reporting entity is required to evaluate the remaining useful lives of intangible assets not being amortized each reporting period, in order to determine whether events and circumstances continue to support indefinite useful lives. Intangible assets not being amortized, but subsequently determined to have finite useful lives, are tested for impairment, as discussed next. The assets are then amortized prospectively over their estimated remaining useful lives and accounted for the same way as other intangible assets subject to amortization.

Intangible assets not subject to amortization are to be tested for impairments annually, or more frequently if events or changes in circumstances indicate that the assets might have become impaired. The impairment tests consist of making comparisons of the fair values of the assets with their respective carrying amounts. If the carrying amount for a given intangible asset exceeds its fair value, an impairment loss is recognized in an amount equal to the excess.

After an impairment loss is recognized, the asset's adjusted carrying amount is the intangible asset's new accounting basis. A previously recognized impairment loss cannot be reversed.

In EITF Issue No. 02-7, "Unit of Accounting for Testing Impairment of Indefinite-Lived Intangible Assets," there was a consensus that separately recorded indefinite-lived intangible assets should be combined into a single unit of accounting for impairment testing purposes if they are operated as a single asset and are therefore essentially inseparable. EITF Issue No. 02-7 includes indicators and illustrations of when intangible assets should be—and when they should not be—combined.

Indicators that suggest that indefinite-lived intangibles should be combined as a single unit of accounting include the following:

1. The intangibles will be used together to construct or enhance a single asset.
2. If the intangibles had been part of the same acquisition, they would have been recorded as a single asset.
3. The intangibles, as a group, represent "the highest and best use of the assets" (e.g., they could probably realize a higher sales price if sold together than if they were sold separately). Indicators pointing to this situation are
   a. The degree to which it is unlikely that a substantial portion of the assets would be sold separately, or
   b. The fact that should a substantial portion of the intangibles be sold individually, there would be a significant reduction in the fair value of the remaining assets in the group.
4. The marketing or branding strategy of the entity treats the assets as being complementary (e.g., a trademark and its related trade name, formulas, recipes, and patented or unpatented technology can all be complementary to an entity's brand name).

Indicators that imply that indefinite-lived intangibles should not be combined as a single unit of accounting include the following:

1. Each separate intangible generates independent cash flows.
2. In a sale, it would be likely that the intangibles would be sold separately. If the entity had previously sold similar assets separately, this would constitute evidence that combining the assets would not be appropriate.
3. The entity is either considering or has already adopted a plan to dispose of one or more of the intangibles separately.
4. The intangibles are used exclusively by different asset groups (as defined in SFAS No. 144).
5. The assets have different useful economic lives.

EITF 02-7 provided additional guidance regarding the "unit of accounting" determination that must be made for impairment testing purposes.

1. Goodwill and finite-lived intangibles may not be combined in the "unit of accounting" since they are subject to different impairment testing rules (set forth by SFAS Nos. 142 and 144, respectively).
2. If the intangibles collectively constitute a business, they may not be combined into a unit of accounting.

3. If the unit of accounting includes intangibles recorded in the separate financial statements of consolidated subsidiaries, it is possible that the sum of impairment losses recognized in the separate financial statements of the subsidiaries will not equal the consolidated impairment loss.

4. Should a unit of accounting be included in a single reporting unit, that same unit of accounting and associated fair value are to be used in computing the implied fair value of goodwill for measuring any goodwill impairment loss.

Identifiable intangible assets, such as franchise rights, customer lists, trademarks, patents and copyrights, and licenses, are to be amortized over their expected useful economic lives, even if they exceed the former 40-year ceiling. However, if longer amortization periods (useful lives) are elected, impairment reviews of the assets' recoverability are required when necessitated by changes in facts and circumstances in the same manner as set forth in SFAS No. 144 for tangible long-lived assets. SFAS No. 144 also requires consideration of the intangible assets' residual values (which are analogous to salvage values for tangible assets) in determining the amounts of the intangibles to amortize. Residual value is defined as the value of the intangible to the entity at the end of its (entity-specific) useful life reduced by any estimated disposition costs. The residual value of an amortizable intangible is assumed to be zero unless the intangible will continue to have a useful life to another party after the end of its useful life to its current holder, and one or both of the following criteria are met:

1. The current holder has received a third-party commitment to purchase the intangible at the end of its useful life, *or*

2. A market for the intangible exists and is expected to continue to exist at the end of the asset's useful life as a means of determining the residual value of the intangible by reference to marketplace transactions.

A broadcast license is nominally subject to expiration in five years, but might be indefinitely renewable at little additional cost to the broadcaster. If cash flows can be projected indefinitely, and assuming a market exists for the license, no amortization is to be recorded until such time as a finite life is predicted. However, it is required that the asset be tested for impairment at least annually, to ensure that it is carried at no greater than its fair value.

20A.5 CERTAIN IDENTIFIABLE INTANGIBLE ASSETS

(a) PATENTS   Accounting for patents is affected by the laws governing the legal rights of a patent holder. A U.S. patent is a nonrenewable right granted by the federal government that enables the recipient to exclude others from the manufacture, sale, or other use of an invention for a period of 17 years from the date of grant. Enforceability of a patent begins only on its grant, and the exclusive right of use is not retroactive. However, the filing of a patent application provides protection from the claims of a later inventor for the same item so that the period of partial protection may be considered to extend from the date of the original application. While the legal term of the patent is 17 years, the effective period of competitive advantage may extend beyond the original 17-year patent term if additional patents are obtained as improvements are made. Many patent holders do endeavor to create various modifications and improvements that can be patented in their own right, to accomplish this de facto extension of protection for many years. The rights to a patent may be assigned in whole or in part, as can the right to use the patent (i.e., licenses under the patent) on a royalty or other basis.

(i) Capitalizable Amounts for Patents   Patents may be purchased from others or developed internally as a result of research and development activities. The cost of a purchased patent includes the purchase price and any related expenditures, such as attorneys' fees. If a patent is developed internally, its cost includes legal fees in connection with patent applications, patent fees, litigation fees, litigation costs, costs of sale or licensing, and filing fees. Any related research, experimental, and developmental expenditures, including the cost of models and drawings not specifically required for a patent application, are research and development costs and should be expensed as incurred in accordance with SFAS No. 2.

The grant of a patent through the U.S. Patent Office is no guarantee of protection. It is often necessary to defend the patent's validity in court tests and also to refute allegations of infringement of other patents and to prosecute infringement of the patent by others. The costs of successful court tests may be capitalized as additional costs of the patent, and then amortized over the remaining useful life of the underlying patent. However, if the litigation is unsuccessful, the costs of the litigation should be written off immediately, as should any carrying value of the patent that has been stripped of its economic value.

(ii) Amortization of Patents   A U.S. patent has a specified legal life. It provides protection for 17 years, and that is the maximum amortization period. The period used in practice is often less because of technological or market obsolescence factors, such as the issuance of new patents to competitors, improved models, substitutes, or general technological progress. These factors must be taken into account in determining the original useful life and during the subsequent reviews of remaining economic life. The amortization period should not extend beyond the market life of the product with which the patent is associated, unless it is demonstrable that the patent can also be used in other applications. However, if it is possible to extend a patent's economic life by obtaining additional patents, it is permissible to amortize the remaining balance of the costs of the old patent over the estimated economic lives of the new ones. (For example, if a patent is half amortized when a successor patent is issued and the estimated life of the successor is 10 years, the unamortized carrying value of the original patent should be added to the cost of the new one, with the entire sum then amortized over 10 years.)

The impairment accounting guidance in SFAS No. 144 is applicable to patents. Once it is determined that the monopolistic advantage offered by use and ownership of the patent no longer exists, the remaining unamortized balance should be written off. Also, any increases in separately identified deferred costs, due to such factors as an additional lawsuit establishing the validity of the patent, should be written off over the remaining estimated economic life of the patent.

(b) COPYRIGHTS   A copyright is the exclusive right to reproduce, publish, and sell a literary product or artistic work. The term of the copyright in the United States is now the life of the author plus 50 years (formerly 28 years with a single renewal option). As in the case of a patent, the rights to a copyright may be assigned, licensed, or sold.

(i) Capitalizable Amounts for Copyrights   The costs of developing copyrights and the costs of purchased copyrights may be substantial and should be deferred. For a copyright developed internally, costs include expenditures for government filing fees and attorneys' fees and expenses, along with outlays for wages and materials in the preparation of the material to be copyrighted and expenditures incurred to establish the right. If a copyright is purchased, the initial valuation includes the acquisition price plus any costs incurred in establishing the right.

(ii) Amortization of Copyrights   Copyrighted materials, for various reasons, often do not have an active market past the first few years after the issuance of the copyright. It is rare that copyrighted materials will have lengthy economic lives, although there are exceptions. The capitalized amounts are to be amortized over the number of years in which sales or royalties related to the copyright can be expected to occur.

SFAS No. 144, "Accounting for the Impairment or Disposal of Long-Lived Assets," provides guidance on the impairment of intangible assets with finite lives, such as copyrights. Continuing review of the status of copyrights is essential to determine whether they have continuing value. If the copyrighted material will no longer be used, it should be written off.

(c) CUSTOMER AND SUPPLIER LISTS   Customer and supplier lists can be particularly valuable to a business, as they represent groups of customers or suppliers with whom business relations have been established. The value of such lists is based on the assumption of continuing business relationships, as well as possibly reducing the marketing costs that would otherwise be necessary (e.g., to develop customer lists).

(i) Capitalizable Amounts for Customer and Supplier Lists   Customer or supplier lists often are developed internally, and the cost specifically identified with development generally is impossible to determine. These costs are often analogous to research and development expenditures; accordingly, such costs are not deferred. However, when lists are purchased from others, the acquisition cost should be deferred. While generally these are identifiable assets and thus separately recognizable, a customer or supplier list acquired in a business combination would not meet the criteria for recognition apart from goodwill if there are terms of confidentiality or other agreements that prohibit the selling, leasing, or otherwise exchanging of the acquired customer or supplier information.

(ii) Amortization of Customer and Supplier Lists   The value of customer or supplier lists decreases as customers or suppliers are lost or cease to exist. Ideally, the cost of a list should be written off based on these factors—that is, on a units-lost basis. However, since it is often difficult to track lost customers or suppliers precisely, straight-line amortization over a reasonable average customer or supplier retention period is commonly used. The estimate of the useful life should consider all available information and should be reevaluated each reporting period. To the extent that there is a rapid turnover of customers or suppliers, this suggests that little or even no value should have been attributed to the acquired lists.

(d) FRANCHISES   Franchises may be granted by governmental units, individuals, or corporate entities. Public utilities are granted franchises by the communities they serve. These franchises establish the right to operate and specify the conditions under which utilities must function. Such franchises may place certain restrictions on the enterprise concerning rates and operating conditions, but they also confer certain privileges, ranging from minor ones to the granting of a full monopoly.

Private franchises are contracts for the exclusive right to perform certain functions or to sell certain (usually branded) products or services. Such agreements involve the use by the franchisee of a trademark, trade name, patent, process, or know-how of the franchisor for the term of the franchise. For example, a manufacturer may grant a dealer a franchise to market a product within a given territory and agree not to allow other dealers to market the same product in that area.

Costs of obtaining a franchise include any fees paid to the franchisor along with legal and other expenditures incurred in obtaining the franchise. If a franchise agreement covers a specified period of time, the cost of the franchise should be written off over that period unless the economic life is anticipated to be less. If the franchise is perpetual, the franchisee should evaluate the expected useful life of the franchise, considering the effect of obsolescence, demand, competition, and other relevant economic factors. Additional periodic payments based on revenues or other factors may be required in addition to initial fees. These period costs should be expensed as incurred, because they pertain to only the current period and represent no future benefit. The franchise agreement may also require certain property improvements that should be capitalized and included in property, plant, and equipment.

(e) LEASES AND LEASEHOLD RIGHTS   A favorable lease is one in which the property rights obtained under the lease could presently be obtained only at a higher rental. This concept is not to be mistaken for the issue of capitalized leases or capital additions classified as leasehold improvements. Favorable leases may be recognized when a business is purchased or when a payment is made to an existing lessee for the right to sublease, if indeed there is sufficient evidence to demonstrate a below-market rate of rental payments.

(i) Capitalizable Amounts for Favorable Leases and Leasehold Rights   The favorable lease usually is measured by the present value of the cost differential between the terms of the lease and the amount that could be obtained currently in an arm's-length transaction. This corresponds to the economic or fair value of the favorable terms.

(ii) Amortization of Favorable Leases   The cost assigned to a favorable lease is amortized over the lease term. A lump-sum payment at the inception of the lease should be amortized to rent expense over the life of the lease.

(f) ORGANIZATION COSTS   Organization costs are expenditures made to promote and organize a concern, including costs (i.e., legal and state filing fees) of establishing the entity's existence. Under Statement of Position (SOP) 98-5, "Reporting on the Costs of Start-Up Activities," start-up activities include organization costs. This SOP concludes that costs of start-up activities, including organization costs, should be expensed as incurred.

(g) REGISTRATION COSTS   The Securities and Exchange Commission staff in Staff Accounting Bulletin (SAB) Topic 5A stated that specific incremental costs directly attributable to a proposed or actual offering of securities may properly be deferred and charged against the gross proceeds of the offering. Management salaries or other general and administrative expenses may not be allocated as costs of the offering. Costs of an aborted offering may not be deferred and charged against a subsequent offering. According to SEC staff, a short postponement of up to 90 days does not represent an aborted offering.

(h) RESEARCH AND DEVELOPMENT COSTS   So-called R&D expenses have long been a controversial accounting topic. Prior to the imposition of current GAAP, it had been common to defer such costs, and investors often were dismayed at sporadic "big baths" when the hoped-for developments failed to be consummated or proved to have less economic value than expected. In reaction to the formerly liberal practices of deferring R&D costs, therefore, one of the FASB's first acts was to impose SFAS No. 2, "Accounting for Research and Development Costs," which requires that all R&D costs be charged to expense as incurred.

SFAS No. 142 did not change the stringent accounting requirements of SFAS No. 2. It includes the following definitions of research and development:

> Research is planned search or critical investigation aimed at discovery of new knowledge with the hope that such knowledge will be useful in developing a new product or service . . . or a new process or technique . . . or in bringing about a significant improvement to an existing product or process.
>
> Development is the translation of research findings or other knowledge into a plan or design for a new product or process or for a significant improvement to an existing product or process whether intended for sale or use. It includes the conceptual formulation, design, and testing of product alternatives, construction of prototypes, and operation of pilot plants. It does not include routine or periodic alterations to existing products, production lines, manufacturing processes, and other on-going operations even though those alterations may represent improvements, and it does not include market research or market testing activities. (SFAS No. 2, para. 8)

The distinction between "research" and "development" is more than semantic. For example, under International Financial Reporting Standards, while research costs must be expensed at once, as under U.S. GAAP, development costs are to be deferred and amortized over the economic lives of the resultant products or processes. Even under U.S. GAAP the distinction between "research" and "development" is germane, albeit not as a general principle. However, for certain categories of software development costs, costs incurred before technological feasibility has been demonstrated (i.e., those that are analogous to research costs) are expensed, whereas those incurred after feasibility has been demonstrated (which are, arguably, more suggestive of development costs) are capitalized and amortized.

Given the huge economic significance of R&D expenditures and the growing recognition that substantial amounts of assets are being omitted from many reporting entities' balance sheets (with an equivalent understatement of net stockholders' equity), this is likely to receive renewed attention. Particularly given the FASB's commitment to "converge" U.S. GAAP and International Financial Reporting Standards (IFRS), there would appear to be some possibility that future GAAP will permit or require deferral of development-type expenses, subject to amortization and, perhaps, impairment assessments.

Research and development costs, according to SFAS No. 2, include the following elements:

> *Materials, Equipment and Facilities.* The cost of materials . . . and equipment or facilities that are acquired or constructed for research and development activities and that have alternative future uses . . . shall be capitalized as tangible assets when acquired or constructed. The cost of such materials consumed in research and development activities and the depreciation of such equipment or facilities used in those activities are research and development costs. However, the costs of materials, equipment, or facilities that are acquired or constructed for a particular research and development project and that have no alternative future uses . . . are research and development costs at the time the costs are incurred.
>
> *Personnel.* Salaries, wages, and other related costs of personnel engaged in research and development activities shall be included in research and development costs.

Intangibles Purchased from Others. The costs of intangibles that are purchased from others for use in research and development activities and that have alternative future uses . . . shall be accounted for in accordance with FASB Statement No. 142, "Goodwill and Other Intangible Assets." . . . The amortization of those intangible assets used in research and development activities is a research and development cost. However, the costs of intangibles that are purchased from others for a particular research and development project and that have no alternative future uses . . . are research and development costs at the time the costs are incurred.

Contract Services. The costs of services performed by others in connection with the research and development activities of an enterprise, including research and development conducted by others in behalf of the enterprise, shall be included in research and development costs.

Indirect Costs. Research and development costs shall include a reasonable allocation of indirect costs. However, general and administrative costs that are not clearly related to research and development activities shall not be included as research and development costs. SFAS No. 2 requires that all costs of activities identified as R&D be charged to expense as incurred. The only exception is that government-regulated enterprises may be required to defer certain costs for rate-making purposes. This occurs when the rate regulator reasonably assures the recovery of R&D costs by permitting the inclusion of the costs in allowable costs for rate-making purposes. SFAS No. 2 also requires disclosure of total R&D costs charged to expense in each period. (SFAS No. 2, paras. 11–13.)

There are three ways in which R&D costs may be incurred by a reporting entity:

1. Conducting R&D activities for the benefit of the reporting entity itself
2. Conducting R&D for others under a contractual arrangement
3. Purchasing R&D from other entities

As noted, under SFAS No. 2 all research and development expenditures must be expensed as incurred. Examples of such R&D costs include

1. Laboratory research to discover new knowledge
2. Formulation and design of product alternatives:
   a. Testing for product alternatives
   b. Modification of products or processes
3. Preproduction prototypes and models:
   a. Tools, dies, and so on, for new technology
   b. Pilot plants not capable of commercial production
4. Engineering activity performed until the product is ready for manufacture

Not all costs that appear related to research and development are to be accounted for as such, however. Examples of costs that are *not* considered R&D include

1. Engineering during an early phase of commercial production
2. Quality control for commercial production
3. Troubleshooting during a commercial production breakdown
4. Routine, ongoing efforts to improve products
5. Adaptation of existing capacity for a specific customer or other requirements

6. Seasonal design changes to products

7. Routine design of tools, dies, and so on

8. Design, construction, start-up, and so on, of equipment except that used solely for R&D

In many cases, entities will pay other parties to perform R&D activities on their behalf. In some instances, these are simply rational business decisions and are not undertaken with any financial reporting motive ("earnings management") in mind. In some instances, however, the intent of "outsourcing" certain R&D activities is to try to avoid the immediate expensing requirement of SFAS No. 2, and to instead disguise these expenditures as capital asset purchases.

In applying substance over form in evaluating these arrangements, a financial reporting result cannot be obtained indirectly if it would not have been permitted if accomplished directly. Thus, if costs incurred to engage others to perform R&D activities that, in substance, could have been performed by the reporting entity itself, those costs must be expensed as incurred. On the other hand, if the payment is to acquire intangibles for use in R&D activities, and these assets have other uses, then the expenditure is capitalized and accounted for in accordance with SFAS No. 142.

When R&D costs are incurred as a result of contractual arrangements, the nature of the agreement dictates the accounting treatment of the costs involved. The key determinant is the transfer of the risk associated with the R&D expenditures. If the business receives funds from another party to perform R&D and is obligated to repay those funds regardless of the outcome, a liability must be recorded and the R&D costs must be expensed as incurred. In order to conclude that a liability does not exist, the transfer of the financial risk must be substantive and genuine.

The SEC staff has stated that if a significant portion of the purchase price in a business combination is expensed as purchased R&D, the SEC staff may raise issues such as the following:

- Purchased R&D must be valued based on appropriate assumptions and valuation techniques; it may not be determined as a residual amount similar to goodwill.
- Allocation of purchase price to purchased R&D will be questioned if it differs significantly from the estimated replacement cost for the acquiring enterprise.
- Policies used for internally developed products should be used to determine whether R&D is in process or complete and whether alternative future uses exist.
- If substantially all of the purchase price is allocated to purchase R&D, the staff will challenge whether some should be allocated to other identifiable intangible assets and goodwill and would object to useful lives of those intangible assets and goodwill exceeding five to seven years.

The AICPA has issued the following Practice Aid on accounting for R&D projects acquired in a business combination: "Assets Acquired in a Business Combination to Be Used in Research and Development Activities: A Focus in Software, Electronic Devices, and Pharmaceutical Industries."

(i) RESEARCH AND DEVELOPMENT ARRANGEMENTS   Research and development arrangements may take a variety of forms, but a central feature of each of these is to conduct R&D that is to be financed by another entity. According to SFAS No. 68, certain of these arrangements are actually financing transactions, and funds to be repaid, irrespective of the outcome of the research, must be reported as liabilities, with actual research or development costs expensed as incurred by the reporting entity. Only if there is a substantive risk transfer to the entity providing financing will it be appropriate not to record such a liability.

The actual obligation can take various forms, including an outright unconditional commitment to repay the funds advanced; an option giving the other entity the right to require that the reporting entity purchase the other party's interest in the outcome of the R&D efforts; and a firm obligation to issue debt or equity instruments to the funding party at completion. In all such instances, the payment for R&D is actually a loan, not a purchase of R&D services. Accordingly, the reporting entity (the party conducting R&D) must currently expense all R&D expenditures.

On the other hand, to the extent that the financial risk associated with the research and development has been transferred because repayment of any of the funds provided is conditioned on the results of the R&D having future economic benefit, the reporting entity is to account for its obligation as a contract to perform research and development for others, not as debt.

(j) ACQUIRED IN-PROCESS RESEARCH AND DEVELOPMENT   So-called in-process research and development (IPRD) has long been a difficult financial reporting issue. On one hand, purchase business combination accounting suggests that the purchase cost be allocated to the fair value of all assets acquired; on the other hand, to allow capitalization of IPRD would result in deferral of costs that would have to be immediately expensed under SFAS No. 2 if incurred directly by the reporting entity.

In many business combinations, a part of the premium (i.e., the amounts in excess of the fair value of tangible net assets) paid is in recognition of the value of the acquiree's previously expensed research and development efforts. Since what is banned under GAAP (e.g., capitalization of R&D costs) if accomplished directly cannot be attained indirectly (e.g., via a business combination), it was logical to prohibit the creation of an intangible asset in purchase business combinations to reflect the value of research and development already completed by the acquiree entity.

IPRD is virtually the only asset acquired in a purchase business combination transaction that is expensed rather than being capitalized. This includes not only the amount paid for actual in-process work (which was, per SFAS No. 2, already expensed as incurred by the acquiree entity), but also certain tangible assets used in research and development. As stated in FASB Interpretation No. 4, "Applicability of FASB Statement No. 2 to Business Combinations Accounted for by the Purchase Method," any identifiable assets of the acquiree to be used in research and development (R&D) projects that do not also have an alternative future use should be first valued as part of the purchase price allocation, and then charged to expense of the combined companies simultaneous with consummation of acquisition. This matter was considered by the EITF (in Issue 86-14, "Purchased Research and Development Projects in a Business Combination"), but no changes to the requirement were made.

In the mid- to late 1990s, overly aggressive use of the mandate that "in-process research and development" costs be immediately expensed upon consummation of a purchase business combination became something of a concern. In many acquisitions a disproportionately large part of the premium paid was assigned to in-process R&D, on the assumption that immediate charge-offs as part of purchase accounting were less of a concern to stockholders and other stakeholding parties than would be regular periodic charges against earnings lasting many years. There were even some instances, in fact, where more than 99 percent of the entire purchase cost was allocated to in-process R&D cost, and then immediately written off. This phenomenon drew the attention of the SEC as well as of accounting standard setters.

The elimination of goodwill amortization by SFAS No. 142 reduced the motivation for exaggerated allocations to IPRD, but this remains a concern.

In response to this perceived problem, the FASB at first indicated an intent to develop a new requirement that, it was widely presumed, would have imposed a requirement that purchased in-process R&D costs be capitalized and amortized. However, upon further reflection, it became clear that to have a diametrically opposite rule for in-process R&D costs, as distinguished from internally generated R&D, would be neither logical nor defensible. Consequently, no action was taken by the FASB, and the requirement that purchased in-process R&D be immediately expensed, after purchase cost is first allocated to it, remained.

Clearly, the last chapter has not yet been written regarding proper accounting for research and/or development costs in general, or regarding in-process R&D acquired in purchase transactions in particular.

(k) ROYALTY AND LICENSE AGREEMENTS   Royalty and license agreements are contracts allowing the use of patented, copyrighted, or proprietary (trade secrets) material in return for royalty payments. An example is the licensing of a patented chemical process for use in a customer's operating system.

The costs to be assigned to royalty and license agreements include any initial payments required plus legal costs incurred in establishing the agreements. Royalty or usage fees are expensed as incurred, because they relate to services of products and not to future benefits.

The capitalized costs of royalty and license agreements should be amortized over the lesser of the life of the agreement or the expected economic life, with the useful life reassessed each reporting period. Unamortized costs of royalty and license agreements should be written off when it is determined that they have become worthless.

(l) SECRET FORMULAS AND PROCESSES   A formula or process known only to a particular producer may be a valuable asset, even if not patented. As in the case of a patent, the value of a trade secret is derived from the exclusive control that it gives. Trade secrets, like patents and copyrights, are recognized legal property and are transferable. Costs that can be directly identified with secret formulas and processes are properly capitalized, except that costs of activities constituting R&D as defined by SFAS No. 2 must be expensed. Costs are normally assigned only to acquired secret formulas and processes. Because secret formulas and secret processes have unlimited lives in a legal sense, costs capitalized are amortized over the useful life of the secret formula or are not amortized if the secret formula is determined to have an indefinite useful life. Whether the value of the formula or process is impaired because of lack of demand for the related product, development of a substitute product or process, loss of exclusivity, or other factors should be determined as discussed in Section 20A.4(b) or 4(c), as appropriate.

(m) START-UP ACTIVITIES   Under SOP 98-5, "Reporting on the Costs of Start-Up Activities," costs of start-up activities, including organization costs, should be expensed as incurred. For purposes of the SOP, start-up activities are defined broadly as those one-time activities related to opening a new facility, introducing a new product or service, conducting business in a new territory, conducting business with a new class of customer or beneficiary, initiating a new process in an existing facility, or commencing some new operation. Start-up activities include activities related to organizing a new entity (commonly referred to as organization costs). The SOP applies to all nongovernmental entities and would apply to development-stage entities as well as established operating entities.

(n) TOOLING COSTS   Initial tooling costs are sometimes treated as an intangible asset, but they are more often considered an element of property, plant, and equipment or, in the case of certain long-term contracts, inventory. SFAS No. 2 states that the design of tools, jigs, molds, and dies involving new technology is a R&D cost, which must be expensed as incurred. However, routine design of those items is not R&D, and the cost may be deferred and amortized over the periods expected to benefit. Deferred tooling may be written off over a period of time (generally less than five years, with shorter periods used when tooling relates to products with frequent style or design obsolescence) or anticipated production (using the unit-of-production method). Replacements of parts of tooling for reasons other than changes in the product are usually expensed.

If deferred initial tooling costs are material, the accounting policy regarding those costs should be disclosed. SEC registrants are required to state, if practicable, the amount of unamortized deferred tooling costs applicable to long-term contracts or programs (Regulation S-X, Rule 5.02-6(d)(i)).

EITF Issue No. 99-5, "Accounting for Pre-Production Costs Related to Long-Term Supply Arrangements," provides guidance on design and development and tooling costs related to new long-term supply arrangements. The Task Force concluded that

- Design and development costs for products to be sold under long-term supply arrangements should be expensed as incurred.
- Design and development costs for molds, dies, and other tools that a supplier will own and that will be used in producing the products under the long-term supply arrangements should, in general, be capitalized as part of the cost of the molds, dies, and other tools. However, if the molds, dies, and tools involve new technology, their costs should be expensed as incurred.
- If the supplier will not own the molds, dies, and other tools, the design and development costs should be capitalized only if the supply arrangement provides the supplier the noncancelable right to use them during the supply arrangement. Otherwise, the design and development costs should be expensed as incurred, including costs incurred before the supplier receives a noncancelable right to use the molds, dies, and other tools during the supply arrangement.
- Design and development costs that would otherwise be expensed should be capitalized if the supplier has a contractual guarantee for reimbursement of those costs. A contractual guarantee means a legally enforceable agreement under which the amount of the reimbursement can be objectively measured and verified.

SEC registrants are expected to disclose their accounting policy for preproduction design and development costs and the aggregate amount of the following:

- Assets recognized pursuant to agreements that provide for contractual reimbursement of preproduction design and development costs
- Assets recognized for molds, dies, and other tools that the supplier owns
- Assets recognized for molds, dies, and other tools that the supplier does not own

Design and development costs for molds, dies, and other tools that are capitalized are subject to impairment assessment under SFAS No. 144.

(o) TRADEMARKS AND TRADE NAMES   Broadly defined, a trademark is any distinguishing label, symbol, or design used by a concern in connection with a product or service. A trade name identifies the entity.

Trademarks can be registered with the U.S. Patent Office to provide access to the federal courts for litigation and to serve as notice of ownership. Proof of prior and continuing use of the trademark is required to obtain and retain the right to use the registered item. Protection of trademarks and trade names that cannot be registered or are not registered can also be sought through common law. These assets have an unlimited life as long as they are used continuously, although technically the term of registration at the U.S. Patent Office is 20 years with indefinite renewal for additional 20-year periods.

They may also be registered under the laws of most states. It is customary to consider trademarks and trade names as being of value only as long as they are used. The value of a trademark or trade name consists of the product differentiation and identification that it provides, which theoretically contributes to revenue by enabling a business to sell such products at a higher price than unbranded products. Although closely related to goodwill, trademarks and trade names are property rights that are separately identifiable and, as such, can be assigned or sold.

(i) Capitalizable Amounts for Trademarks and Trade Names Costs   The cost of a trademark or trade name developed internally consists of legal fees associated with successful litigation involving the trademark or trade name, registration fees, and all developmental expenditures that can be reasonably associated with trademarks, such as payments to design firms. The cost of a purchased trademark or trade name is its purchase price, along with any other costs required to maintain exclusive use of the mark or name. Obviously, much of the value of a trademark or trade name is established by continuing operations that create a reputation with customers. Some of that reputation, however, may have been gained through the use of advertising and other marketing techniques.

The costs should be amortized over the trademark's or trade name's useful life to the entity, unless the trademark or trade name is determined to have an indefinite useful life, in which case it is not amortized, as discussed in Section 20A.4(c). The expected useful life should be reassessed each reporting period. These expenditures should be accounted for under SOP 93-7, which is discussed next.

(ii) Amortization of Trademarks and Trade Names   Because of the legal status of trademarks and trade names, established trademarks and trade names have unlimited legal lives as long as they are used. There is no specified statutory life that restricts the amortization period.

(p) ADVERTISING   While many, if not most, businesses engage in some forms of advertising, it has long been held that demonstrating the actual effectiveness of such efforts is too speculative to warrant deferral of costs to future periods. Put another way, advertising has been held to be a "sunk cost," and thus must be expensed as incurred. However, SOP 93-7, "Reporting on Advertising Costs," did provide a limited exception to this general principle.

Under this SOP, the costs of advertising should be expensed either as incurred or the first time the advertising takes place, unless the advertising is direct-response advertising that meets specific, rather rigorous criteria, in which case deferral and amortization is prescribed. Examples of first-time advertising include the first public showing of a television commercial for its intended purpose or the first appearance of a magazine advertisement for its intended purpose. The cost of direct-response advertising is deferred and reported as an asset, subject to amortization, if the primary purpose of the advertising is to elicit sales to customers who can be shown to have responded specifically to the advertising, *and* if the advertising results in *probable* future benefits. Showing that a customer responded to specifically identifiable direct-response advertising requires documentation, including a record that can identify the name of the customer and the advertising that elicited the direct response. Such documentation could include, for example, files listing the customer names and the related direct-response advertisement, a coded order form, coupon, or response card included with the advertisement that would indicate the customer's name, or a log of customers who made phone calls responding to a number appearing in an advertisement.

Probable future benefits are highly likely future primary revenues resulting from the direct-response advertising, net of future costs to realize the revenues. Probable future primary revenues are limited to revenues from sales to customers receiving and responding to the direct-response advertising. To demonstrate that direct-response advertising will result in probable future benefits, an entity is required to provide persuasive evidence that the results of the advertising will be similar to the results of its past direct-response advertising activities that had future benefits. The evidence should include verifiable historical patterns of results specific to the entity. To determine if results will be similar, attributes to consider include the demographics of the audience, the method of advertising, the product, and economic conditions. Industry statistics would not provide objective evidence of probable future benefits in the absence of the entity's own operating history.

Other requirements of the SOP include the following:

- Costs of direct-response advertising should include only incremental direct costs incurred in transactions with independent third parties plus payroll and payroll-related costs for the activities of employees that are directly associated with the direct-response advertising project. Allocated administrative costs, rent, depreciation, and other occupancy costs are not costs of direct-response advertising activities.
- The costs of the direct-response advertising directed to all prospective customers, not just the cost related to the portion of the potential customers that is expected to respond to the advertising, should be deferred.
- Deferred direct-response advertising costs should be amortized using a cost-pool method over the period during which the future benefits are expected to be received. The amortization should be the ratio that current period revenues for a cost pool bear to the total current and estimated future period revenues for that cost pool. The amount of estimated future revenues should not be discounted, but it may be adjusted in subsequent periods. The ratio should be recalculated at each reporting date.
- The realizability of the deferred advertising should be evaluated, at each balance sheet date, by comparing, on a cost-pool by cost-pool basis, the carrying amount of the deferred advertising with the probable remaining future net revenues expected to result directly from such advertising. Only probable future primary revenues should be used to determine the probable remaining future net revenues.
- There are certain disclosures required, such as the accounting policy selected for advertising, the total amount charged to advertising, a description of the direct-response advertising reported as assets (if any), the accounting policy and amortization period of direct-response advertising, the total amount of advertising reported as assets, and the amounts, if any, written down to net realizable income.

The SEC staff considers the requirements for deferral of direct-response advertising costs to be met only if the advertising results in a direct revenue-generating response—for example, if the respondent orders the product when placing the call to the advertised number. The staff believes capitalization is not appropriate for advertising that results not in sales but only in sales opportunities, even if these are likely to produce results. For example, an advertisement for aluminum siding that includes a phone number to call to schedule a visit from a sales representative would not qualify for capitalization as direct-response advertising because the advertisement leads only indirectly to the revenue-generating transaction. The SEC staff also would object to the classification of deferred advertising costs as current assets, because such costs do not meet the definition of a current asset in ARB No. 43.

(q) WEB SITE DEVELOPMENT COSTS   With the rapid growth in so-called e-commerce in the late 1990s, many reporting entities incurred costs to develop and maintain Web sites.

EITF Issue No. 00-2 provided the following guidance for accounting for Web site development costs:

- During the planning phase, an entity develops a project plan, determines the desired functionalities of the Web site, identifies the needed hardware and software applications, and determines whether suitable technology exists. All costs incurred in the planning stage should be expensed as incurred.
- During the Web site development phase, the entity acquires or develops hardware and software to operate its Web site and develops appropriate graphics. Costs related to software and graphics should be accounted for under SOP 98-1 as software for internal use unless the entity has or is developing a plan to market the software. Software, including graphics, to be marketed should be accounted for under SFAS No. 86, "Computer Software to Be Sold, Leased, or Otherwise Marketed." See Section 20A.6(f) for a discussion of SOP 98-1 and SFAS No. 86. Costs incurred for Web site hosting should generally be expensed over the period of benefit.

20A.6   INTANGIBLE ASSETS IN SPECIALIZED INDUSTRIES

Intangible assets are particularly significant or receive unique accounting treatment in certain industries. These requirements are generally to be found in AICPA Industry Audit and Accounting Guides or in Statements of Position.

(a) AIRLINES   Under the AICPA Industry Audit Guide, *Audits of Airlines,* as amended by SOP 88-1, "Accounting for Developmental and Pre-operating Costs, Purchases and Exchanges of Take-off and Landing Slots, and Airframe Modifications," and SOP 98-5, "Reporting on the Costs of Start-Up Activities," the capitalization of preoperating costs related only to the integration of new types of aircraft. The costs of acquiring take-off and landing slots, whether by exchange of stock or through purchase, are identifiable intangible assets. Developmental costs related to preparation of new routes should not be capitalized.

(b) BANKING AND THRIFTS   During the thrift and banking crises of the late 1980s and early 1990s, precipitated in part by the high interest rate environment and negative interest rate spreads of those years, many insured financial institutions, when evaluated on a fair value basis, were threatened with insolvency or already were insolvent. The federal insurers (FDIC and FSLIC) were themselves facing insolvency, and would likely have been unable to repay all depositors of closed institutions from available reserves. It was hoped that, with an anticipated return to a normal interest rate environment, many of these banks and thrifts would regain solvency and survive, sparing the insurers (and ultimately the taxpayers) these losses.

Given this situation, there was a concerted political effort to postpone bank and thrift closings, and one perhaps ill-conceived solution was to encourage the takeovers of failing banks and thrifts by offering the acquirers the ability to treat the net liabilities acquired (measured at fair value) as so-called supervisory goodwill. Although this did not comport with the traditional GAAP concept of goodwill, the profession accommodated this regulatory mandate. Under SFAS No. 72, "Accounting for Certain Acquisitions of Banking or Thrift Institutions," this goodwill was to be amortized over the terms set forth in the assisted, supervisory mergers (often 20 or more years), even though the so-called core deposit intangible (related to the expected holding term of deposits acquired) would have a much shorter expected life.

The elimination of goodwill amortization by SFAS No. 142 necessitated a change to many of the SFAS No. 72 provisions. SFAS No. 147, "Acquisitions of Certain Financial Institutions," eliminates the special accounting imposed by SFAS No. 72, with the exception that mergers between mutual enterprises continue to be governed by that standard. Thus, as amended, SFAS No. 72 applies only to acquisitions of financial institutions that are mutual enterprises by other financial institutions that are also mutual enterprises. For those acquisitions, goodwill that is created by an excess of the fair value of liabilities assumed over the fair value of tangible and identified intangible assets acquired is to be amortized by the interest method over a period no greater than the estimated remaining life of the long-term, interest-bearing assets acquired. If the assets acquired do not include a significant amount of long-term, interest-bearing assets, such goodwill is to be amortized over a period not exceeding the estimated average life of the existing customer (deposit) base acquired.

At the effective date of SFAS No. 147, any remaining unidentified intangible other than that arising from a business combination continued to be amortized, while that arising from business combinations (the assisted supervisory mergers, for example) was to be reclassified as goodwill and thereafter tested for impairment per SFAS No. 142. Transitional impairment testing procedures were also specified.

(c) MORTGAGE BANKING   Under SFAS No. 140, "Accounting for Transfers and Servicing of Financial Assets and Extinguishments of Liabilities," servicing of mortgage loans becomes a distinct asset or liability only when contractually separated from the underlying amounts by sale or securitization of the assets with servicing retained, or through the separate purchase or assumption of the servicing rights.

An entity that undertakes a contract to service financial assets shall recognize either a servicing asset or a servicing liability, unless the transferor transfers the assets in a guaranteed mortgage securitization, retains all of the resulting securities, and classifies them as debt securities held to maturity in accordance with SFAS No. 115, in which case the servicing asset or liability may be reported together with the asset being serviced. Each sale or securitization with servicing retained or separate purchase or assumption of servicing results in a servicing contract. Each servicing contract results in a servicing asset (when the benefits of servicing are expected to be more than adequate compensation to the servicer for performing the servicing) or a servicing liability (when the benefits of servicing are not expected to compensate the servicer adequately for performing the servicing). If the servicer is more than adequately compensated and if the servicing was retained in a sale or securitization, the servicer shall account for the contracts to service the mortgage loans separately from the loans by initially measuring the servicing assets at their allocated previous carrying amounts based on relative fair value at the date of sale or securitization. If the servicing asset is purchased or servicing liability assumed, it is measured at fair value. If the servicer is not adequately compensated, a servicing liability undertaken in a sale or securitization is measured at fair value.

Servicing assets are amortized in proportion to and over the period of estimated net servicing income—the excess of service revenues over servicing costs. Servicing liabilities are amortized in proportion to and over the period of estimated net servicing loss—the excess of servicing costs over servicing revenues, if practicable.

Impairment of servicing assets should be measured as follows:

1. Stratify servicing assets based on one or more of the predominant risk characteristics of the underlying assets.
2. Recognize impairment through a valuation allowance for an individual stratum for the amount by which the carrying amount of the servicing assets for the stratum exceeds their fair value.
3. Adjust the valuation allowance to reflect changes in the measurement of impairment subsequent to the initial measurement of impairment.

Rights for future income from the serviced assets that exceed contractually specified servicing fees should be accounted for separately. Those rights are not servicing assets; they are financial assets, effectively interest-only strips to be accounted for in accordance with paragraph 14 of SFAS No. 140.

In EITF No. 95-5, "Determination of What Risks and Rewards, If Any, Can Be Retained and Whether Any Unresolved Contingencies May Exist in a Sale of Mortgage Loan Servicing Rights," the issue addressed was whether the inclusion of any provision that results in the seller's retention of specified risk (1) precludes recognition of a sale at the date title passes or (2) allows recognition of the sale at that date if (a) the seller can reasonably estimate, and record a liability for, the costs related to protection provisions, or (b) the sale agreement provides for substantially all risks and rewards to irrevocably pass to the buyer, and the seller can reasonably estimate, and record a liability for, the minor protection provisions.

The EITF consensus was that sales of rights to service mortgage loans should be recognized when the following conditions are met: (1) title has passed, (2) substantially all risks and rewards of ownership have irrevocably passed to the buyer, and (3) any protection provisions retained by the seller are minor and can be reasonably estimated. If a sale is recognized and minor protection provisions exist, a liability should be accrued for the estimated obligation associated with those provisions. The seller retains only minor protection provisions if (a) the obligation associated with those provisions is estimated to be no more than 10 percent of the sales price and (b) risk of prepayment is retained for no longer than 120 days. Mortgage banking is covered in more detail in Chapter 29.

(d) BROADCASTING INDUSTRY The principal intangible assets in the broadcasting industry are Federal Communications Commission (FCC) licenses, broadcast rights (license agreement to program material), and network affiliation agreements. Television and radio stations may not operate without a FCC license, which specifies, for example, the frequency to be used. A broadcasting license is granted for a 10-year period and is renewable for additional 10-year periods if the entity provides at least an average level of service to its customers and complies with applicable FCC rules and policies. Licenses thus may be renewed indefinitely at little cost.

If the entity intends to renew the license indefinitely and has the ability to do so, a broadcast license would be deemed to have an indefinite useful life. It would not be amortized until its useful life was no longer deemed to be indefinite. Impairment would be tested as provided in Section 20A.4(c). On the other hand, if the entity does not intend to renew a broadcast license indefinitely, if would amortize the license over its remaining useful life and follow the impairment guidance in SFAS No. 144.

(i) Broadcast Rights SFAS No. 63, "Financial Reporting by Broadcasters," contains industry-specific GAAP. Its primary mandate is that broadcasters must account for license agreements for program materials as purchases of rights, thus necessitating the presentation of assets and liabilities on the entities' balance sheets. Broadcast rights result from a contract or license to exhibit films, programs, or other works and permit one or more exhibitions during a specified license period. Compensation is ordinarily payable in installments over a period shorter than the period of the licensing contract, but it may also take the form of a lump-sum payment at the beginning of the period. The license expires at the end of the contract period.

Amounts recorded for broadcasting rights are to be segregated on the balance sheet as current and noncurrent assets based on estimated usage within one year. Rights should be amortized based on the estimated number of future showings. Items that may be used on an unlimited basis, rather than a limited number of showings, may be amortized over the period covered by the agreement. An accelerated method of amortization is required when the first showing is more valuable than reruns, as is usually the case. Straight-line amortization is allowable only when each telecast or broadcast is expected to generate approximately the same revenue.

Feature programs are to be amortized on a program-by-program basis; however, amortization as a package may be appropriate if it approximates the amortization that would have been provided on a program-by-program basis. The capitalized costs of rights to program material should be reported in the balance sheet at the lower of unamortized cost or estimated net realizable value on a program-by-program, series, package, or "daypart" basis, as appropriate. If management's expectations of the programming usefulness of a program, series, package, or daypart are revised downward, it may be necessary to write down unamortized cost to estimated net realizable value. *Daypart* is defined in SFAS No. 63 as an aggregation of programs broadcast during a particular time of day (e.g., daytime, evening, late night) or programs of a similar type (e.g., sports, news, children's shows). A write-down from unamortized cost to a lower estimated net realizable value establishes a new cost basis.

(ii) Revoked or Nonrenewed Broadcast Licenses When broadcasting licenses are not renewed or are revoked, unamortized balances should be written off. If a network affiliation is terminated and is not immediately replaced or under agreement to be replaced, the unamortized balance of the amount originally allocated to the network affiliation agreement should be charged to expense. If a network affiliation is terminated and immediately replaced or is under agreement to be replaced, a loss is recognized to the extent that the unamortized cost of the terminated affiliation exceeds the fair value of the new affiliation. Gain is not to be recognized if the fair value of the new network affiliation exceeds the unamortized cost of the terminated affiliation.

(e) CABLE TELEVISION   Cable television companies experience a long preoperating and development period. SFAS No. 51, "Financial Reporting by Cable Television Companies," defines the "pre-maturity period" as that during which a cable television system is partially under construction and partially in service. Costs incurred during this period that relate to both current and future operations are partially expensed and partially capitalized. In a cable system, portions or segments that are in the pre-maturity period and can be clearly distinguished from the remainder of the system should be accounted for separately. Costs incurred to obtain and retain subscribers and general and administrative expenses incurred during the pre-maturity period are to be expensed as period costs. Programming costs and other system costs that will not vary significantly regardless of the number of subscribers are allocated between current and future operations. The amount currently expensed is based on a relationship of subscribers during the current month (as prescribed in the SFAS) and the total number of subscribers expected at the end of the pre-maturity period. The capitalized portions decrease each month as the cable company progresses toward the end of the pre-maturity period. Prior to the pre-maturity period, system-related costs are capitalized; subsequent thereto, none of these costs is deferred. Capitalized costs should be amortized over the same period used to depreciate the main cable television plant. Costs of successful franchise applications are capitalized and amortized in accordance with SFAS No. 142. Costs of unsuccessful applications and abandoned franchises are charged to expense.

(f) COMPUTER SOFTWARE   SFAS No. 86, "Computer Software to Be Sold, Leased, or Otherwise Marketed," prescribes the accounting for the costs of computer software purchased or internally developed as a marketable product by itself. Costs incurred to establish the technological feasibility are charged to expense when incurred. Technological feasibility is established on completion of all planning design, coding, and testing activities necessary to establish that the product can be produced. The completion of a detailed program design or completion of a working model provides evidence of the establishment of technological feasibility.

Costs incurred subsequent to the establishment of technological feasibility are capitalized. Software used as an integral part of product or process is not capitalized until both technological feasibility has been established and all R&D activities for the other components have been completed. When the product is available for release to customers, capitalization ceases. Costs of maintenance and customer support are expensed when the related revenue is recognized or when the costs are incurred, whichever occurs first. Purchased software that has alternative future uses should be capitalized but subsequently accounted for according to its use.

Amortization of capitalized software costs is based on the ratio that current gross revenues bear to the total current and anticipated revenues with a minimum amortization equivalent to straight-line over the remaining estimated economic life of the product. The excess of unamortized capitalized costs over a product's net realizable value is written off (and not subsequently restored).

The unamortized computer costs included in the balance sheet, the total amortization charged to expense in each income statement presented, and amounts written down to net realizable value should be disclosed.

FIN (FASB Interpretations) No. 6 (par. 4) states that to the extent the acquisition, development, or improvement of a process for use in selling and administrative activities includes costs for computer software, these costs are not R&D costs. Examples given of excluded costs are the development by an airline of a computerized reservation system or the development of a general management information system. SFAS No. 86 does not cover accounting for costs of software used internally. For that subject, see the discussion of SOP 98-1 in this subsection.

In Issue No. 96-6, "Accounting for the Film and Software Cost Associated with Developing Entertainment and Educational Software Products," the EITF considered the issue of how companies should account for the film and software costs associated with developing entertainment and educational software (EE) products such as computer games, interactive videos, and other multimedia products. The SEC staff announced that EE products that are sold, leased, or otherwise marketed are subject to the accounting requirements of SFAS No. 86. The SEC staff believes that the film costs incurred in development of an EE product should be accounted for under the provisions of SFAS No. 86. In addition, exploitation costs should be expensed as incurred unless those costs include advertising costs that qualify for capitalization in accordance with SOP 93-7. Because of the SEC staff's position, the EITF was not asked to reach a consensus on this issue.

In EITF No. 97-13, "Accounting for Costs Incurred in Connection with a Consulting Contract or an Internal Project That Combines Business Process Reengineering and Information Technology Transformation," the EITF addressed the accounting for business process reengineering costs. These costs may be included in a contract that combines business process reengineering and a project to acquire, develop, or implement internal-use software. The issue does not address the accounting for internal-use software development costs (which was, however, dealt with subsequently by SOP 98-1). The EITF reached a consensus that costs of business process reengineering, whether done internally or by third parties, should be expensed as incurred. If the project is carried out by a third party and some of the costs are capitalizable, such as fixed asset costs, the EITF concluded that the total contract cost should be allocated to various activities based on the relative fair value of the separate activities. The allocation should be based on the objective evidence of the fair value of the elements in the contract, not separate prices stated within the contract. The consensus opinion identified the following as third-party or internally generated costs typically associated with business process reengineering activities that should be expensed as incurred:

- Preparation of request for proposal
- Current state assessment
- Process reengineering
- Restructuring the workforce

The cost of software used internally is accounted for under SOP 98-1, "Accounting for the Costs of Computer Software for Internal Use." The SOP divides the process of computer software development into three stages: (1) preliminary project stage (conceptual formulation and evaluation of alternatives, determination of existence of needed technology, and final selection of alternatives); (2) application development stage (design of chosen path, coding, installation to hardware, and testing); and (3) postimplementation/operation stage (training and application maintenance). Computer software costs that are incurred in the preliminary project stage should be expensed as incurred.

Once the capitalization criteria of the SOP have been met, external direct costs of materials and services consumed in developing or obtaining internal-use computer software, payroll costs for employees who are directly associated with and who devote time to the project, and interest costs incurred in developing the software should be capitalized. Capitalization should cease no later than the point at which a computer software project is substantially complete and ready for its intended use.

Internal and external training costs and maintenance costs incurred in the postimplementation/ operation stage should be expensed as incurred. General and administrative costs and overhead costs should not be capitalized as costs of internal-use software.

(g) EXTRACTIVE INDUSTRIES   Intangible assets in the extractive industries include leased or purchased rights to exploit mineral and other natural resources based on lump-sum, periodic, or production-based payments. The rights are usually included in the property section of the balance sheet.

A comprehensive discussion of the accounting for these and other assets in the extractive industries is given in Chapter 27.

(h) PRODUCERS OR DISTRIBUTORS OF FILMS   SOP 00-2, "Accounting by Producers or Distributors of Films," provides guidance on the accounting for costs related to all types of films and is applicable to both producers and distributors of films. The costs of producing a film include film costs, participation costs, exploitation costs, and manufacturing costs. Marketing and other exploitation costs, other than advertising, should be expensed as incurred. Advertising costs should be accounted for under SOP 93-7, "Reporting on Advertising Costs." Entities are required to amortize film costs using the individual-film-forecast-computation method. That method provides for amortization of costs in the same ratio that current-period actual revenue bears to estimated remaining unrecognized ultimate revenue as of the beginning of the current fiscal year. Amortization begins when a film is released and the entity begins to recognize revenue from the film.

Certain events or changes in circumstances, such as an adverse change in the expected performance of a film or a substantial delay in completion of the film, indicate that the fair value of the film may be less than the related unamortized film costs. If such an event occurs, an entity should assess whether the fair value of the film is less than its unamortized film costs. If the unamortized capitalized film costs exceed the film's fair value, the excess should be written off and may not be subsequently restored. See Chapter 30 for more on this topic.

(i) PUBLIC UTILITIES   The general provisions of accounting for intangible assets of various types apply to public utilities. However, since public utilities are required by regulatory agencies to maintain their accounts in accordance with accounting practices that may vary from GAAP, certain differences in treatment may result. An example is R&D costs, which certain regulatory agencies allow to be deferred.

The rate regulator may reasonably assure the existence of an asset by permitting the inclusion of a cost in allowable costs for rate-making purposes. SFAS No. 71, "Accounting for the Effects of Certain Types of Regulation," sets forth two criteria that must both be met in order for a utility to capitalize a cost that would otherwise be required, under GAAP, to be expensed currently:

1.   It is probable that future revenue in an amount at least equal to the capitalized cost will result from inclusion of that cost in allowable costs for rate-making purposes.
2.   Based on available evidence, the future revenue will be provided to permit recovery of the previously incurred cost rather than to provide for expected levels of similar future costs. If the revenue will be provided through an automatic rate-adjustment clause, this criterion requires that the regulator's intent clearly be to permit recovery of the previously incurred cost.

If at any time the capitalized cost no longer meets those two criteria, it is to be expensed. The value of an asset may be impaired by a regulator's rate actions. If a rate regulator excludes all or part of a capitalized cost from allowable costs and the cost was capitalized based on the foregoing criteria, the asset should be reduced to the extent of the excluded cost. Whether other assets have been impaired is determined under the general rules for impairment, which are described in Sections 20A.4(b) and 20A.4 (c).

If an enterprise discontinues application of SFAS No. 71 because, for example, its operations have been deregulated, it would eliminate from its GAAP balance sheet assets consisting of costs capitalized that would not have been capitalized by unregulated entities. Numerous state legislatures and/or regulatory commissions have approved or are considering deregulating utilities' generation (production) cost of electricity, although the portion of the kilowatt charge attributable to transmission of the electricity to the local area and the distribution cost to the customer are not being deregulated. If some, but not all, of a utility's operations are regulated, SFAS No. 71 should be applied to the portion of the operations that continue to meet the requirements of SFAS No. 71 for regulatory accounting. SFAS No. 101, "Regulated Enterprises—Accounting for the Discontinuation of Application of FASB Statement No. 71," addresses how an entity that ceases to meet the criteria for application of SFAS No. 71 to all or part of its operations should report that event in its financial statements.

An issue related to the current deregulation environment is when an entity should cease to apply the regulated enterprise accounting model prescribed by SFAS No. 71 to the generation portion of its operations if deregulation is under consideration. In Issue No. 97-4, "Deregulation of the Price of Electricity—Issues Related to the Application of FASB Statements No. 71 and 101," the EITF reached a consensus that when deregulatory legislation or a rate order is issued that contains sufficient detail to determine how the deregulatory plan will affect the portion of the business being deregulated, the entity should stop applying SFAS No. 71 to that separable portion of its business. The Task Force considered the following fact situation: If legislation is passed requiring deregulation of generation charges at the end of five years, the date the legislation is passed is the latest date that the entity can discontinue application of the SFAS No. 71 accounting model to the generation portion of its operations. The consensus does not address whether an entity should stop applying SFAS No. 71 at an earlier time. The Task Force also observed that the financial statements should segregate, either on their face or in the notes, the amounts that pertain to the separable portion.

With regard to goodwill, a regulator may permit a utility to amortize purchased goodwill over a specified period, may direct a utility not to amortize goodwill, or may direct the utility to write off goodwill. SFAS No. 71 requires the goodwill to be amortized for financial reporting purposes over the period during which it will be allowed for rate-making purposes. If the regulator either excludes amortization from allowable costs for rate-making purposes or directs the utility to write off goodwill, goodwill should not be amortized, and it should be accounted for under SFAS No. 142.

(j) RECORD AND MUSIC INDUSTRY   Significant intangible assets in the record and music industry include record masters, recording artist contracts, and copyrights. Accounting for copyrights generally follows that used in other industries, but the accounting for record masters and recording artist contracts is unique.

SFAS No. 50, "Financial Reporting in the Record and Music Industry," is the primary source of accounting principles in this area. Costs of producing a record master include the costs of musical talent; technical talent for engineering, directing, and mixing; equipment to record and produce the master; and studio facility charges. When past performance of an artist provides a reasonable basis for estimating that the cost of a record master borne by the record company will be recovered from future sales, that cost should be recorded as an asset and, when material, should be separately disclosed. The cost of record masters should be amortized by a method that reasonably relates the cost to the net revenue expected to be realized. Ordinarily, amortization occurs over a very short period. Unamortized amounts should be written off when it becomes apparent that they will not be recovered through future sales. The cost of the record master recoverable from the artist's royalties is to be accounted for as an advance royalty.

A recording artist contract is an agreement for personal services. A major portion of the artist's compensation consists of participation in earnings (measured by sales and license fee income, commonly referred to as a "royalty") or of a nonrefundable advance against royalties. Advances should be recorded as an asset (as a prepaid royalty, classified as current or noncurrent depending on when amounts are expected to be realized) if it is anticipated that they will be recovered against royalties otherwise payable to the artist. When it is determined that a prepayment will not be recovered, the balance should be written off.

(k) TIMBER INDUSTRY   Companies in the forest products industry may make lump-sum payments for timber-cutting rights, which allow them to remove trees for a specified period or in specified quantities. Lump-sum payments made at the inception of an agreement are properly deferred and amortized over the period of the agreement or on the basis of estimates of recoverable timber. Periodic or production-based payments are expensed as they do not represent future benefits. Cutting rights are ordinarily included in the Property section of the balance sheet and are stated at cost less amortization. The amortization policy should be disclosed.

20A.7   ACCOUNTING FOR GOODWILL

(a) INITIAL VALUATION   SFAS Nos. 141, "Business Combinations," and 142, "Goodwill and Other Intangible Assets," were both issued in June 2001 and replaced Accounting Principles Board (APB) Opinions Nos. 16 and 17. In these standards, goodwill is defined as

> The excess of the cost of an acquired entity over the net of the amounts assigned to assets acquired and liabilities assumed. The amount recognized as goodwill includes acquired intangible assets that do not meet the criteria in SFAS No. 141, "Business Combinations," for recognition as an asset apart from goodwill.

The previously referenced criteria for separate recognition of intangibles are discussed in Section 20A.3(a). For accounting purposes, the cost of purchased goodwill is the residual cost remaining after all other identifiable assets and liabilities have been valued.

(b) SUBSEQUENT ACCOUNTING   Goodwill is not amortized. It is tested for impairment at a level of reporting referred to as a reporting unit (see Section 20A.7(b)(iv) for a definition of a reporting unit). Impairment is the condition that exists when the carrying amount of goodwill is greater than its implied fair value. A two-step impairment test, discussed next, is used to identify potential goodwill impairment and measure the amount of a goodwill impairment loss to be recognized, if any.

(i) Recognition and Measurement of an Impairment Loss   The first step of a goodwill impairment test compares the fair value of a reporting unit with its carrying amount, including goodwill, applying the guidance provided in Section 20A.7(b)(ii). If the fair value of the

reporting unit is more than its carrying amount, goodwill of the reporting unit is considered not impaired, and the second step of the impairment test is not performed. If the carrying amount of the reporting unit is more than its fair value, the second step of the goodwill impairment test, discussed next, is performed to measure the amount of impairment, if any.

The second step of the goodwill impairment test compares the implied fair value of reporting unit goodwill (explained in the next paragraph) with the carrying amount of the goodwill. If the carrying amount of reporting unit goodwill is more than the implied fair value of the goodwill, an impairment loss is recognized in an amount equal to the excess. The loss recognized cannot exceed the carrying amount of goodwill. When a goodwill impairment loss is recognized, the adjusted carrying amount of goodwill is its new accounting basis. Subsequent to the measurement and recognition of the goodwill impairment loss, a later recovery in value cannot be recognized. Thus, goodwill impairments cannot be reversed.

The implied fair value of goodwill is determined in the same way as is the amount of goodwill to be recognized in a business combination. The reporting entity allocates the fair value of the reporting unit to all of the assets and liabilities of the unit, including any unrecognized intangible assets, the same way it would be allocated had the reporting unit been acquired in a business combination and had the fair value of the reporting unit been the price paid to acquire the reporting unit. The excess of the fair value of the reporting unit over the amounts assigned to its assets and liabilities is the *implied fair value of goodwill*.

The allocation process just described is performed only for the purpose of testing goodwill for impairment. A reporting entity does not write up or down a recognized asset or liability, and it does not recognize a previously unrecognized intangible asset as a result of the allocation process exercise.

If the second step of the goodwill impairment test is not complete before the financial statements are issued and a goodwill impairment loss is probable and can be reasonably estimated, the best estimate of the loss is recognized in those financial statements. Any adjustment to the estimated loss based on completion of the measurement of the impairment loss is recognized in the next reporting period.

(ii) Fair Value Measurements   SFAS No. 142 defines *fair value* the same way FASB Statement of Concepts No. 7 does:

> The amount at which that asset (or liability) could be bought (or incurred) or sold (settled) in a current transaction between willing parties, that is, other than in a forced or liquidation sale.

According to that definition, the fair value of a reporting unit is the amount at which the unit as a whole could be bought or sold in a current transaction between willing parties. Quoted market prices in active markets are the best evidence of fair value and are used as the basis for measurement, if available. However, the market price of an individual equity security and thus the market capitalization of a reporting unit with publicly traded equity securities may not be representative of the fair value of the reporting unit as a whole, because of a control premium. The quoted market price of an individual equity security, therefore, need not be the sole measurement basis of the fair value of a reporting unit. SEC registrants should be aware that the SEC staff has sometimes questioned valuations not based on the market price of the equity security.

If quoted market prices are not available, the estimate of fair value is based on the best information available, including prices for similar assets and liabilities and the results of using other valuation techniques. A present value technique is often the best available technique with which to estimate the fair value of a group of net assets (i.e., a reporting unit). If a present value technique is used to measure fair value, estimates of future cash flows used in the technique are to be consistent with the objective of measuring fair value. The cash flow estimates should incorporate assumptions that marketplace participants would use in their estimates of fair value. If that information is not available without undue cost and effort, a reporting entity may use its own assumptions.

An entity should base the cash flow estimates on reasonable and supportable assumptions after consideration of all available evidence. The weight given to the evidence should be commensurate with the extent to which the evidence can be verified objectively. If the entity estimates a range for the amount or timing of possible cash flows, it should consider the likelihood of possible outcomes. FASB Concepts Statement No. 7 gives guidance. It states that an "expected present value technique" which uses the sum of probability-weighted present values in a range of estimated cash flows adjusted for risk, all discounted using the same interest rate convention, is the preferred—but not required—approach. The FASB has indicated that such a technique is a more effective measurement tool than was the traditional present value approach, especially in situations in which the timing or the amount of estimated cash flows is uncertain, as is the case in measuring nonfinancial assets and liabilities.

In estimating the fair value of a reporting unit, a valuation technique based on multiples of earnings or revenue or a similar performance measure may be used if that technique is consistent with the objective of measuring fair value. Use of such multiples may be appropriate, for example, when the fair value of an entity that has comparable operations and economic characteristics is observable and the relevant multiples of the comparable entity are known. Conversely, such multiples are not used in situations in which the operations or activities of an entity whose multiples are known are not of a comparable nature, scope, or size as the reporting unit for which fair value is being estimated.

(iii) ***When to Test Goodwill for Impairment***   Goodwill of a reporting unit is tested for impairment annually and between annual tests in certain circumstances, as discussed subsequently. The annual goodwill impairment test may be performed any time during the fiscal year provided the timing of the test is consistent from year to year. Different reporting units may be tested for impairment at different times.

A detailed determination of the fair value of a reporting unit may be carried forward from one year to the next if all of the following criteria have been met:

- The assets and liabilities that make up the reporting unit have not changed significantly since the most recent fair value determination.
- The most recent fair value determination resulted in an amount that exceeded the carrying amount of the reporting unit by a substantial margin.
- Based on an analysis of events that have occurred and circumstances that have changed since the most recent fair value determination, the likelihood that a current fair value determination would be less than the current carrying amount of the reporting unit is remote.

Goodwill of a reporting unit is tested for impairment between annual tests if an event occurs or circumstances change that would more likely than not reduce the fair value of a reporting unit below its carrying amount.

Examples of such events or circumstances include the following:

- A significant adverse change in legal factors or in the business climate
- An adverse action or assessment by a regulator
- Unanticipated competition
- A loss of key personnel
- A more-likely-than-not expectation that a reporting unit or a significant portion of a reporting unit will be sold or otherwise disposed of
- Testing for recoverability under SFAS No. 144 of a significant asset group within a reporting unit
- Recognition of a goodwill impairment loss in the financial statements of a subsidiary that is a component of a reporting unit

Also see Section 20A.7(b)(vii) for the need to test goodwill for impairment after a portion of goodwill has been allocated to a business to be disposed of.

If goodwill and another asset or asset group of a reporting unit are tested for impairment at the same time, the other asset or asset group is tested before goodwill. If the asset or asset group is found to be impaired, the impairment loss is recognized before goodwill is tested for impairment.

(iv) Reporting Unit A reporting unit is an operating segment or one level below an operating segment, referred to as a component. An operating segment is defined by SFAS No. 131, "Disclosures about Segments of an Enterprise and Related Information." A component of an operating segment is a reporting unit if the component constitutes a business, as discussed in EITF Issue No. 98-3, for which discrete financial information is available and segment management, as defined by SFAS No. 131, regularly reviews the operating results of that component.

Segment management may consist of one or more segment managers. Two or more components of an operating segment are aggregated and deemed a single reporting unit if the components have similar economic characteristics, as discussed in SFAS No. 131. An operating segment is deemed a reporting unit if all of its components are similar, if none of its components is a reporting unit, or if it comprises only a single component.

Because considerable judgment is required for entities to determine their reporting units and the guidance in SFAS No. 142 is quite limited, the FASB staff provided further clarification of that guidance in EITF Topic No. D-101. The basic guidance is that a component of an operating segment is a reporting unit if (1) it constitutes a business, (2) discrete financial information on the component is available, and (3) segment management regularly reviews the results of the reporting unit. A fourth requirement provides that components with similar economic characteristics should be combined into one reporting unit. Topic No. D-101 provides that the first three factors are required for a component to be a reporting unit, but no one factor is individually determinative.

The determinative factors are how an entity manages its operations and how an acquired entity is integrated with the acquiring entity. Topic No. D-101 provides the following clarification of each factor:

- *Component constitutes a business.* Judgment is required to determine whether a component constitutes a business, and entities are required to consider the guidance in EITF Issue No. 98-3 in determining that. To be a business under the guidance in EITF Issue No. 98-3, the activities and assets should include "all the inputs and processes necessary" to conduct normal operations. The fact that operating information may be available does not mean the operations constitute a business. They may be just a part of a business, such as one product line.

- *Discrete financial information.* For purposes of both SFAS No. 131 and SFAS No. 142, discrete financial information can consist of just operating information, with no balance sheet information prepared for the component. However, if the component is a reporting unit, the entity would be required to identify and allocate assets and liabilities applicable to the component to test goodwill for impairment.
- *Reviewed by segment management.* Under SFAS No. 131, segment management may be one level below the chief operating decision maker, and there may be one or more segment managers. The focus of SFAS No. 142 is on how operating segments are managed rather than on how the entity as a whole is managed.
- *Similar economic characteristics.* The evaluation of whether two components have similar economic characteristics requires consideration of the factors in paragraph 17 of SFAS No. 131: similar economic characteristics, such as similar long-term average gross margins; the nature of the products and/or services; the nature of production processes; the type or class of customers; the methods used to distribute products and provide services; and the nature of any regulatory environment. Topic No. D-101 provides that not all factors have to be met for economic similarity to exist, and the evaluation should be more qualitative than quantitative.

Topic No. D-101 also provides additional factors to consider when evaluating whether components should be combined in a reporting unit because they are economically similar:

- How an entity operates its business and the nature of the operations
- Whether goodwill is recoverable from the separate operations of each component business or from the components working together because, for example, the components are economically interdependent
- The extent to which the component businesses share assets and other resources
- Whether the components provide support and receive benefits from the same R&D projects

Components of different operating segments for purposes of SFAS No. 131 cannot be combined into the same reporting unit, even if they have similar economic characteristics. This might occur, for example, if the entity organized its operating segments on a geographic basis.

Questions have arisen about whether one or more components of operating units aggregated into one reporting unit under SFAS No. 131 could be economically dissimilar and therefore be in separate reporting units under SFAS No. 142. Topic No. D-101 provides two explanations of why that could happen:

1. The determination of reportable segments under SFAS No. 131 requires identification of operating segments and subsequent determination of whether economically similar operating segments should be aggregated. However, the determination of reporting units under SFAS No. 142 begins with operating segments and then requires an analysis of whether economically dissimilar components of an operating segment should be disaggregated.
2. For a component of an operating segment to be an operating segment under SFAS No. 131, its operating performance must be regularly reviewed by the chief operating decision maker. That same component, however, could be a reporting unit if a segment manager regularly reviews its operating performance.

For the purpose of testing goodwill for impairment, acquired assets and assumed liabilities are assigned to a reporting unit as of the acquisition date if both of the following criteria are met:

1. The asset will be employed in or the liability relates to the operations of a reporting unit.
2. The asset or liability will be considered in determining the fair value of the reporting unit.

Assets or liabilities that an entity considers part of its corporate assets or liabilities are also assigned to a reporting unit if both of the preceding criteria are met. Examples are environmental liabilities that relate to an existing operating facility of the reporting unit and a pension obligation that would be included in the determination of the fair value of the reporting unit. Some assets or liabilities may be employed in or relate to the operations of multiple reporting units. The methodology used to determine the amount of those assets or liabilities to assign to a reporting unit is on a reasonable and supportable basis and applied in a consistent manner. For example, this would include assets and liabilities not directly related to a specific reporting unit but from which the reporting unit benefits could be allocated according to the benefit received by the different reporting units or based on the relative fair values of the different reporting units. A pro rata allocation based on payroll expense might be used for pension items.

For the purpose of testing goodwill for impairment, all goodwill acquired in a business combination is assigned to one or more reporting units as of the acquisition date. Goodwill is assigned to reporting units of the acquiring entity expected to benefit from the synergies of the combination even though other assets or liabilities of the acquired entity may not be assigned to that reporting unit. The total amount of acquired goodwill may be divided among a number of reporting units. The methodology used to determine the amount of goodwill to assign to a reporting unit should be reasonable and supportable and applied in a consistent manner. Also, the methodology has to be consistent with the objectives of the process of assigning goodwill to reporting units, described next. In concept, the amount of goodwill assigned to a reporting unit would be determined in a manner similar to how the amount of goodwill recognized in a business combination is determined.

The fair value of the acquired business or portion of the acquired business that will be included in a particular reporting unit is, in essence, the purchase price of that business. The entity allocates that purchase price to the assets acquired and liabilities incurred related to (the portion of) the acquired business assigned to the reporting unit. Any excess purchase price is the amount of goodwill assigned to that reporting unit. However, if the goodwill is to be assigned to a reporting unit that has not been assigned any of the assets acquired or liabilities assumed in that acquisition, the amount of goodwill to be assigned to that unit might be determined by applying a "with and without" computation. That is, the difference between the fair value of that reporting unit before the acquisition and its fair value after the acquisition represents the amount of goodwill to be assigned to that reporting unit.

When an entity reorganizes its reporting structure in a manner that changes the composition of one or more of its reporting units, the guidance given earlier in this section for assigning acquired assets and assumed liabilities to reporting units is used to reassign assets and liabilities to the reporting units affected. However, goodwill is reassigned to the reporting units affected using a relative fair value allocation approach similar to that used when a portion of a reporting unit is to be disposed of, which is discussed in Section 20A.7(b)(vii). For example, if existing reporting unit A is to be integrated with reporting units B, C, and D, goodwill of reporting unit A would be assigned to units B, C, and D based on the relative fair values of the three portions of reporting unit A before those portions are integrated with reporting units B, C, and D.

(v) Goodwill Impairment Testing by a Subsidiary   All goodwill recognized by a public or nonpublic subsidiary in its separate financial statements prepared in conformity with GAAP, known as subsidiary goodwill, is accounted for in conformity with SFAS No. 142. It is tested for impairment at the subsidiary level using the subsidiary's reporting units. If a goodwill impairment loss is recognized at the subsidiary level, goodwill of the reporting unit or units at the consolidated level in which the subsidiary's reporting unit with impaired goodwill resides is tested for impairment if the event that gave rise to the loss at the subsidiary level more likely than not would reduce the fair value of the reporting unit at the consolidated level below its carrying amount. A goodwill impairment loss is recognized at the consolidated level only if goodwill at the consolidated level is impaired.

(vi) Goodwill Impairment Testing When a Noncontrolling Interest Exists   Goodwill from a business combination with a continuing noncontrolling (minority) interest is tested for impairment using an approach consistent with the approach used to measure the noncontrolling interest at the acquisition date. For example, if goodwill is first recognized based on only the controlling interest of the parent, the fair value of the reporting unit used in the impairment test is based on the controlling interest and does not reflect the portion of fair value attributable to the noncontrolling interest. Similarly, the implied fair value of goodwill determined in the second step of the impairment test used to measure the impairment loss reflects only the parent's interest in the goodwill.

(vii) Disposal of All or a Portion of a Reporting Unit   When a reporting unit is to be disposed of in its entirety, the carrying amount of goodwill of the reporting unit is included in the carrying amount of the reporting unit in determining the gain or loss on disposal. When a portion of a reporting unit that constitutes a business is to be disposed of, the carrying amount of goodwill associated with the business is included in the carrying amount of the business in determining the gain or loss on disposal. The portion of the carrying amount of goodwill to be included in that carrying amount is based on the relative fair values of the business to be disposed of and the portion of the reporting unit to be retained. However, if the business to be disposed of was never integrated into the reporting unit after its acquisition and thus the benefits of the acquired goodwill were never realized by the rest of the reporting unit, the current carrying amount of the acquired goodwill is included in the carrying amount of business to be disposed of. When only a portion of goodwill is allocated to a business to be disposed of, the goodwill remaining in the portion of the reporting unit to be retained is tested for impairment.

(viii) Equity Method Investments   The portion of the difference between the cost of an investment and the amount of underlying equity in net assets of an equity method investee recognized as goodwill in conformity with paragraph 19(b) of APB Opinion No. 18, "The Equity Method of Accounting for Investments in Common Stock," known as equity method goodwill, is not amortized. However, equity method goodwill is not tested for impairment in conformity with SFAS No. 142.

Equity method investments continue to be reviewed for impairment in conformity with paragraph 19(h) of APB Opinion No. 18.

(ix) Entities Emerging from Bankruptcy   SOP 90-7, "Financial Reporting by Entities in Reorganization Under the Bankruptcy Code," provides that when an entity applies fresh-start accounting on emerging from bankruptcy, the reorganization value should be allocated to all tangible and intangible assets following the procedures in APB Opinion No. 16, "Business

Combinations." SFAS No. 142 stipulates that entities should report the excess reorganization value as goodwill and account for it in the same manner as other elements of goodwill.

20A.8 DEFERRED INCOME TAXES

SFAS No. 142 does not change the requirements in SFAS No. 109, "Accounting for Income Taxes," paragraphs 30, 261, and 262, for recognition of deferred income taxes related to goodwill and intangible assets.

20A.9 FINANCIAL STATEMENT PRESENTATION

(a) INTANGIBLE ASSETS   All intangible assets are aggregated and presented as a separate line item in the statement of financial position. In addition, individual intangible assets or classes of intangible assets may be presented as separate line items. Amortization expense and impairment losses for intangible assets are presented in income statement line items within continuing operations as deemed appropriate for each entity. An impairment loss resulting from such an impairment test should not be recognized as a change in accounting principle.

(b) GOODWILL   The aggregate amount of goodwill is presented as a separate line item in the statement of financial position. The aggregate amount of goodwill impairment losses are presented as a separate line item in the income statement before the subtotal *income from continuing operations,* or a similar caption, unless a goodwill impairment loss is associated with a discontinued operation. A goodwill impairment loss associated with a discontinued operation is included net of tax within the results of discontinued operations.

20A.10 DISCLOSURES

The following information is disclosed in the notes to the financial statements in the period of acquisition of intangible assets acquired either individually or with a group of assets:

    A. For intangible assets subject to amortization:
        1. The total amount assigned and the amount assigned to any major intangible asset class
        2. The amount of any significant residual value, in total and by major intangible asset class
        3. The weighted-average amortization period, in total and by major intangible asset class
    B. For intangible assets not subject to amortization, the total amount assigned and the amount assigned to any major intangible asset class
    C. The amount of R&D assets acquired and written off in the period and the line item in the income statement in which the amounts written off are aggregated

The following information is disclosed in the financial statements or the notes to the financial statements for each period for which a statement of financial position is presented:

    A. For intangible assets subject to amortization:
        1. The gross carrying amount and accumulated amortization, in total and by major intangible asset class
        2. The aggregate amortization expense for the period

3. The estimated aggregate amortization expense for each of the five succeeding fiscal years
B. For intangible assets not subject to amortization, the total carrying amount and the carrying amount for each major intangible asset class
C. The changes in the carrying amount of goodwill during the period, including:
   1. The aggregate amount of goodwill acquired
   2. The aggregate amount of impairment losses recognized on goodwill
   3. The amount of goodwill included in the gain or loss on disposal of all or a portion of a reporting unit

Reporting entities that report segment information in conformity with SFAS No. 131 should provide the preceding information about goodwill in total and for each reportable segment and should disclose any significant changes in the allocation of goodwill by reportable segment. If any portion of goodwill has not yet been allocated to a reporting unit at the date the financial statements are issued, that unallocated amount and the reasons for not allocating the amount are disclosed. For each impairment loss recognized related to an intangible asset, the following information is disclosed in the notes to the financial statements that include the period in which the impairment loss is recognized:

- Description of the impaired intangible asset and the facts and circumstances leading to the impairment
- Amount of the impairment loss and the method for determining fair value
- Caption in the income statement or the statement of activities in which the impairment loss is aggregated
- If applicable, the segment in which the impaired intangible asset is reported under SFAS No. 131

For each goodwill impairment loss recognized, the following information is disclosed in the notes to the financial statements that include the period in which the impairment loss is recognized:

- A description of the facts and circumstances leading to the impairment
- The amount of the impairment loss and the method of determining the fair value of the associated reporting unit
- If a recognized impairment loss is an estimate that has not yet been finalized, that fact and the reasons for it and, in subsequent periods, the nature and amount of any significant adjustments made to the initial estimate of the impairment loss

20A.11   EFFECTIVE DATE AND TRANSITION PROVISIONS OF SFAS NO. 142

The provisions of SFAS No. 142 were initially applied in fiscal years beginning after December 15, 2001, to all goodwill and other intangible assets recognized in a reporting entity's statement of financial position at the beginning of that fiscal year, regardless of when those previously recognized assets were first recognized. Early application was permitted for entities with fiscal years beginning after March 15, 2001, provided that the first interim financial statements had not been issued previously. The provisions of the statement were to be first applied at the beginning of a fiscal year. They were not to be applied retroactively.

SFAS No. 142's provisions are not to be applied to previously recognized goodwill and intangible assets acquired in a combination between two or more mutual enterprises, acquired in a combination between not-for-profit organizations, or from the acquisition of a for-profit business entity by a not-for-profit organization until interpretive guidance related to the application of the purchase method to those transactions is issued. As of late 2005, this guidance has yet to be promulgated, although this is anticipated to occur in the near future.

See Section 10.3(o) for transition provisions related to goodwill and intangible assets acquired in business combination for which the acquisition date was before July 1, 2001, that were accounted for by the purchase method.

(a) GOODWILL AND INTANGIBLE ASSETS ACQUIRED AFTER JUNE 30, 2001
Goodwill acquired in a business combination for which the acquisition date is after June 30, 2001 is not amortized. Intangible assets other than goodwill acquired in a business combination or other transaction for which the date of acquisition is after June 30, 2001 are amortized or not amortized in conformity with the discussion in Sections 20A.4(b) and 20A.4(c). Goodwill and intangible assets acquired in a transaction for which the acquisition date is after June 30, 2001 but before the date that SFAS No. 142 was first applied in its entirety were to be reviewed for impairment in conformity with APB Opinion No. 17 or SFAS No. 121 (as appropriate) until the date SFAS No. 142 was applied in its entirety. The financial statement presentation and disclosure provisions of SFAS No. 142 were not to be applied to those assets until SFAS No. 142 was applied in its entirety.

Goodwill and intangible assets acquired in a combination between two or more mutual enterprises, acquired in a combination between not-for-profit organizations, or from the acquisition of a for-profit business entity by a not-for-profit organization for which the acquisition date is after June 30, 2001, continue to be accounted for in conformity with APB Opinion No. 17 until the FASB provides guidance on issues related to the application of the purchase method to such transactions.

(b) PREVIOUSLY RECOGNIZED INTANGIBLE ASSETS   To apply SFAS No. 142 to previously recognized intangible assets (those acquired in a transaction for which the acquisition date is on or before June 30, 2001), the useful lives of those assets are reassessed using the guidance in Section 20A.4(a) and the remaining amortization periods are adjusted accordingly. For example, the amortization period for a previously recognized intangible asset might be increased if its original useful life was estimated to be longer than the 40-year maximum amortization period allowed by APB Opinion No. 17. The reassessment was to be completed before the end of the first interim period of the fiscal year in which SFAS No. 142 was first applied.

Previously recognized intangible assets deemed to have indefinite useful lives were to be tested for impairment as of the beginning of the fiscal year in which SFAS No. 142 was first applied. The transitional intangible asset impairment test was to be completed in the first interim period in which SFAS No. 142 was first applied, and any resulting impairment loss was to be recognized as the effect of a change in accounting principle. The effect of the accounting change and related income tax effects were to be presented in the income statement between the captions extraordinary items and net income. The per-share information presented in the income statement included the per-share effect of the accounting change.

(c) PREVIOUSLY RECOGNIZED GOODWILL   At the date SFAS No. 142 was first applied, the reporting entity was required to establish its reporting units based on its reporting structure at that date and the guidance described in Section 20A.7(b)(iv). Recognized net assets and liabilities that did not relate to a reporting unit, such as an environmental liability for an operation previously disposed of, did not need to be assigned to a reporting unit. All goodwill recognized in a reporting entity's statement of financial position at the date that SFAS No. 142 was first applied was to be assigned to one or more reporting units. Goodwill was to be assigned in a reasonable and supportable manner. The sources of previously recognized goodwill were to be considered in making that initial assignment as well as the reporting units to which the related acquired net assets were assigned. Section 20A.7(b)(iv) provides guidance on assigning goodwill to reporting units on initial application of SFAS No. 142.

Goodwill in each reporting unit was tested for impairment as of the beginning of the fiscal year in which SFAS No. 142 was first applied in its entirety. The first step of the test was to be completed within six months from the date the reporting entity first applied SFAS No. 142. The amounts used in the transitional goodwill impairment test were measured as of the beginning of the year of first application. If the carrying amount of the net assets of a reporting unit (including goodwill) exceeded the fair value of the reporting unit, the second step of the transitional goodwill impairment test was completed as soon as possible, but no later than the end of the year of first application.

An impairment loss as a result of a transitional goodwill impairment test was recognized as the effect of a change in accounting principle. The effect of the accounting change and related income tax effects were to be presented in the income statement between the captions extraordinary items and net income. The per-share information presented in the income statement included the per-share effect of the accounting change. Though a transitional impairment loss for goodwill could be measured in other than the first interim reporting period, it was to be recognized in the first interim period regardless of the period in which it was measured, consistent with paragraph 10 of SFAS No. 3, "Reporting Accounting Changes in Interim Financial Statements."

The financial information for the interim periods of the fiscal year that preceded the period in which the transitional goodwill impairment loss was measured was to be restated to reflect the accounting change in those periods. The aggregate amount of the accounting change is included in restated net income of the first interim period of the year of first application (and in any year-to-date or last-12-months-to-date financial reports that included the first interim period). Whenever financial information is presented that includes the periods that precede the period in which the transitional goodwill impairment loss was measured, that financial information should be presented on the restated basis.

A reporting entity was required to perform the required annual goodwill impairment test in the year that SFAS No. 142 was first applied in its entirety, in addition to the transitional goodwill impairment test, unless the reporting entity designated the beginning of its fiscal year as the date for its annual goodwill impairment test.

(d) EQUITY METHOD GOODWILL   When SFAS No. 142 was first applied, the portion of the excess of cost over the underlying equity in net assets of an investee accounted for using the equity method that had been recognized as goodwill was no longer to be amortized. However, equity method goodwill is not to be tested for impairment under SFAS No. 142.

Rather, the guidance under APB No. 18 continues to be applicable in assessing impairment of equity method investments.

(e) TRANSITIONAL DISCLOSURES   Expanded disclosures were mandated during the initial implementation period for SFAS No. 142. Since all entities have now fully adopted this standard, and since comparative disclosures including pre-implementation periods are now unlikely to be encountered in practice, this will not be described in detail.

20A.12   SOURCES AND SUGGESTED REFERENCES

Accounting Principles Board, "Restatement of Revision of Accounting Research Bulletins," Accounting Research Bulletin No. 43. New York: AICPA, 1968.

Accounting Principles Board, "Disclosure of Accounting Policies," APB Opinion No. 22. New York: AICPA, 1973.

Accounting Principles Board, "Reporting the Results of Operations," APB Opinion No. 30. New York: AICPA, 1973.

American Accounting Association Financial Accounting Standards Committee, "Equity Valuation Models and Measuring Goodwill Impairment," *Accounting Horizons,* June 2001.

American Institute of Certified Public Accountants, "Push Down Accounting," Issues Paper. New York: AICPA, 1979.

American Institute of Certified Public Accountants, "Accounting for Developmental and Preoperating Costs, Purchases and Exchanges of Take-off and Landing Slots, and Airframe Modifications," Statement of Position 88-1. New York: AICPA, 1988.

American Institute of Certified Public Accountants, "Financial Reporting by Entities in Reorganization Under the Bankruptcy Code," Statement of Position 90-7. New York: AICPA, November 19, 1990.

American Institute of Certified Public Accountants, "Reporting on Advertising Costs," Statement of Position 93-7. New York: AICPA, December 29, 1993.

American Institute of Certified Public Accountants, "Accounting for the Costs of Computer Software Developed or Obtained for Internal Use," Statement of Position 98-1. New York: AICPA, 1998.

American Institute of Certified Public Accountants, "Reporting on the Cost of Start-Up Activities," Statement of Position 98-5. New York: AICPA, 1998.

American Institute of Certified Public Accountants, "Accounting by Producers or Distributors of Films," Statement of Position 00-2. New York: AICPA, 2000.

American Institute of Certified Public Accountants, "Assets Acquired in a Business Combination to Be Used in R&D Activities: A Focus on Software, Electronic Devices, and Pharmaceutical Industries," AICPA Practice Aid Series. New York: AICPA, 2001.

American Institute of Certified Public Accountants: "The Fair Value Measurement Valuation Toolkit for Financial Accounting Standards Board Statements of Financial Accounting Standards No. 141, Business Combinations, and No. 142, Goodwill and Other Intangible Assets. New York: AICPA, 2002.

Financial Accounting Standards Board, "Accounting for Research and Development Costs," Statement of Financial Accounting Standards No. 2. Norwalk, CT: FASB, 1974.

Financial Accounting Standards Board, "Applicability of FASB Statement No. 2 to Computer Software (An Interpretation of FASB Statement No. 2)," FASB Interpretation No. 6. Norwalk, CT: FASB, 1975.

Financial Accounting Standards Board, "Accounting for Franchise Fee Revenue," Statement of Financial Accounting Standards No. 45. Norwalk, CT: FASB, 1981.

Financial Accounting Standards Board, "Financial Reporting in the Record and Music Industry," Statement of Financial Accounting Standards No. 50. Norwalk, CT: FASB, 1981.

Financial Accounting Standards Board, "Financial Reporting by Cable Television Companies," Statement of Financial Accounting Standards No. 51. Norwalk, CT: FASB, 1981.

Financial Accounting Standards Board, "Financial Reporting by Broadcasters," Statement of Financial Accounting Standards No. 63. Norwalk, CT: FASB, 1982.

Financial Accounting Standards Board, "Accounting for the Effects of Certain Types of Regulation," Statement of Financial Accounting Standards No. 71. Norwalk, CT: FASB, 1982.

Financial Accounting Standards Board, "Accounting for Certain Acquisitions of Banking or Thrift Institutions," Statement of Financial Accounting Standards No. 72. Norwalk, CT: FASB, 1983.

Financial Accounting Standards Board, "Accounting for the Costs of Computer Software to Be Sold, Leased, or Otherwise Marketed," Statement of Financial Accounting Standards No. 86. Norwalk, CT: FASB, 1985.

Financial Accounting Standards Board, "Statement of Cash Flows," Statement of Financial Accounting Standards No. 95. Norwalk, CT: FASB, 1987.

Financial Accounting Standards Board, "Issues Relating to Accounting for Leases," FASB Technical Bulletin No. 88-1. Norwalk, CT: FASB, 1988.

Financial Accounting Standards Board, "Accounting for Income Taxes," Statement of Financial Accounting Standards No. 109. Norwalk, CT: FASB, February, 1992.

Financial Accounting Standards Board, "Recognition of Liabilities in Connection with a Purchase Business Combination," EITF Issue No. 95-3. Norwalk, CT: FASB, 1995.

Financial Accounting Standards Board, "Determination of What Risks and Rewards, If Any, Can Be Retained and Whether Any Unresolved Contingencies May Exist in a Sale of Mortgage Loan Servicing Rights," EITF Issue No. 95-5. Norwalk, CT: FASB, 1995.

Financial Accounting Standards Board, "Accounting for Contingent Consideration Paid to the Shareholders of an Acquired Enterprise in a Purchase Business Combination," EITF Issue No. 95-8. Norwalk, CT: FASB, 1995.

Financial Accounting Standards Board, "Accounting for the Film and Software Costs Associated with Developing Entertainment and Educational Software Products," EITF Issue No. 96-6. Norwalk, CT: FASB, 1996.

Financial Accounting Standards Board, "Disclosures about Segments of an Enterprise and Related Information," Statement of Financial Accounting Standards No. 131. Norwalk, CT: FASB, 1997.

Financial Accounting Standards Board, "Deregulation of the Price of Electricity—Issues Related to the Application of FASB Statements 71 and 101," EITF Issue No. 97-4. Norwalk, CT: FASB, 1997.

Financial Accounting Standards Board, "Accounting for Contingent Consideration Issued in a Purchase Business Combination," EITF Issue No. 97-8. Norwalk, CT: FASB, 1997.

Financial Accounting Standards Board, "Accounting for Costs Incurred in Connection with a Consulting Contract or an Internal Project That Combines Business Process Reengineering and Information Technology Transformation," EITF Issue No. 97-13. Norwalk, CT: FASB, 1997.

Financial Accounting Standards Board, "Accounting for Transfers and Servicing of Financial Assets and Extinguishments of Liabilities—A Replacement of FASB Statement No. 125," Statement of Financial Accounting Standards No. 140. Norwalk, CT: FASB, 2000.

Financial Accounting Standards Board, "Business Combinations," Statement of Financial Accounting Standards No. 141. Norwalk, CT: FASB, June 2001.

Financial Accounting Standards Board, "Goodwill and Other Intangible Assets," Statement of Financial Accounting Standards No. 142. Norwalk, CT: FASB, June 2001.

Financial Accounting Standards Board, "Accounting for the Impairment or Disposal of Long-Lived Assets," Statement of Financial Accounting Standards No. 144. Norwalk, CT: FASB, June 2001.

Financial Accounting Standards Board, "Accounting for Costs Associated with Exit or Disposal Activities," Statement of Financial Accounting Standards No. 146. Norwalk, CT: FASB, June 2002.

Financial Accounting Standards Board, "Acquisitions of Certain Financial Institutions," Statement of Financial Accounting Standards No. 147. Norwalk, CT: FASB, October 2002.

Financial Accounting Standards Board, "Unit of Accounting for Testing Impairment of Indefinite-Lived Assets," EITF Issue No. 02-7. Norwalk, CT: FASB, 2002.

Financial Accounting Standards Board, "Deferred Income Tax Considerations in Applying the Goodwill Impairment Test in FASB Statement No. 142," EITF Issue No. 02-13. Norwalk, CT: FASB, 2002.

Financial Accounting Standards Board, "Recognition of Customer Relationship Intangible Assets Acquired in a Business Combination," EITF Issue No. 02-17. Norwalk, CT: FASB, 2002.

Financial Accounting Standards Board, "Interaction of Paragraphs 11 and 12 of FASB Statement No. 142 Regarding Determination of the Useful Life and Amortization of Intangible Assets," EITF Issue No. 03-9. Norwalk, CT: FASB, 2003.

Financial Accounting Standards Board, "Interaction of FASB Statements No. 141, *Business Combinations,* and No. 142, *Goodwill and Other Intangible Assets,* and EITF Issue No. 04-2, *Whether Mineral Rights Are Tangible or Intangible Assets,*" FASB Staff Positions 141-1 and 142-1. Norwalk, CT: FASB, 2003.

Financial Accounting Standards Board, "Accounting for Pre-Existing Contractual Relationships Between the Parties to a Business Combination," EITF Issue No. 04-1. Norwalk, CT: FASB, 2004.

Financial Accounting Standards Board, "Whether Mineral Rights Are Tangible or Intangible Assets and Related Issues," EITF Issue No. 04-2. Norwalk, CT: FASB, 2004.

Financial Accounting Standards Board, "Fair Value Measurements," Exposure Draft. Norwalk, CT: FASB, June 2004.

Financial Accounting Standards Board, "Business Combinations (a Replacement of FASB Statement No. 141," Exposure Draft SFAS No. 141(R). Norwalk, CT: FASB, June 2005.

Financial Accounting Standards Board, "Selected Issues Relating to Assets and Liabilities with Uncertainties," Invitation to Comment. Norwalk, CT: FASB, September 2005.

Securities and Exchange Commission, "Expenses of Offering," Staff Accounting Bulletin Topic 5A. Washington, DC: SEC: 1975.

Securities and Exchange Commission, "Acquisitions Involving Financial Institutions," Staff Accounting Bulletin Topic 2-A3. Washington, DC: SEC: 1981.

Securities and Exchange Commission, "Push Down Basic of Accounting Required in Certain Limited Circumstances," Staff Accounting Bulletin Topic 5J. Washington, DC: SEC: 1983.

CHAPTER 21

PROPERTY, PLANT, EQUIPMENT, AND DEPRECIATION (REVISED)

GEORGE I. VICTOR, CPA

Holtz Rubenstein Reminick LLP[†]

[†]   The information contained in this chapter does not necessarily represent the views of Holtz Rubenstein Reminick LLP.

21.1 NATURE OF PROPERTY, PLANT, AND EQUIPMENT

(a) DEFINITION   Property, plant, and equipment are presented as noncurrent assets in a classified balance sheet. The category includes such items as land, buildings, equipment, furniture, fixtures, tools, machinery, and leasehold improvements. It excludes intangibles and investments in affiliated companies.

(b) CHARACTERISTICS   Property, plant, and equipment have several important characteristics:

- A relatively long life
- The production of income or services over its life
- Tangibility—having physical substance

(c) AUTHORITATIVE LITERATURE   Generally accepted accounting principles (GAAP) for property, plant, and equipment have evolved without the promulgation of any Level A or B GAAP rule making on a comprehensive basis. Because of this lack of authoritative literature, many believe that diversity in practice has developed with respect to both the type of costs capitalized and the amounts.

In 2001, the Accounting Standards Executive Committee (AcSEC) of the American Institute of CPAs (AICPA) issued an exposure draft (ED) of a Statement of Position (SOP) titled *Accounting for Certain Costs and Activities Related to Property, Plant and Equipment.* The proposal was not adopted, since the FASB indicated that it addressed significant issues that should be addressed by the FASB. Nevertheless, in the absence of subsequent action by the FASB, this document reflects the "best thinking" of the AcSEC at the time.

The proposal addresses accounting for costs related to initial acquisition, construction, improvements, betterments, additions, repairs and maintenance, planned major maintenance, turnaround, overhauls and other similar costs related to property, plant, and equipment (PP&E). The ED proposed a project stage framework consisting of the following:

1.   *Preliminary stage*
This stage occurs before the acquisition of any specific PP&E asset and before it is probable that a specific PP&E asset will be acquired or constructed. All costs, with the exception of costs related for payment of an option to acquire PP&E, should be charged to expense during the preliminary stage.

2.   *Preacquisition stage*
This stage is similar to the preliminary stage as no PP&E asset has yet been acquired. However, acquisition or construction of a specific PP&E asset is considered probable. All costs related to PP&E incurred during this stage should be charged to expense unless the costs are directly identifiable with the specific PP&E. Directly identifiable costs include only (a) incremental direct costs incurred in transactions with independent third parties and (b) payroll and payroll-benefit-related costs for employees who devote time to the PP&E activity. All general and administrative and overhead costs should be charged to expense and not capitalized as a cost of PP&E.

3.   *Acquisition-or-construction stage*
This stage begins when the entity obtains ownership of the PP&E. Only directly identifiable costs as outlined in the previous paragraph are capitalizable along with depreciation of machinery and equipment used directly in the construction of PP&E and inventory

used directly in the construction or installation of PP&E. All general and administrative and overhead costs should also be charged to expense and not capitalized as a cost of PP&E.

4. *In-service stage*

This stage begins when a PP&E asset is substantially complete and ready for its intended use. All costs incurred in this stage are charged to expense except for costs relating to replacement of existing components of a PP&E asset or acquisition of additional components. The principles outlined under the acquisition-or-construction stage are used to determine what costs of the replacements or additional components are capitalizable. Accordingly, all costs of repairs and maintenance are charged to expense, because they cannot be considered replacements or additional components. In conjunction with the replacement of a component of PP&E, an estimate of the remaining net book value of that replaced component should be charged to expense in the period of replacement.

5. *Planned major maintenance activities*

The ED prohibited the following accounting methods for planned major maintenance activities:

- Accrual of a liability before incurring the costs for a planned major maintenance activity
- Deferral and amortization of the cost of a planned major maintenance activity
- Current recognition of additional depreciation to cover future costs of a planned major maintenance activity

6. *Component accounting*

A *component* of a PP&E asset is defined as a tangible part or portion that can be separately identified as an asset, and it is expected to provide economic benefit for more than one year. The ED provided that if a component has an expected useful life that differs from the expected useful life of the PP&E asset to which it relates, the cost of the component should be accounted for separately and depreciated over its separate expected useful life.

7. *Current practice*

Over 400 comment letters were received by AcSEC in response to this proposed SOP. The ED would have made the following major changes in existing practice:

- The capitalization criteria would have prohibited capitalization of indirect costs, overhead, and general and administrative costs, which many entities capitalize currently as a part of their PP&E cost.
- Many entities currently use the methods prohibited under the section titled "Planned Major Maintenance Activities" to account for plant turnarounds and other major maintenance activities.
- Requirements to use component accounting would have effectively prohibited entities from using group and composite methods of accounting for depreciation.

Since the withdrawal of this ED, the FASB has not taken action in providing guidance on these issues.

21.2 COST

Property, plant, and equipment usually are recorded at *cost*, defined as the amount of consideration paid or incurred to acquire or construct an asset. Cost consists of several elements. Welsch and Zlatkovich explain:

The capitalizable costs include the invoice price (less discounts), plus other costs such as sales tax, insurance during transit, freight, duties, ownership searching, ownership registration, installation, and break-in costs.[1]

(a) DETERMINING COST   Generally, three principles are followed for determining the cost of an asset:

1. An asset acquired by exchanging cash or other assets is recorded at cost—that is, at the amount of cash disbursed or the fair value of other assets distributed.
2. An asset acquired by incurring liabilities is recorded at cost—that is, at the present value of the future amounts to be paid.
3. An asset acquired by issuing shares of stock of the acquiring corporation is recorded at the fair value of the asset—that is, shares of stock issued are recorded at the fair value of the consideration received for the stock. That fair value is considered cost.

(i) Acquisition by Exchange   Property, plant, and equipment may be acquired by exchange, as well as by purchase. In that case, the applicable accounting requirements are set forth in Accounting Principles Board (APB) Opinion No. 29, *Accounting for Nonmonetary Transactions*, which defines an exchange (par. 3c) as "a reciprocal transfer between an enterprise and another entity that results in the enterprise's acquiring assets or services or satisfying liabilities by surrendering other assets or services or incurring other obligations."

After defining nonmonetary assets (par. 3b) to include property, plant, and equipment, Opinion No. 29 further provides (par. 18) the general rule:

> Accounting for nonmonetary transactions should be based on the fair values of the assets (or services) involved. . . . Thus, the cost of a nonmonetary asset acquired in exchange for another nonmonetary asset is the fair value of the asset surrendered to obtain it, and a gain or loss should be recognized on the exchange. The fair value of the asset received should be used to measure the cost if it is more clearly evident than the fair value of the asset surrendered.

However, the Opinion recognizes (par. 21) an exception to its general rule if an exchange of nonmonetary assets "is not essentially the culmination of an earning process." In that case, the accounting "should be based on the recorded amount (after reduction, if appropriate, for an indicated impairment of value) of the nonmonetary asset relinquished."

Among the exchanges of nonmonetary assets that do not culminate the earning process, the Opinion includes (par. 21b) "an exchange of a productive asset [defined to include property, plant, and equipment] not held for sale in the ordinary course of business for a similar productive asset or an equivalent interest in the same or similar productive asset."

However, the rule about basing exchanges of productive (nonmonetary) assets on recorded amounts has its own exception if the exchange includes monetary consideration. In that case, the Opinion (par. 22) states:

> The Board believes that the recipient of the monetary consideration has realized gain on the exchange to the extent that the amount of the monetary receipt exceeds a proportionate share of the recorded amount of the asset surrendered.

---

1.   Glenn A. Welsch and Charles T. Zlatkovich, *Intermediate Accounting, Eighth Edition* (Homewood, IL: Irwin, 1989).

The portion of the cost applicable to the realized amount should be based on the ratio of the monetary consideration to the total consideration received (monetary consideration plus the estimated fair value of the nonmonetary asset received) or, if more clearly evident, the fair value of the nonmonetary asset transferred. The Board further believes that the entity paying the monetary consideration should not recognize any gain on [an exchange not culminating the earning process] but should record the asset received at the amount of the monetary consideration paid plus the recorded amount of the nonmonetary asset surrendered. If a loss is indicated by the terms of [an exchange not culminating the earning process], the entire indicated loss on the exchange should be recognized.

The Financial Accounting Standards Board (FASB)'s Emerging Issues Task Force (EITF) later reached a consensus (EITF Issue No. 86-29) that an exchange of nonmonetary assets should be considered a monetary (rather than nonmonetary) transaction if monetary consideration is significant, and agreed that *significant* should be defined as at least 25 percent of the fair value of the exchange.

(ii) Acquisition by Issuing Debt   If property, plant, and equipment are acquired in exchange for payables or other contractual obligations to pay money (referred to collectively as *notes*), APB Opinion No. 21, *Interest on Receivables and Payables* (par. 12), states:

There should be a general presumption that the rate of interest stipulated by the parties to the transaction represents fair and adequate compensation to the supplier for the use of the related funds.

However, the Opinion continues:

That presumption . . . must not permit the form of the transaction to prevail over its economic substance and thus would not apply if (1) interest is not stated, or (2) the stated interest rate is unreasonable . . . or (3) the stated face amount of the note is materially different from the current cash sales price for the same or similar items or from the market value of the note at the date of the transaction.

In any of these circumstances, both the assets acquired and the note should be recorded at the fair value of the assets or at the market value of the note, whichever can be more clearly determined. If the amount recorded is not the same as the face value of the note, the difference is a discount or premium, which should be accounted for as interest over the life of the note. If there is no established price for the assets acquired and no evidence of the market value of the note, the amount recorded should be determined by discounting all future payments on the note using an imputed rate of interest.

In selecting the imputed rate of interest to be used, APB Opinion No. 21 (par. 14) states that consideration should be given to:

(a) An approximation of the prevailing market rates for the source of credit that would provide a market for sale or assignment of the note; (b) the prime or higher rate for notes which are discounted with banks, giving due weight to the credit standing of the maker; (c) published market rates for similar quality bonds; (d) current rates for debentures with substantially identical terms and risks that are traded in open markets; and (e) the current rate charged by investors for first or second mortgage loans on similar property.

(iii) Acquisition by Issuing Stock   Assets acquired by issuing shares of stock should be recorded at either the fair value of the shares issued or the fair value of the property acquired, whichever is more clearly evident.

Smith and Skousen further explain:

> When securities do not have an established market value, appraisal of the acquired assets by an independent authority may be required to arrive at an objective determination of their fair market value. If satisfactory market values cannot be obtained for either securities issued or the assets acquired, values may have to be established by the board of directors for accounting purposes. The source of the valuation should be disclosed on the balance sheet.[2]

(iv) Mixed Acquisition for Lump Sum   Several assets may be acquired for a lump-sum payment. This type of acquisition is often called a *basket purchase*. It is essential to allocate the joint cost carefully, because the assets may include both depreciable and nondepreciable assets, or the depreciable assets may be depreciated at different rates.

Welsch and Zlatkovich discuss the methods of allocating joint costs:

> The allocation of the purchase price should be based on some realistic indicator of the relative values of the several assets involved, such as current appraised values, tax assessment, cost savings, or the present value of estimated future earnings.[3]

(v) Donated Assets   Property, plant, and equipment may be donated to an entity. The accounting for such donations is addressed by Statement of Financial Accounting Standards (SFAS) No. 116, *Accounting for Contributions Received and Contributions Made.* Paragraph 8 of SFAS No. 116 concludes that donated property, plant, and equipment should be measured at fair value.

Paragraph 19 provides guidance for determining the fair value of donated assets and indicates that quoted market prices, if available, are the best evidence of the fair value. It further indicates that if quoted market prices are not available, fair value may be estimated based on quoted market prices for similar assets, independent appraisals, or valuation techniques, such as the present value of estimated cash flows.

(b) OVERHEAD ON SELF-CONSTRUCTED ASSETS   Companies often construct their own buildings and equipment. Materials and labor directly identifiable with the construction are part of its cost.

As to whether overhead should be included in the cost of construction, Lamden, Gerboth, and McRae suggest:

> In the absence of compelling evidence to the contrary, overhead costs considered to have "discernible future benefits" for the purpose of determining the cost of inventory should be presumed to have "discernible future benefits" for the purpose of determining the cost of a self-constructed depreciable asset.[4]

---

2.   Jay M. Smith and K. Fred Skousen, *Intermediate Accounting, Comprehensive Volume, Ninth Edition* (Cincinnati: Southwestern Publishing, 1987).

3.   Welch and Zlatkovich.

4.   Charles Lamden, Dale L. Gerboth, and Thomas McRae, "Accounting for Depreciable Assets," *Accounting Research Monograph,* No. 1 (New York: AICPA, 1975).

Mosich and Larsen agree and go on to discuss two alternative views as to what overhead should be included:

Allocate Only Incremental Overhead Costs to the Self-Constructed Asset. This approach may be defended on the grounds that incremental overhead costs represent the relevant cost that management considered in making the decision to construct the asset. Fixed overhead costs, it is argued, are period costs. Because they would have been incurred in any case, there is no relationship between the fixed overhead costs and the self-constructed project. This approach has been widely used in practice because it does not distort the cost of normal operations.

Allocate a Portion of All Overhead Costs to the Self-Constructed Asset. The argument for this approach is that the proper function of cost allocation is to relate all costs incurred in an accounting period to the output of that period. If an enterprise is able to construct an asset and still carry on its regular activities, it has benefited by putting to use some of its idle capacity, and this fact should be reflected in larger income. To charge the entire overhead to only a portion of the productive activity is to disregard facts and to understate the cost of the self-constructed asset. This line of reasoning has considerable merit.[5]

(c) INTEREST CAPITALIZATION   SFAS No. 34, *Capitalization of Interest Cost* (par. 6), states:

The historical cost of acquiring an asset includes the costs necessarily incurred to bring it to the condition and location necessary for its intended use. If an asset requires a period of time in which to carry out the activities necessary to bring it to that condition and location, the interest cost incurred during that period as a result of expenditures for the asset is a part of the historical cost of acquiring the asset.

Paragraph 9 describes the assets that qualify for interest capitalization:

- Assets that are constructed or otherwise produced for an enterprise's own use (including assets constructed or produced for the enterprise by others for which deposits or progress payments have been made)
- Assets intended for sale or lease that are constructed or otherwise produced as discrete projects (e.g., ships or real estate developments)

The amount of interest capitalized is computed by applying an interest rate to the average amount of accumulated expenditures for the asset during the period. To the extent that specific borrowings are associated with the asset, the interest rate on those borrowings may be used. Otherwise, the interest rate should be the weighted average rate applicable to other borrowings outstanding during the period. In no event should the total interest capitalized exceed total interest costs incurred for the period. Imputing interest costs on equity is not permitted.

---

5.   A. N. Mosich and John E. Larsen, *Intermediate Accounting, Sixth Edition* (New York: McGraw-Hill, 1986).

Descriptions of capitalized interest are often seen in footnotes, such as the following example from 1989 financial statements:

Delta Air Lines, Inc.

Notes to Consolidated Financial Statements

Note 1. Summary of Significant Accounting Policies

Interest Capitalized—Interest attributable to funds used to finance the acquisition of new aircraft and construction of major ground facilities is capitalized as an additional cost of the related asset. Interest is capitalized at the Company's average interest rate on long-term debt or, where applicable, the interest rate related to specific borrowings. Capitalization of interest ceases when the property or equipment is placed in service.

(d) COST OF LAND   Determining the cost of land presents particular problems, as described by Pyle and Larson:

When land is purchased for a building site, its cost includes the amount paid for the land plus real estate commissions. It also includes escrow and legal fees, fees for examining and insuring the title, and any accrued property taxes paid by the purchaser, as well as expenditures for surveying, clearing, grading, draining, and landscaping. All are part of the cost of the land. Furthermore, any assessments incurred at the time of purchase or later for such things as the installation of streets, sewers, and sidewalks should be debited to the Land account because they add a more or less permanent value to the land.[6]

Excavation of land for building purposes, however, is chargeable to buildings rather than to land.

See Chapter 30 for a discussion of the accounting for land acquired as part of a real estate operation.

(i) Purchase Options   If a company acquires an option to purchase land and later exercises that option, the cost of the option generally becomes part of the cost of the land. Even if an option lapses without being exercised, its cost can be capitalized if the option is one of a series of options acquired as part of an integrated plan to acquire a site. In that case, if any one of the options is exercised, the cost of all may be capitalized as part of the cost of the site.

(ii) Interest   SFAS No. 34 (par. 11) describes the proper accounting for interest cost related to land:

Land that is not undergoing activities necessary to get it ready for its intended use is not [an asset qualifying for interest capitalization]. If activities are undertaken for the purpose of developing land for a particular use, the expenditures to acquire the land qualify for interest capitalization while those activities are in progress. The interest cost capitalized on those expenditures is a cost of acquiring the asset that results from those activities. If the resulting asset is a structure,

6.   William W. Pyle and Kermit D. Larson, *Fundamental Accounting Principles, Tenth Edition* (Homewood, IL: Irwin, 1984).

such as a plant or a shopping center, interest capitalized on the land expenditures is part of the acquisition cost of the structure. If the resulting asset is developed land, such as land that is to be sold as developed lots, interest capitalized on the land expenditures is part of the acquisition cost of the developed land.

(iii) Other Carrying Charges   SFAS No. 67, *Accounting for Costs and Initial Rental Operations of Real Estate Projects* (par. 6), states:

> Costs incurred on real estate for property taxes and insurance shall be capitalized as property cost only during periods in which activities necessary to get the property ready for its intended use are in progress. Costs incurred for such items after the property is substantially complete and ready for its intended use shall be charged to expense as incurred.

Even though the scope of the Statement excludes "real estate developed by an enterprise for use in its own operations, other than for sale or rental," this guidance is followed in capitalizing carrying charges generally.

(e) COST OF ASSETS HELD FOR RESEARCH AND DEVELOPMENT ACTIVITIES

Although SFAS No. 2, *Accounting for Research and Development Costs* (par. 12), generally requires that research and development costs be charged to expense when incurred, it makes an exception (par. 11a) for "the costs of materials (whether from the enterprise's normal inventory or acquired specially for research and development activities) and equipment or facilities that are acquired or constructed for research and development activities and that have alternate future uses (in research and development projects or otherwise)." These costs, the Statement says, "shall be capitalized as tangible assets when acquired or constructed."

21.3   IMPAIRMENT OF VALUE

(a) AUTHORITATIVE PRONOUNCEMENTS

SFAS No. 144, *Accounting for the Impairment or Disposal of Long-Lived Assets*, prescribes the accounting for the impairment of long-lived assets, including property, plant, and equipment. The SFAS applies to property, plant, and equipment that is "held and used" and to property, plant, and equipment that is held for disposal (referred to in the Statement as *assets to be disposed of*).

(b) ASSETS TO BE HELD AND USED

SFAS No. 144 requires the following three-step approach for recognizing and measuring the impairment of assets to be held and used:

1. Consider whether indicators of impairment of property, plant, and equipment are present.
2. If indicators of impairment are present, determine whether the sum of the estimated undiscounted future cash flows attributable to the assets in question is less than their carrying amounts.
3. If less, recognize an impairment loss based on the excess of the carrying amount of the assets over their fair values.

(i) Recognition   SFAS No. 144 requires that property, plant, and equipment that are used in operations be reviewed for impairment whenever events or changes in circumstances indicate that the carrying amount of the assets might not be recoverable—that is, information indicates

that an impairment might exist. Accordingly, companies do not need to perform a periodic assessment of assets for impairment in the absence of such information. Instead, companies would assess the need for an impairment write-down only if an indicator of impairment is present. The SFAS lists the following examples of events or changes in circumstances that may indicate to management that an impairment exists:

- A significant decrease in the market value of an asset
- A significant adverse change in the extent or manner in which an asset is used or in its physical condition
- A significant adverse change in legal factors or in the business climate that affects the value of an asset or an adverse action or assessment by a regulator
- An accumulation of costs significantly in excess of the amount originally expected to acquire or construct an asset
- A current period operating or cash flow loss combined with a history of operating or cash flow losses or a projection or forecast that demonstrates continuing losses associated with an income-producing asset
- A current expectation that an asset will be sold before the end of its previously estimated useful life

The preceding list is not all-inclusive, and there may be other events or changes in circumstances, including circumstances that are peculiar to a company's business or industry, indicating that the carrying amount of a group of assets might not be recoverable and thus impaired. If indicators of impairment are present, companies must then disaggregate the assets by grouping them at the lowest level for which there are identifiable cash flows that are largely independent of the cash flows of other groups of assets. Then future cash flows expected to be generated from the use of those assets and their eventual disposal must be estimated. That estimate is comprised of the future cash inflows expected to be generated by the assets less the future cash outflows expected to be necessary to obtain those inflows. If the estimated undiscounted cash flows are less than the carrying amount of the assets, an impairment exists and an impairment loss must be calculated and recognized.

The FASB recognized that certain long-lived assets could not be readily identified with specific cash flows (e.g., a corporate headquarters building and certain property and equipment of not-for-profit organizations). In those situations, the assets should be evaluated for impairment at an entity-wide level. If management estimates that the entity as a whole will generate cash flows sufficient to recover the carrying amount of all assets used in its operations, including its corporate headquarters building, no impairment loss would be recognized.

The SFAS No. 144 provides little guidance for estimating future cash flows, even though the accounting consequences of small changes in those estimates could be significant. Accordingly, estimating future undiscounted cash flows requires a great deal of judgment. Companies must make their best estimate based on reasonable and supportable assumptions and projections that are applied on a consistent basis. SFAS No. 144 indicates that all available evidence should be considered in developing the cash flow estimates, and the weight given that evidence should be commensurate with the extent to which the evidence can be verified objectively.

(ii) Measurement   Once it is determined that an impairment exists, an impairment loss is calculated based on the excess of the carrying amount of the asset over the asset's *fair value.*

In September 2006, the FASB issued FASB Statement of Financial Accounting Standards (SFAS) No. 157, *Fair Value Measurements.* FAS 157 defines fair value, establishes a framework for measuring fair value in generally accepted accounting principles (GAAP), and expands disclosure about fair value measurements. The effective date of SFAS No. 157 is for financial statements of fiscal years beginning after November 15, 2007. FAS 157 defines *fair value* as "the price that would be received to sell an asset or paid to transfer a liability in an orderly transaction between market participants at the measurement date." FAS 157 changes to current practice related to the definition of fair value, the methods used to measure fair value, and expands the disclosures about fair value measurements.

FAS 157 clarifies that the exchange price is the price in an orderly transaction between market participants to sell the asset or transfer the liability in the market in which the reporting entity would transact for the asset or liability, that is, the principal or most advantageous market for the asset or liability. The transaction to sell the asset or transfer the liability is a hypothetical transaction at the measurement date, considered from the perspective of a market participant that holds the asset or owes the liability. Therefore, the definition focuses on the price that would be received to sell the asset or paid to transfer the liability (an exit price), not the price that would be paid to acquire the asset or received to assume the liability (an entry price).

Once management determines that an asset (or a group of assets) is impaired and the asset is written down to fair value, the reduced carrying amount represents the new cost basis of the asset. As a result, subsequent depreciation of the asset is based on the revised carrying amount, and companies are prohibited from reversing the impairment loss should facts and circumstances change or conditions improve in the future.

(c) ASSETS TO BE DISPOSED OF   SFAS No. 144 indicates that assets to be disposed of other than by sale (e.g., abandonment, exchange for another long-lived asset) shall continue to be classified as held and used until they are disposed of. An asset or asset group to be disposed of by sale should be classified as held for sale during the period in which all of the following criteria are met:

- Management commits to a plan of disposal.
- The asset is available for immediate sale.
- An active program to locate a buyer has been initiated.
- Sale of the asset within one year is probable.
- The asset is being actively marketed for sale at a reasonable price.
- Actions required to complete the plan indicate that it is unlikely the plan will be significantly modified or withdrawn.

If at any time while an asset is classified as held for sale any of the above criteria are no longer met or the entity's plans change, the asset should be reclassified to the held and used category. The asset should be reclassified at the lower of the original carrying amount immediately before the asset is transferred to held for sale (adjusted for any depreciation expense that would have been recognized had the asset been continuously classified as held and used) or fair value at the date of the change in status. An asset classified as held for sale should be measured at the lower of its carrying amount or fair value less incremental direct costs of sale. An asset classified as held for sale should not be depreciated. SFAS No. 144 requires subsequent revisions to the carrying amount of assets classified as held for sale if the estimate of fair value less cost to sale changes during the holding period. After an initial write-down of an asset to fair value less cost to sell, the carrying amount can be increased or decreased depending on changes in the fair value less cost to sell of the asset. However, an increase in carrying value cannot exceed the carrying amount of the asset immediately before its classification into the held for sale category.

SFAS No. 144 also supersedes APB Opinion No. 30 with respect to discontinued operations. The Statement indicates that the results of operations relating to assets to be disposed of comprising a component of an entity should be classified as discontinued operations if both of the following conditions are met:

1. The operations and cash flows of the component have been eliminated or will be eliminated from the ongoing operations of the entity as a result of the disposal.
2. The entity will not have any continuing involvement in the operations of the component after the disposal.

A *component* of an entity is defined as operations and cash flows that can be clearly distinguished from the rest of the entity both operationally and for financial reporting purposes. The definition of component of an entity under SFAS No. 144 is much broader than the APB Opinion No. 30 definition of a segment of a business. Accordingly, many more discontinued operations will be reported under SFAS No. 144 than previously. For example, if a real estate entity disposes of an individual property, that property would likely qualify as a component of an entity under SFAS No. 144 but would generally not have qualified as a disposal of a segment of a business under APB Opinion No. 30.

21.4 EXPENDITURES DURING OWNERSHIP

(a) DISTINGUISHING CAPITAL EXPENDITURES FROM OPERATING EXPENDITURES
After property, plant, and equipment have been acquired, additional expenditures are incurred to keep the assets in satisfactory operating condition. Certain of these expenditures—capital expenditures—are added to the asset's cost. The remainder—operating expenditures (sometimes called *revenue expenditures*)—are charged to expense.

Kohler defines a *capital expenditure* in the following two ways:

1. An expenditure intended to benefit future periods, in contrast to a revenue expenditure, which benefits a current period; an addition to a capital asset. The term is generally restricted to expenditures that add fixed-asset units or that have the effect of increasing the capacity, efficiency, life span, or economy of operation of an existing fixed asset.
2. Hence, any expenditure benefiting a future period.[7]

Although the distinction is important, immaterial capital expenditures can be charged to expense.

Expenditures during ownership fall into four categories: (1) maintenance and repairs; (2) replacements, improvements, and additions; (3) rehabilitation; (4) rearrangement and reinstallation.

---

7. Eric Louis Kohler, *Kohler's Dictionary for Accountants, Sixth Edition* (Englewood Cliffs, NJ: Prentice-Hall, 1983).

(b) MAINTENANCE AND REPAIRS   The terms *maintenance* and *repairs* generally are used interchangeably. However, Kohler defines them separately, and his definitions are useful in identifying expenditures that should be accounted for as maintenance and repairs. He defines *maintenance* as follows:

> The keeping of property in operable condition; also, the expense involved. Maintenance costs include outlays for (a) labor and supplies; (b) the replacement of any part that constitutes less than a retirement unit; and (c) major overhauls the items of which may involve elements of the first two classes. Items falling under (a) and (b) are always regarded as operating costs, chargeable to current expense directly or through the medium of a maintenance reserve. . . . Costs under (c) are similarly treated unless they include the replacement of a retirement unit the outlay for which is normally capitalized.[8]

He defines *repairs* (p. 428) as follows:

> The restoration of a capital asset to its full productive capacity, or a contribution thereto, after damage, accident, or prolonged use, without increase in the asset's previously estimated service life or productive capacity. The term includes maintenance primarily "preventive" in character, and capitalizable extraordinary repairs.

(i) Accounting Alternatives   As Kohler states, except for extraordinary repairs (or major overhauls), discussed below, maintenance and repairs expenditures are accounted for in two ways:

1.   Charge to expense when the cost is incurred
2.   Charge to a maintenance allowance account[9]

> *Charge to Expense When the Cost Is Incurred.* Since ordinary maintenance and repairs expenditures are regarded as operating costs, they are usually charged directly to expense when incurred.
> *Charge to a Maintenance Allowance Account.* The charge to expense may be accomplished through an allowance account. In some cases, the purpose of an allowance account is equalize monthly repair costs within a year. Total repair costs are estimated at the beginning of the year, and the total is spread evenly throughout the year. The difference between the estimated and actual amounts at the end of the year is usually spread retroactively over all months of the year rather than being absorbed entirely by the last month. In the balance sheet, this allowance account may be treated as a reduction of the related asset account.

This latter approach is supported by APB Opinion No. 28, *Interim Financial Reporting* (par. 16a):

> When a cost that is expensed for annual reporting purposes clearly benefits two or more interim periods (e.g., annual major repairs), each interim period should be charged for an appropriate portion of the annual cost by the use of accruals or deferrals.

In other cases, the purpose of a maintenance allowance account is to charge the costs of major repairs over the entire period benefited, which may be longer than one year. When

---

8.   Id., p. 315.
9.   Id., p. 428.

airlines acquire new aircraft, for example, they begin immediately to accrue the cost of the first engine overhaul, which usually is scheduled for more than one year hence. As illustrated by the following example from 1987 financial statements, the accrual charges are credited to a maintenance allowance account, which is then charged for cost of the overhaul.

Stateswest Airlines, Inc. and Subsidiaries

Notes to Consolidated Financial Statements

Summary of Significant Accounting Policies

Engine Overhaul Reserve. For all the leased aircraft, the Company accrues maintenance expense, on the basis of hours flown, for the estimated cost of engine overhauls.

(ii) Extraordinary Repairs   Welsch, Anthony, and Short define *extraordinary repairs* as repairs that

> . . . occur infrequently, involve relatively large amounts of money, and tend to increase the economic usefulness of the asset in the future because of either greater efficiency or longer life, or both. They are represented by major overhauls, complete reconditioning, and major replacements and betterments.[10]

Because expenditures for extraordinary repairs increase the future economic usefulness of an asset, they benefit future periods and are therefore capital expenditures. Ordinarily, they are added to the related asset account, as illustrated in the following example from 1987 financial statements.

Air Midwest, Inc. and Subsidiaries

Notes to Consolidated Financial Statements

Note 1. Summary of Significant Accounting Policies

d. Maintenance and Repairs

Major renewals and betterments are capitalized and depreciated over the remaining useful life of the asset.

Some authorities recommend that the expenditures for extraordinary repairs be charged against the accumulated depreciation account. The rationale for charging accumulated depreciation is provided by Smith and Skousen:

> Often it is not possible to identify the cost related to a specific part of an asset. In these instances, by debiting accumulated depreciation, the undepreciated book value is increased without creating a build-up of the gross asset values.[11]

Other authorities argue against debiting accumulated depreciation for extraordinary repairs because the accumulated depreciation on the asset may be less than the cost of the repairs and because the practice allows the original cost of any parts replaced to remain in the asset account.

---

10.   Glenn A. Welsch, Robert N. Anthony, and Daniel G. Short, *Fundamentals of Financial Accounting* (Homewood, IL: Irwin, 1984).

11.   Smith and Skousen.

(c) Replacements, Improvements, and Additions   Replacements, improvements, and additions are related concepts. Kohler defines a *replacement* as "the substitution of one fixed asset for another, particularly of a new asset for an old, or of a new part for an old part." He defines an *improvement* (which he calls a *betterment*) as "an expenditure having the effect of extending the useful life of an existing fixed asset, increasing its normal rate of output, lowering its operating cost, increasing rather than merely maintaining efficiency or otherwise adding to the worth of benefits it can yield."[12] Improvements ordinarily do not increase the physical size of the productive facility. Such an increase is an *addition*.

The distinctions among *replacement, improvement,* and *addition* notwithstanding, the accounting for all three is substantially the same. Expenditures for them are capital expenditures, that is, additions to property, plant, and equipment. (In practice, immaterial amounts are often charged to expense.) The cost of existing assets that are replaced, together with their related accumulated depreciation accounts, is eliminated from the accounts.

(d) Rehabilitation   Expenditures to rehabilitate buildings or equipment purchased in a rundown condition with the intention of rehabilitating them should be capitalized. Normally the acquisition price of a rundown asset is less than that of a comparable new asset, and the rehabilitation expenditures benefit future periods. Capitalization of the expenditures is therefore appropriate. However, the total capitalized cost of the asset should not exceed the amount recoverable through operations.

When rehabilitation takes place over an extended period, care should be taken to distinguish between the cost of rehabilitation and the cost of maintenance.

(e) Rearrangement and Reinstallation   Kieso and Weygandt describe *rearrangement and reinstallation costs* and the accounting for them:

> Rearrangement and reinstallation costs, which are expenditures intended to benefit future periods, are different from additions, replacements and improvements. An example is the rearrangement and reinstallation of a group of machines to facilitate future production. If the original installation cost and the accumulated depreciation taken to date can be determined or estimated, the rearrangement and reinstallation cost can be handled as a replacement. If not, which is generally the case, the new costs if material in amount should be capitalized as an asset to be amortized over those future periods expected to benefit. If these costs are not material, if they cannot be separated from other operating expenses, or if their future benefit is questionable, they instead should be expensed in the period in which they are incurred.[13]

(f) Asbestos Removal or Containment   Removal or containment of asbestos is regulated and required by various federal, state, and local laws. The diversity of practice in capitalizing or expensing the cost of asbestos removal or containment resulted in asbestos removal being considered by the EITF. Issue No. 89-13 asked "whether the costs incurred to treat asbestos when a property with a known asbestos problem is acquired should be capitalized or charged

12.   Kohler.
13.   Donald E. Kieso and Jerry J. Weygandt, *Intermediate Accounting, Fifth Edition* (New York: John Wiley & Sons, 1986).

to expense" and "whether the costs incurred to treat asbestos in an existing property should be capitalized or charged to expense."

The EITF reached a conclusion that the costs incurred to treat asbestos within a reasonable time period after a property with a known asbestos problem is acquired should be capitalized as part of the cost of the acquired property subject to an impairment test for that property. The consensus on existing property was not as conclusive and stated the costs "may be capitalized as a betterment subject to an impairment test for that property."

The EITF also reached a consensus that when costs are incurred in anticipation of a sale of property, they should be deferred and recognized in the period of the sale to the extent that those costs can be recovered from the estimated sales price.

The Standards Executive Committee (SEC) observer at the EITF meeting noted that regardless of whether asbestos treatment costs are capitalized or charged to expense, SEC registrants should disclose significant exposure for asbestos treatment costs in "Management's Discussion and Analysis."

The EITF in Issue No. 90-8 affirmed the Issue No. 89-13 consensus but did not provide further guidance on capitalizing or charging to expense the costs incurred on existing properties. In practice, there continues to be wide diversity of the types of costs capitalized, if any, and the accrual of costs to remove or contain asbestos in existing properties.

(g) Costs to Treat Environmental Contamination Costs to remove, contain, neutralize, or prevent existing or future environmental contamination may be incurred voluntarily or as required by federal, state, and local laws. In Issue No. 90-8, the EITF considered whether environmental contamination treatment costs should be capitalized or charged to expense.

The EITF reached a consensus that, in general, environmental contamination treatment costs should be charged to expense unless the costs are recoverable and meet one of the following three criteria:

1. The costs extend the life, increase the capacity, or improve the safety or efficiency of property owned by the company. For purposes of this criterion, the condition of that property after the costs are incurred must be improved as compared with the condition of that property when originally constructed or acquired, if later.
2. The costs mitigate or prevent environmental contamination that has yet to occur and that otherwise may result from future operations or activities. In addition, the costs improve the property compared with its condition when constructed or acquired, if later.
3. The costs are incurred in preparing for sale property currently held for sale.

Costs to remediate environmental contamination that do not meet one of the criteria above should be expensed under the provisions of the AICPA's SOP 96-1, *Environmental Remediation Liabilities*. SOP 96-1 provides authoritative guidance on the recognition, measurement, display, and disclosure of environmental remediation liabilities. The AICPA issued SOP 96-1 to improve and narrow the manner in which existing authoritative accounting literature, principally SFAS No. 5, *Accounting for Contingencies*, is applied in recognizing, measuring, and disclosing environmental liabilities.

SFAS No. 5 generally requires loss contingencies to be accrued when they are both probable and estimable. According to SOP 96-1, the probability criterion of SFAS No. 5 is met for environmental liabilities if both of the following conditions have occurred on or before the date the financial statements are issued:

- Litigation, a claim, or an assessment has been asserted, or is probable of being asserted.
- It is probable that the outcome of such litigation, claim, or assessment will be unfavorable.

The AICPA concluded that there is a presumption that the outcome will be unfavorable if litigation, a claim, or an assessment has been asserted, or is probable of assertion, and if the entity is associated with the site. Assuming that both of the above conditions are met, a company would need to accrue at least the minimum amount that can reasonably be estimated as an environmental remediation liability.

Once a company has determined that it is probable that a liability has been incurred, the entity should estimate the remediation liability based on available information. In estimating its allocable share of costs, a company should include incremental direct costs of the remediation effort and postremediation monitoring costs that are expected to be incurred after the remediation is complete. An entity also should include in its estimate costs of compensation and related benefit costs for employees who are expected to devote a significant amount of their time directly to the remediation effort. The accrual of expected legal defense costs related to remediation is not required.

In cases in which joint and several liability exists and the company is one of several parties responsible for remediation, which often will be the case, the entity is required to estimate the percentage of the liability that it will be allocated. The entity also must assess the likelihood that each of the other parties will pay their allocable share of the remediation liability. An entity would accrue its estimated share of amounts related to the site that will not be paid by other parties or the government.

SOP 96-1 provides that discounting environmental liabilities is permitted, but not required, only if the aggregate amount of the obligation and the amount and timing of the cash payments are fixed or reliably determinable. Because of the nature of the remediation process and the inherent subjectivity involved in estimating remediation liabilities, most companies will find it difficult to meet the criteria for discounting.

An asset relating to recoveries can be recognized only when realization of the claim for recovery is deemed probable. If a claim for recovery is the subject of litigation, a rebuttable presumption exists that realization of the claim is not probable. An environmental liability should be evaluated independently from any potential claim for recovery. SOP 96-1 requires that probable recoveries be recorded at fair value. However, discounting a recovery claim is not required in determining the value of the recovery when the related liability is not discounted and the timing of the recovery is dependent on the timing of the payment of the liability.

The EITF provided examples of applying the consensus in Issue No. 90-8.

21.5   DISPOSALS

Asset disposals may be voluntary, through retirement, sale, or trade-in, or involuntary, from fire, storm, flood, or other casualty. In general, these terms have the same meaning for accounting purposes as they do in ordinary discourse. The one exception is *retirement*, which for accounting purposes means the removal of an asset from service, whether or not the asset is removed physically. This is clear from Kohler's (1983) definition of *retirement* as "the removal of a fixed asset from service, following its sale or the end of its productive life, accompanied by the necessary adjustment of fixed asset and depreciation-reserve accounts."

(a) RETIREMENTS, SALES, AND TRADE-INS Davidson, Stickney, and Weil describe the accounting for retirements, which applies also to assets that are sold or traded in:

> When an asset is retired from service, the cost of the asset and the related amount of accumulated depreciation must be removed from the books. As part of this entry, the amount received from the sale or trade-in and any difference between that amount and book value must be recorded. The difference between the proceeds received on retirement and book value is a gain (if positive) or a loss (if negative).[14]

As discussed in the following, when composite or group rate depreciation is used, no gain or loss on disposal is recognized.

When an asset is traded in, the amount that should in theory be recorded as received from the trade-in is the asset's fair market value (which is not necessarily the amount by which the cash purchase price of the replacement asset is reduced). However, in practice, a reliable market value for the old asset may not be available. In that case, the usual practice is to recognize no gain or loss on the exchange, but to record as the acquisition cost of the replacement asset the net book value of the old asset plus the cash or other consideration paid.

(b) CASUALTIES Casualties, the accidental loss or destruction of assets, can give rise to gain or loss, even when the assets are replaced. The FASB Interpretation No. (FIN) No. 30, *Accounting for Involuntary Conversions of Nonmonetary Assets to Monetary Assets* (par. 2), makes this clear:

> Involuntary conversions of nonmonetary assets to monetary assets are monetary transactions for which gain or loss shall be recognized even though an enterprise reinvests or is obligated to reinvest the monetary assets in replacement nonmonetary assets.

21.6 ASSET RETIREMENT OBLIGATIONS

SFAS No. 143, *Accounting for Asset Retirement Obligations*, was issued in June 2001. This project was undertaken by the FASB because diversity in practice had developed in accounting for the obligations associated with the retirement of long-lived assets. Some entities were accruing the obligations over the life of the related asset either as a liability or a reduction of the carrying amount of the asset while others did not recognize the liability until the asset was retired. The Statement requires that a liability be recorded for legal obligations resulting from the acquisition, construction, or development and normal operations of a long-lived asset.

(a) INITIAL RECOGNITION AND MEASUREMENT If a reasonable estimate of an asset retirement obligation can be made, an entity shall recognize the fair value of the liability in the period in which it is incurred. Fair value is usually defined as the amount at which the liability could be settled in a current transaction between willing parties. (That definition is ambiguous. See Section 1.3(b)(v).) Quoted market prices in active markets are the best evidence of fair value. However, when such prices are not available, fair value should be based on the best available information, including prices for similar liabilities and the results of present value techniques. SFAS No. 143 indicates that if present value techniques are used to estimate

---

14. Sidney Davidson, Clyde P. Stickney, and Roman L. Weil, *Financial Accounting: An Introduction to Concepts, Methods and Uses, Fifth Edition* (Hinsdale, IL: Dryden Press, 1988).

fair value, estimates of future cash flows should be consistent with the expected cash flow approach outlined in Concepts Statement No. 7.

When an asset retirement obligation is initially recognized, the entity should capitalize an asset retirement cost by increasing the carrying amount of the related long-lived asset by the same amount. This cost should be charged to expense over the estimated useful life of the asset. When the asset is tested for impairment under SFAS No. 144, the asset retirement cost should be included in the carrying value tested for impairment.

(b) SUBSEQUENT RECOGNITION AND MEASUREMENT   Subsequent to initial recognition, an entity should recognize period-to-period changes in the asset retirement liability for the passage of time and revisions to either the timing or amount of the original estimate of undiscounted cash flows. Adjustments for the passage of time should use an interest method based on the credit-adjusted risk-free rate at the time of initial recognition of the liability. The adjustment should increase the amount of the liability and be charged to accretion expense. Adjustments relating to revisions in the timing or amounts of cash flows will increase or decrease the asset retirement liability and the related asset.

21.7 DEPRECIATION

Property, plant, and equipment used by a business in the production of goods and services is a depreciable asset. That is, its cost is systematically amortized by charges to goods produced or to operations over the asset's estimated useful service life. That meaning is captured by International Accounting Standards (IAS) No. 4, *Depreciation Accounting*, which defines depreciable assets as "assets that (a) are expected to be used during more than one accounting period, and (b) have a limited useful life, and (c) are held by an enterprise for use in the production or supply of goods and services, for rental to others, or for administrative purposes."

(a) *DEPRECIATION* DEFINED   Despite its widespread use, *depreciation* has no single, universal definition. Economists, engineers, the courts, accountants, and others have definitions that meet their particular needs. Seldom are the definitions identical.

The generally accepted accounting definition is set forth in Accounting Terminology Bulletin No. 1:

> Depreciation accounting is a system of accounting which aims to distribute the cost or other basic value of tangible capital assets, less salvage (if any), over the estimated useful life of the unit (which may be a group of assets) in a systematic and rational manner. It is a process of allocation, not of valuation. Depreciation for the year is the portion of the total charge under such a system that is allocated to the year.

As the definition says, the depreciation accounting is "a process of allocation, not of valuation." That is, its purpose is to allocate the net cost (cost less salvage) of an asset over time, not to state the asset at its current or long-term value.

Depreciation, as accountants use the term, applies only to buildings, machinery, and equipment. It is thus distinguished first from *depletion*, which is a process of allocating the cost of wasting resources, such as mineral deposits, and second from *amortization*, which is a process of allocating the cost of intangible assets.

(b) BASIC FACTORS IN THE COMPUTATION OF DEPRECIATION   Three basic factors enter into the computation of depreciation:

1.   The estimate of the service life (sometimes called the *useful life*) of the asset
2.   The determination of the depreciation base
3.   The choice of a depreciation method

21.8 SERVICE LIFE

(a) SERVICE LIFE AS DISTINGUISHED FROM PHYSICAL LIFE   Depreciation allocates the net cost of an asset over its service life, not its physical life. The *service* life of an asset represents the period of usefulness to its present owner. The *physical* life of an asset represents its total period of usefulness, perhaps to more than one owner. For any given asset, and any given owner, physical and service life may be identical, or service life may be shorter. For example, a company that supplies automobiles to its sales force may replace its automobiles every 50,000 miles. An automobile's physical life is usually longer than 50,000 miles. But to this particular company, the service life of an automobile in their fleet is 50,000 miles, and the company's depreciation policies would allocate the net cost of its automobiles over 50,000 miles.

(b) FACTORS AFFECTING SERVICE LIFE   Service life may be affected by two factors— *physical* or *functional*—as follows:

1.   Physical factors:
   a.   Wear and tear
   b.   Deterioration and decay
   c.   Damage or destruction
2.   Functional factors:
   a.   Inadequacy
   b.   Obsolescence

(i) Physical Factors   Mosich and Larsen discuss physical factors:

> Physical deterioration results largely from wear and tear from use and the forces of nature. These physical forces terminate the usefulness of plant assets by rendering them incapable of performing the services for which they were intended and thus set the maximum limit on economic life.[15]

Wear and tear and deterioration and decay act gradually and are reasonably predictable. They are ordinarily taken into consideration in estimating service life. Damage or destruction, however, usually occurs suddenly, irregularly, infrequently, and unpredictably. Either one is ordinarily not taken into consideration in estimating service life. Its effects are therefore usually not recognized in the depreciation charge but as a charge to expense when the damage or destruction occurs.

(ii) Functional Factors   Asset inadequacy may result from business growth, requiring the company to replace existing assets with larger or more efficient assets. Or assets may become inadequate because of changes in the market, in plant location, in the nature or variety of products manufactured, or in the ownership of the business. For example, a warehouse may be in

---

15.   Mosich and Larsen.

good structural condition, but if more space is needed and cannot be economically provided by adding a wing or a separate building, the warehouse has become inadequate, and its remaining service life to its present owner is ended.

Obsolescence usually arises from events that are more clearly external, such as progress, invention, technological advances, and improvements. For example, the Boeing 707 and the Douglas DC-8 jet aircraft made many propeller-driven airplanes obsolete, at least as to major airlines, because propeller-driven planes were no longer economical in long-range service, compared to more modern and efficient jets.

A distinction should be made between ordinary obsolescence and extraordinary obsolescence. Ordinary obsolescence is due to normal, reasonably predictable technical progress; extraordinary obsolescence arises from unforeseen events that result in an asset being abandoned earlier than expected. For example, computers and related software generally have a short service life span in anticipation of more advanced computers and software releases in the market within a few years.

The American Accounting Association (AAA) publication, "A Statement of Basic Accounting Theory" (1966), states: "Obsolescence, to the extent it can be quantified by equipment replacement studies or similar means, should be recognized explicitly and regularly." Thus ordinary obsolescence, like wear and tear, should be considered in estimating useful life so that it can be recognized in the annual depreciation charge. But extraordinary obsolescence, like damage or destruction, is recognized outside depreciation accounting as a charge when it occurs.

(c) THE EFFECT OF MAINTENANCE   As Welsch and Zlatkovich note, "The useful life of operational assets also is influenced by the repair and maintenance policies of the company."[16] The expected effect of a company's maintenance policy is therefore considered in estimating service lives.

(d) STATISTICAL METHODS OF ESTIMATING SERVICE LIVES   In several industries, notably utilities, estimates of service lives have been based on historical analyses of retirement rates for specific groups of assets, such as telephone or electric wire poles. These analyses have resulted in the development of statistical techniques for predicting retirement rates and service lives. Utilities have used such techniques in defending depreciation practices, replacement needs and policies, and investment valuations for rate-making purposes. Statistical techniques are appropriate for any group of homogeneous assets where estimating individual service lives is not possible or practical (e.g., mattresses and linens in a hotel, overhead and underground cables of telephone companies, and rails and ties for railroads).

Grant and Norton mention two other statistical approaches to determining service lives:

1. *Actuarial methods*, which aim at determining survivor curves and frequency curves for annual retirements, as well as giving estimates of average life. These methods are generally similar to the methods developed by life insurance actuaries for the study of human mortality. They require plant records in sufficient detail so that the age of each unit of plant is known at all times.

2. *Turnover methods*, which aim only at estimating average life. Since turnover methods require only information about additions and retirements, they require less detail in the plant records than do actuarial methods.[17]

---

16.   Welsch and Zlatkovich.
17.   E. Grant and P. Norton, *Depreciation* (New York: Ronald Press, 1955).

(e) SERVICE LIVES OF LEASEHOLD IMPROVEMENTS   Leasehold improvements are depreciated over the shorter of the remaining term of the lease or the expected life of the asset. Lease renewal terms are usually not considered unless renewal is probable.

In February 2005, almost concurrent with the filing of the first wave of SOX Section 404 filings, the SEC clarified that certain accounting principles for leasehold improvements, rent holidays, and landlord/tenant incentives should be followed, despite "industry practice" that had arisen where these principles were not always being adhered to. This clarification forced a spate of restatements and material weakness determinations by some larger retail establishments. The timing of this announcement made it difficult for some companies to remediate the control deficiency in time to avoid reporting a material weakness in internal controls. At the time of this edition, the letter from the SEC Chief Accountant Don Nicolaison could be found at www.sec.gov/info/accountants/staffletters/cpcaf020705.htm.

(f) REVISIONS OF ESTIMATED SERVICE LIVES   Service life estimates should be reviewed periodically and revised as appropriate. The National Association of Accountants (NAA) Statement on Management Accounting Practices No. 7, *Fixed Asset Accounting: The Allocation of Costs*, suggests that reviews of estimates involve operations, management, engineering, and accounting personnel.

A change in the estimated useful lives of depreciable assets should be accounted for as a change in an accounting estimate. As prescribed by APB Opinion No. 20, *Accounting Changes*, the change is recognized in the period of change and in future periods affected. If future periods are affected, the Opinion also requires disclosure of the effect on income before extraordinary items, on net income, and on related per-share amounts of the current period. The following is an example of this disclosure from 2007 financial statements:

EXAMPLE

TANGER PROPERTIES LTD PARTNERSHIP /FORM 10-K (PERIOD END 12/31/07)

CHANGE IN ACCOUNTING ESTIMATE
During the first quarter of 2007, the general partner's Board of Trustees formally approved a plan to reconfigure our center in Foley, Alabama. As a part of this plan, approximately 42,000 square feet was relocated within the property by September 2007. The depreciable useful lives of the buildings demolished were shortened to coincide with their demolition dates throughout the first three quarters of 2007 and the change in estimated useful life was accounted for as a change in accounting estimate. Approximately 28,000 relocated square feet had opened as of December 31, 2007 with the remaining 14,000 square feet expected to open in the next two quarters. Accelerated depreciation recognized related to the reconfiguration reduced income from continuing operations and net income by approximately $6.0 million for the year ended December 31, 2007. The effect on income from continuing operations per diluted unit and net income per diluted unit was a decrease of $.32 per unit for the year ended December 31, 2007.

21.9 DEPRECIATION BASE

The cost to be depreciated, otherwise known as the *depreciation base*, is the total cost of an asset less its estimated net salvage value. When immaterial, net salvage value is commonly ignored.

(a) NET SALVAGE VALUE   *Kohler's Dictionary for Accountants* defines *salvage* as: "Value remaining from a fire, wreck, or other accident or from the retirement or scrapping of an asset."[18] Salvage value may be determined by reference to quoted market prices for similar items or to estimated reproduction costs, reduced by an allowance for usage. Salvage value reduced by the cost to remove the asset is net salvage value.

Net salvage value can be taken into account in either of two ways: directly, by reducing the depreciation base; or indirectly, by adjusting the depreciation rate.

To illustrate the latter, assume an asset with a total cost of $1,000, a service life of 10 years, and an estimated net salvage value of $250. A 7.5 percent rate applied to the cost will yield the same annual depreciation charge as a 10 percent rate applied to cost less estimated net salvage value. This point should be borne in mind in interpreting stated rates of depreciation; the rates may be applied to the asset cost or to cost less net salvage value.

(b) PROPERTY UNDER CONSTRUCTION   Assets are generally not depreciated during construction, which includes any necessary pilot testing or breaking in. Such assets are not yet placed in service, and the purpose of depreciation accounting is to allocate the cost of an asset over its service life.

An exception to the general rule arises when an asset under construction is partially used in an income-producing activity. In that case, the part in use should be depreciated. An example is a building that is partially rented while still under construction.

(c) IDLE AND AUXILIARY EQUIPMENT   NAA Statement on Management Accounting Practices No. 7 recommends that depreciation be continued on idle, reserve, or standby assets. When the period of idleness is expected to be long, the assets should be separately disclosed in the balance sheet; however, depreciation should continue.

EITF Issue No. 84-28 raises the question of how idle facilities or facilities operating significantly below normal operating levels should be depreciated. Some EITF members stated that they were aware of a limited number of cases in which the depreciation method for such assets was changed to one of the usage methods (see below), but none expressed knowledge of cases in which depreciation of the assets was totally suspended. The EITF reached no consensus.

(d) ASSETS TO BE DISPOSED OF   SFAS No. 144 prohibits depreciation from being recorded during the period in which the asset is being held for disposal, even if the asset is still generating revenue.

(e) USED ASSETS   The depreciation base of a used asset is the same as for a new asset, that is, cost less net salvage value. The carrying value of a used asset in the accounts of the previous owner should not be carried over to the accounts of the new owner. See, however, Chapter 22 for the accounting for assets acquired in a business combination.

21.10   DEPRECIATION METHODS

Assets are depreciated by a variety of methods, including the following five:

1. Straight-line method
2. Usage methods:

---

18.   Kohler.

    a. Service-hours method
    b. Productive-output method
3. Decreasing-charge methods:
    a. Sum-of-digits method
    b. Fixed-percentage-of-declining-balance method
    c. Double-declining-balance method
4. Interest methods:
    a. Annuity method
    b. Sinking-fund method
5. Other methods:
    a. Appraisal method
    b. Retirement method
    c. Replacement method
    d. Arbitrary assignment

(a) STRAIGHT-LINE METHOD   This method recognizes equal periodic depreciation charges over the service life of an asset, thereby making depreciation a function solely of time without regard to asset productivity, efficiency, or usage. The periodic depreciation charge is computed by dividing the cost of the asset, less net salvage value, by the service life expressed in months or years:

$$\frac{\text{Cost} - \text{Net salvage value}}{\text{Service life}} = \text{Depreciation charge per period}$$

Assuming an asset cost \$15,000 and has an estimated net salvage value of \$750 (5 percent of cost) and a service life of 10 years, the annual depreciation charge would be \$1,425, calculated as follows:

$$\frac{\$15,000 - \$750}{10 \text{ years}} = \$1,425$$

When the use or productivity of an asset differs significantly over its life, the straight-line method produces what some believe is a distorted allocation of costs. For example, if an asset is more productive during its early life than later, some view an equal amount of depreciation in each year as distorted. Nevertheless, the method is widely used because of its simplicity.

A survey reported by Lamden, Gerboth, and McRae showed that the straight-line method is most frequently used for financial statement purposes by companies with the following five characteristics:

1. Relatively large investments in depreciable assets
2. Relatively high depreciation charges
3. Stock traded on one of the major stock exchanges or in the over-the-counter market
4. Managements with a high level of concern for (a) matching costs with revenues and (b) maintaining comparability with other firms in the industry
5. Managements with a low level of concern for conforming depreciation for financial statement to depreciation for tax purposes[19]

---

19.   Lamden, Gerboth, and McRae.

(b) USAGE METHODS   Two other methods, the service-hours method and the productive-output method, vary the periodic depreciation charge to recognize differences in asset use or productivity.

(i) Service-Hours Method   This method assumes that if an asset is used twice as much in period 1 as in period 2, the depreciation charge should differ accordingly. The depreciation rate is calculated as it is for the straight-line method, except that service life is expressed in terms of hours of use:

$$\frac{\text{Cost} - \text{Net salvage value}}{\text{Service life}} = \text{Rate per hour of use}$$

If an asset cost $15,000 and had an estimated net salvage value of $750 and an estimated service life of 38,000 hours, the calculation would be as follows:

$$\frac{\$15,000 - \$750}{38,00 \text{ hours}} = \$0.375 \text{ per hour of use}$$

If the asset is used 4,000 hours in the first year, the annual depreciation charge would be $1,500 (4,000 hours × $0.375 per hour).

Welsch and Zlatkovich state, "The service hours method usually is appropriate when obsolescence is not a primary factor in depreciation and the economic service potential of the asset is used up primarily by running time."[20]

(ii) Productive-Output Method   This method is essentially the same as the service-hours method, except that service life is expressed in terms of units of production rather than hours of use. If the asset described above had a service life of 95,000 units of production rather than 38,000 hours of use, the depreciation rate would be calculated as follows:

$$\frac{\$15,000 - \$750}{95,00 \text{ units}} = \$0.15 \text{ per unit of product}$$

Depreciation by the productive-output method is illustrated by the following example from 1987 financial statements:

McDermott International, Inc.

Notes to Consolidated Financial Statements

Note 3. Change in Depreciation Method

Effective April 1, 1986, McDermott International changed the method of depreciation for major marine vessels from the straight-line method to a units-of-production method based on the utilization of each vessel. Depreciation expense calculated under the units-of-production method may be less than, equal to, or greater than depreciation expense calculated under the straight-line method in any period. McDermott International employs utilization factors as a key element in the management of marine construction operations and believes the units-of-production method, which recognizes both time and utilization factors, accomplishes a better matching of costs and revenues than the straight-line method. The cumulative effect of the change on prior years at March 31, 1986, of $25,711,000,

---

20.   Welsch and Zlatkovich.

net of income taxes of $17,362,000 ($0.70 per share), is included in the accompanying Consolidated Statement of Income (Loss) and Retained Earnings for the fiscal year ended March 31, 1987. The effect of the change on the fiscal year ended March 31, 1987, was to increase Income from Continuing Operations before Extraordinary Items and Cumulative Effect of Accounting Change and decrease Net Loss $6,556,000 ($0.18 per share). Pro forma amounts showing the effect of applying the units-of-production method of depreciation retroactively, net of related income taxes, are presented in the Consolidated Statement of Income (Loss) and Retained Earnings.

The productive-output method is sometimes used to adjust depreciation calculated by the straight-line method, when asset usage varies from normal. The adjustment may be limited to a specified range, as illustrated in the following example drawn from 1986 financial statements:

Wheeling-Pittsburgh Steel Corporation

Notes to Financial Statements

Note G. Property, Plant, and Equipment

The Corporation utilizes the modified units-of-production method of depreciation which recognizes that the depreciation of steelmaking machinery is related to the physical wear of the equipment as well as a time factor. The modified units-of-production method provides for straight-line depreciation charges modified (adjusted) by the level of production activity. On an annual basis, adjustments may not exceed a range of 60% (minimum) to 110% (maximum) of related straight-line depreciation. The adjustments are based on the ratio of actual production to a predetermined norm. Eighty-five percent of capacity is considered the norm for the Corporation's primary steelmaking facilities; 80% of capacity is considered the norm for finishing facilities. No adjustment is made when the production level is equal to norm. In 1986 depreciation under the modified units of production method exceeded straight-line depreciation by $1.5 million or 3.2%. For 1985 and 1984 aggregate straight-line depreciation exceeded that recorded under the modified units-of-production method by $10.1 million or 18.3%, $7.0 million or 12.6%, respectively.

The productive-output method recognizes that not all hours of use are equally productive. Therefore, the theory underlying the preference for a usage method would point to the productive-output method as the better of the two.

(c) DECREASING-CHARGE METHODS Decreasing-charge methods allocate a higher depreciation charge to the early years of an asset's service life. These methods are justified on the following grounds:

- Most equipment is more efficient (hence more productive) in its early life. Therefore, the early years of service life should bear more of the asset's cost.
- Repairs and maintenance charges generally increase as an asset gets older. Therefore, depreciation charges should decrease as the asset gets older so as to produce a more stable total charge (repairs and maintenance plus depreciation) for the use of the asset during its service life.

(i) Sum-of-Digits Method   This method applies a decreasing rate to a constant depreciation base (cost less net salvage value). The rate is a fraction. The denominator is the sum of the digits representing periods (years or months) of asset life. The numerator, which changes each period, is the digit assigned to the particular period. Digits are assigned in reverse order. For example, if an asset has an estimated service life of five years, the denominator would be 15, calculated as follows:

$$1 + 2 + 3 + 4 + 5 = 15$$

In the first year the rate fraction would be 5/15, in the second year 4/15, in the third year 3/15, and so on. The denominator may be calculated by means of the following formula, where n is the service life in years or months:

$$\frac{n + 1}{2} \times n = \text{Denominator}$$

For example, if the service life is estimated to be 25 years:

$$\frac{25 + 1}{2} \times 25 = 325$$

(ii) Fixed-Percentage-of-Declining-Balance Method   This method produces results similar to the sum-of-digits method. However, whereas the sum-of-digits method multiplies a declining rate times a fixed balance, the fixed-percentage-of-declining-balance method multiplies a fixed rate times a declining balance. The rate is calculated by means of the following formula, where n equals the service life in years:

$$\text{Depreciation rate} = 1 - \sqrt{\frac{\text{Net salvage value}}{\text{Cost}}}$$

The rate thus determined is then applied to the cost of the asset, without regard to salvage value, reduced by depreciation previously recognized. The result is to reduce the cost of the asset to its estimated net salvage value at the end of the asset's service life. (Some salvage value must be assigned to the asset, since it is not possible to reduce an amount to zero by applying a constant rate to a successively smaller remainder. In the absence of an expected salvage value, a nominal value of $1 can be assumed.)

To illustrate, assume an asset with a cost of $10,000, an estimated salvage value of $1,296, and an estimated service life of four years:

$$\text{Depreciation rate} = 1 - \sqrt[4]{\frac{\$1,296}{\$10,000}} = 1 - \frac{6}{10} = 40\%$$

The first year's depreciation will be $4,000 ($10,000 × 40%), the second year's $2,400 [($10,000 − $4,000) × 40%], and so on, leaving at the end of the fourth year a net asset of $1,296.

(iii) Double-Declining-Balance Method   The double-declining-balance method was introduced into the income tax laws in 1954. Since then, it has gained increased acceptability for financial reporting as well. This method differs from the fixed-percentage-of-declining-balance method by specifying that the fixed rate should be twice the straight-line rate. Otherwise, the two methods are identical: The fixed rate is applied to the undepreciated book value of the asset—a declining balance.

To illustrate, assume an asset with a cost of $15,000, an estimated net salvage value of $750, and an estimated service life of 10 years. Twice the straight-line rate would be 20 percent. Exhibit 21.1 shows the calculation for the first four years.

Note that, as with the fixed-percentage-of-declining-balance method, the rate is applied to the cost of the asset without regard to net salvage value. This means that by the end of the

Year	Book Value Beginning of Period	Rate (%)	Annual Depreciation Charge	Book Value End of Period
1	$15,000	20	$3,000	$12,000
2	12,000	20	2,400	9,600
3	9,600	20	1,920	7,680
4	7,680	20	1,536	6,144

Exhibit 21.1 Depreciation Using the Double-Declining-Balance Method

asset's estimated service life, some amount of undepreciated book value will be left in the asset account. But since the depreciation rate is determined without regard to estimated net salvage value, the undepreciated amount left in the account will likely differ from net salvage value. For example, at the end of the 10-year service life of the asset illustrated in Exhibit 21.1, the asset's book value would be $1,611, which is $861 greater than estimated net salvage value. To avoid such differences, companies usually switch from the double-declining-balance method to the straight-line method sometime during an asset's service life.

To calculate the straight-line depreciation charge at the time of the switch, the net book value (cost less accumulated depreciation), less estimated net salvage value, is divided by the estimated remaining service life. For example, if an asset has a remaining depreciation base (cost less estimated net salvage value) of $4,620 and seven years of remaining service life, a straight-line charge of $660 for the next seven years will depreciate the asset to its net salvage value.

The optimal time to make a switch is when the year's depreciation computed using the straight-line method exceeds depreciation computed using the double-declining-balance method. That is usually sometime after the midpoint of the asset's life.

Exhibit 21.2 compares the annual depreciation charges computed by the straight-line method, the sum-of-digits method, and the double-declining-balance method with switch to straight-line.

Year	Straight-Line	Sum-of-Digits	Double-Declining-Balance, Switch to Straight-Line
1	$ 14,250	$ 2,591	$ 3,000
2	1,425	2,322	2,400
3	1,425	2,073	1,920
4	1,425	1,814	1,536
5	1,425	1,555	1,229
6	1,425	1,295	983
7	1,425	1,036	796
8	1,425	777	796
9	1,425	518	795
10	1,425	259	795
	$14,250	$14,250	$14,250

Exhibit 21.2 Comparison of Annual Depreciation Charges: Straight-Line, Sum-of-Digits, and Declining-Balance with Switch to Straight Line

Note that although all three methods charge the same total amount to expense over the same service life, the amounts charged at the midpoint of the asset's service life differ:

1. Straight-line has charged 50 percent of the total.
2. Sum-of-digits has charged nearly 73 percent.
3. Double-declining-balance with switch to straight-line has charged about 71 percent.

(d) INTEREST METHODS   Two methods, the annuity method and the sinking-fund method, compute depreciation using compound interest factors. Both methods produce an increasing annual depreciation charge. Neither method is used much in practice.

(i) Annuity Method   The annuity method equalizes each year's sum of depreciation and an imputed interest charge calculated at a constant rate on the asset's undepreciated book value. Each year's sum of depreciation and imputed interest is calculated by the following formula, where n is the estimated service life of the asset in years and i is the imputed rate of interest:

$$\frac{\text{Cost of asset less present value of net salvage value}}{\text{Present value of an ordinary of annuity of } n \text{ payments of 1 at } i}$$

Assume, for example, that an asset with an economic life of five years and a net salvage value of $67,388 is acquired at a cost of $800,000. Using an imputed rate of interest of 10 percent, each year's sum of depreciation and imputed interest would be computed as follows:

$$\frac{\$800,000 - (\$67,388 \times 0.620921^*)}{3.790787}$$

$$\frac{\$800,000 - \$41,843}{3.790787}$$

$$= \$200,000$$

*Present value of $1 for five periods at 10%.

The result is presented in Exhibit 21.3.

Imputed interest is computed only for purposes of computing depreciation; it is not charged to expense.

(ii) Sinking-Fund Method   The sinking-fund method produces a depreciation pattern that is identical to that of the annuity method but by means of a different rationale and a different formula. Under the sinking-fund method, the amount of annual depreciation is equal to the increase in a hypothetical interest-earning asset-replacement fund. The increase in the fund consists of assumed equal periodic deposits to the fund plus interest at the assumed rate on the fund balance.

Each year's depreciation charge is calculated by the following formula, where n is the remaining service life of the asset in years and i is the assumed rate of interest:

$$\text{Depreciation} = \frac{\text{Cost of asset less net residual value}}{\text{Ordinary annuity of } n \text{ payments of 1 at } i}$$

Year	Combined Depreciation and Imputed Interest	Imputed Interest (10% of Carrying Amount)	Depreciation	Accumulated Depreciation	Carrying Amount of Asset
0					$800,000
1	$ 200,000	$ 80,000	$120,000	$120,000	680,000
2	200,000	68,000	132,000	252,000	548,000
3	200,000	54,800	145,200	397,200	402,800
4	200,000	40,280	159,720	556,920	243,080
5	200,000	24,308	175,692	732,612	67,388
	$1,100,000	$267,388	$732,612		

Exhibit 21.3 Depreciation Using the Annuity Method

Source: Mosich and Larsen, *Intermediate Accounting*, McGraw-Hill, 1986, p. 627 [adapted].

Using the same facts as in Exhibit 21.3 (an asset cost of $800,000, a 5-year life, a net salvage value of $67,388, and a 10 percent interest rate), the first year's depreciation would be computed as follows:

$$\text{Depreciation} = \frac{\text{Cost of asset less net residual value}}{\text{Ordinary annuity of 5 payments of 1 at 10\%}}$$

$$\frac{\$800,000 - \$67,388}{6.1051}$$

$$= \$120,000$$

(e) DEPRECIATION FOR PARTIAL PERIODS   Since assets are often acquired and disposed of throughout the year, companies must compute depreciation for partial periods. Five computation alternatives are found in practice:

1. Depreciation is recognized to the nearest whole month. Assets acquired on or before the 15th of the month or sold after the 15th are reduced by a full month's depreciation; assets acquired after the 15th or sold on or before the 15th are excluded from the month's depreciation computation.
2. Depreciation is recognized to the nearest whole year. Assets acquired during the first six months or sold during the last six months are reduced by a full year's depreciation; assets acquired during the last six months or sold during the first six months are excluded from the year's depreciation computation.
3. One-half year's depreciation only is recognized on all assets purchased or sold during the year.
4. No depreciation is recognized on all assets purchased or sold during the year.
5. A full year's depreciation is recognized on assets acquired during the year; none is recognized on assets retired during the year.

(f) CHANGE IN DEPRECIATION METHOD   A change in depreciation method is a change in an accounting principle. In accordance with APB Opinion No. 20 (par. 18), the cumulative effect of the change is recognized in net income of the period of change. Accounting changes are discussed more fully in Chapter 9.

21.11   DEPRECIATION RATES

(a) SOURCES OF DEPRECIATION RATES   Information concerning depreciation rates for various classes of business property is available from several sources. Depreciation rates have been given attention by authors of manuals on accounting, engineering, management, rate making, and other aspects of the business process. They have been the subject of special investigation by industry through individual studies and studies conducted under the auspices of manufacturing and other trade associations.

The choice of depreciation rates has also been influenced by the requirements of tax law and regulation, discussed later in this chapter.

(b) GROUP AND COMPOSITE RATES   A group of assets may be depreciated at a single rate. Assets of electrical utilities and hotels are sometimes depreciated in this manner. The two most common methods of depreciating asset groups are the group depreciation method and the collective depreciation method.

(i) Group Depreciation   Mosich and Larsen define *group depreciation* as the "process of averaging the economic lives of a number of plant assets and computing depreciation on the entire class of assets as if it were an operating unit."[21] Smith and Skousen elaborate:

> Because the accumulated depreciation account under the group procedure applies to the entire group of assets, it is not related to any specific asset. Thus, no book value can be calculated for any specific asset and there are no fully depreciated assets. To arrive at the periodic depreciation charge, the depreciation rate is applied to the recorded cost of all assets remaining in service, regardless of age.[22]

To illustrate, assume that a company purchased a group of 100 similar machines having an average expected service life of five years at a total cost of $200,000. Of this group, 30 machines are expected to be retired at the end of four years, 40 at the end of five years, and the remaining 30 at the end of six years. Under the group depreciation method, depreciation is based on the average expected service life of five years, which converts to an annual depreciation rate of 20 percent. This rate is applied to those assets in service each year. Assuming the machines are retired as expected, the charges for depreciation and the changes in the group asset and accumulated depreciation accounts are summarized in Exhibit 21.4.

---

21.   Mosich and Larsen.
22.   Smith and Skousen.

END OF YEAR	DEPRECIATION (20% OF COST)	ASSET DEBIT	ASSET CREDIT	ASSET BALANCE	ACCUMULATED DEPRECIATION DEBIT	ACCUMULATED DEPRECIATION CREDIT	ACCUMULATED DEPRECIATION BALANCE	ASSET BOOK VALUE
		$200		$200				$200
1	$ 40			200		$ 40	$ 40	160
2	40			200		40	80	120
3	40			200		40	120	80
4	40		$ 60	140	$ 60	40	100	40
5	28		80	60	80	28	48	12

EXHIBIT 21.4   GROUP DEPRECIATION (ALL AMOUNTS IN THOUSANDS)

It should be noted that the depreciation charge per machine-year is $400—one-fifth of the unit price of $2,000. In each of the first four years, 100 machines are in use, and the annual depreciation charge is $40,000. In the fifth year, when the number of machines in use drops to 70, the charge is $28,000. In the sixth year, when only 30 units are in use, the charge is $12,000.

When an asset in the group is disposed of, no gain or loss is recognized. The asset's cost is removed from the group asset account, and the difference between the cost and the asset's actual net salvage value is removed from the accumulated depreciation account.

The advantage of group depreciation, according to Smith and Skousen, is "an annual charge that is more closely related to the quantity of productive facilities being used. Gains and losses due solely to normal variations in asset lives are not recognized, and operating results are more meaningfully stated."[23]

But what Smith and Skousen see as an advantage, Geiger sees as a weakness:

> Since, for all practical purposes, the actual depreciation rate of an item is unknown and is not used, the true gain or loss at time of its sale or disposal cannot be computed. Accordingly, gain or loss on disposal of fixed assets is not recognized in the income accounts.[24]

But Smith and Skousen counter: "With normal variations in asset lives, the losses not recognized on early retirements are offset by the continued depreciation charges on those assets still in service after the average life has elapsed."[25]

(ii) Composite Depreciation   Composite depreciation applies group depreciation procedures to groups of dissimilar assets with varying service lives.

---

23.   Smith and Skousen.
24.   H. Dwight Geiger, "Composite Depreciation under Depreciation Guidelines," *AAA Bulletin*, Vol. 44, No. 11, July 1963.
25.   Smith and Skousen.

Asset Item	Cost	New Salvage Value	Depreciation Base	Annual Rate	Depreciation
A	$ 2,000	$ —	$ 2,000	20.0%	$ 400
B	5,000	500	4,500	12.0	540
C	8,000	1,000	7,000	10.0	700
D	15,000	1,000	14,000	8.0	1,120
Group	$30,000	$2,500	$27,500		$2,760

Composite life: $27,500 ÷ $2,760 = 9.96 years.
Composite rate: $2,760 ÷ $30,000 = 9.2%.

EXHIBIT 21.5   COMPOSITE DEPRECIATION

Exhibit 21.5 illustrates the calculation of composite rates. The composite life of the assets is 9.96 years; the resulting composite depreciation rate is 9.2 percent. To determine the annual depreciation, the composite rate of 9.2 percent is applied to the asset account balance at the beginning of the year. The total acquisition cost of $30,000 is thus reduced to the estimated salvage value of $2,500 in 9.96 years.

As in group depreciation, when an asset is disposed of, no gain or loss is recognized. The asset's cost is removed from the group asset account, and the difference between cost and actual net salvage value is removed from the accumulated depreciation account.

Once a composite rate has been established, it is usually continued until a significant event indicates the need for a new rate. Such an event may be a material change in the service lives of the assets included in the group, a major asset addition, or a major asset retirement. Composite depreciation is based on the assumptions that assets are regularly retired near the end of their service lives and that the retired assets are replaced with similar assets. If replacements do not take place according to the assumptions, if the service lives of replacement assets differ substantially from the service lives of the assets replaced, or if the cost of replacement assets differs materially from the cost of the assets replaced, continued use of the same composite rate is inappropriate.

Mosich and Larsen discuss the advantages and disadvantages of composite depreciation:

> The primary disadvantage . . . is that the averaging procedure may obscure significant variations from average. The accuracy of the . . . composite depreciation rate may be verified by recomputing depreciation on the straight-line basis for individual plant assets. Any significant discrepancies between the two results require a change in the composite depreciation rate.
>
> The advantages . . . are simplicity, convenience, and a reduction in the amount of detail involved in plant asset records and depreciation computations. The availability of computers has reduced the force of this argument.[26]

(c) THE EFFECTS OF REPLACEMENTS, IMPROVEMENTS, AND ADDITIONS   As stated in Subsection 21.4(c), major expenditures that extend the service lives of assets or otherwise benefit future years are capitalized. Such expenditures require new depreciation computations.

---

26.   Mosich and Larsen.

The new periodic depreciation charge is determined by dividing the asset's new book value by the new remaining service life, illustrated for straight-line depreciation, as follows:

Original asset cost (original estimated life, 10 years)	$8,000
Six years' depreciation	–4,800
Net book value before capital expenditure	3,200
Net increase in book value resulting from capital expenditure	2,400
New book value (new estimated life, 8 years)	$5,600
New annual depreciation charge ($5,600 ÷ 8)	$ 700

Retroactive adjustment of previous years' depreciation is not appropriate, since the expenditures benefit future years only.

(d) TOOLS AND RELATED ASSETS   Tools are sometimes divided into two classes: *semidurable* (lives of five years or more) and *perishable*. The cost of semidurable tools is capitalized and depreciated, usually at a group or composite rate. The rate is usually high because tools are hard to control.

Perishable tools may be handled in a variety of ways. Their cost may be charged directly to the appropriate expense or production cost account. Or the cost may be capitalized, often at some arbitrarily reduced amount, and written down when periodic inventories reveal shrinkage and deterioration. A third method is to capitalize the original cost and charge all subsequent expenditures for replacements to expense.

21.12   DEPRECIATION FOR TAX PURPOSES

Tax regulations contain their own depreciation requirements. Before 1954, the Internal Revenue Service generally allowed only the straight-line method of depreciation. Subsequently, the tax laws and regulations have been amended several times to permit accelerated depreciation methods and arbitrarily short asset lives. As a result, depreciation for financial reporting purposes and depreciation for tax purposes commonly differ. The difference between an asset's tax and accounting basis is a temporary difference that requires interperiod tax allocation under SFAS No. 109, *Accounting for Income Taxes* (see Chapter 24).

(a) CURRENT REQUIREMENTS   Depreciation for tax purposes is currently determined under the *accelerated cost recovery system* (ACRS), enacted in the Economic Recovery Act of 1981, and the *modified accelerated cost recovery system* (MACRS), enacted in the Tax Reform Act of 1986. ACRS and MACRS provide for accelerated write-offs. In many cases, the asset service lives allowable for tax purposes under ACRS and MACRS are shorter than the realistic economic service lives used for financial reporting purposes.

(b) MODIFIED ACCELERATED COST RECOVERY SYSTEM   MACRS is mandatory for most tangible depreciable property placed in service after December 31, 1986, but not if the taxpayer uses a depreciation method, such as the service-hours method, based on a service life expressed other than in years.

Under MACRS, property other than real estate is depreciated over 3, 5, 7, 10, 15, or 20 years, depending on its classification. Real estate is classified as residential rental property, which is depreciated over 27.5 years, or nonresidential real property, which is depreciated over 39 years, for purchases made after May 13, 1993. Prior to that date, nonresidential real property will be depreciated over 31.5 years.

Most property can be depreciated using an alternative method, which computes depreciation using the straight-line method with no salvage value over the applicable MACRS class life.

(c) ADDITIONAL FIRST-YEAR DEPRECIATION   The Internal Revenue Code also allows, with certain limitations, up to $17,500 of qualified tangible personal property to be deducted as an expense in the year acquired. The additional expense must be deducted from cost to determine the asset's depreciable base for tax purposes.

21.13   FINANCIAL STATEMENT PRESENTATION AND DISCLOSURE

(a) GENERAL REQUIREMENTS   APB Opinion No. 12, *Omnibus Opinion—1967* (par. 5), requires the following four disclosures in the financial statements or notes:

1. Depreciation expense for the period
2. Balances of major classes of depreciable assets, by nature or function, at the balance sheet date
3. Accumulated depreciation, either by major asset classes or in total, at the balance sheet date
4. A general description of the method or methods used in computing depreciation for major classes of depreciable assets

Special disclosures may also include the method of accounting for fully depreciated assets, liens against property, impairments, and property held for sale. Ordinarily, the basis of valuation is also disclosed.

(b) CONSTRUCTION IN PROGRESS   Payments to contractors for construction in progress are usually recorded as advances, since the payor does not acquire ownership until completion of the construction. Self-constructed assets are normally classified separately as construction in progress until construction is complete.

(c) GAIN OR LOSS ON RETIREMENT   Under APB Opinion No. 30, *Reporting the Results of Operations* (par. 23), gains or losses from the sale or abandonment of property, plant, or equipment used in the business are usually not reported as extraordinary items. They are expected to recur as a consequence of customary and continuing business activities. Exceptions are recognized for gains and losses that are "a direct result of a major casualty (such as an earthquake), an expropriation, or a prohibition under a newly enacted law or regulation" and that clearly meet both criteria of unusual nature and infrequency of occurrence.

(d) FULLY DEPRECIATED AND IDLE ASSETS   Many authorities recommend that the cost and accumulated depreciation of fully depreciated assets still in use be kept in the accounts until the assets are sold or retired. Stettler recommends disclosure not only of fully depreciated assets in use, but also of idle assets:

> Disclosure should also be made if there are material amounts of fully depreciated assets still in use or material amounts of assets still subject to depreciation that are not currently in productive use.[27]

---

27.   Howard F. Stettler, *Auditing Principles, Fifth Edition* (Englewood Cliffs, NJ: Prentice-Hall, 1982).

(e) IMPAIRMENT OF ASSETS

(i) Presentation   The SFAS No. 144 requires that impairment losses related to assets to be held and used in operations and that impairment losses from initial adjustments (and gains and losses from subsequent adjustments) of the carrying amount of assets to be disposed of be reported as a component of income from continuing operations, before income taxes. However, it provides the following options as to how such losses may be presented within the financial statements:

- As a separate line item in the income statement
- Aggregated in an appropriate line item in the income statement (e.g., as part of "other expenses") with the amount of the loss noted parenthetically on the face of the income statement
- Aggregated in an appropriate line item in the income statement supplemented by disclosure in the notes to the financial statements of the amount of impairment loss and the income statement caption in which the loss is included

If a company presents a subtotal in its income statement (e.g., income from operations, or operating income), the impairment loss must be included in such subtotal.

(ii) Disclosures for Assets to Be Held and Used   The SFAS No. 144 requires the following disclosures in the notes to the financial statements when an impairment loss is reported:

- A description of the assets that are impaired and the facts and circumstances leading to the impairment
- The amount of the impairment loss and how the fair value of the impaired assets was determined
- The caption in the income statement (or statement of activities for a not-for-profit organization) in which impairment gains or losses are aggregated if those gains or losses have not been presented in a separate caption or reported parenthetically on the face of the statement
- If applicable, the business segment(s) affected

(iii) Disclosures for Assets to Be Disposed Of   The SFAS No. 144 requires that an entity that holds assets to be disposed of should disclose the following in financial statements that include a period during which those assets are held:

- A description of the assets to be disposed of, the facts and circumstances leading to the expected disposal, the expected disposal date, and the carrying amount of those assets, if not separately presented on the face of the balance sheet
- If applicable, the business segment(s) in which assets to be disposed of are being held
- In the period in which an initial impairment loss is recorded, the amount of the impairment loss, and in years after the initial impairment is recorded, the gain or loss, if any, resulting from subsequent changes in the carrying amounts of the assets
- The caption in the income statement (or statement of activities for a not-for-profit organization) in which impairment gains or losses are aggregated if those gains or losses have not been presented in a separate caption or reported parenthetically on the face of the statement
- If applicable, amounts of revenue and pretax profit or loss reported in discontinued operations

(f) SEGMENT INFORMATION   The SFAS No. 131, *Disclosures about Segments of an Enterprise and Related Information*, requires disclosure of two items of information about property, plant, and equipment for each reportable segment:

1. Total assets, for each reportable segment
2. The aggregate amount of depreciation, depletion, and amortization expense and the amount of capital expenditures for each reportable segment

21.14   SOURCES AND SUGGESTED REFERENCES

Accounting Principles Board, "Omnibus Opinion—1967," APB Opinion No. 12, AICPA, New York, 1967.

Accounting Principles Board, "Accounting Changes," APB Opinion No. 20, AICPA, New York, 1971.

Accounting Principles Board, "Interest on Receivables and Payables," APB Opinion No. 21, AICPA, New York, 1971.

Accounting Principles Board, "Interim Financial Reporting," APB Opinion No. 28, AICPA, New York, 1973.

Accounting Principles Board, "Accounting for Nonmonetary Transactions," APB Opinion No. 29, AICPA, New York, 1973.

Accounting Principles Board, "Reporting the Results of Operations," APB Opinion No. 30, AICPA, New York, 1973.

American Accounting Association, "A Statement of Basic Accounting Theory," AAA, Sarasota, FL, 1966.

American Institute of Certified Public Accountants, "Accounting Research and Terminology Bulletins—Final Edition," AICPA, New York, 1961.

American Institute of Certified Public Accountants, "Accounting for the Inability to Fully Recover the Carrying Amount of Long-Lived Assets," Issues Paper, AICPA, New York, July 15, 1980.

American Institute of Certified Public Accountants, "Illustrations of Accounting for the Inability to Fully Recover the Carrying Amounts of Long-Lived Assets," AICPA, New York, April 1987.

American Institute of Certified Public Accountants, "Environmental Remediation Liabilities," Statement of Position 96-1, AICPA, New York, October 1996.

American Institute of Certified Public Accountants, "Accounting for Certain Costs and Activities Related to Property, Plant, and Equipment," Proposed Statement of Position, AICPA, New York, 2001.

Bendel, C. W., "Streamlining the Property Accounting Procedures," *NACA Bulletin*, Vol. 31, No. 11, 1950.

Davidson, Sidney, Stickney, Clyde P., and Weil, Roman L., *Financial Accounting, An Introduction to Concepts, Methods and Uses, Fifth Edition,* Dryden Press, Hinsdale, IL, 1988.

Financial Accounting Standards Board, "Fair Value Measurements," Statement of Financial Accounting Standards No. 157, FASB, Norwalk, CT, 2006.

Financial Accounting Standards Board, "Impairment of Long-Lived Assets and Depreciation of Idle Facilities," EITF Issue No. 84-28, FASB, Stamford, CT, October 18, 1984, December 19, 1985, and February 6, 1986.

Financial Accounting Standards Board, "Nonmonetary Transactions: Magnitude of Boot and the Exceptions to the Use of Fair Value," EITF Issue No. 86-29, FASB, Stamford, CT, December 3–4, 1986, January 15, 1987, and February 26, 1987.

Financial Accounting Standards Board, "Applicability of FASB Statement No. 2 to Business Combinations Accounted for by the Purchase Method," FASB Interpretation No. 4, FASB, Stamford, CT, 1975.

Financial Accounting Standards Board, "Accounting for the Cost of Asbestos Removal," EITF Issue No. 89-13, FASB, Norwalk, CT, October 26, 1989.

Financial Accounting Standards Board, "Capitalization of Costs to Treat Environmental Contamination," EITF Issue No. 90-8, FASB, Norwalk, CT, May 31, 1990, and July 12, 1990.

Financial Accounting Standards Board, "Accounting for Involuntary Conversions of Nonmonetary Assets to Monetary Assets," FASB Interpretation No. 30, FASB, Stamford, CT, 1979.

Financial Accounting Standards Board, "Accounting for Research and Development Costs," Statement of Financial Accounting Standards No. 2, FASB, Stamford, CT, 1974.

Financial Accounting Standards Board, "Financial Reporting for Segments of a Business Enterprise," Statement of Financial Accounting Standards No. 14, FASB, Stamford, CT, 1976.

Financial Accounting Standards Board, "Capitalization of Interest Cost," Statement of Financial Accounting Standards No. 34, FASB, Stamford, CT, 1979.

Financial Accounting Standards Board, "Accounting for Costs and Initial Rental Operations of Real Estate Projects," Statement of Financial Accounting Standards No. 67, FASB, Stamford, CT, 1982.

Financial Accounting Standards Board, "Accounting for Income Taxes," Statement of Financial Accounting Standards No. 109, FASB, Norwalk, CT, 1992.

Financial Accounting Standards Board, "Disclosures about Segments of an Enterprise and Related Information," Statement of Financial Accounting Standards No. 131, FASB, Norwalk, CT, 1997.

Financial Accounting Standards Board, "Accounting for Asset Retirement Obligations," Statement of Financial Accounting Standards No. 143, FASB, Norwalk, CT, 2001.

Financial Accounting Standards Board, "Accounting for the Impairment or Disposal of Long-Lived Assets," Statement of Financial Accounting Standards No. 144, FASB, Norwalk, CT, 2001.

Financial Accounting Standards Board, "Using Cash Flow Information and Present Value in Accounting Measurements," Statement of Financial Accounting Concepts No. 7, FASB, Norwalk, CT, 2000.

Financial Executives Institute, "Survey of Unusual Charges," Morristown, NJ, September 26, 1986.

Geiger, H. Dwight, "Composite Depreciation under Depreciation Guidelines," *NAA Bulletin*, Vol. 44, No. 11, July 1963.

Grant, E., and Norton, P., *Depreciation*. Ronald Press, New York, 1955.

International Accounting Standards Committee, "Depreciation Accounting," International Accounting Standards No. 4, IASC, London, 1977.

Kieso, Donald E., and Weygandt, Jerry J., *Intermediate Accounting, Fifth Edition*, John Wiley & Sons, New York, 1986.

Kohler, Eric Louis, *Kohler's Dictionary for Accountants, Sixth Edition*, Prentice-Hall, Englewood Cliffs, NJ, 1983.

Lambert, S. J., III, and Lambert, Joyce C., "Concepts and Applications in APB Opinion No. 29," *Journal of Accountancy*, March 1977, pp. 60–68.

Lamden, Charles, Gerboth, Dale L., and McRae, Thomas, "Accounting for Depreciable Assets," *Accounting Research Monograph*, No. 1, AICPA, New York, 1975.

Mosich, A. N., and Larsen, E. John, *Intermediate Accounting, Sixth Edition*, McGraw-Hill, New York, 1986.

National Association of Accountants, Management Accounting Practices Committee, "Fixed Asset Accounting: The Capitalization of Costs," Statement on Management Accounting Practices No. 4, NAA, New York, 1973.

National Association of Accountants, Management Accounting Practices Committee, "Fixed Asset Accounting: The Allocation of Costs," Statement on Management Accounting Practices No. 7, NAA, New York, 1974.

Pyle, William W., and Larson, Kermit D., *Fundamental Accounting Principles, Tenth Edition*, Irwin, Homewood, IL, 1984.

Smith, Jay M., and Skousen, K. Fred, *Intermediate Accounting, Comprehensive Volume, Ninth Edition*, South-Western Publishing, Cincinnati, OH, 1987.

Stettler, Howard F., *Auditing Principles, Fifth Edition*, Prentice-Hall, Englewood Cliffs, NJ, 1982.

Welsch, Glenn A., Anthony, Robert N., and Short, Daniel G., *Fundamentals of Financial Accounting*, Irwin, Homewood, IL, 1984.

Welsch, Glenn A., and Zlatkovich, Charles T., *Intermediate Accounting, Eighth Edition*, Irwin, Homewood, IL, 1989.

VOLUME **2**

ACCOUNTANTS' HANDBOOK

ELEVENTH EDITION

SPECIAL INDUSTRIES AND SPECIAL TOPICS

CHAPTER 34

STATE AND LOCAL GOVERNMENT ACCOUNTING† (REVISED)

Cynthia Pon, CPA
Macias Gini O'Connell LLP
Kevin J. O'Connell, CPA
Macias Gini O'Connell LLP
Ernest J. Gini, CPA, CGFM
Macias Gini O'Connell LLP

---

† We would like to acknowledge the efforts of the contributors of the previous edition—Andrew J. Blossom, KPMG LLP; Andrew Gottschalk, KPMG LLP; John R. Miller, KPMG LLP; and Warren Ruppel, DiTomasso & Ruppel—and thank them for their undertaking. We also are indebted to Lynford Graham, whose thoughtful feedback helped raise our own understanding of governmental accounting.

34.1   INTRODUCTION

Governmental accounting has changed dramatically in recent years in response to changes in the state and local government environment. Subject to greater scrutiny by federal and state agencies and faced with budgetary challenges, governments must also negotiate an ever-increasing level of sophistication required to manage their operations—operations which are on par with the largest and most complex business organizations and are as diverse as airports, hospitals, schools, and fire protection. Add to that concerns involving deteriorating infrastructure, an aging workforce, public health care, and the spread of terrorism, and it is no surprise that governments are finding themselves addressing increasing demands for public accountability and transparency.

Before discussing the specifics of governmental accounting principles and practices, it is important to have an overall sense of the nature and organization of state and local government activities. The goal of this chapter is to provide insight on the current governmental accounting landscape and to shed light on future trends to explore. Continued examination is critical in light of the fact that governments are no longer able to be slow adopters, following behind business-related trends and regulations; they must be innovative and proactive in order to secure the quality of their service delivery, now and in the future.

34.2   THE NATURE AND ORGANIZATION OF STATE AND LOCAL GOVERNMENT ACTIVITIES

(a) STRUCTURE OF GOVERNMENT   For the most part, government is structured on three levels: federal, state, and local. This chapter deals only with state and local governments.

States are specific identifiable entities in their own right, but accounting at the state level is associated more often than not with the individual state functions, such as departments of revenue, retirement systems, turnpike authorities, and housing finance agencies.

Local governments exist as political subdivisions of states, and the rules governing their types and operation are different in each of the 50 states. There are, however, three basic types of local governmental units: general-purpose local governments (counties, cities, towns, villages, and townships), special-purpose local governments, and authorities.

The distinguishing characteristics of general-purpose local governments are that they

- Have broad powers in providing a variety of government services—for example, public safety, fire prevention, and public works
- Have general taxing and bonding authority
- Are headed by elected officials

Special-purpose local governments are established to provide specific services or construction. They may or may not be contiguous with one or more general-purpose local governments.

Authorities and agencies are similar to special-purpose governments except that they have no taxing power and are expected to operate with their own revenues. They typically can issue only revenue bonds, not general obligations bonds.

(b) OBJECTIVES OF GOVERNMENT   The purpose of government is to provide the citizenry with the highest level of services possible given the available financial resources and the legal requirements under which it operates. The services are provided as a result of decisions made during a budgeting process that considers the desired level and quality of services. Resources are then made available through property taxes, sales taxes, income taxes, general and categorical grants from the federal and state governments, charges for services, fines, licenses, and other sources. However, there is generally no direct relationship between the cost of the services rendered to an individual and the amount that the individual pays in taxes, fines, fees, and so on.

Governmental units also conduct operations that are financed and operated in a manner similar to private business enterprises, where the intent is that the costs of providing the goods or services be financed or recovered primarily through charges to the users. In such situations, governments have many of the features of ordinary business operations.

(c) ORGANIZATION OF GOVERNMENT   A government's organization depends on its constitution (state level) or charter (local level) and on general and special statutes of state and local legislatures. When governments were simpler and did not provide as many services as they do today, there was less of a tendency toward centralization. The commission and weak-mayor forms of governments were common. The financial function was typically divided among several individuals.

As government has become more complex, however, the need for strong professional management and for centralization of authority and responsibility has grown. There has been a trend toward the strong-mayor and council-manager forms of government. In these forms, a chief financial officer, usually called the *director of finance* or *controller*, is responsible for maintaining the financial records and preparing financial reports; assisting the chief executive officer (CEO) in the preparation of the budget; performing treasury functions such as collecting revenues, managing cash, managing investments, and managing debt; and overseeing the tax-assessment function. Other functions that may report to the director of finance are purchasing, data processing, and personnel administration.

Local governments are also making greater use of the internal audit process. In the past, the emphasis by governmental internal auditors was on preaudit—that is, reviewing invoices and other documents during processing for propriety and accuracy. The internal auditors reported to the director of finance. Today, however, governmental internal auditors have been removing themselves from the preaudit function by transferring this responsibility to the department responsible for processing the transactions. They have started to provide the more traditional internal audit function—that is, conducting reviews to ensure the reliability of data and the safeguarding of assets and to become involved in performance auditing (i.e., reviewing the efficiency and effectiveness of the government's operations). They have also started to report, for professional (as opposed to administrative) purposes, to the CEO or directly to the governing board. Finally, internal auditors are becoming more actively involved in the financial statement audit and single audit of their government.

(d) SPECIAL CHARACTERISTICS OF GOVERNMENT   Several characteristics associated with governments have influenced the development of governmental accounting principles and practices:

- Governments do not have any owners or proprietors in the commercial sense. Accordingly, measurement of earnings attributable or accruing to the direct benefit of an owner is not a relevant accounting concept for governments.
- Governments frequently receive substantial financial inflows for both operating and capital purposes from sources other than revenues and investment earnings, such as taxes and grants.
- Governments frequently obtain financial inflows subject to legally binding restrictions that prohibit or seriously limit the use of these resources for other than the intended purpose.
- A government's authority to raise and expend money results from the adoption of a budget that, by law, usually must balance (e.g., the estimated revenues plus any prior years' surpluses need to be sufficient to cover the projected expenditures).
- The power to raise revenues through taxes, licenses, fees, and fines is generally defined by law.
- There are usually restrictions related to the tax base that govern the purpose, amount, and type of indebtedness that can be issued.
- Expenditures are usually regulated less than revenues and debt, but they can be made only within approved budget categories and must comply with specified purchasing procedures when applicable.
- State laws may dictate the local government accounting policies and systems.
- State laws commonly specify the type and frequency of financial statements to be submitted to the state and to the government's constituency.
- Federal law, the Single Audit Act of 1984 and as amended in 1996, defines the audit requirements for state and local governments.

In short, the environment in which governments operate is complex and legal requirements have a significant influence on their accounting and financial reporting practices.

34.3 SOURCE OF ACCOUNTING PRINCIPLES FOR STATE AND LOCAL GOVERNMENT ACCOUNTING

Governmental accounting principles are not a complete and separate body of accounting principles, but rather are part of the whole body of generally accepted accounting principles (GAAP). Since the accounting profession's standard-setting bodies have been concerned primarily with the accounting needs of profit-seeking organizations, these principles have been defined primarily by groups formed by the state and local governments. In 1934, the National Committee on Municipal Accounting published "A Tentative Outline—Principles of Municipal Accounting." In 1968, the National Committee on Governmental Accounting (the successor organization) published *Governmental Accounting, Auditing, and Financial Reporting* (GAAFR), which was widely used as a source of governmental accounting principles. The American Institute of Certified Public Accountants (AICPA) Industry Audit Guide, "Audits of State and Local Governmental Units," published in 1974, stated that the accounting principles outlined in the 1968 GAAFR constituted GAAP for government entities.

The financial difficulties experienced by many governments in the mid-1970s led to a call for a review and modification of the accounting and financial reporting practices used by governments. Laws were introduced in Congress, but never enacted, that would have given the federal government the authority to establish governmental accounting principles. The Financial Accounting Standards Board (FASB), responding to pressures, commissioned a research study to define and explain the issues associated with accounting for all nonbusiness enterprises, including governments. This study was completed in 1978, and the Board developed Statement of Financial Accounting Concepts (SFAC) No. 4 for nonbusiness organizations. The Statement defined nonbusiness organizations, the users of the statements, the financial information needs of these users, and the information that is necessary to meet these needs.

(a) NATIONAL COUNCIL ON GOVERNMENT ACCOUNTING   The National Council on Governmental Accounting (NCGA) was the successor of the National Committee on Municipal Accounting reconstituted as a permanent organization. One of its first projects was to "restate," that is, update, clarify, amplify, and reorder, the GAAFR to incorporate pertinent aspects of "Audits of State and Local Governmental Units." The restatement was published in March 1979 as NCGA Statement No. 1, "Governmental Accounting and Financial Reporting Principles." Shortly thereafter, the AICPA Committee on State and Local Government Accounting recognized NCGA Statement No. 1 as authoritative and agreed to amend the Industry Audit Guide accordingly. This restatement was completed, and a new guide was published in 1986. Thus NCGA Statement No. 1 became the primary reference source for the accounting principles unique to governmental accounting. However, in areas not unique to governmental accounting, the complete body of GAAP still needed to be considered.

(b) GOVERNMENTAL ACCOUNTING STANDARDS BOARD   In 1984, the Financial Accounting Foundation (FAF) established the Governmental Accounting Standards Board (GASB) as the primary standard setter for GAAP for governmental entities. Under the jurisdictional agreement, the GASB has the primary responsibility for establishing accounting and reporting principles for government entities. The GASB's first action was to issue Statement No. 1, "Authoritative Status of NCGA Pronouncements and AICPA Industry Audit Guide," which recognized the NCGA's statements and interpretations and the AICPA's audit guide as authoritative. The Statement also recognized the pronouncements of the FASB issued prior to the date of the agreement as applicable to governments. FASB pronouncements issued after the organization of GASB do not become effective unless the GASB specifically adopts them.

The GASB has operated under this jurisdictional arrangement since 1984. However, the arrangement came under scrutiny during the GASB's mandatory five-year review conducted in 1988. In January 1989 the Committee to Review Structure of Governmental Accounting Standards released its widely read report on the results of its review and proposed to the FAF, among other recommendations, a new jurisdictional arrangement and GAAP hierarchy for governments. These two recommendations prompted a great deal of controversy within the industry. The issue revolved around the Committee's recommended jurisdictional arrangement for the separately issued financial statements of certain "special entities." (Special entities are organizations that can either be privately or governmentally owned and include colleges and universities, hospitals, and utilities.) The Committee recommended that the FASB be the primary accounting standard setter for these special entities when they issue separate, stand-alone financial statements and that the GASB be allowed to require the presentation of "additional data" in these stand-alone statements. This arrangement would allow for greater comparability between entities in the same industry (e.g., utilities) regardless of whether the entities were privately or governmentally owned and still allow government-owned entities to meet their "public accountability" reporting objective.

This recommendation and a subsequent compromise recommendation were unacceptable to many and especially to the various public interest groups, such as the Government Finance Officers Association (GFOA), which, 10 months after the Committee's report, began discussions to establish a new body to set standards for state and local government. These actions prompted the FAF to consider whether a standard-setting schism was in the interest of the public and the users of financial statements. Based on this consideration, the FAF decided that the jurisdictional arrangement established in 1984 should remain intact.

In response to the jurisdictional arrangement just described, the AICPA issued Statement on Auditing Standards No. 69, "The Meaning of Present Fairly in Conformity with Generally Accepted Accounting Principles in the Independent Auditor's Report," which creates a hierarchy of GAAP specifically for state and local governments. SAS No. 69 raises AICPA Statement of Positions (SOPs) and audit and accounting guides to a level of authority above that of industry practice. As a result, FASB pronouncements will not apply to state and local governments unless the GASB issues a standard incorporating them into GAAP for state and local government. In September 1993, the GASB issued Statement No. 20, "Accounting and Financial Reporting for Proprietary Funds and Other Governmental Entities That Use Proprietary Fund Accounting."

Statement No. 20 requires proprietary activities to apply all applicable GASB Statements as well as FASB pronouncements, Accounting Principles Board (APB) Opinions, and Accounting Research Bulletins issued on or before November 30, 1989, unless those pronouncements conflict or contradict with a GASB pronouncement. A proprietary activity may also apply, at its option, all FASB pronouncements issued after November 30, 1989, except those that conflict or contradict with a GASB pronouncement.

The GASB subsequently issued Statement No. 29, "The Use of Not-for-Profit Accounting and Financial Reporting Principles by Governmental Entities," which amended Statement No. 20 to indicate that proprietary activities could apply only those FASB statements that were developed for business enterprises. The FASB statements and interpretations whose provisions are limited to not-for-profit organizations or address issues primarily of concern to those organizations may not be applied. These actions, along with the increased activity of the FASB in setting standards for not-for-profit organizations, have resulted in increasing differences in GAAP between nongovernmental entities and state and local governments.

These differences also highlight the importance of determining whether a particular entity is a state or local government. While it is obvious that states, cities, and counties are governments, other units of government are less clear. Is a university considered a government if it is supported 70 percent by taxes allocated by the state? What if the percentage is only 15 percent? If a hospital is created by a county but the county has no continuing involvement with the hospital, is the hospital a government? The GASB acknowledged these concerns in the Basis for Conclusions of Statement No. 29 in stating

> Some respondents believe that the fundamental issue underlying this Statement—identifying those entities that should apply the GAAP hierarchy applicable to state and local governmental entities—will continue to be troublesome until there is an authoritative definition of such "governmental entities." The Board agrees—but does not have the authority to unilaterally establish a definition—and intends to continue to explore alternatives for resolving the issue.

The decision as to whether a particular entity should follow the hierarchy for state and local governments or nongovernmental entities is a matter of professional judgment based on the individual facts and circumstances for the entity in question. The AICPA audit and accounting guide for not-for-profit organizations provides guidance to distinguish between governmental and nongovernmental organizations. It defines governmental organizations as

> Public corporations and bodies corporate and politic. . . . Other organizations are governmental organizations if they have one or more of the following characteristics:
>
> **a.** Popular election of officers or appointment (or approval) of a controlling majority of the members of the organization's governing body by officials of one or more state or local governments;
> **b.** The potential for unilateral dissolution by a government with the net assets reverting to a government; or
> **c.** The power to enact and enforce a tax levy.

Furthermore, organizations are presumed to be governmental if they have the ability to issue directly (rather than through a state or municipal authority) debt that pays interest exempt from federal taxation. However, organizations possessing only that ability (to issue tax-exempt debt) and none of the other governmental characteristics may rebut the presumption that they are governmental if their determination is supported by compelling, relevant evidence.

In 2006, the GFOA questioned the continued role of the GASB in response to its project on Service Efforts and Accomplishments (SEA) Reporting (see Section 34.4(b), Users and Uses of Financial Reports). However, in 2006 FAF reaffirmed that the GASB has the jurisdictional authority to include "service efforts and accomplishments" in its financial accounting and reporting standard-setting activities.

Recently Texas passed legislation that would give the state and any of its public entities permission to ignore GASB Statement 45, an accounting standard requiring state and local governments to disclose their liability for "other post-employment benefits," which include retiree health, dental, and vision benefits as well as some forms of life insurance. Texas CPAs are worried that this is a first step down a road where all 50 states will start developing their own set of accounting standards.

34.4 GOVERNMENTAL ACCOUNTING PRINCIPLES AND PRACTICES

(a) SIMILARITIES TO PRIVATE SECTOR ACCOUNTING   Since the accounting principles and practices of governments are part of the whole body of GAAP, certain accounting concepts and conventions are as applicable to governmental entities as they are to accounting in other industries:

- *Consistency.* Identical transactions should be recorded in the same manner both during a period and from period to period.
- *Conservatism.* The uncertainties that surround the preparation of financial statements are reflected in a general tendency toward early recognition of unfavorable events and minimization of the amount of net assets and net income.
- *Historical cost.* Amounts should be recognized in the financial statements at the historical cost to the reporting entity. Changes in the general purchasing power should not be recognized in the basic financial statements.
- *Matching.* The financial statements should provide for a matching, but in government it is a matching of revenues and expenditures with a time period to ensure that revenues and the expenditures they finance are reported in the same period.
- *Reporting entity.* The focus of the financial report is the economic activities of a discrete individual entity for which there is a reporting responsibility.
- *Materiality.* Financial reporting is concerned only with significant information.
- *Full disclosure.* Financial statements must contain all information necessary to understand the presentation of financial position and results of operations and to prevent them from being misleading.

(b) USERS AND USES OF FINANCIAL REPORTS   Users of the financial statements of a governmental unit are not identical to users of a business entity's financial statements. The GASB Concepts Statement No. 1 identifies three groups of primary users of external governmental financial reports:

1. *Those to whom government is primarily accountable—the citizenry.* The citizenry group includes citizens (whether they are classified as taxpayers, voters, or service recipients), the media, advocate groups, and public finance researchers. This user group is concerned with obtaining the maximum amount of service with a minimum amount of taxes and wants to know where the government obtains its resources and how those resources are used.
2. *Those who directly represent the citizens—legislative and oversight bodies.* The legislative and oversight officials group includes members of state legislatures, county commissions, city councils, boards of trustees, and school boards, along with those executive branch officials with oversight responsibility over other levels of government. These groups need timely warning of the development of situations that require corrective action, financial information that can serve as a basis for judging management performance, and financial information on which to base future plans and policies.
3. *Those who lend or participate in the lending process—investors and creditors.* Investors and creditors include individual and institutional investors and creditors, municipal security underwriters, bond-rating agencies (Moody's Investors Service, Standard & Poor's, etc.), bond insurers, and financial institutions.

The uses of a government's financial reports are also different. GASB Concepts Statement No. 1 also indicates that governmental financial reporting should provide information to assist users in (1) assessing accountability and (2) making economic, social, and political decisions by

- *Comparing actual financial results with the legally adopted budget.* All three user groups are interested in comparing original or modified budgets with actual results to get some assurance that spending mandates have been complied with and that resources have been used for the intended purposes.

- *Assisting in determining compliance with finance-related laws, rules, and regulations.* In addition to the legally mandated budgetary and fund controls, other legal restrictions may control governmental actions. Some examples are bond covenants, grant restrictions, and taxing and debt limits. Financial reports help demonstrate compliance with these laws, rules, and regulations.
  - Citizens are concerned that governments adhere to these regulations because noncompliance may indicate fiscal irresponsibility and could have severe financial consequences, such as acceleration of debt payments, disallowance of questioned costs, or loss of grants.
  - Legislative and oversight officials are also concerned with compliance as a follow-up to the budget formulation process.
  - Investors and creditors are interested in the government's compliance with debt covenants and restrictions designed to protect their investment.
- *Assisting in evaluating efficiency and effectiveness.* Citizen groups and legislators, in particular, want information about service efforts, costs, and accomplishments of a governmental entity. This information, when combined with information from other sources, helps users assess the economy, efficiency, and effectiveness of government and may help form a basis for voting on funding decisions.
- *Assessing financial condition and results of operations.* Financial reports are commonly used to assess a state or local government's financial condition—that is, its financial position and its ability to continue to provide services and meet its obligations as they come due.
  - Investors and creditors need information about available and likely future financial resources, actual and contingent liabilities, and the overall debt position of a government to evaluate the government's ability to continue to provide resources for long-term debt service.
  - Citizens' groups are concerned with financial condition when evaluating the likelihood of tax or service fee increases.
  - Legislative and oversight officials need to assess the overall financial condition, including debt structure and funds available for appropriation, when developing both capital and operating budget and program recommendations.

With the users and the uses of financial reports clearly defined, the GASB developed the following three overall objectives of governmental financial reporting:

1. Financial reporting should assist in fulfilling a government's duty to be publicly accountable and should enable users to assess that accountability by
   a. Providing information to determine whether current-year revenues were sufficient to pay for current-year services.
   b. Demonstrating whether resources were obtained and used in accordance with the entity's legally adopted budget and in compliance with other finance-related legal or contractual requirements.
   c. Providing information to assist users in assessing the service efforts, costs, and accomplishments of the governmental entity.
2. Financial reporting should assist users in evaluating the operating results of the governmental entity for the year by providing information

    a. About sources and uses of financial resources.

    b. About how the governmental entity financed its activities and met its cash requirements.

    c. Necessary to determine whether the entity's financial position improved or deteriorated as a result of the year's operations.

3. Financial reporting should assist users in assessing the level of services that can be provided by the governmental entity and its ability to meet its obligations as they become due by

    a. Providing information about the financial position and condition of a governmental entity. Financial reporting should provide information about resources and obligations, both actual and contingent, current and noncurrent, and about tax sources, tax limitations, tax burdens, and debt limitations.

    b. Providing information about a governmental entity's physical and other non-financial resources having useful lives that extend beyond the current year, including information that can be used to assess the service potential of those resources.

    c. Disclosing legal or contractual restrictions on resources and risks of potential loss of resources.

In April 1994, the GASB issued Concepts Statement No. 2, "Service Efforts and Accomplishments Reporting," which expands on the consideration of service efforts and accomplishments (SEA) reporting included in Concepts Statement No. 1. The GASB believes that the government's duty to be publicly accountable requires the presentation of SEA information. Concepts Statement No. 2 identifies the objective of SEA reporting as providing "more complete information about a governmental entity's performance that can be provided by the operating statement, balance sheet, and budgetary comparison statements and schedules to assist users in assessing the economy, efficiency, and effectiveness of services provided." The Concepts Statement also indicates that SEA information should meet the characteristics of relevance, understandability, comparability, timeliness, consistency, and reliability. In April 2007, the GASB started work on the SEA project, which will include future guidelines for SEA performance reporting issues and measures.

In April 2005, the GASB issued Concepts Statement No. 3, "Communication Methods in General Purpose External Financial Reports That Contain Basic Financial Statements," which provides a conceptual basis for selecting communication methods to present items of information within general-purpose external financial reports that contain basic financial statements. Preparers should select an appropriate communication method to convey information that enhances the consistency, comparability, and understandability of general-purpose external financial reports. The hierarchy for selecting communications methods is as follows:

    a. Recognition in the basic financial statements

    b. Disclosure in notes to basic financial statements

    c. Presentation as required supplementary information

    d. Presentation as supplementary information

In June 2007, the GASB issued Concepts Statement No. 4, "Elements of Financial Statements," which establishes definitions for the seven elements of historically based financial statements of state and local governments. These elements are the fundamental components of financial statements. The five statements of financial position elements are defined as follows:

- *Assets* are resources with present service capacity that the government presently controls.
- *Liabilities* are present obligations to sacrifice resources that the government has little or no discretion to avoid.
- A *deferred outflow* of resources is a consumption of net assets by the government that is applicable to a future reporting period.
- A *deferred inflow* of resources is an acquisition of net assets by the government that is applicable to a future reporting period.
- *Net position* is the residual of all other elements presented in a statement of financial position.

The two resource flows elements are defined as follows:

- An *outflow of resources* is a consumption of net assets by the government that is applicable to the reporting period.
- An *inflow of resources* is an acquisition of net assets by the government that is applicable to the reporting period.

Each element's inherent characteristics provides the primarily basis for these definitions. Central to these definitions is a resource, which in the governmental context is an item that can be drawn on to provide services to the citizenry. These definitions apply to an entity that is a governmental unit (i.e., a legal entity) and are applicable to any measurement focus under which financial statements may be prepared.

(c) SUMMARY STATEMENT OF PRINCIPLES   Because governments operate under different conditions and have different reporting objectives than commercial entities, basic principles applicable to government accounting and reporting have been developed. These principles are generally recognized as being essential to effective management control and financial reporting. In other words, understanding these principles and how they operate is extremely important to the understanding of governments.

(i) Accounting and Reporting Capabilities   A governmental accounting system must make it possible to both (1) present fairly the basic financial statements in conformity with GAAP, which include both government-wide and fund financial statements with full disclosure, and to provide adequately the required supplementary information, including the management's discussion and analysis (MD&A) and required budgetary comparison information; and (2) determine and demonstrate compliance with finance-related legal and contractual provisions.

(ii) Government-Wide and Fund Accounting Systems   Governmental accounting systems should provide information that permits reporting on a fund basis and provide conversion information that facilities reporting on a government-wide basis. A "fund" is defined as a fiscal and accounting entity with a self-balancing set of accounts recording cash and other financial resources, together with all related liabilities and residual equities or balances, and changes therein, which are segregated for the purpose of carrying on specific activities or attaining certain objectives in accordance with special regulations, restrictions, or limitations.

Under GASB Statement No. 34, government-wide financial statements should be presented in addition to fund financial statements. They should report information about the reporting government as a whole, except for its fiduciary activities. The statements should include separate columns for governmental activities, business-type activities, total activities, and component units, which are legally separate organizations for which the elected officials of the primary government (PG) are financially accountable, or other organizations for which the nature and significance of its relationship with a PG are such that exclusion from the financial statements of the PG would cause them to be misleading or incomplete. The government-wide financial statements should be prepared using the economic resources measurement focus and the accrual basis of accounting.

(iii) Types of Funds   The following three types of funds should be used by state and local governments.

(A) GOVERNMENTAL FUNDS (EMPHASIZING MAJOR FUNDS)

1. *The general fund.* To account for all financial resources except those required to be accounted for in another fund.
2. *Special revenue funds.* To account for the proceeds for specific revenue sources (other than expendable trusts, or major capital projects) that are legally restricted to expenditures for specified purposes.
3. *Capital projects funds.* To account for financial resources to be used for the acquisition or construction of major capital facilities (other than those financed by proprietary funds and trust funds).
4. *Debt service funds.* To account for the accumulation of resources for, and the payment of, general long-term debt principal and interest.
5. *Permanent funds.* To account for the resources used to make earnings, of which only the earnings may be used for the benefit of the government or its citizenry, such as a cemetery perpetual-care fund.

(B) PROPRIETARY FUNDS

1. *Enterprise funds (emphasizing major funds).* To account for operations (a) that are financed and operated in a manner similar to private business enterprises, where the intent of the governing body is that the cost (expenses, including depreciation) of providing goods or services to the general public, on a continuing basis, be financed or recovered primarily through user charges; or (b) where the governing body has decided that periodic determination of revenues earned, expenses incurred, and/or net income is appropriate for capital maintenance, public policy, management control, accountability, or other purposes.
2. *Internal service funds.* To account for the financing of goods or services provided by one department or agency to other departments or agencies of the governmental unit, or to other governmental units, on a cost-reimbursement basis.

(C) FIDUCIARY FUNDS (AND SIMILAR COMPONENT UNITS)

1. *Pension and other employee benefit trust funds.* To account for resources that are required to be held in trust for the members and beneficiaries of defined-benefit pension plans, defined contribution plans, other postemployment benefit (OPEB) plans, or other employee benefit plans.
2. *Investment trust funds.* To account for the external portion of external investment pools that the government sponsors.

3. *Private-purpose trust funds.* To account for all other trust arrangements under which the principal and income benefit individuals, private organizations, or other governments.
4. *Agency funds.* To account for resources held in a custodial capacity for individuals, private organizations, or other governments.

(iv) Number of Funds   Governmental units should establish and maintain those funds required by law and sound financial administration. Only the minimum number of funds consistent with legal and operating requirements should be established, since unnecessary funds result in inflexibility, undue complexity, and inefficient financial administration.

(v) Accounting for Capital Assets   A clear distinction should be made between proprietary capital assets and general capital assets. Capital assets related to specific proprietary funds should be accounted for through both the government-wide and proprietary funds statements. All other capital assets of a governmental unit should be accounted for only in the government-wide capital assets account, except for fiduciary fund capital assets that should be accounted for only in the fiduciary funds' statements.

(vi) Valuation of Capital Assets   Capital assets should be accounted for at cost or, if the cost is not practicably determinable, at estimated cost. Donated capital assets should be recorded at their estimated fair value at the time received.

(vii) Depreciation and Impairment of Capital Assets   While some assets are not depreciated, such as land, most assets are depreciated over their useful lives. An exception is also those assets accounted for using the modified approach, as outlined in GASB 34. Depreciation of capital assets should be recorded in the government-wide statement of activities; the proprietary fund statement of revenues, expense, and changes in fund net assets; and the statement of changes in fiduciary net assets. Capital assets should be evaluated for impairment when events or changes in circumstances suggest that the service utility of a capital asset may have significantly and unexpected declined.

(viii) Accounting for Long-Term Liabilities   Similar to reporting capital assets, a clear distinction should be made between proprietary fund and fiduciary long-term liabilities and general long-term liabilities. Long-term liabilities of proprietary funds should be accounted both in those funds and in the government-wide statement of net assets. All other outstanding general long-term liabilities should be accounted for in the government activities column in the government-wide statement of net assets, except for fiduciary funds long-term liabilities that should be accounted for only in the fiduciary funds' statements.

(ix) Measurement Focus and Basis of Accounting   The modified accrual or accrual basis of accounting, as appropriate, should be used in measuring financial position and operating results.

- Governmental fund revenues and expenditures should be recognized on the modified accrual basis using the current financial resources measurement focus. Revenues should be recognized in the accounting period in which they become available and measurable. Expenditures should be recognized in the accounting period in which the fund liability is incurred, if measurable, except for unmatured long-term indebtedness and other obligations not due for payment in the current period, which should be recognized when mature or due.

- Proprietary fund revenues and expenses should be recognized using the economic resources measurement focus and the accrual basis. Revenues should be recognized in the accounting period in which they are earned and become measurable; expenses should be recognized in the period incurred, if measurable.
- Fiduciary fund revenues/additions and expenses/reductions should be recognized using the economic resources measurement focus and the accrual basis.
- Transfers should be recognized in the period in which the inter-fund receivable and payable arise.

(x) Budgeting, Budgetary Control, and Budgetary Reporting   An annual budget should be adopted by every governmental unit. The accounting system should provide the basis for appropriate budgetary control. Budgetary comparisons should be presented for the general fund and for each major special revenue fund that has a legally adopted annual budget.

(xi) Transfer, Revenue, Expenditure, and Expense Account Classification   The statement of activities should present activities accounted for in governmental funds by function and activities accounted for in enterprise funds by different identifiable activities.

Governmental fund revenues should be classified by fund and source. Expenditures should be classified by fund, function (or program), organization unit, activity, character, and principal classes of objects.

Proprietary fund revenues and expenses should be classified in essentially the same manner as those of similar business organizations, functions, or activities.

Contributions to term and permanent endowments, contributions to permanent fund principal, other capital contributions, special and extraordinary items, and transfers should each be reported separately.

(xii) Common Terminology and Classification   A common terminology and classification should be used consistently throughout the budget, the accounts, and the financial reports of each fund or activity.

(xiii) Interim and Annual Financial Reports   Appropriate interim financial statements and reports of financial position, operating results, and other pertinent information should be prepared to facilitate management control of financial operations, legislative oversight, and, where necessary or desired, external reporting.

A comprehensive annual financial report (CAFR) covering all funds of the governmental unit may be prepared and published, including appropriate government-wide financial statements; combined, combining, and individual fund statements; notes to the financial statements; required supplementary information; schedules; narrative explanations; and statistical tables.

Basic financial statements may be issued separately from the CAFR. Such statements should include the financial statements, notes to the financial statements, and any required supplementary information essential to a fair presentation of financial position and operating results and cash flows of proprietary funds.

(d) DISCUSSION OF THE PRINCIPLES   To enable readers to more fully understand the principles, a discussion follows.

(e) ACCOUNTING AND REPORTING CAPABILITIES

(i) Legal Compliance   *Principle 1* of governmental accounting (GASB Codification Section 1100.101) states

> A governmental accounting system must make it possible both: (a) to present fairly and with full disclosure the funds of the governmental unit in conformity with GAAPs; and (b) to determine and demonstrate compliance with finance-related legal and contractual provisions.

Several state and local governments have accounting requirements that differ from GAAP—for example, cash basis accounting is required, and capital projects must be accounted for in the general fund. Because of this situation, the legal compliance principle used to be interpreted as meaning that, when the legal requirements for a particular entity differed from GAAP, the legal requirements became GAAP for the entity. This interpretation is no longer viewed as sound. When GAAP and legal requirements conflict, governments should present their basic financial report in accordance with GAAP and, if the legal requirements differ materially from GAAP, the legally required reports can be published as supplemental data to the basic financial report or, if these differences are extreme, it may be preferable to publish a separate legal-basis report.

However, conflicts that arise between GAAP and legal provisions do not require maintaining two sets of accounting records. Rather, the accounting records typically would be maintained in accordance with the legal requirements but would include sufficient additional information to permit preparation of reports in accordance with GAAP.

(ii) Reporting Requirements   Under GASB Statement No. 34, the typical local government's set of basic financial statements consists of three components: (1) Government-wide financial statements; (2) Fund financial statements; and (3) Notes to the financial statements. Governments will also have other supplementary information in addition to the basic financial statements themselves. An example of how the various elements of a local government's financial statement are related is shown in Exhibit 34.1.

The table in Exhibit 34.2 summarizes the major features of the City and County of San Francisco's financial statements.

(f) GOVERNMENT-WIDE AND FUND ACCOUNTING SYSTEMS   Principle 2, fund accounting, is used by governments because of (1) legally binding restrictions that prohibit or seriously limit the use of much of a government's resources for other than the purposes for which the resources were obtained, and (2) the importance of reporting the accomplishment of various objectives for which the resources were entrusted to the government.

GASB Codification Section 1100.102 defines a fund for accounting purposes as

> A fiscal and accounting entity with a self-balancing set of accounts recording cash and other financial resources, together with all related liabilities and residual equities or balances, and changes therein, which are segregated for the purposes of carrying on specific activities or obtaining certain objectives in accordance with special regulations, restrictions, or limitations.

Thus a fund may include accounts for assets, liabilities, fund balance or net assets, revenues, expenditures, or expenses. Accounts may also exist for appropriations and encumbrances, depending on the budgeting system used.

INTRODUCTORY SECTION

Introductory
Section

+

Management's Discussion and Analysis

Government-wide
Financial
Statements

Fund Financial Statements

Governmental Funds	Proprietary Funds	Fiduciary Funds
Balance sheet	Statement of net assets	Statement of fiduciary net assets
Statement of revenues, expenditures, and changes in fund balances	Statement of revenues, expenses, and changes in fund net assets	Statement of changes in fiduciary net assets
Budgetary comparison statement	Statement of cash flows	

Statement of
net assets

Statement of
activities

Financial
Section

CAFR

Notes to the Financial Statements

Required Supplementary Information Other than MD&A

Information on individual non-major funds and other
supplementary information that is not required

+

Statistical
Section

STATISTICAL SECTION

EXHIBIT 34.1 ORGANIZATION OF THE CITY AND COUNTY OF SAN FRANCISCO COMPREHENSIVE
ANNUAL FINANCIAL REPORT

Source: City and County of San Francisco, California, Comprehensive Annual Financial
Report for the Year Ended June 30, 2006, pp. 4–5

A government should report separately on its most important, or "major," funds, including its general fund. A major fund is one whose revenues, expenditures/expenses, assets, or liabilities (excluding extraordinary items) are at least 10 percent of the corresponding totals for all governmental or enterprise funds and at least 5 percent of the aggregate amount for all governmental and enterprise funds. Any other fund may be reported as a major fund if the government's officials believe information about the fund is particularly important to the users of the statements. Other funds should be reported in the aggregate in a separate column. Internal service funds should be reported in the aggregate in a separate column on the proprietary fund statements. Separate fund financial statements should be presented for governmental and proprietary funds.

	Government-wide Statements	Fund Financial Statements		
		Governmental	Proprietary	Fiduciary
Scope	Entire entity (except fiduciary funds)	The day-to-day operating activities of the City for basic governmental services	The day-to-day operating activities of the City for business-type enterprises	Instances in which the City administers resources on behalf of others, such as employee benefits
Accounting basis and measurement focus	Accrual accounting and economic resources focus	Modified accrual accounting and current financial resources focus	Accrual accounting and economic resources focus	Accrual accounting and economic resources focus; except agency funds do not have measurement focus
Type of asset and liability information	All assets and liabilities, both financial and capital, short term and long term	Current assets and liabilities that come due during the year or soon thereafter	All assets and liabilities, both financial and capital, short term and long term	All assets held in a trustee or agency capacity for others
Type of inflow and outflow information	All revenues and expenses during year, regardless of when cash is received or paid	Revenues for which cash is received during the year or soon thereafter; expenditures when goods or services have been received and the related liability is due and payable	All revenues and expenses during year, regardless of when cash is received or paid	All additions and deductions during the year, regardless of when cash is received or paid

Exhibit 34.2   Summary of the Major Features of the City and County of San Francisco's Financial Statements

A government should present a summary reconciliation to the government-wide financial statements at the bottom of the fund financial statements or in a separate schedule. Fund balances for governmental funds should be segregated into reserved and unreserved categories. Proprietary fund net assets should be reported in the same categories required for the government-wide financial statements. Proprietary fund statements of net assets should distinguish between current and noncurrent assets and liabilities and should display restricted assets.

(g) TYPES AND NUMBER OF FUNDS   Because of the various nature of activities carried on by government, it is often important to be able to account for certain activities separately from others (i.e., when required by law). Principles 3 and 4 define seven basic fund types in which to account for various governmental activities. The purpose and operation of each fund type differs, and it is important to understand these differences and why they exist. Every fund maintained by a government should be classified into one of these three fund categories:

1. Governmental funds, emphasizing major funds:
   - The general fund
   - Special revenue funds
   - Capital projects funds
   - Debt service funds
   - Permanent funds
2. Proprietary funds:
   - Enterprise funds, emphasizing major funds
   - Internal service funds

3. Fiduciary funds and similar component units:
- o Pension and other employee benefit trust funds
- o Investment trust funds
- o Private-purpose trust funds
- o Agency funds

The general fund, special revenue funds, debt service funds, capital projects funds, and permanent funds are considered governmental funds since they record the transactions associated with the general services of a local governmental unit (i.e., police, public works, fire prevention) that are provided to all citizens and are supported primarily by general revenues. For these funds, the primary concerns, from the financial statement reader's point of view, are the types and amounts of resources that have been made available to the governmental unit and the uses to which they have been put.

The enterprise funds and internal services funds are considered proprietary funds because they account for activities for which the determination of operating income is important.

The trust and agency funds are considered fiduciary funds. There are basically three types of trust funds: pension (and other employee benefit) trust funds, investment trust funds and private-purpose trust funds that operate in a manner similar to proprietary funds, and agency funds that account for funds held by a government entity in an agent capacity. Agency funds consist of assets and liabilities only and do not involve the measurement of operations.

Although a government should establish and maintain those funds required by law and sound financial administration, it should set up only the minimum number of funds consistent with legal and operating requirements. The maintenance of unnecessary funds results in inflexibility, undue complexity, and inefficient financial administration. For instance, in the past, the proceeds of specific revenue sources or resources that financed specific activities as required by law or administrative regulation had to be accounted for in a special revenue fund. However, governmental resources restricted to purposes usually financed through the general fund should be accounted for in the general fund, provided that all legal requirements can be satisfied. Examples include state grants received by an entity for special education. If a separate fund is not legally required, the grant revenues and the grant-related expenditures should be accounted for in the fund for which they are to be used.

Another way to minimize funds is by accounting for debt service payments in the general fund and not establishing a separate debt service fund unless it is legally mandated or resources are actually being accumulated for future debt service payments (i.e., for term bonds or in sinking funds).

Furthermore, one or more identical accounts for separate funds should be combined in the accounting system, particularly for funds that are similar in nature or are in the same fund group. For example, the cash accounts for all special revenue funds may be combined, provided that the integrity of each fund is preserved through a distinct equity account for each fund.

(i) Governmental Funds
(A) GENERAL FUND

The general fund accounts for the revenues and expenditures not accounted for in other funds and finances most of the current normal functions of governmental units: general government, public safety, highways, sanitation and waste removal, health and welfare, culture, and recreation. It is usually the largest and most important accounting activity for state and local governments. Property taxes are often the principal source of general fund revenues, but substantial revenues may also be received from other financing sources.

The general fund balance sheet is typically limited to current assets and current liabilities. The GASB Codification emphasizes this practice by using the terms *expendable assets* and *current liabilities* when describing governmental funds, of which the general fund is one. Thus the fund balance in the general fund is considered available to finance current operations.

A governmental unit, however, often makes long-term advances to independent governmental agencies, such as redevelopment authorities or housing agencies, or provides the capital necessary to establish an internal service fund. The advances are recorded in the general fund as an advance receivable. Although in most cases collectibility is assured, repayment may extend over a number of years. The inclusion of a noncurrent asset in the general fund results in a portion of the general fund's fund balance not being readily available to finance current operations.

To reflect the unavailability of an advance to finance current activities, a fund balance reserve is established to segregate a portion of the fund balance from the general fund in an amount equal to the advance that is not considered currently available. Establishing this reserve does not require a charge to operations; rather, it is a segregation of the fund balance in the available general fund and is established by debiting unreserved fund balance and crediting reserved fund balance. The reserve is reported in the fund balance section of the balance sheet.

(B) SPECIAL REVENUE FUNDS

Special revenue funds should be established to account for the proceeds of specific revenue sources (other than expendable trusts or major capital projects) that are legally restricted to expenditure for specified purposes and for which a separate fund is legally required. Examples are parks, schools, and museums, as well as particular functions or activities, such as highway construction or street maintenance.

A special revenue fund may have a definite limited life, or it may remain in effect until discontinued or revoked by appropriate legislative action. It may be used for a very limited purpose, such as the maintenance of a historic landmark, or it may finance an entire function of government, such as public education or highways.

A special revenue fund may be administered by the regularly constituted administrative and financial organization of the government; by an independent body or special-purpose local district, such as a park board or the board of directors of a water district; or by a quasi-independent body. In some cases, the fund may be administered by an independent board, but the government maintains the accounting records because the independent board does not have the necessary personnel or other facilities.

(C) DEBT SERVICE FUNDS

Debt service funds exist to account for the accumulation of resources for, and the payment of, long-term debt principal and interest other than that which it is issued for and serviced primarily by an enterprise or similar trust fund. A debt service fund is necessary only if it is legally required or if resources are being accumulated for future payment. Although governments may incur a wide variety of debt, the more common types are described below.

Term (or sinking fund) bonds are being replaced by serial bonds as the predominant form of state and local government debt. For term bonds, debt service consists of annual additions of resources being made to a cumulative "investment fund" for repayment of the issue at maturity. The additions, also called *sinking fund installments,* are computed on an actuarial basis, which includes assumptions that certain rates of interest will be earned from investing the resources accumulating in the investment fund. If the actual earnings are less than the planned earnings, subsequent additions are increased; if the earnings are greater than planned, the excess is carried forward until the time of the final addition of the fund. Because term bond principal is due at the end of the bond's term, the expenditure for repayment of principal is recognized at that time.

Debt service on serial bonds, however, generally consists of preestablished principal payments that are due on an annual basis and interest payments based on either fixed or variable rates that are due on a semiannual basis. No sinking fund is involved in the repayment of serial bonds.

The revenues for a debt service fund come from one or more sources, with property taxes being the predominant source. Taxes that are specified for debt service appear as a revenue of the debt service fund. Taxes for general purposes (i.e., not specified but nevertheless used for debt service) are considered to be a transfer to the debt service fund from the fund in which the revenue is recorded, oftentimes the general fund.

Enterprise activity earnings may be another resource for servicing general obligation debt. In these instances, the general obligation debt should be classified as enterprise debt (a liability of the enterprise fund), and the debt service payments should be recorded in the enterprise fund as a reduction of the liability, not in the debt service fund. The debt service transactions would be recorded in the debt service fund only if the enterprise fund was not expected to be responsible for repaying the debt on an ongoing basis. Essentially, if the enterprise fund became unable to service the principal and interest and the general governmental unit assumed responsibility for servicing the debt, then the debt service fund would be used.

In addition, governmental units have been utilizing alternative financing activities, including lease-purchase arrangements and issuance of zero-coupon or deep-discount debt. The issues surrounding lease-purchase arrangements involve legal questions about whether such arrangements constitute debt of a government since they often do not require voter approval prior to incurring the debt. Zero-coupon and deep-discount debt issues center on the manner of presenting and amortizing the bond discount amount in the government's financial statements.

In other instances, governmental units have been securitizing specific receivables and future revenues in order to receive cash upfront for current outlays. GASB recently issued Statement No. 48, "Sales and Pledges of Receivables and Future Revenues and Intra-Entity Transfers of Assets and Future Receivables," to address a divergence in practice as to whether these securitizations should be reported as a revenue or as a liability. For example, in January 2007 the County of Santa Clara, California, sold its future Tobacco Settlement Revenues scheduled to be earned in the years 2026 through 2056 and recognized $102 million as a source of funds in 2007 in its governmental funds prior to the effective date of GASB Statement No. 48. As a result, the county was able under prior guidance to record this as an inflow of resources in its governmental funds.

Recently, governments are examining the possibility of issuing debt to fund their unfunded actuarial accrued liability (UAAL) for their Other Postemployment Benefits (OPEB) as has sometimes been done with UAAL for their pension obligations. These are taxable debt issues that are used to fund all or part of a government entity's UAAL. This shifts the liability from one owed to the pension plan to one owed to bondholders and brings the liability onto the government's financial statements. The rationale for issuing this type of debt is to invest the proceeds in investments that provide a rate of return higher than the debt interest costs. Governments should exercise caution when evaluating the possibility of issuing OPEB or pension obligation bonds, given the volatility of the computation of the actuarial liabilities, the increase in the government's debt burden, and the dependence on a higher rate of earnings on investments.

Quite often, a refunding bond is issued to replace or consolidate prior debt issues. Determining the appropriate accounting principles to apply to refunding bonds depends primarily on whether the bonds are enterprise fund obligations or general obligations. GASB Statement No. 7, "Advance Refundings Resulting in Defeasance of Debt," outlines the appropriate accounting and reporting principles. For the refunding of debt, the proceeds of the refunding issue become an "other financing source" of the fund receiving the proceeds of the refunding bond (oftentimes a debt service fund created to service the original issue or a capital projects fund). Since the proceeds are used to liquidate the original debt, an "other financing use" is also recorded in the debt service or capital projects fund in an amount equal to the remaining principal, interest, and other amounts due on the original debt.

If, as a result of the refunding, the liability to the bondholders is satisfied, the refunding is referred to as a *legal defeasance of debt* or *current refunding*. However, refundings often do not result in the immediate repayment of the debt; rather, assets are placed in a trust to be used to repay the debt as it matures. These refundings are called *advance refundings* or *in-substance defeasances*. To qualify for an in-substance defeasance, the proceeds of the refunding bonds are placed in an irrevocable trust and invested in essentially risk-free securities, usually obligations of the U.S. Treasury or other government agencies, so that the risk-free securities, together with any premiums on the defeased debt and expenses of the refunding operation, will be sufficient for the trust to pay off the debt to the bondholders when it becomes due. The accounting for an in-substance defeasance is identical to legal defeasances except that payment is made to a trustee rather than to bondholders. The trustee then pays principal and interest to the bondholders based on the maturity schedule of the bond. In addition, the recording of payments of proceeds to the trustee as another financing use is limited to the amount of proceeds.

Advance refundings of debt follow the accounting principles outlined in GASB Statement No. 23, "Accounting and Financial Reporting for Refundings of Debt Reported by Proprietary Activities." Statement No. 23 requires that the difference between the reacquisition price and the net carrying amount of the old debt be deferred and amortized as a component of interest expense over the remaining life of the old or the life of the new debt, whichever is shorter.

In addition, GASB Statement No. 7 requires the disclosure of a description of the refunding transaction; the cash flow gain or loss, which is the difference between the total cash outflow of the new debt (i.e., principal, interest, etc.) and the remaining cash outflow of the old debt; and the economic gain or loss, which is the difference between the present values of the cash flows of the new and old debt.

For advance refundings, each year after the defeasance, the footnotes to the financial statements should disclose the remaining amount of debt principal that the trustee has to pay to bondholders.

(D) CAPITAL PROJECTS FUNDS
The purpose of a capital projects fund is to account for the receipt and disbursement of resources used for the acquisition of major capital facilities other than those financed by enterprise funds. Capital projects are defined as outlays for major, permanent fixed assets having a relatively long life (e.g., buildings), as compared with those of limited life (e.g., office equipment). Capital projects are usually financed by bond proceeds, but they can also be financed from other resources, such as current revenues or grants from other governments.

Capital outlays financed entirely from the direct revenues of the general fund or a special revenue fund and not requiring long-term borrowing may be accounted for in the fund providing such resources rather than in a separate capital projects fund. Assets with a relatively short life—hence not capital projects—are usually financed from current revenues or by short-term obligations and are accounted for in the general or special revenue fund.

Accounting for Capital Projects Fund Transactions. Bonds are issued and capital projects are started under a multiyear capital program. In some instances, it is necessary to secure referendum approval to issue general obligation bonds. Obligations are then incurred and expenditures made according to an annual capital projects budget.

When a project is financed entirely from general obligation bond proceeds, the initial entry to be made in the capital projects fund when the bonds are sold is as follows:

Cash	$XXX
Other financing source—	
Proceeds of general obligation bonds	$XXX

Whereas the proceeds of the bonds are accounted for in the capital projects funds, the liability for the face amount of the bonds is recorded in the government-wide statement of net assets.

If bonds are sold at a premium (i.e., above par value), the premium increases the other financing sources. Often, the premium is transferred—by a debit to "other financing sources" and a credit to "cash"—to the debt service fund established to service the debt for the project. If the bonds are sold at a discount (i.e., below par value), the discount reduces the amount recorded as other financing sources in the capital projects fund. Bond issuance costs either paid out of available funds or withheld from the bond proceeds usually are accounted as debt service expenditures in the capital projects or debt service funds operating statement.

Bond Anticipation Notes (BANs). Governments sometimes issue BANs prior to the sale of bonds, planning to retire the notes with the proceeds of the bond issue to which the notes are related. The reasons would include

- The governmental unit wants to accelerate initiation of a project, and issuance of the long-term bonds will require more time than is required to issue BANs.
- The governmental unit does not want to undertake long-term financing until the project is complete and ready for use. Hence BANs are used to provide construction financing.
- The current and projected interest rates make it prudent to issue short-term notes first and to defer issuance of long-term bonds.
- The individual capital projects to be financed from the proceeds of the bond sale are so small as to make the sale of bonds to finance each project impracticable.

The cash proceeds and the liabilities resulting from the sale of BANs should be recorded in the capital projects fund as follows:

Cash	$XXX
Bond anticipation notes payable	$XXX

When the long-term bonds are sold, an "other financing source" should be recorded and the BANs payable debited in an amount equal to the portion of the BANs redeemed as follows:

Bond participation notes payable	$XXX
Other financing source	$XXX

If the BANs are not redeemed with long-term bond proceeds or other funds by the end of the year, and the governmental unit has both the intent and the ability (as those terms are defined in Statement of Financial Accounting Standards (SFAS) No. 6, "Classification of Short-Term Obligations Expected to Be Refinanced," pars. 10 and 11) to redeem the BANs with long-term debt, the BANs payable account should be debited and an "other financing source" should be credited. If the governmental unit does not have the intent or ability to redeem the BANs with long-term debt, it is appropriate to leave the liability in the capital projects fund. The ability to redeem the BANs could be demonstrated by a post–balance sheet issuance of long-term debt or the entering into of a long-term financing arrangement for the BANs.

Project Budgets.   When debt is issued to finance an entire capital project, it is usually done at the beginning of the project in an amount equal to the total estimated project cost. Accordingly, a portion of the proceeds may remain unexpended over a considerable period of time. To the maximum extent possible, these excess proceeds should be invested in interest-bearing investments. However, consideration should be given to the federal arbitrage regulations that limit the amount of interest that can be earned from investing the proceeds of a tax-exempt bond issue. If certain limits are exceeded, the bond's tax-exempt status may be lost or severe penalties could be imposed on the issuer.

Project budgets are typically established for capital projects to control costs and to guard against cost overruns. All expenditures needed to place the project in readiness—that is, indirect as well as direct costs—should be recorded against this budget. The actual expenditures, however, will probably be either less or greater than the amounts authorized. Therefore, in the absence of any legal restrictions, any unspent balance should be transferred to the appropriate sources. If the project was financed only from bond proceeds, the transfer should be to the debt service fund from which the bond issue is to be repaid. If the resources were drawn from more than one source, such as bond proceeds and current revenues, the transfer should be split among the sources in proportion to their contributions. If the expenditures were greater than authorized and a deficit exists, sufficient funds must be transferred to liquidate any commitments.

As construction of the project is completed, the costs should be recorded in the capital account as Construction in Progress and then transferred to the final building account when construction is completed.

(E) PERMANENT FUNDS

Permanent funds should be used to report assets legally restricted so that only earnings, not principal, may be spent for the government's programs—that is, for the benefit of the government or its citizens.

(ii) Proprietary Funds
(A) ENTERPRISE FUNDS

Enterprise funds *may be* used to report any activity for which fees are charged to external users in exchange for goods or services. They are *required* to be used if *any one* of the following criteria is met in the context of the activity's principal revenue sources (insignificant activities, such as fees charged for frivolous small-claims suits, are excluded):

- The activity is financed with debt secured solely by a pledge of the net revenues from fees and charges of the activity. (This is met if the debt is secured in part by a portion of its own proceeds.)
- Laws or regulations require that the activity's costs of providing goods or services, including capital costs such as depreciation or debt service, be recovered by its fees and charges, not by taxes or similar revenues.
- The pricing policies of the activity result in fees and charges intended to recover the activity's costs, including capital costs such as depreciation or debt service.
- The primary focus of these criteria is on fees charged to external users.

Proprietary (enterprise) activities are frequently administered by departments of the general-purpose government—for example, a municipal water department or a state parks department. They can also be the exclusive function of a local special district, such as a water district, power authority, or bridge and tunnel authority.

User charges are one significant source of enterprise fund resources; revenue bond proceeds are another. Revenue bonds are long-term obligations, the principal and interest of which are paid from the earnings of the enterprise for which the bond proceeds were spent. The enterprise revenues may be pledged to the payment of the debt, and the physical properties may carry a mortgage that is to be liquidated in the event of default.

Revenue bond indentures usually also contain several requirements concerning the use of the bond proceeds, the computation and reporting of revenue bond coverage, and the establishment and use of restricted asset accounts for handling revenue bond debt service requirements. For instance, a revenue bond indenture may require the establishment of various bond accounts, including a construction account, operations and maintenance account, current debt service account, future debt service account, and revenue and replacement account. This does not necessarily mean establishing individual accounting funds for each bond issue. Instead, the accounting and reporting requirements can be met through the use of various accounts within an accounting fund.

The revenue bond construction account normally represents cash and investments (including interest receivable) segregated by the bond indenture for construction. Construction liabilities payable from restricted assets should be reported as "contracts payable from restricted assets." If there are significant unspent debt proceeds at year-end, the portion of the debt attributable to the unspent proceeds should not be included in the calculation of amounts invested in capital assets, net of related debt. Instead, that portion of the debt should be included as the same net assets component as the unspent proceeds.

A revenue bond operations and maintenance account often is established pursuant to a bond indenture. Resources for this account are provided through bond proceeds and/or operating income or net income. This account generally accumulates assets equal to operating costs for one month. Once this account has been established, additional proceeds from future bond issues generally are necessary only to the extent the costs associated with these expanded operations are expected to increase. This account is normally balanced by a restricted net asset account for revenue bond operations and maintenance.

Bond indentures may also include a covenant requiring the establishment of a restricted account for the repayment of bond principal and interest. Resources for this account also are provided through bond proceeds and/or operating income or net income. Normally, assets accumulated for debt service payments (i.e., principal and interest) due within one year are classified in the revenue bond current debt service account. This account is at least partially associated with the bonds payable—current account and the accrued interest payable account. Any difference between the revenue bond current debt service account and related current bonds payable and accrued interest payable should be reported as restricted net assets. When accounts are restricted for debt service payments beyond the next 12 months, a revenue bond future debt service account should be established.

The final restricted account typically established pursuant to a covenant within a bond indenture is the revenue bond renewal and replacement account. Net income is often restricted for payments of unforeseen repairs and replacements of assets originally acquired with bond proceeds. Provided that liabilities have not been incurred for this purpose, the revenue bond renewal and replacement account is balanced by net assets restricted for revenue bond renewal and replacement.

The following general rule should be considered when determining the amount of restricted net assets to record: Unless otherwise required by the bond indenture, net assets should be restricted only for amounts of restricted assets in excess of related liabilities and the balance of restricted assets funded by bond proceeds.

Another restricted asset often found in enterprise funds for utility operations is the amount resulting from the deposits customers are required to make to ensure payment of their final charges and to protect the utility against damage to equipment located on the customer's property. These funds are not available for the financing of current operations and, generally, the amount, less the charges outstanding against the account, must be returned when the customer withdraws from the system. Also, these deposits may, depending on legal and policy requirements, draw interest at some stipulated rate.

In some instances, revenue bonds are also secured by the full faith and credit of the governmental unit. This additional security enables the bonds to obtain better acceptance in the securities market. If the bonds are to be serviced by the enterprise activity, the cash, liability, principal, and interest payments should be accounted for in the enterprise fund. Even if the bonds are secured only by full faith and credit and not by a revenue pledge but the intention is to use enterprise revenues to service the bonds, they should be accounted for as if they were revenue bonds. If, however, general obligation bond proceeds are used to finance the enterprise activity and there is no intention to service the bonds with enterprise fund resources, the amounts provided to the enterprise fund should be recorded as a transfer from the fund recording the proceeds of the bond—typically, the general fund.

Other sources of contributions also provide significant resources for enterprise activities. Such resources include capital contributions by other funds or other governmental bodies; capital contributions by customers or other members of the general public; the aforementioned proceeds of a bond issue to be repaid from general fund revenues, federal grants, or state grants; connection charges to users of utility services; payments by real estate developers for installing utility lines; and similar receipts.

Another resource is the support provided by or to other funds of the government. For instance, an enterprise fund will frequently use the services or commodities of a central facility operated as an internal service fund. Conversely, the general fund departments will use the services of an electric utility fund.

It is important to handle these relationships on a businesslike basis. All services rendered by an enterprise fund for other funds of the government should be billed at predetermined rates, and the enterprise should pay for all services received from other funds on the same basis that is utilized to determine charges for other users. The latter will often include payments in lieu of taxes to the general fund in amounts comparable to the taxes that would have been paid by the enterprise were it privately owned and operated, or an "administrative charge" if the enterprise does not have its own management capacity and instead uses management services provided by the general government. Unless this is done, the financial operations of a government-owned enterprise will be distorted, and valid comparisons of operating results with those for a similar privately owned enterprise cannot be made. However, other considerations, such as the amount of planned idle capacity, have an impact on the comparability of public and private enterprise funds.

Interfund transfers may also occur between an enterprise fund and governmental funds. Operating subsidy transfers from the general fund or special revenue fund are possible. There may also be transfers from an enterprise to finance general fund expenditures.

Finally, there are the nonoperating income and expenses, which are incidental to, or by-products of, the enterprise's primary service function. Nonoperating income consists of such items as interest earnings, rent from nonoperating properties, intergovernmental revenues, and sale of excess supplies. Nonoperating expenses include items such as interest expense and fiscal agents' fees.

(B) INTERNAL SERVICE FUNDS

Internal service funds finance and account for special activities that are performed and commodities that are furnished by one department or agency of a governmental unit to other departments or agencies of that unit or to other governmental units on a cost-reimbursement basis. The services differ from those rendered to the public at large, which are accounted for in general, special revenue, or enterprise funds. Examples of activities in which internal service funds are established include central motor pools, duplication services, central purchasing and stores departments, and insurance and risk-management activities.

When an internal service fund is established, resources are typically obtained from contributions from other operating funds, such as the general fund or an enterprise fund, or from long-term advances from other funds that are to be repaid from operating income. The entry to be made when the fund is created varies depending on the source of the contributions.

The cost of services rendered and commodities furnished, including labor, depreciation on all capital assets used by the funds other than buildings financed from capital projects, and overhead, are charged to the departments served. These departments reimburse the internal service fund by recording expenditures against their budgeted appropriations. The operating objective of the fund is to recover costs incurred to provide the service, including depreciation. Accordingly, the operations of the fund should not result in any significant profit or loss. Whenever it uses the services of another fund, such as an enterprise fund, the fund pays for and records the costs just as if it had dealt with an outside organization.

Since exact overhead charges are usually not known when bills are prepared, the departments being served are usually billed for direct costs plus a uniform rate for their portion of estimated overhead. Any difference in actual overhead expenses may be charged or credited to the departments at fiscal year-end or adjusted for in a subsequent year. At the end of each fiscal year, net income or loss must be determined. The excess of net billings to the department over costs is closed to the net assets account.

(iii) Fiduciary Funds   The purpose of fiduciary (trust and agency) funds is to account for assets held by a governmental unit in a trustee capacity or as an agent for other individuals, private organizations, or other governmental units.

Usually in existence for an extended period of time, trust funds deal with substantial vested interests and involve complex administrative problems. The government's records must provide adequate information to permit compliance with the terms of the trust as defined in the trust document, statutes, ordinances, or governing regulations.

(A) PENSION (AND OTHER EMPLOYEE BENEFIT) TRUST FUNDS

In pension (and other employee benefit) trust funds, governments account for resources held for the future retirement and other postemployment benefits (defined benefit and defined contribution) of their employees. The resources of these funds are the members' contributions, contributions from the government employer, and earnings on investments in authorized securities. The expenses are the authorized retirement allowances and other benefits, refunds of contributions to members who resign prior to retirement, and administrative expenses. Professional actuaries make periodic actuarial studies of the retirement systems and compute the amounts that should be provided so that the benefits can be paid as required.

The proper accounting for pension trust funds has been on the GASB's agenda since its creation. The GASB initially allowed governments to choose from three different methods of accounting and financial reporting but required certain disclosures from all governments. The GASB has finally completed its consideration of pensions and other postemployment employee benefits (OBEB), and the current statements include: Statement No. 25, "Financial Reporting for Defined Benefit Pension Plans and Note Disclosures for Defined Contribution Plans," Statement No. 27, "Accounting for Pensions by State and Local Government Employers," Statement No. 43, "Financial Reporting for Postemployment Benefit Plans Other Than Pension Plans," Statement No. 45, "Accounting and Financial Reporting by Employers for Postemployment Benefits Other Than Pensions," and Statement No. 50, "Pension Disclosures—an Amendment of GASB Statements No. 25 and No. 27." Statements No. 25 and 43 address issues related to accounting by pension and other employee benefit plans along with pension and other employee benefit trust funds. Statements Nos. 27 and 45 address accounting and financial reporting for those employers who participate in a pension and other employee benefit plans.

Statements Nos. 25 and 43 describe two basic financial statements for pension (and other employee benefit) plans: the statement of plan net assets and the statement of changes in plan net assets. These two financial statements are designed to provide current information about plan assets and financial activities. Statements Nos. 25 (as amended by No. 50) and 43 have other requirements for note disclosure that include a brief plan description, a summary of significant accounting principles, and information about contributions, legally required reserves, investment concentrations, funded status of the plan as of the most recent actuarial valuation date, and the actuarial methods and significant assumptions used in the most recent actuarial valuation.

The accounting guidance is directed at employers which participate in a pension (and other employee benefit) plans and reflects two underlying principles. First, the pension or OPEB cost recognized should be related to the annual required contribution (ARC) as determined by an actuary for funding purposes. Second, the actuarial methods and assumptions used by employers should be consistent with those used by the plan in its separate reporting.

In implementing these basic principles, Statements Nos. 27 and 45 require the ARC to be recognized as pension or OPEB expense in government-wide financial statements and in the proprietary funds. Governmental funds will recognize pension expenditure to the extent that the ARC is expected to be liquidated with expendable available resources. If an employer does not contribute to the ARC (or has contributed in excess of the ARC), pension or OPEB expense/expenditure no longer equals the ARC. In these cases the ARC is adjusted to remove the effects of the actuarial adjustments included in the ARC and to reflect interest on previous under or over funding.

Although Statements Nos. 27 and 45 try to minimize the differences between accounting for pensions (and other employee benefits) and funding pensions (and other employee benefits), it does place certain limits or "parameters" on the actuary's modified calculation of the ARC. These parameters are consistent with parameters established for accounting for the plan itself in Statements Nos. 25 and 43. These parameters relate to the pension/OPEB obligation, actuarial assumptions, economic assumptions, actuarial cost method, actuarial valuation of assets, and amortization of unfunded actuarial accrued liability.

Statements Nos. 27 and 45 establish disclosure requirements that vary depending on whether the government merely participates in a pension (and other employee benefits) plan administered by another entity or includes a pension (and other employee benefits) trust fund(s). Disclosure requirements also vary for governments with a pension (and other employee benefits) trust fund based on whether the pension (and other employee benefits) plan issues separate publicly available financial statements. These disclosure requirements generally include a plan description, funding policy, pension cost components, actuarial valuation information, and trend data.

Resources accumulated for OPEB should be accounted for in a trust fund separate from resources accumulated for pension benefits.

(B) INVESTMENT TRUST FUNDS
Investment trust funds should be used by the sponsoring government to report the external part of investment pools, as required by GASB Statement No. 31, paragraph 18.

(C) PRIVATE-PURPOSE TRUST FUNDS
Private-purpose trust funds, such as one used to report escheat property, should be used to report all other trust arrangements under which principal and income benefit individuals, private organizations, or other governments.

(D) AGENCY FUNDS
Used by governments to handle cash resources held in an agent capacity, agency funds require relatively simple administration. The typical agency funds used by state and local governments include (1) tax collection funds, under which one local government collects a tax for an overlapping governmental unit and remits the amount collected less administrative charges to the recipient, and (2) payroll withholdings, under which the government collects the deductions and periodically remits them in a lump sum to the appropriate recipient.

(iv) Special Assessment Activities   Special assessment activities pertain to (1) the financing and construction of certain public improvements, such as storm sewers, which are to be paid for wholly or partly from special assessments levied against the properties benefited by such improvements, or (2) the providing of services that are normally provided to the public as general governmental functions and that would otherwise be financed by the general fund or a special revenue fund. Those services may include street lighting, street cleaning, and snow

plowing. The payment by the property owners or taxpayers receiving the benefit distinguishes these activities from activities that benefit the entire community and are paid for from general revenues or general obligation bond proceeds. Sometimes, however, a special assessment bond, which is often used to finance the special assessment improvement, also carries the additional pledge of the full faith and credit of the governmental unit.

It should be emphasized that whereas GASB Statement No. 6 eliminated the requirement to report special assessment funds in an entity's basic financial statement, accounting for special assessment activities is still an important part of governmental accounting.

Capital improvement special assessment projects have two distinct and functionally different phases. The initial phase consists of financing and constructing the project. In most cases, this period is relatively short in duration, sometimes lasting only a few months, and rarely more than a year or two. The second phase, which may start at the same time as, during, or after the initial phase, consists of collecting the assessment principal and interest levied against the benefited properties and repaying the cost of financing the construction. The second phase is usually substantially longer than the first.

There are many ways of financing a capital improvement special assessment project. Assessments may be levied and collected immediately. Funds will then be available to pay construction costs, and it will not be necessary to issue special assessment bonds. Alternatively, a project may be constructed using the proceeds from short-term borrowing. When the project is complete and the exact cost is known, special assessment bonds are issued to provide the exact amount of money, and the short-term borrowings are repaid. A third—and perhaps the most common—financing alternative is for the government to levy a special assessment for the estimated cost of the improvement, issue bonds to provide the funds, construct the improvement using the bond proceeds, and then collect the assessments over a period of years, using the collections to service the bonds.

Five basic types of transactions are associated with a capital-project type special assessment:

1. Levying the special assessment
2. Issuing special assessment bonds
3. Constructing the capital project
4. Collecting the special assessment
5. Paying the bond principal and interest

Because the special assessment fund has been eliminated for financial reporting purpose, the transactions related to special assessment activities are typically reported in the same manner and on the same basis of accounting as any other capital improvement and financing transaction. Transactions of the construction phase of the project should generally be reported in a capital projects fund, and transactions of the debt service phase should be reported in a debt service fund, if one is required.

At the time of the levy, the governmental fund should recognize the special assessments receivable with the deferred revenue; the deferred revenue should be reduced as the assessments become measurable and available in the fund financial statements.

The entry for the retirement of special assessment bonds and for the construction of the special assessment project would follow the accounting principles outlined in the discussion on capital projects. The usual entries are made for expenditures and for encumbrances, if such a system exists. At the end of the year, the revenues and expenditures should be closed to the fund balance to reflect the balance that may be expended in future periods.

Although the accounting for special assessment construction activities is quite similar to other financing and construction activities, the major issue relating to special assessment activities involves the definition of special assessment debt. Special assessment debt is often defined as those long-term obligations, secured by a lien on the assessed properties, for which the primary source of repayment is the assessments levied against the benefiting properties.

However, the nature and composition of debt associated with special assessment–related capital improvements is not always consistent with this definition. Rather, it can vary significantly from one jurisdiction to another. Capital improvements involving special assessments may be financed by debt that is

1. General obligation debt that is not secured by liens on assessed properties but nevertheless will be repaid in part by special assessment collections
2. Special assessment debt that is secured by liens on assessed properties and is also backed by the full faith and credit of the government as additional security
3. Special assessment debt that is secured by liens on assessed properties and is not backed by the full faith and credit of the government but is, however, fully or partially backed by some other type of general governmental commitment
4. Special assessment debt that is secured by liens on assessed properties, is not backed by the full faith and credit of the government, and is not backed by any other type of general governmental commitment, the government not being liable under any circumstance for the repayment of this category of debt should the property owner default

In some cases special assessment debt is payable entirely by special assessment collections from the assessed property owners; in other cases the debt may be repaid partly from special assessment collections and partly from the general resources of the government, either because the government is a property owner benefiting from the improvements or because the government has agreed to finance part of the cost of the improvement as a public benefit. The portion of special assessment debt that will be repaid directly with governmental resources is, in essence, a general obligation of the government. If the government owns property that benefits from the improvements financed by special assessment debt as in item 4 in the preceding list, or if a public benefit assessment is made against the government, the government is obligated for the public benefit portion and the amount assessed against its property, even though it has no liability for the remainder of the debt issue.

Because the special assessment debt can have various characteristics, the extent of a government's liability for debt related to a special assessment capital improvement can also vary significantly. For example, the government may be primarily liable for the debt, as in the case of a general obligation issue; it may have no liability whatsoever for special assessment debt; or it may be obligated in some manner to provide a secondary source of funds for repayment of special assessment debt in the event of default by the assessed property owners. A government is obligated in some manner for special assessment debt if (1) it is legally obligated to assume all or part of the debt in the event of default or (2) the government may take certain actions to assume secondary liability for all or part of the debt—and the government takes, or has given indications that it will take, those actions.

Stated differently, the phrase *obligated in some manner* is intended to include all situations other than those in which (1) the government is prohibited (by constitution, charter, statute, ordinance, or contract) from assuming the debt in the event of default by the property owner or (2) the government is not legally liable for assuming the debt and makes no statement, or gives no indication, that it will, or may, honor the debt in the event of default.

Debt issued to finance capital projects that will be paid wholly or partly from special assessments against benefited property owners should be reported in one of the following three ways:

1. General obligation debt that will be repaid, in part, from special assessments should be reported like any other general obligation debt.

2. Special assessment debt for which the government is obligated in some manner should be reported in the capital projects fund, except for the portion, if any, that is a direct obligation of a proprietary fund or that is expected to be repaid from operating revenues of a proprietary fund.

3. Special assessment debt for which the government is not obligated in any manner should not be displayed in the government's financial statements. However, if the government is liable for a portion of that debt (the public benefit portion, or as a property owner), that portion should be reported as previously stated.

(h) CAPITAL ASSETS REPORTING AND ACCOUNTING   The term *capital assets* includes land, improvements to land, easements, buildings, building improvements, vehicles, machinery, equipment, works of art and historical treasures, infrastructure, and all other tangible or intangible assets used in operations and that have initial useful lives beyond a single reporting period. Infrastructure assets are capital assets that are normally stationary and normally can be preserved for a significantly greater number of years than most other capital assets—for example, roads, bridges, tunnels, drainage systems, water and sewer systems, dams, and lighting systems. Buildings that are not ancillary parts of networks of infrastructure assets are not infrastructure assets.

Purchased capital assets should be reported at their acquisition costs, which should include ancillary charges needed to place the assets in their intended locations and conditions for use. Ancillary charges include costs directly attributable to asset acquisition, such as freight and transportation charges, site preparation costs, and professional fees. Donated capital assets should be reported at their fair values at their times of acquisition plus ancillary charges.

In general, capital assets should be depreciated. They should be reported net of accumulated depreciation in the statement of net assets, with accumulated depreciation reported on the face of the statement or in the notes. Capital assets not depreciated, such as land and infrastructure assets reported using the modified approach, discussed subsequently, should be reported separately if they are significant.

Capital assets, such as infrastructure, buildings and improvements, vehicles, machinery, and equipment may also be reported in greater detail. Capital assets should be depreciated over their useful lives based on their net costs less salvage values in a systematic and rational manner unless they are either inexhaustible, such as land and land improvements, or are infrastructure reported using the modified approach. Depreciation, reported in the statement of activities as discussed in the following text, may be calculated for (1) a class of assets, (2) a network of assets (all the assets that provide a particular kind of service for a government; a network of infrastructure assets may be only one infrastructure asset composed of many components—e.g., a dam composed of a concrete dam, a concrete spillway, and a series of locks), (3) a subsystem of a network (all assets that make up a similar portion or segment of a network of assets—e.g., interstate highways, state highways, and rural roads could each be a subsystem of a network of all the roads of a government), or (4) individual assets.

Eligible infrastructure assets—infrastructure assets that are part of a network or subsystem of a network—need not be depreciated but may be treated by a modified approach if both of the following are met:

1. The government manages them using an asset management system that has these characteristics:
    o   It has an up-to-date inventory of eligible infrastructure assets.
    o   It performs condition assessments of the eligible infrastructure assets and summarizes the results using a measurement scale. The assessments must be documented so they can be replicated—based on sufficiently understandable and complete measurement methods so that different measurers using the same methods would reach substantially similar results—performed by the government or by contract.
    o   It estimates each year the annual cost to maintain and preserve the eligible infrastructure assets at the condition level established and disclosed by the government.
2. The government documents that the eligible infrastructure assets are being preserved approximately at or above a condition level established and documented by administrative or executive policy or by legislative action and documented by the government. Adequate documentation requires professional judgment and may vary within governments for different eligible infrastructure assets. Nevertheless, documentation should include
    o   Complete condition assessments of eligible infrastructure assets performed consistently at least every three years. Statistical sampling may be used, and eligible infrastructure assets may be assessed on a cyclical basis. A complete assessment on a cyclical basis requires all or statistical samples of all eligible infrastructure assets in the network or subsystem to be assessed.
    o   The three most recent complete condition assessments provide reasonable assurance that the eligible infrastructure assets are being preserved approximately at or above the condition level established and disclosed by the government. The condition level could be measured either by a condition index or as the percentage of a network of infrastructure assets in good or poor condition.

All expenditures other than for additions and improvements made for eligible infrastructure assets that meet the two requirements and are not depreciated should be reported as expense in the periods incurred. Additions and improvements increase the capacity or efficiency of infrastructure assets; expenditures for them should be capitalized. A change from depreciation to the modified approach should be reported as a change in an accounting estimate.

When and if the requirements to report capital assets by the modified approach are no longer met, they should be depreciated in subsequent periods. The change should be reported as a change in accounting estimate.

Governments should in general capitalize individual or collections of works of art, historical treasures, and similar assets at their acquisition costs or fair values at the dates of acquisition or donation (estimated if necessary). They are encouraged but not required to capitalize a collection and all additions to the collection, whether donated or purchased, that meet all three of the following conditions (but collections capitalized by June 30, 1999, should remain capitalized and additions to them should be capitalized regardless of whether they meet the conditions):

1. The collection is held for public exhibition, education, or research for public service, not financial gain.
2. The collection is protected, kept unencumbered, cared for, and preserved.
3. The collection is subject to an organizational policy that requires that the proceeds from sales of collection items are used to acquire other items for collections.

Governments that receive donations of works of art, historical treasures, and similar assets should report revenues in conformity with GASB Statement No. 33. Governments should report program expense equal to the revenue reported on donated assets added to noncapitalized collections.

Capitalized collections or individual items of works of art, historical treasures, and similar assets that are exhaustible, such as exhibits whose useful lives decrease because of display or educational or research use, should be depreciated over their estimated useful lives. Depreciation is not required for collections or individual items of works of art, historical treasures, and similar assets that are inexhaustible.

(i) Methods for Calculating Depreciation   Governments may use any established depreciation method. It may be based on the estimated useful life of a class of assets, a network of assets, a subsystem, a network, or individual assets. Estimated useful lives may be obtained from general guidelines obtained from professional or industry organizations, information for comparable assets of other governments, or internal information.

A government may use a composite method, applying one rate, to calculate depreciation—for example, for similar assets or dissimilar assets of the same class, such as all the roads and bridges of the government. Depreciation is determined as the product of the total cost times the rate. The rate can be determined based on a weighted average or an unweighted average estimate of the useful lives of the assets included. Alternatively, it may be based on condition assessment or experience with the useful lives of the group of assets. It is generally used throughout the life of the group of assets, but it should be recalculated if the composition of the assets or the estimate of average useful lives changes significantly.

(ii) Subsidiary Property Records   The maintenance of subsidiary property records aids in the control of fixed assets. The subsidiary records should contain such information as classification code, date of acquisition, name and address of vendor, unit charged with custody, location, cost, fund and account from which purchased, method of acquisition, estimated life, and repair and maintenance data.

(iii) Disposal or Retirement of Capital Assets   In the disposal or retirement of a capital asset, the book value of the asset must be removed from the asset side and the gain or loss must be recorded in the statement of activities or the proprietary fund statements. If the asset is sold, the amount obtained in cash or by evidence of indebtedness should be recorded as another financing source in the appropriate governmental fund.

(iv) Impairment of Capital Assets   Governments should evaluate prominent events or changes in circumstances affecting capital assets to determine whether impairment of a capital asset has occurred. Indicators of impairment include physical damage, enactment or approval of laws or regulations or other changes in environmental factors, technological changes or evidence of obsolescence, changes in the manner or duration of use of a capital asset, and construction stoppage. A capital asset generally should be considered impaired if (1) the decline in service utility of the capital asset is large in magnitude and (2) the event or change in circumstance is outside the normal life cycle of the capital asset.

(i) REPORTING AND ACCOUNTING FOR LONG-TERM LIABILITIES   General long-term liabilities need to be clearly distinguished from fund long-term liabilities. General long-term liabilities are the unmatured principal of bonds, warrants, notes, or other forms of long-term general obligation indebtedness. They may arise from debt issuances, lease–purchase agreements, and other commitments that are not liabilities properly reported in governmental funds. Other general long-term liabilities include capital leases, operating judgments, pensions and other postemployment benefits, special termination benefits, and landfill closure and postclosure care liabilities that are not due.

General long-term liabilities should be reported in the governmental activities column in the government-wide statement of net assets, not in governmental funds.

Typically, the general long-term debt of a state or local government is secured by the general credit and revenue-raising powers of the government rather than by the assets acquired for specific fund resources. Furthermore, just as general capital assets do not represent financial resources available for appropriation and expenditure, general long-term liabilities do not require current appropriation and expenditure of a governmental fund's current financial resources. Thus, to include it as a governmental fund liability would be misleading for management control and accountability functions for the current period.

(j) MEASUREMENT FOCUS AND BASIS OF ACCOUNTING The accounting and financial reporting treatment applied to the government-wide financial statements and the fund financial statements is determined by its measurement focus. The measurement focus refers to what is being expressed in reporting an entity's financial performance and position. A particular measurement focus is accomplished by considering not only which resources are measured but also when the effects of transactions or events involving those resources are recognized (the basis of accounting). This principle describes the measurement focus and basis of accounting used by governments.

(i) Measurement Focus The government-wide and proprietary funds financial statements should be prepared using the economic resources measurement focus and the accrual basis of accounting. Assets, liabilities, revenues, expenses, and gains and losses that result from exchange transactions and exchange-like transactions should be reported when the transactions occur. (In an exchange-like transaction, the resources or services exchanged, though related, may not be quite equal or the direct benefits may not be exclusively for the parties to the transactions. Nevertheless, the transactions are similar enough to exchanges to justify treating them as exchanges.) Assets, liabilities, revenues, expenses, and gains and losses that result from nonexchange transactions should be reported as discussed further on in this chapter.

(ii) Basis of Accounting The basis of accounting determines when revenues, expenditures, expenses, and transfers—along with the related assets and liabilities—are recognized in the accounts and reported in the financial statements. Specifically, it relates to the timing of the measurements made, regardless of the measurement focus. For example, whether depreciation is recognized depends on whether expenses or expenditures are being measured rather than on whether the cash or accrual basis is used.

CASH BASIS
Under the cash basis of accounting, revenues and transfers in are not recorded in the accounts until cash is received, and expenditures or expenses and transfers out are recorded only when cash is disbursed.

The cash basis is frequently encountered, but its use is not generally accepted for any governmental unit. With the cash basis, it is difficult to compare expenditures with services rendered, because the disbursements relating to those services may be made in the fiscal period following that in which the services occurred. Also, statements prepared on a cash basis do not show financial position and results of operations on a basis that is generally accepted.

ACCRUAL BASIS

Under the accrual basis of accounting, most transactions are recorded when they occur, regardless of when cash is received or disbursed. Items not measurable until cash is received or disbursed are accounted for at that time.

The accrual basis is considered a superior method of accounting for the economic resources of any organization because it results in accounting measurements that are based on the substance of transactions and events, rather than merely on the receipt or disbursement of cash.

MODIFIED ACCRUAL BASIS

As indicated previously, the financial flows of governments, such as taxes and grants, typically do not result from a direct exchange for goods or services and thus cannot be accrued based on the completion of the earnings process and an exchange taking place. Governments have thus devised the "susceptible to accrual" concept as the criterion for determining when inflows are accruable as revenue. A revenue is susceptible to accrual when it is both measurable and available to finance current operations. An amount is measurable when the precise amount is known because the transaction is completed or when it can be accurately estimated using past experience or other available information. An amount is available to finance operations when it is (1) physically available—that is, collectible within the current period or soon enough thereafter to be used to pay liabilities of the current period, and (2) legally available—that is, authorized for expenditure in the current fiscal period and not applicable to some future period.

On the expenditure side, a government's main concern, for governmental funds at least, is to match the financial resources used with the financial resources obtained. This measure of whether current-year revenues were sufficient to pay for current-year services is referred to as *interperiod equity*. A measure of interperiod equity shows whether current-year citizens received services but shifted part of the payment burden to future-year citizens or used up previously accumulated resources. Conversely, such a measure would show whether current-year revenues were not only sufficient to pay for current-year services but also increased accumulated net resources.

This adaptation of the accrual basis to the conditions surrounding government activities and financing has been given the term *modified accrual*. Modified accrual is currently used in all governmental fund types (i.e., the general fund, special revenue funds, etc.) where the intent is to determine the extent to which provided services have been financed by current resources.

In proprietary funds the objective is to determine net income, and the accounting should be essentially the same as commercial accounting. Hence, proprietary funds use the economic resources measurement focus and the accrual basis without the need for modification described above.

(iii) Revenue Transactions   The modified accrual basis of accounting is applied in practice for five different revenue transactions as follows:

1. Property taxes are recorded as revenue when the taxes are levied, provided that they apply to and are collected in the current period or soon enough thereafter to finance the current period's expenditures. The period after year-end generally should not exceed 60 days. The amount recorded as revenue should be net of estimated uncollectible taxes, abatements, discounts, and refunds. (Property taxes that are

measurable but not available—and hence not susceptible to accrual—should be deferred and recognized as revenue in the fiscal year they become available.)

2. Taxpayer-assessed income, gross receipts, and sales taxes should be recorded as revenues when susceptible to accrual.

3. Miscellaneous revenues such as fines and forfeits, athletic fees, and inspection charges are generally recognized when cash is received because they are usually not measurable and available until they are received.

4. Grants should be recorded when the government has an irrevocable right to the grant. If expenditure of funds is the prime factor for determining eligibility for the grant funds, revenue should be recognized when the expenditure is made.

5. Interest earned on special assessment levies may be accrued when due rather than when earned if it approximately offsets interest expenditures on special assessment indebtedness that is also recorded when due.

Escheat property, which consists of assets reverted to a governmental entity in the absence of legal claimants or heirs, should be reported in government-wide and fund financial statements generally as an asset in the governmental or proprietary fund to which the property ultimately escheats. If held for individuals, private organizations, or another government, it should be reported in a private-purpose trust fund or an agency fund, as appropriate (or in the governmental or proprietary fund in which escheat property is otherwise reported, with a corresponding liability).

Escheat revenue on escheat property reported in governmental or proprietary funds should be reduced and a governmental or proprietary fund liability reported to the extent that it is probable that escheat property will be reclaimed and paid to claimants. The liability should represent the best estimate of the amount ultimately expected to be reclaimed and paid, giving effect to such factors as previous and current trends and anticipated changes in those trends. The liability may differ from the amount specified in law to be held separately for payments to claimants.

Escheat-related transactions reported in the government-wide financial statements should be measured using the economic resources measurement focus and the accrual basis of accounting. Escheat transactions reported in private-purpose trust funds or in agency funds should be excluded from the government-wide financial statements.

(iv) Expenditure Transactions Expenditure transactions under the modified accrual basis are treated as follows:

• If there is no explicit requirement to do otherwise, a governmental fund liability and expenditure should be accrued in the period in which the government incurs the liability. They include liabilities that normally are paid in a timely manner and in full from available financial resources, such as salaries, professional services, supplies, utilities, and travel. Unpaid, they represent claims against current financial resources and should be reported as governmental fund liabilities.

• Debt issue costs paid from debt proceeds, such as underwriter fees, should be reported as expenditures. Issue costs, such as attorneys' fees, rating agency fees, or bond insurance, paid from existing resources, should be reported as expenditures when liabilities for them are incurred.

• Inventory items may be considered expenditures either when purchased (the purchases method) or when used (the consumption method). Under either method, significant amounts of inventory at the end of a fiscal year should be reported as an asset on the balance sheet.

- Expenditures for insurance and similar services extending over more than one accounting period need not be allocated between or among accounting periods, but they may be accounted for as expenditures of the period of acquisition.
- Interest expenditures on special assessment indebtedness may be recorded when due if they are approximately offset by interest earnings on special assessment levies that are also recorded when due.
- Compensated absences, claims and judgments, special termination benefits, landfill closure and postclosure care costs, and "other obligations" should be recorded as a governmental fund liability when they are due for payment in the current period.

(v) Reporting on Nonexchange Transactions   As with a nonreciprocal transaction discussed in APB Statement No. 4, in a nonexchange transaction, a government of any level other than the federal government gives or receives financial or capital resources, not including contributed services, without directly receiving or giving equal value in exchange. Such transactions are divided into four classes:

1. *Derived tax revenues.* These result from assessments imposed by governments on exchange transactions, such as personal and corporate income taxes and retail sales taxes. Some legislation enabling such a tax provides purpose restrictions, requirements that a particular source of tax be used for a specific purpose or purposes—for example, motor fuel taxes required to be used for road and street repairs.

2. *Imposed nonexchange revenues.* These result from assessments on nongovernmental entities, including individuals, other than assessments on exchange transactions, such as property taxes, fines, and penalties, or property forfeitures, such as seizures and escheats. Such a tax is imposed on an act committed or omitted by the payor, such as property ownership or the contravention of a law or a regulation that is not an exchange. Some enabling legislation provides purpose restrictions; some also provides time requirements, specification of the periods in which the resources must be used or when their use may begin.

3. *Government-mandated nonexchange transactions.* These occur when a government, including the federal government, at one level provides resources to a government at another level and provides purpose restrictions on the recipient government established in the provider's enabling legislation. Transactions other than cash or other advances are contingent on fulfillment of certain requirements, which may include time requirements, which are called *eligibility requirements*.

4. *Voluntary nonexchange transactions.* These result from legislative or contractual agreements but are not deemed an exchange (unfunded mandates are excluded, because they are not transactions), entered into willingly by two or more parties, at least one of which is a government, such as certain grants, certain entitlements, and donations by nongovernmental entities including individuals (private donations). Providers often establish purpose restrictions and eligibility requirements and require return of the resources if the purpose restrictions or the eligibility requirements are contravened after reporting of the transaction.

Labels such as *tax, grant, contribution,* or *donation* do not necessarily indicate which of those classes nonexchange transactions belong to and therefore what principles should be applied. In addition, labels such as *fees, charges,* and *grants* do not always indicate whether exchange or nonexchange transactions are involved. Principles for reporting on nonexchange transactions depend on their substance, not merely their labels, and determining that requires analysis.

The following expense (or expenditure, for public colleges or universities) reporting principles for nonexchange transactions apply to both the accrual and the modified accrual basis, unless the transactions are not measurable or are not probable of collection. Such transactions that are not measurable should be disclosed.

Time requirements affect the timing of reporting of the transactions. The effect on the timing of reporting depends on whether a nonexchange transaction is an imposed nonexchange revenue transaction or a government-mandated or voluntary nonexchange transaction. Purpose restrictions do not affect the timing of reporting of the transactions. However, recipients should report resulting net assets, equity, or fund balance as restricted until the resources are used for the specified purpose or for as long as the provider requires the resources to be maintained intact, such as endowment principal.

Award programs commonly referred to as *reimbursement-type* or *expenditure-driven* grant programs may be either government mandated or voluntary nonexchange transactions. The provider stipulates an eligibility requirement that a recipient can qualify for resources only after incurring allowable costs under the provider's program. The provider has no liability and the recipient has no asset (receivable) until the recipient has met the eligibility requirements. Assets provided in advance should be reported as advances (assets) by providers and as deferred revenues (liabilities) by recipients until eligibility requirements have been met.

Assets should be reported from derived tax revenue transactions in the period in which the exchange transaction on which the tax is imposed occurs or in which the resources are received, whichever occurs first. Revenues net of estimated refunds and estimated uncollectible amounts should be reported in the period the assets are reported, provided that the underlying exchange transaction has occurred. Resources received in advance should be reported as deferred revenues (liabilities) until the period of the exchange.

Assets from imposed nonexchange revenue transactions should be reported in the period in which an enforceable legal claim to the assets arises or in which the assets are received, whichever occurs first. The date on which an enforceable legal claim to taxable property arises is generally specified in the enabling legislation, sometimes referred to as the *lien date*, though a lien is not formally placed on the property on that date. Others refer to it as the *assessment date*. (An enforceable legal claim by some governments arises in the period after the period for which the taxes are levied. Those governments should report assets in the same period they report revenues, as discussed next.)

Revenues from property taxes, net of estimated refunds and estimated uncollectible amounts, should be reported in the period for which the taxes are levied, even if the enforceable legal claim arises or the due date for payment occurs in a different period. All other imposed nonexchange revenues should be reported in the same period as the assets unless the enabling legislation includes time requirements. If it does, revenues should be reported in the period in which the resources are required to be used or in which use is first permitted. Resources received or reported as receivable before then should be reported as deferred revenues.

The following are the kinds of eligibility requirements for government-mandated and voluntary nonexchange transactions:

- The recipient and secondary recipients, if applicable, have the characteristics specified by the provider. For example, under a certain federal program, recipients are required to be states and secondary recipients are required to be school districts.

- Time requirements specified by enabling legislation or the provider have been met—that is, the period in which the resources are required to be sold, disbursed, or consumed or in which use is first permitted has begun, or the resources are being maintained intact, as specified by the provider.
- The provider offers resources on an "expenditure-driven" basis and the recipient has incurred allowable costs under the applicable program.
- The offer of resources by the provider in a voluntary nonexchange transaction is contingent on a specified action of the recipient—for example, to raise a specific amount of resources from third parties or to dedicate its own resources for a specified purpose, and that action has occurred.

Providers should report liabilities or decreases in assets and expenses from government-mandated or voluntary nonexchange transactions, and recipients should report receivables or decreases in liabilities and revenues, net of estimated uncollectible amounts, when all applicable eligibility requirements have been met (the need to complete purely routine requirements such as filing of claims for allowable costs under a reimbursement program or the filing of progress reports with the provider should not delay reporting of assets and revenues). Resources transmitted before the eligibility requirements are met should be reported as advances by the provider and as deferred revenue by recipients, except as indicated next for recipients of certain resources transmitted in advance. The exception does not cover transactions in which, for administrative or practical reasons, a government receives assets in the period immediately before the period the provider specifies as the one in which sale, disbursement, or consumption of resources is required or may begin.

A provider in some kinds of government-mandated and voluntary nonexchange transactions transmits assets stipulating that the resources cannot be sold, disbursed, or consumed until after a specified number of years have passed or a specific event has occurred, if ever. The recipient may nevertheless benefit from the resources in the interim—for example, by investing or exhibiting them. Examples are permanently nonexpendable additions to endowments and other trusts, term endowments, and contributions of works of art, historical treasures, and similar assets to capitalized collections. The recipient should report revenue when the resources are received if all eligibility requirements have been met. Resulting net assets, equity, or fund balance, should be reported as restricted as long as the provider's purpose restrictions or time requirements remain in effect.

If a provider in a government-mandated or voluntary nonexchange transaction does not specify time requirements, the entire award should be reported as a liability and an expense by the provider and as a receivable and revenue net of estimated uncollectible amounts by the recipients in the period in which all applicable eligibility requirements are met (applicable period). If the provider is a government, that period for both the provider and the recipients is the provider's fiscal year and begins on the first day of that year, and the entire award should be reported as of that date. But if the provider government has a biennial budgetary process, each year of the biennium should be treated as a separate applicable period. The provider and the recipients should then allocate one-half of the resources appropriated for the biennium to each applicable period, unless the provider specifies a different allocation.

Promises of assets including entities individuals voluntarily make to governments may include permanently nonexpendable additions to endowments and other trusts, term endowments, contributions of works of art and similar assets to capitalized collections, or other kinds of capital or financial assets, with or without purpose restrictions or time requirements. Recipients of such promises should report receivables and revenue net of estimated uncollectible amounts when all eligibility requirements have been met if the promise is verifiable and the resources are measurable and probable of collection. If the promise involves a stipulation (time requirement) that the resources cannot be sold, disbursed, or consumed until after a specified number of years have passed or a specific event has occurred, if ever, the recipient does not meet the time requirement until the assets have been received.

After a nonexchange transaction has been reported in the financial statements, it may become apparent that (1) if the transaction was reported as a government-mandated or voluntary nonexchange transaction, the eligibility requirements are no longer met, or (2) the recipient will not comply with the purpose restrictions within the specified time limit. If it then is probable that the provider will not provide the resources or will require the return of all or part of the resources already provided, the recipient should report a decrease in assets or an increase in liabilities and an expense, and the provider should report a decrease in liabilities or an increase in assets and a revenue for the amount involved in the period in which the returned resources become available.

A government may collect derived tax revenue or imposed nonexchange revenue on behalf of another government, the recipient, that imposed the revenue source—for example, sales tax collected by a state, part of which is a local option sales tax. The recipient should be able to reasonably estimate the accrual-basis information needed to comply with the requirements previously stated for derived tax revenue or imposed nonexchange revenue. However, if a government shares in a portion of the revenue resulting from a tax imposed by another government, it may not be able to reasonably estimate the accrual-basis information nor obtain sufficient timely information from the other government needed to comply with the previously stated requirements for derived tax revenue or imposed nonexchange revenue. If it cannot, the recipient government should report revenue for a period in the amount of cash received during the period. Cash received afterward should also be reported as revenue of the period, less amounts reported as revenue in the previous period, if reliable information is consistently available to identify the amounts that apply to the current period.

Revenue from nonexchange transactions reported on the modified accrual basis should be reported as follows:

- Recipients should report derived tax revenue in the period in which the underlying exchange transaction has occurred and the resources are available.
- Recipients should report property taxes in conformity with NCGA Interpretation No. 3, as amended.
- Recipients should report other imposed nonexchange revenue in the period in which an enforceable legal claim has arisen and the resources are available.
- Recipients should report government-mandated nonexchange transactions and voluntary nonexchange transactions in the period in which all applicable eligibility requirements have been met and the resources are available.

(k) BUDGETING, BUDGETARY CONTROL, AND BUDGETARY REPORTING ACCOUNTING

(i) Types of Operating Budgets   Several types of annual operating budgets are used in contemporary public finance. Among the more common are the following:

- Line item budget
- Program budget
- Performance budget
- Zero-base budget

LINE ITEM BUDGETING

Listing the inputs for resources that each organizational unit requests for each line (or object) of expenditure is referred to as *line item budgeting*. This simple approach produces a budget that governing bodies and administrators can understand, based on their own experience. It provides for tight control over spending and is the most common local government budgeting approach, although this popularity is due primarily to tradition.

Line item budgeting is criticized because it emphasizes inputs rather than outputs, analyzes expenditures inadequately, and fragments activities among accounts that bear little relation to purposes of the government. However, all budgeting systems use objects for the buildup of costs and for execution of the budget.

Overcoming criticisms of a line item budgeting system can be accomplished by:

- Improving the budget structure to encompass all funds and organizational units in a manner that enables the total resources available to a particular organizational unit or responsibility center to be readily perceived
- Developing a level of detail for the object categories that permits adequate analysis of proposed expenditures and effective control over the actual expenditures
- Improving the presentation of historical data to stimulate the analysis of trends
- Providing a partial linking of outputs to the objects of expenditures

PROGRAM BUDGETING

Formulating expenditure requests on the basis of the services to be performed for the various programs the government provides is known as *program budgeting*. A program budget categorizes the major areas of citizen needs and the services for meeting such needs into programs. Goals and objectives are stated for each program, normally in relatively specific, quantified terms. The costs are estimated for the resources required (e.g., personnel and equipment) to accomplish the objective for each program. The governing body can then conduct a meaningful review of budget requests by adding or deleting programs or placing different emphasis on the various programs.

Program budgeting has existed for many years, but relatively few governments have adopted it, partly because line item budgeting is so familiar and comprehensible. Lack of acceptance also results from the difficulty of developing operationally useful program budgets that meet the governmental notion of accountability, that is, control of the number of employees and other expense items, rather than achievement of results in applying such resources.

The operational usefulness of program budgeting has also been questioned as a result of the complexity of the program structure, the vagueness of goals and objectives, the lack of organizational or individual responsibility for program funds that span several departments or agencies, and the inadequacy of accounting support to record direct and indirect program costs.

Nevertheless, program budgeting can be an extremely effective approach for a government willing to devote the effort. The steps that departments should take to implement the system are as follows:

- Identify programs and the reasons for their existence.
- Define the goals of programs.
- Define kinds and levels of services to be provided in light of budgetary guidelines (council- or CEO-furnished guidelines, e.g., budget priorities, budget assumptions, and budget constraints).

- Develop budget requests in terms of resources needed, based on the programs' purposes, the budgetary guidelines, the projected levels of services, and the previous years' expenditure levels for the programs.
- Submit budget requests for compilation, review, and approval.

PERFORMANCE BUDGETING

Formulating expenditure requests based on the work to be performed is the primary function of performance budgeting. It emphasizes the work or service performed, described in quantitative terms, by an organizational unit performing a given activity—for example, number of tons of waste collected by the Sanitation Department and case workload in the Department of Welfare. These performance data are used in the preparation of the annual budget as the basis for increasing or decreasing the number of personnel and the related operating expenses of the individual departments.

The development of a full-scale performance budget requires a strong budget staff, constructive participation at all levels, special accounting and reporting methods, and a substantial volume of processed statistical data. Primarily for these reasons, performance budgeting has been less widely used than line item budgeting.

The approach to developing a performance budgeting system is as follows:

- Decide on the extent to which functions and activities will be segmented into work units and services for formulation and execution of the budget.
- Define the functions in services performed by the government, and assemble them into a structure.
- Identify and assemble or develop workload and efficiency measures that relate to service categories.
- Estimate the total costs of the functions and services.
- Analyze resource needs for each service in terms of personnel, equipment, and so on.
- Formulate the first-year performance budget (for the first year, set the budget appropriations and controls at a higher level than the data indicate).
- Perform cost accounting for the functional budget category; initiate statistical reporting of the workload measures; match resources utilized to actual results.

ZERO-BASE BUDGETING

In the preparation of a budget, zero-base budgeting projects funding for services at several alternative levels, both lower and higher than the present level, and allocates funds to services based on rankings of these alternatives. It is an appropriate budgeting system for jurisdictions whose revenues are not sufficient for citizen demands and inflation-driven expenditure increases, where considerable doubt exists as to the necessity and effectiveness of existing programs and services, and where incremental budgeting processes have resulted in existing programs and their funding being taken as a given, with attention devoted to requests for new programs.

Zero-base budgeting can be used with any existing budgeting system, including line item, program, or performance budgeting. The budget format can remain unchanged.

The steps to implement zero-base budgeting are as follows:

- Define decision units—that is, activities that can be logically grouped for planning and providing each service.

- Analyze decision units to determine alternative service levels, determine the resources required to operate at alternative levels, and present this information in decision packages.
- Rank the decision packages in a priority order that reflects the perceived importance of a particular package to the community in relation to other packages.
- Present the budget to the governing body for a review of the ranking of the decision packages.

(ii) Budget Preparation   The specific procedures involved in the preparation of a budget for a governmental unit are usually prescribed by state statute, local charter, or ordinance. There are, however, certain basic steps:

- Preparation of the budget calendar
- Development of preliminary forecasts of available revenues, recurring expenditures, and new programs
- Formulation and promulgation of a statement of executive budget policy to the operating departments
- Preparation and distribution of budget instructions, budget forms, and related information
- Review of departmental budget requests and supporting work sheets
- Interviews with department heads for the purpose of adjusting or approving their requests in a tentative budget
- Final assembly of the tentative budget, including fixing of revenue estimates and the required tax levy
- Presentation of the tentative budget to the legislative body and the public
- Conduction of a public hearing, with advance legal notice
- Adoption of final budget by the legislative body

REVENUE AND EXPENDITURE ESTIMATES

The property tax has been the traditional basic source of revenue for local government. The amount to be budgeted and raised is determined by subtracting the estimated nonproperty taxes and other revenues, plus the reappropriated fund balance, from budgeted expenditures. This amount, divided by the assessed valuation of taxable property within the boundaries of the governmental unit, produces the required tax rate.

Many jurisdictions have legal ceilings on the property tax rates available for general operating purposes. Additionally, taxpayer initiatives have forced governments to seek new revenue sources. Accordingly, governmental units have turned increasingly to other types of revenue, such as sales taxes; business and nonbusiness license fees; charges for services; state-collected, locally shared taxes; and grants-in-aid from the federal and state governments. Department heads, however, ordinarily have little knowledge of revenue figures. As a result, the primary responsibility for estimating these revenues usually lies with the budget officer and the chief finance officer.

Most governmental units, as a safeguard against excessive accumulation of resources, require that any unappropriated amounts carried over from a previous year be included as a source of financing in the budget of that fund for the succeeding fiscal year. Most controlling laws or ordinances provide for inclusion of the estimated surplus (fund balance) at the end of the current year, although many require that the includable surplus be the balance at the close of the last completed fiscal year.

Departmental estimates of expenditures and supporting work programs or performance data generally are prepared by the individual departments, using forms provided by the central budget agency. Expenditures are customarily classified to conform to the standard account classification of the governmental unit and thus permit comparison with actual performance in the current and prior periods.

PERSONAL SERVICES

Generally, personal services are supported by detailed schedules of proposed salaries for individual full-time employees. Nonsalaried and temporary employees are usually paid on an hourly basis, and the budget requests are normally based on the estimated number of hours of work.

Estimates of materials and supplies and other services, ordinarily quite repetitive in nature, are most often based on current experience, plus an allowance, if justified, for rising costs. Capital outlay requests are based on demonstrated need for specific items of furniture or equipment by individual departments.

In recent years, governmental units, particularly at the county, state, and federal levels, have disbursed substantial sums annually that are unlike the usual current operating expenditures. These sums include welfare or public assistance payments, contributions to other governmental units, benefit payments, and special grants. They are properly classified as "other charges." Estimates of these charges are generally based on unit costs for assistance, legislative allotments, requests from outside agencies or governmental units, and specified calculations.

In addition to departmental expenditures, the budget officer must estimate certain nondepartmental or general governmental costs not allocated to any department or organizational unit. Examples include pension costs and retirement contributions, which are not normally allocated, election costs, insurance and surety bonds, and interest on tax notes.

Although most governments still operate under laws that require the budget to be balanced precisely, an increasing number permit a surplus or contingency provision in the expenditure section of the budget. This is usually included to provide a reserve to cover unforeseen expenditures during the budget year.

The expenditure budget may be approved by a board, a commission, or other governing body before presentation to the central budget-making authority.

PRESENTATION OF THE BUDGET

To present a comprehensive picture of the proposed fund operations for a budget year, a budget document is prepared that is likely to include a budget message, summary schedules and comparative statements, detailed revenue estimates, detailed expenditure estimates, and drafts of ordinances to be enacted by the legislative body.

The contents of a budget message should set forth concisely the salient features of the proposed budget of each fund and will generally include the following: (1) a total amount showing amounts of overall increase and decrease, (2) detailed amounts and explanations of the increases and decreases, and (3) a detailed statement of the current financial status of each fund for which a budget is submitted, together with recommendations for raising the funds needed to balance the budget of each fund. It should identify the relationship of the operating budget to the capital program and capital budget, which are submitted separately.

ADOPTION OF THE BUDGET

Most states adopt the budget by the enactment of one or more statutes. Many cities require the formality of an ordinance for the adoption of the budget. In other cases, the budget is adopted by resolution of the governing body.

APPROPRIATIONS

Because appropriations constitute maximum expenditure authorizations during the fiscal year, they cannot be exceeded legally unless subsequently amended by the legislative body (although some governments permit modifications up to a prescribed limit to be made by the executive branch). Unexpended or unencumbered appropriations may lapse at the end of a fiscal year or may continue as authority for subsequent period expenditures, depending on the applicable legal provisions.

It may be necessary for the legislative agency to adopt a separate appropriation resolution or ordinance, or the adoption of the budget may include the making of appropriations for the items of expenditure included therein. Provision for the required general property tax levy is usually made at this time, either by certifying the required tax rates to the governmental unit that will bill and collect the general property tax or by enacting a tax levy ordinance or resolution.

(iii) Budget Execution   The budget execution phase entails obtaining the revenues, operating the program, and expending the money as authorized. The accounts are usually structured on the same basis on which the budget was prepared. Many governments maintain budgetary control by integration of the budgetary accounts into the general and subsidiary ledger. The entry is as follows:

Estimated revenues	$XXX
Appropriations	$XXX

If estimated revenues exceed appropriations, a credit for the excess is made to "budgetary fund balance"; if they are less the appropriations, the difference is debited to "budgetary fund balance."

Individual sources of revenues are recognized in subsidiary revenue accounts. A typical revenue ledger report is illustrated in Exhibit 34.3. This format provides for the comparison, at any date, of actual and estimated revenues from each source.

To control expenditures effectively, the individual amounts making up the total appropriations are recorded in subsidiary expenditures accounts, generally called *appropriation ledgers*. Exhibit 34.4 presents an example of an appropriation ledger. It should be noted that this format provides for recording the budget appropriation and for applying expenditures and encumbrances (see the following text) relating to the particular classification against the amount appropriated at any date.

When the managerial control purposes of integrating the budgetary accounts into the general ledger have been served, the budgetary account balances are reversed in the process of closing the books at year-end. Budgetary accounting procedures thus have no effect on the financial position or results of operations of a governmental entity.

ENCUMBRANCES

An encumbrance, which is unique to governmental accounting, is the reservation of a portion of an applicable appropriation that is made because a contract has been signed or a purchase order issued. The encumbrance is usually recorded in the accounting system to prevent

NAME OF GOVERNMENTAL UNIT
BUDGET VERSUS ACTUAL REVENUE
BY REVENUE SOURCE
FOR ACCOUNTING PERIOD JUNE 30, 20XX
FUND TYPE: THE GENERAL FUND

REVENUES		BUDGETED	ACTUAL	VARIANCE
015	Real & per. revenue recognized			
0110	Real & per. prop rev. recognized	$ 459,449,213	$ 460,004,317	$ (555,104)
	Revenue class total	459,449,213	460,004,317	(555,104)
020	Motor vehicle & other excise			
0121	M/V taxes—current year	16,000,000	22,727,905	(6,727,905)
0122	M/V taxes—prior 2007	0	2,886,605	(2,886,605)
0123	M/V taxes—2006	0	32,051	(32,051)
0124	M/V taxes—2005	0	45,378	(45,378)
0125	M/V taxes—2004	0	85,393	(85,393)
0126	M/V taxes—2003 and prior	0	2	(2)
0127	Boat excise—cur yr 2008	15,000	40,414	(25,414)
0128	Boat excise—2007	0	155	(155)
0131	M.V. lessor surcharge	200	60	139
	Revenue class total	16,015,200	25,817,963	(9,802,764)
025	Local excise taxes			
0129	Hotel/motel room excise	13,500,000	13,580,142	(80,142)
0130	Aircraft fuel excise	12,400,000	12,960,966	(560,966)
	Revenue class total	25,900,000	26,541,108	(641,108)
030	Departmental & other revenue			
0133	Penalties & int—prop. taxes	1,000,000	1,746,007	(746,007)
0134	Penalties & int.—M/V taxes	525,000	620,124	(95,124)
0135	Penalties & int.—sidewalk	0	115	(115)
0136	Penalties & interest/tax title	5,000,000	3,835,517	1,164,483
0138	Penalties & int./boat excise	0	3	(3)
3101	Data processing services	100	6,849	(6,749)
3103	Purchasing services	50,000	69,038	(19,038)
3104	Recording of legal instruments	150	291	(141)
3105	Registry division—fees	750,000	761,238	(11,238)
3107	City record/sale of publication	10,000	25,353	(15,353)
3108	Assessing fees	1,600	914	686
3109	Liens	400,000	373,410	26,590
3120	City clerk—fees	250,000	231,970	18,030
3130	Election—fees	12,000	10,633	1,367
3140	City council/sale of publication	200	310	(110)
3199	Other general services	35,000	18,691	16,309
3202	Police services	350,000	365,102	(15,102)
3211	Fire services	1,150,000	1,582,355	(432,355)
3221	Civil defense	40,000	161,835	(121,835)
3301	Parking facilities	3,350,000	3,775,810	(425,810)
	Revenue class total	$12,924,050	$13,585,565	$(661,515)

EXHIBIT 34.3 TYPICAL REVENUE LEDGER REPORT

NAME OF GOVERNMENTAL UNIT
BUDGET VERSUS ACTUAL EXPENDITURES
AND ENCUMBRANCES BY ACTIVITY
FOR ACCOUNTING PERIOD JUNE 30, 20XX
FUND TYPE: THE GENERAL FUND

EXPENDITURES		BUDGETED	ACTUAL [1]	VARIANCE
1100 Human services				
011-384-0384	Rent equity board	$1,330,977	$1,274,531	$56,446
011-387-0387	Elderly commission	2,534,005	2,289,549	244,456
011-398-0398	Physically handicapped comm	180,283	159,768	20,515
011-503-0503	Arts & humanities office	211,916	207,219	4,697
011-740-0741	Vet serv—veterans serv div	2,871,616	2,506,363	365,253
011-740-0742	Vet serv—veterans graves reg	158,270	146,392	11,878
011-150-1505	Jobs & community services	370,053	369,208	845
Activity total		7,657,120	6,953,030	704,090
1200 Public safety				
011-211-0211	Police department	116,850,000	117,145,704	(295,704)
011-221-0221	Fire department	80,594,068	79,587,423	1,006,645
011-222-0222	Arson commission	189,244	175,670	13,574
011-251-0251	Transportation—traffic div	13,755,915	13,707,890	48,025
011-252-0252	Licensing board	542,007	449,825	92,182
011-251-0253	Transportation—parking clerk	7,520,539	7,474,462	46,077
011-261-0260	Inspectional services dept	10,004,470	10,003,569	901
Activity total		229,456,243	228,544,543	911,700
1300 Public works				
011-311-0311	Public works department	64,900,000	60,281,837	4,618,163
011-331-0331	Snow removal	2,250,000	2,360,326	(110,326)
Activity total		67,150,000	62,642,163	4,507,837
1400 Property & development				
011-180-0180	RPD—general administration div	432,740	416,569	16,171
014-180-0183	Real property dept county	1,027,660	354,328	673,332
011-180-0184	RPD—buildings division	6,010,155	6,038,464	(28,309)
011-180-0185	RPD—property division	1,847,650	1,806,427	41,223
011-188-0186	PFD—code enforcement division	504,013	458,984	45,029
011-188-0187	PFD—administration division	4,677,365	4,697,167	(19,802)
011-188-0188	PFD—construction & repair div	3,063,637	2,808,266	255,371
Activity total		$17,563,220	$16,580,205	$983,015

[1] This example actual is presented as a non-GAAP budgetary basis that includes both expenditures plus encumbrances as a budgetary use of resources.

EXHIBIT 34.4   TYPICAL APPROPRIATION LEDGER REPORT

overspending the appropriation. When the goods or services are received, the expenditure is recorded and the encumbrance is reversed. The entry to record an encumbrance is as follows:

Encumbrances	$XXX
Reserve for encumbrances	$XXX

The entries that are made when the goods or services are received are as follows:

Reserve for encumbrances	$XXX
Encumbrances	$XXX
Expenditures	$XXX
Vouchers payable	$XXX

Many governments report encumbrances that are not liquidated at year-end in the same way as expenditures because the encumbrances are another use of budgetary appropriations. The total amount of encumbrances not liquidated by year-end may be considered as a reservation of the fund balance for the subsequent year's expenditures, based on the encumbered appropriation authority carried over.

ALLOTMENTS
Another way to maintain budgetary control is to use an allotment system. With an allotment system, the annual budget appropriation is divided and allotted among the months or quarters in the fiscal year. A department is not permitted to spend more than its allotment during the period.

The International City Managers' Association lists the following four purposes of an allotment system:

1. To make sure that departments plan their spending so as to have sufficient funds to carry on their programs throughout the year, avoiding year-end deficiencies and special appropriations
2. To eliminate or reduce short-term tax anticipation borrowing by making possible more accurate forecast control of cash position throughout the fiscal year
3. To keep expenditures within the limits of revenues that are actually realized, avoiding an unbalanced budget in the operation of any fund as a whole
4. To give the chief administrator control over departmental expenditures commensurate with the administrative responsibility, allowing the administrator to effect economies in particular activities as changes in workload and improvements in methods occur

INTERIM REPORTS
The last element in the budget execution process is interim financial reports. These are prepared to provide department heads, senior management, and the governing body with the information needed to monitor and control operations, demonstrate compliance with legal and budgetary limitations, anticipate changes in financial resources and requirements due to events or developments that are unknown or could not be foreseen at the time the budget was initially developed, or take appropriate corrective action. Interim reports should be prepared frequently enough to permit early detection of variances between actual and planned operations, but not so frequently as to adversely affect practicality and economy. For most governmental units, interim reports on a monthly basis are necessary for optimum results. With smaller units, a bimonthly or quarterly basis may be sufficient. With sophisticated data-processing equipment, it may be possible to automatically generate the appropriate information daily.

Governmental units should prepare interim financial reports covering the following:

- Revenues
- Expenditures
- Cash projections
- Proprietary funds
- Capital projects
- Grant programs

The form and content of these reports should reflect the government's particular circumstances and conditions.

PROJECT BUDGETS

When debt is issued to finance an entire capital project, it is usually done at the beginning of the project in an amount equal to the total estimated project cost. Accordingly, a portion of the proceeds may remain unexpended over a considerable period of time. To the maximum extent possible, these excess proceeds should be invested in interest-bearing investments. However, consideration should be given to the federal arbitrage regulations that limit the amount of interest that can be earned from investing the proceeds of a tax-exempt bond issue. If certain limits are exceeded, the bond's tax-exempt status may be lost or severe penalties could be imposed on the issuer.

Project budgets are typically established for capital projects to control costs and to guard against cost overruns. All expenditures needed to place the project in readiness—that is, indirect as well as direct costs, should be recorded against this budget. The actual expenditures, however, will probably be either less or greater than the amounts authorized. Therefore, in the absence of any legal restrictions, any unspent balance should be transferred to the appropriate sources. If the project was financed only from bond proceeds, the transfer should be to the debt service fund from which the bond issue is to be repaid. If the resources were drawn from more than one source, such as bond proceeds and current revenues, the transfer should be split among the sources in proportion to their contributions. If the expenditures were greater than authorized and a deficit exists, sufficient funds must be transferred to liquidate any commitments.

As construction of the project is completed, the costs should be recorded in the capital account as Construction in Progress and then transferred to the final building account when construction has been completed.

(iv) Proprietary Fund Budgeting   The nature of most operations financed and accounted for through proprietary funds is such that the demand for the goods or services largely determines the appropriate level of revenues and expenses. Increased demand causes a higher level of expenses to be incurred but also results in a higher level of revenues. Thus, as in commercial accounting, flexible budgets prepared for several levels of possible activity typically are better for planning, control, and evaluation purposes than are fixed budgets.

Accordingly, budgets are not typically adopted for proprietary funds. Furthermore, even when flexible budgets are adopted, they are viewed not as appropriations but as approved plans. The budgetary accounts are generally not integrated into the ledger accounts because it is considered unnecessary. Budgetary control and evaluation are achieved by comparing interim actual revenues and expenses with planned revenues and expenses at the actual level of activity for the period.

In some instances, fixed dollar budgets are adopted for proprietary funds either to meet local legal requirements or to control certain expenditures (e.g., capital outlay). In such cases, it may be appropriate to integrate budgetary accounts into the proprietary fund accounting system in a manner similar to that discussed for governmental funds.

(v) Capital Budget Many governments also prepare a capital budget. A capital budget is a plan for capital expenditures to be incurred during a single budget year from funds subject to appropriation for projects scheduled under the capital program. The annual capital budget is adopted concurrently with the operating budgets of the governmental unit, being subject to a public hearing and the other usual legal procedures.

The capital budget should not be confused with a capital program or capital project budget. A capital program is a plan for capital expenditures to be incurred over a period of years, usually five or six years. The capital project budget represents the estimated amount to be expended on a specific project over the entire period of its construction. The capital budget authorizes the amounts to be expended on all projects during a single year. Controlling this amount is important for the proper use of available funds.

(vi) Budgetary Comparison Information Under GASB Statement No. 34, the general fund's and the major special revenue funds' budgetary comparison schedules should present: (1) the original appropriated budgets; (2) the final appropriated budgets; and (3) actual inflows, outflows, and balances, stated on the governmental budgetary basis as discussed in NCGA Statement No. 1, paragraph 154. Separate columns may be provided comparing the original budget amounts with the actual amounts, the final budget amounts with the actual amounts, or both. The original budget is the first complete appropriated budget, which may be adjusted by reserves, transfers, allocations, supplementary appropriations, and other legally authorized legislative and executive changes made before the beginning of the reporting year. It also includes appropriation amounts automatically carried over from prior years by law. The final budget is the original budget adjusted by all legally authorized legislative and executive changes whenever signed into law or otherwise legally authorized. Governments may elect to report the budget comparison information in a budgetary comparison statement as part of the financial statements or as required supplementary disclosure as discussed in Section 34.4(m)(ii)(G), Required Supplementary Information (see Exhibit 34.5).

(l) CLASSIFICATION AND TERMINOLOGY A common terminology and classification should be used consistently throughout the budget, the accounts, and the financial reports of each fund.

(i) Classification of Government Fund Revenues Governmental fund revenues should be classified by fund and source. The major revenue source classifications are taxes, licenses and permits, intergovernmental revenues, charges for services, fines and forfeits, and miscellaneous. Governmental units often classify revenues by organizational units. This classification may be desirable for purposes of management control and accountability, as well as for auditing purposes, but it should supplement rather than supplant the classifications by fund and source.

(ii) Classification of Government Fund Expenditures There are many ways to classify governmental fund expenditures in addition to the basic fund classification. Function, program, organizational unit, activity, character, and principal class of object are examples. Typically, expenditures are classified by character (current, intergovernmental, capital outlay, and/or debt service). Current expenditures are further classified by function and/or program.

| | BUDGETED AMOUNTS | | ACTUAL AMOUNTS (BUDGETARY BASIS) (SEE NOTE A) | VARIANCE WITH FINAL BUDGET POSITIVE (NEGATIVE) |
	ORIGINAL	FINAL		
Budgetary fund balance, January 1	$3,528,750	$2,742,799	$2,742,799	$ —
Resources (inflows):				
Property taxes	52,017,833	51,853,018	51,173,436	(679,582)
Franchise taxes	4,546,209	4,528,750	4,055,505	(473,245)
Public service taxes	8,295,000	8,307,274	8,969,887	662,613
Licenses and permits	2,126,600	2,126,600	2,287,794	161,194
Fines and forfeitures	718,800	718,800	606,946	(111,854)
Charges for services	12,392,972	11,202,150	11,374,460	172,310
Grants	6,905,898	6,571,360	6,119,938	(451,422)
Sale of land	1,355,250	3,500,000	3,476,488	(23,512)
Miscellaneous	3,024,292	1,220,991	881,874	(339,117)
Interest received	1,015,945	550,000	552,325	2,325
Transfers from other funds	939,525	130,000	129,323	(677)
Amounts available for appropriation	96,867,074	93,451,742	92,370,775	(1,080,967)
Charges to appropriations (outflows)				
General government:				
Legal	665,275	663,677	632,719	30,958
Mayor, legislative, city manager	3,058,750	3,192,910	2,658,264	534,646
Finance and accounting	1,932,500	1,912,702	1,852,687	60,015
City clerk and elections	345,860	354,237	341,206	13,031
Employee relations	1,315,500	1,300,498	1,234,232	66,266
Planning and economic development	1,975,600	1,784,314	1,642,575	141,739
Public safety:				
Police	19,576,820	20,367,917	20,246,496	121,421
Fire department	9,565,280	9,559,967	9,559,967	—
Emergency medical services	2,323,171	2,470,127	2,459,866	10,261
Inspections	1,585,695	1,585,695	1,533,380	52,315
Public works:				
Public works administration	388,500	385,013	383,397	1,616
Street maintenance	2,152,750	2,233,362	2,233,362	—
Street lighting	762,750	759,832	759,832	—
Traffic operations	385,945	374,945	360,509	14,436
Mechanical maintenance	1,525,685	1,272,696	1,256,087	16,609
Engineering services:				
Engineering administration	1,170,650	1,158,023	1,158,023	—
Geographical information system	125,625	138,967	138,967	—
Health and sanitation:				
Garbage pickup	5,756,250	6,174,653	6,174,653	—
Cemetery:				
Personal services	425,000	425,000	422,562	2,438
Purchases of goods and services	299,500	299,500	283,743	15,757
Culture and recreation:				
Library	985,230	1,023,465	1,022,167	1,298
Parks and recreation	9,521,560	9,786,397	9,756,618	29,779
Community communications	552,350	558,208	510,361	47,847
Nondepartmental:				
Miscellaneous	—	259,817	259,817	—
Contingency	2,544,049	—	—	—
Transfers to other funds	2,970,256	2,163,759	2,163,759	—
Funding for school district	22,000,000	22,000,000	21,893,273	106,727
Total charges to appropriations	93,910,551	92,205,681	90,938,522	1,267,159
Budgetary fund balance, December 31	$2,956,523	$1,246,061	$1,432,253	$186,192

EXHIBIT 34.5   BUDGET-TO-ACTUAL COMPARISON SCHEDULE FOR THE GENERAL FUND IN THE BUDGET DOCUMENT FORMAT

Source: Illustration G1, GASB Statement 34.

- *Character classification*—reporting expenditures according to the physical period they are presumed to benefit. The major character classifications are: (1) current expenditures, which benefit the current fiscal period; (2) capital outlays, which are presumed to benefit both the present and future fiscal periods; and (3) debt service, which benefits prior fiscal periods as well as current and future periods. Intergovernmental expenditures is a fourth character classification that is used when one governmental unit makes expenditures to another governmental unit.
- *Function classification*—establishing groups of related activities that are aimed at accomplishing a major service or regulatory responsibility. Standard function classifications are as follows:
  - General government
  - Public safety
  - Health and welfare
  - Culture and recreation
  - Conservation of natural resources
  - Urban redevelopment and housing
  - Economic development and assistance
  - Education
  - Debt service
  - Miscellaneous
- *Program classification*—establishing groups of activities, operations, or organizational units that are directed at the attainment of specific purposes or objectives—for example, protection of property or improvement of transportation. Program classification is used by governmental units employing program budgeting.
- *Organizational unit classification*—grouping expenditures according to the governmental unit's organization structure. Organizational unit classification is essential to responsibility reporting.
- *Activity classification*—grouping expenditures according to the performance of specific activities. Activity classification is necessary for the determination of cost per unit of activity, which in turn is necessary for evaluation of economy and efficiency.
- *Object classification*—grouping expenditures according to the types of items purchased or services obtained—for example, personal services, supplies, other services, and charges. Object classifications are subdivisions of the character classification.

Excessively detailed object classifications should be avoided; they complicate the accounting procedure and are of limited use in financial management. The use of a few object classifications is sufficient in budget preparation; control emphasis should be on organizational units, functions, programs, and activities rather than on the object of expenditures.

(iii) Classifications of Other Transactions Certain transactions, although not revenues or expenditures of an individual fund, are increases or decreases in the net assets of an individual fund. These transactions are classified as other financing sources and uses and are reported in the operating statement separately from fund revenues and expenditures. The most common other financing sources and uses are

- *Proceeds of long-term debt issues.* Such proceeds (including leases) are not recorded as fund liabilities—for example, proceeds of bonds and notes expended through the capital project or debt service funds.

- *Transfers.* These are flows of assets such as cash or goods without equivalent flows of assets in return and without a requirement for repayment. They include payments in lieu of taxes that are not payments for, and are not reasonably equivalent in value to, services provided. They should be reported in governmental funds as other financing uses in the funds making transfers and as other financing sources in the funds receiving transfers. They should be reported in proprietary funds after nonoperating revenues and expenses.

Other interfund transactions are

- *Interfund loans and advances.* These are interfund loans, which are amounts provided with a requirement for repayment. They should be reported as interfund receivables and payables. They should not be reported as other financing sources or uses in the fund financial statements. If repayment is not expected within a reasonable time, the interfund balances should be reduced and the amount not expected to be repaid should be reported as a transfer from the fund that made the loan to the fund that received the loan.

  If the advance is long term in nature and the asset will not be available to finance current operations, a governmental fund balance reserve equal to the amount of the advance should be established.
- *Interfund services provided and used.* These are sales and purchases of goods and services between funds at prices that approximate their external exchange values. They should be reported as revenues in the seller funds and expenditures or expenses in purchases funds, except that when the general fund is used to account for risk-financing activity, interfund charges to other funds should be accounted for as reimbursements.

  Amounts should be accounted for as revenues in the recipient fund and as expenditures in the disbursing fund.
- *Interfund reimbursements.* These are repayments from the funds responsible for particular expenditures or expenses to the funds that initially paid for them. They should not be displayed in the financial statements.

(iv) Classifications of Proprietary Fund Revenues and Expenses   Proprietary fund revenues and expenses should be classified in essentially the same manner as those of similar business organizations, functions, or activities.

(v) Classification of Fund Equity   Fund equity is the difference between a fund's assets and its liabilities. The equity reported in the government-wide statement of net assets is called *net assets* and should be displayed in the following three categories:

- *Invested in capital assets, net of related debt*—this category consists of capital assets, including restricted capital assets, reduced by accumulated depreciation and by any outstanding debt incurred to acquire those assets.
- *Restricted net assets*—this category reports those net assets with restrictions on their use, either by external or internal factors.
- *Unrestricted net assets*—this category consists of all other net assets.

INVESTED IN CAPITAL ASSETS, NET OF RELATED DEBT

The amount of this component equals the amount of capital assets, including restricted capital assets, net of accumulated depreciation and less the outstanding balances of bonds, mortgages, notes, or other borrowings attributable to acquiring, constructing, or improving the assets. The portion of debt attributable to significant unspent debt proceeds should be included in the same net assets component as the unspent proceeds—for example, *restricted for capital projects*.

RESTRICTED NET ASSETS

Net assets should be reported as restricted if constraints on their use are either

1. Imposed externally, by creditors, grantors, contributors, or laws or regulations of other governments.
2. Imposed by law by constitutional provisions or enabling legislation that both authorizes the government to assess, levy, charge, or otherwise mandate receipt of resources from external providers and includes a legally enforceable requirement to use the resources for only the purposes stated in the legislation.

Permanent fund's principal amounts included in restricted net assets should be presented in two components—expendable and nonexpendable. Nonexpendable net assets are those required to be retained in perpetuity.

UNRESTRICTED NET ASSETS

Unrestricted net assets are other than net assets invested in capital assets, net of related debt, and other than restricted net assets.

Net assets are often *designated* by the management of the government if they do not consider them available for general operations. Such constraints are internal and can be removed or modified by the management. They are not restricted net assets.

The equity reported in the proprietary fund statement of net assets or balance sheet should be labeled either *net assets* or *fund equity,* using the three net asset components discussed for government-wide net assets.

An important amount in the fund equity account for governmental funds is the amount available for future appropriation and expenditure (i.e., unreserved and undesignated fund balance). The equity reported in the governmental fund balance sheets should be labeled *fund balances* and should be segregated into reserved and unreserved amounts. NCGA Statement 1 notes that fund balance reserves, report the portions of the fund balances that are (1) legally segregated for a specific use or (2) not available for expenditure because the underlying asset is not available for current appropriation or expenditure. Reserves are not intended as valuation allowances but merely demonstrate the current unavailability of the subject assets to pay current expenditures. Reserves and designations are established by debiting unreserved, undesignated fund balance and crediting the reserve or designation. The reserve is not established by a charge to operations.

Designations of fund balance identify tentative plans for or restrictions on the future use of financial resources. Such designations should be supported by definitive plans and approved by either the government's CEO or the legislature. Examples of such designations include the earmarking of financial resources for capital projects and contingent liabilities. Management designations for the use of resources should not be reported in the statement of net assets but may be disclosed in notes to the financial statements.

GASB Statement No. 34 requires reserved fund balances of non-major governmental funds to be displayed in sufficient detail to disclose the purposes of the reservations, and requires unreserved fund balances of the non-major governmental funds to be displayed by fund type. Management designations of fund balances should be reported as part of unreserved fund balances and disclosed as separate line items or disclosed in the financial statement notes. In response, the GASB is currently working on developing new guidance on fund balance reporting and governmental fund type definitions to mitigate the diversity in practice as it relates to this issue.

The equity reported in the fiduciary fund statement of fiduciary net assets should be labeled *net assets* but does not require net assets to be categorized into the three components. GASB Statements No. 25, "Financial Reporting for Defined Benefit Pension Plans and Note Disclosures for Defined Contribution Plans," No. 43, "Financial Reporting for Postemployment Benefit Plans Other Than Pension Plans," and No. 31, "Accounting and Financial Reporting for Certain Investments and for External Investment Pools," contain specific disclosure requirements for these types of funds.

(m) FINANCIAL REPORTING   Prior to 1979, governments traditionally prepared external financial reports by preparing financial statements for every fund maintained by the government. This often resulted in lengthy financial reports. External financial reporting has evolved to require the presentation of financial statements on a more aggregated basis and the inclusion of legally separate entities that have special relationships. Principle 12 relates to financial reporting and is discussed in the following text.

(i) The Financial Reporting Entity   GASB Statement No. 14, "The Financial Reporting Entity," establishes standards for defining and reporting on the financial reporting entity.

The statement indicates that the financial reporting entity consists of (1) the Primary Government (PG), (2) organizations for which the PG is financially accountable, and (3) other organizations that, if omitted from the reporting entity, would cause the financial statements to be misleading.

The Statement also outlines the basic criteria for including organizations in or excluding organizations from the reporting entity. All organizations for which the PG is *financially* accountable should be included in the reporting entity. Such organizations include

- The organizations that make up the PG's legal entity, and
- Component units—that is, organizations that are legally separate from the PG but
  - The PG's officials appoint a voting majority of the organization's governing board, and
  - Either the PG is able to impose its will on that organization or there is a potential for the organization to provide specific financial benefits to, or to impose specific financial burdens on, the PG.

A legally separate, tax-exempt organization should be reported as a component unit of a reporting entity if all of the following criteria are met:

- The economic resources received or held by the separate organization are entirely or almost entirely for the direct benefit of the PG, its component units, or its constituents.
- The PG (or its component units) is entitled to, or has the ability to otherwise access,[2] a majority of the economic resources received or held by the separate organization.

---

2.   *Ability to otherwise access* does not necessarily imply control over the other organization or its resources. It may be demonstrated in several ways. For example, the primary government or its component units historically may have received, directly or indirectly, a majority of

- The economic resources received or held by an individual organization that the specific PG (or its component units) is entitled to or has the ability to otherwise access, are significant to that PG.

Other organizations should be evaluated as potential component units if they are closely related to, or financially integrated[3] with, the PG. It is a matter of professional judgment to determine whether the nature and the significance of a potential component unit's relationship with the PG warrant inclusion in the reporting entity. Organizations not meeting the foregoing criteria are excluded from the reporting entity.

Reporting the inclusion of the various entities comprising the reporting entity can be done using one of two methods—blending or discrete presentation. Most component units should be included in the financial reporting entity by discrete presentation. Some component units, despite being legally separate entities, are so intertwined with the PG that, in substance, they are the same as the PG and should be "blended" with the transactions of the PG.

Certain other entities are not considered component units because the PG, while responsible for appointing the organization's board members, is not financially accountable. Such entities are considered related organizations. These related organizations as well as joint ventures and jointly governed organizations should be disclosed in the reporting entity's footnotes.

REPORTING COMPONENT UNITS
Discrete presentation of component unit financial information should be included in the statement of net assets and the statement of activities. However, information on component units that are fiduciary in nature should be included only in the fund financial statements, together with the PG's fiduciary funds. Information required by paragraph 51 of GASB Statement No. 14 about each major component unit can be given by

- Presenting each major component unit other than those that are fiduciary in nature in separate columns in the statements of net assets and activities,
- Including combining statements of major component units (with non-major component units aggregated in a single column) with the reporting entity's basic statements after the fund financial statements, or
- Presenting condensed financial statements in the notes.

The "aggregated total" component unit information, as discussed in paragraph 14 of GASB Statement No. 14, should be the entity totals derived from the component units' statements of net assets and activities. (Because component units that are engaged in only business-type activities are not required to prepare a statement of activities, this disclosure should be taken from the information provided in the component unit's statement of revenues, expenses, and changes in fund net assets.)

---

the economic resources provided by the organization; the organization may have previously received and honored requests to provide resources to the primary government; or the organization is a financially interrelated organization as defined by FASB Statement No. 136.
3. Financial integration may be exhibited and documented through the policies, practices, or organizational documents of either the primary government or the other organization. More than one column may be used to display components of a program revenue category. Governments may also provide more descriptive category headings to better explain the range of program revenues reported therein—for example, *operating grants, contributions,* and *restricted interest.*

If component unit information is presented in the notes, the following should be included:

- Condensed statement of net assets:
  - o Total assets, distinguishing between capital assets and other assets (Amounts receivable from the PG or from other component units should be reported separately.)
  - o Total liabilities, distinguishing between long-term debt and other liabilities (Amounts payable to the PG or to other component units should be reported separately.)
  - o Total net assets, distinguishing between restricted, unrestricted, and amounts invested in capital assets net of related debt
- Condensed statement of activities:
  - o Expenses by major functions and for depreciation expense if separately reported
  - o Program revenues by type
  - o Net program expense or revenue
  - o Tax revenues
  - o Other nontax general revenues
  - o Contributions to endowments and permanent fund principal
  - o Special and extraordinary items
  - o Change in net assets
  - o Beginning net assets
  - o Ending net assets

The nature and amount of significant transactions with the PG and other component units should be reported in the notes for each component unit.

(ii) Basic Financial Statements   As discussed in Section 34.4(e)(ii), Reporting Requirements, the basic financial statements (BFS) include the financial statements of the governmental activities, the business-type activities, the aggregate discretely presented component units, each major fund, and the aggregate remaining fund information.

The two government-wide financial statements—the statement of net assets and the statement of activities—should report information about the reporting government without displaying individual funds or fund types. The statements should cover the PG and its component units, except for fiduciary funds of the PG and component units that are fiduciary in nature, which should be reported in the statements of fiduciary net assets and changes in fiduciary net assets.

The focus of the government-wide financial statements should be on the PG. The total PG and its discretely presented component units should be distinguished by separate rows and columns. A total column for the government entity and prior year information are optional.

Governmental and business-type activities of the PG should also be distinguished by separate rows and columns. (An activity need not be set out as a proprietary fund if it is not currently reported as such by the management of the government unless it is required to be reported as an enterprise fund, as discussed in Section 34.4(g)(ii)(A), Enterprise Funds.) Governmental and business-type activities are distinguished in general by their methods of financing. Governmental activities are generally financed by taxes, intergovernmental revenues, and other nonexchange-type revenues; they are generally reported in governmental funds and internal service funds. Business-type activities are financed in whole or in part by fees charged for goods or services; they are generally reported in enterprise funds.

These statements measure and report all financial and capital assets, liabilities, revenues, expenses, gains, and losses using the economic resources measurement focus and accrual basis of accounting.

Some amounts reported as interfund activity and balances in the funds should be eliminated or reclassified in aggregating information for the statement of net assets and the statement of activities.

Amounts reported in the funds as interfund receivables and payables should be eliminated in the governmental and business-type activities columns of the PG in the statement of net assets, except for the net residual amount due between the governmental and business-type activities, which should be reported as internal balances. (Amounts reported in the funds as receivable from or payable to fiduciary funds should be reported in the statement of net assets as receivable from and payable to external parties.) Internal balances should be eliminated in the total PG column.

The doubling-up effect of internal service fund activity should be eliminated in the statement of activities. Also, the effects of similar internal events, such as allocations of accounting staff salaries, which are, in effect, allocations of overhead expenses from one function to another or within a single function, should be eliminated so that the allocated expenses are reported by only the function to which they were allocated. (The effect of interfund services provided and used between functions should not be eliminated.)

(A) STATEMENT OF NET ASSETS
The statement of net assets should report all financial and capital resources and all liabilities, preferably in a format that displays *assets less liabilities equal net assets*, though the format *assets equal liabilities plus net assets* may be used. The difference between assets and liabilities should be reported as *net assets*, not *fund balance* or *equity*.

Governments are encouraged to report assets and liabilities in order of their relative liquidity (and subtotals of current assets and current liabilities may be provided). The liquidity of an asset depends on how readily it is expected to be converted to cash and whether restrictions limit the government's ability to use it. The liquidity of a liability depends on its maturity or on when cash is expected to be required to liquidate it. The liquidity of assets and liabilities may be determined by class, though individual assets or liabilities may be significantly more or less liquid than others in the same class, and some may have both current and long-term elements. Liabilities whose average maturities are more than one year should be reported by both the amount due within one year and the amount due in more than one year.

As discussed in Section 34.4(h)(v), Classification of Fund Equity, the three components of net assets are reported as (1) *invested in capital assets, net of related debt*; (2) *restricted*, distinguishing between major categories of restrictions; and (3) *unrestricted*.

Statement of Net Assets Format. The City and County of San Francisco's statement of net assets at June 30, 2006 in Exhibit 34.6 illustrates the statement of net assets format.

(B) STATEMENT OF ACTIVITIES
Some governments have a single function, program, activity, or component unit (together discussed as functions), as discussed subsequently. Most have more than one function. A government with more than one function should present a statement of activities that reports expenses by each function and revenues specifically pertaining to each function, arriving at net expense or net revenue by function. Net expense or net revenue is sometimes referred to as the *net cost* of a function or program and represents the total expenses of the function or program less its program revenues—that is, charges or fees and fines that derive directly from the function or program and grants and contributions that are restricted to the function or

program. That presentation indicates the financial burden (or benefit) each function places on the government's taxpayers and the extent to which each draws on the general revenues of the government or is self-financing. General revenues should be reported after expenses and revenues of the functions, together with contributions to term and permanent endowments, contributions to permanent fund principal, special and extraordinary items, and transfers reported separately, leading to change in net assets for the period.

CITY AND COUNTY OF SAN FRANCISCO
Statement of Net Assets

June 30, 2006
(In Thousands)

	Primary Government			Component Units	
	Governmental Activities	Business- Type Activities	Total	San Francisco Redevelopment Agency	Treasure Island Development Authority
ASSETS					
Current assets					
Deposits and investments City Treasury	$ 1,511, 936	$ 681,935	$ 2,193, 871	$ —	$ 1,268
Deposits and investments outside City Treasury	48,885	9,758	58,643	169,046	-
Receivables (net of allowance for uncollectible amounts of $84,334 for the primary government):					
Property taxes and penalities	42, 586	—	42,586	—	—
Other local taxes	168,457	—	168,457	—	—
Federal and state grants and subventions	154,086	57,707	211,793	—	—
Charges for services	22,194	194,800	216,994	—	—
Interest and other	16,132	43,787	59,919	7,641	4
Loans receivable	7,025	132	7,157	12	—
Capital lease receivable from primary government	—	—	—	14,460	
Due from component unit	782	—	782	—	—
Inventories	—	53,051	53,051	—	—
Deferred charges and other assets	10,423	3,531	13,954	—	—
Restricted assets:					
Deposits and investments with City Treasury	—	54,218	54, 218	—	—
Deposits and investments outside City Treasury	—	45,306	45,306	78,413	—
Grants and other receivables	—	36	36	1,206	—
Total current assets	1,982,506	1,144,261	3,126,767	270,778	1,272
Noncurrent assets:					
Loans receivable (net of allowance for uncollectible amounts of $383,869 and $158, 166 for the primary government and component units, respectively)	67,016	455	67,471	10,455	—
Advance to component unit	4,024	—	4,024	—	—
Capital lease receivable from primary government	—	—	—	175,636	—
Deferred charges and other assets	19,887	72,632	92,519	9,565	—
Restricted assets:					
Deposits and investments with City Treasury	—	617,925	617,925	—	—
Deposits and investments outside City Treasury	—	265,093	265,093	20,797	—
Grants and other receivables	—	61,670	61,670	—	—
Property held for resale	—	—	—	15,988	—
Capital assets:					
Land and other assets not being depreciated	504,527	1,208,435	1,712,962	119,965	—
Facilities, infrastructure, and equipment, net of depreciation	2,170,335	7,320,619	9,490,954	146,638	—
Total capital assets	2,674,862	8,529,054	11,203,916	266,603	—
Total noncurrent assets	2,765,789	9,546,829	12,312,618	499,044	—
Total Assets	$ 4,748,295	$ 10,691,090	$ 15,439,385	$ 769,822	$ 1,272

EXHIBIT 34.6   CITY AND COUNTY OF SAN FRANCISCO STATEMENT OF NET ASSETS (JUNE 30, 2006)

CITY AND COUNTY OF SAN FRANCISCO
Statement of Net Assets (*Continued*)
June 30, 2006
(In Thousands)

	Primary Government			Component Units	
	Governmental Activities	Business-Type Activities	Total	San Francisco Redevelopment Agency	Treasure Island Development Authority
LIABILITIES					
Current liabilities:					
Accounts payable	$ 178,765	$ 121,868	$ 300,633	$ 7,962	$ 3,207
Accrued payroll	64,377	46,498	110,875	—	—
Accrued vacation and sick leave pay	65,948	43,182	109,130	1,254	—
Accrued workers' compensation	41,803	35,466	77,269	—	—
Estimated claims payable	23,811	24,629	48,440	—	—
Bonds, loans, capital leases, and other payable	262,599	142,119	404,718	27,791	—
Capital lease payable to component unit	14,460	—	14,460	—	—
Accrued interest payable	7,764	18,472	26,236	27,207	—
Unearned grant and subvention revenues	2,421	—	2,421	—	—
Due to primary government	—	—	—	782	—
Internal balances	27,966	(27,966)	—	—	—
Deferred credits and other liabilities	125,111	91,061	216,172	750	664
Liabilities payable from restricted assets:					
Bonds, loans, capital leases, and other payables	—	17,393	17,393	—	—
Accrued interest payable	—	26,321	26,321	—	—
Other	—	38,331	38,331	—	—
Total current liabilities	815,025	577,374	1,392,399	65,746	3,871
Noncurrent liabilities:					
Accrued vacation and sick leave pay	66,576	36,381	102,957	1,553	—
Accrued workers' compensation	160,678	126,188	286,866	—	—
Estimated claims payable	45,666	53,154	98,820	—	—
Bonds, loans, capital leases, and other payables	1,690,096	5,438,803	7,128,899	700,942	—
Advance from primary government	—	—	—	4,024	—
Capital lease payable to component unit	175,636	—	175,636	—	—
Accrued interest payable	—	—	—	63,839	—
Deferred credits and other liabilities	—	46,757	46,757	6,117	—
Total noncurrent liabilities	2,138,652	5,701,283	7,839,935	776,475	—
Total liabilities	2,953,677	6,278,657	9,232,334	842,221	3,871
NET ASSETS					
Invested in capital assets, net of related debt	1,438,010	3,438,397	4,876,407	67,463	—
Restricted for:					
Reserve for rainy day	121,976	—	121,976	—	—
Debt service	53,076	256,055	309,131	54,821	—
Capital projects	10,589	148,957	159,546	—	—
Community development	71,207	—	71,207	—	—
Transportation Authority activities	23,727	—	23,727	—	—
Grants and other purposes	148,071	32,354	180,425	15,988	—
Unrestricted (deficit)	(72,038)	536,670	464,632	(210,671)	(2,599)
Total net assets (deficit)	$1,794,618	$4,412,433	$6,207,051	$(72,399)	$(2,599)

EXHIBIT 34.6: (*CONTINUED*)

At a minimum, the statement of activities should present

- Activities accounted for in governmental funds by function, as discussed in NCGA Statement No. 1, paragraph 112, to coincide with the level of detail required in the governmental fund statement of revenues, expenditures, and changes in fund balances.
- Activities accounted for in enterprise funds by different identifiable activities. An activity is identifiable if it has a specific revenue stream and related expenses and gains and losses that are accounted for separately.

Expenses.   All expenses should be reported by function other than special or extraordinary items, defined subsequently. At a minimum, direct expenses, those clearly identifiable with a particular function, should be presented. In addition, some or all indirect expenses of the functions may be reported by function, in columns separate from the direct expenses. A column reporting the total of direct and indirect expenses by function may also be presented. Governments that charge functions for centralized expenses need not identify and eliminate such charges. The fact that they are included in direct expenses should be disclosed in the summary of significant accounting policies.

Depreciation expense on capital assets specifically identifiable with functions should be included in their direct expenses. Depreciation expense on shared capital assets should be assigned ratably to the direct expense of the functions benefiting. Depreciation expense on capital assets that serve all functions, such as city hall, need not be included in the direct expense of the functions but may be reported as a separate line in the statement of activities or as part of the general government function. A government that reports unallocated depreciation on a separate line should state on the face of the statement of activities that this item does not include direct depreciation expenses of the various functions.

Depreciation expense for general infrastructure assets should be reported as a direct expense of the function that the government normally associates with capital outlays for and maintenance of infrastructure assets or on a separate line in the statement of activities.

Interest on long-term liabilities should generally be reported as an indirect expense on a separate line in the statement of activities, clearly indicating that it excludes direct interest expenses, if any, reported in other functions. The amount excluded should be disclosed on the face of the statement or in the notes. However, interest should be included in direct expense on borrowings essential to the creation or continuing existence of a program (e.g., a new, highly leveraged program in its early stages) if excluding it would be misleading.

Revenues.   A government obtains revenue essentially from four sources:

1. Entities that buy, use, or directly benefit from the goods or services of programs, including the citizens of the government or others
2. Entities outside the citizens of the government, including other governments, nongovernmental entities, or persons
3. The government's taxpayers, regardless of whether they benefit from particular programs
4. The government itself—for example, from investing

Type 1 is always a program revenue. Type 2 is a program revenue if restricted to specific programs. If unrestricted, type 2 is a general revenue. Type 3 is always a general revenue, even if restricted to specific programs. Type 4 is usually a general revenue.

Program revenues reduce the net cost of program function required to be financed by general revenue. They should be reported separately in three categories:[4] (1) charges for services, (2) program-specific operating grants and contributions, and (3) program-specific capital grants and contributions. For identifying the function to which a program revenue pertains, the

---

4.   More than one column may be used to display components of a program revenue category. Governments may also provide more descriptive category headings to better explain the range of program revenues reported therein—for example, *operating grants, contributions,* and *restricted interest.*

determining factor for charges for services is which function generates[5] the revenue. For grants and contributions, the determining factor is the function to which the revenues are restricted.

All other revenues are general revenues, including all taxes and all nontax revenues that do not meet the criteria to be reported as program revenues. General revenues should be reported after total net expense of the government's functions.

The following should be reported separately at the bottom of the statement of activities in the same manner as general revenues, to arrive at the all-inclusive change in net assets for the reporting period:

- Contributions to term and permanent endowments
- Contributions to permanent fund principal
- Special and extraordinary items (discussed in the following text)
- Transfers between governmental and business-type activities

Other financing sources and uses include face amount of long-term debt, issuance premium or discount, certain payments to escrow agents for bond refundings, transfers, and sales of capital assets (unless the sale meets the criteria for reporting as a special item).

Special and Extraordinary Items.   Special items, significant events within the control of management that are either unusual or infrequent as defined in APB Opinion No. 30, should be reported separately at the bottom of the statement of activities. Extraordinary items, significant events that are both unusual and infrequent, should also be reported separately at the bottom of the statement of activities.

Statement of Activities Format.   The City and County of San Francisco's statement of activities for the year ended June 30, 2006, illustrates the statement of activities format (see Exhibit 34.7).

(C) BASIC FINANCIAL STATEMENTS—FUND FINANCIAL STATEMENTS
Governmental Fund Balance Statement Format.   Exhibit 34.8 presents the balance sheet presentation of the City and County of San Francisco's General Fund, the only major governmental fund of the City and County of San Francisco. Non-major funds are aggregated in an "Other" column. Note: the City and County of San Francisco's financial statements include optional partial or summarized prior year comparative information.

(D) REQUIRED RECONCILIATION TO GOVERNMENT-WIDE STATEMENTS
The amount of net assets reported for a PG in the government-wide statement of net assets usually will differ from the aggregate amount of equity reported in its fund financial position statements, because the fund statements are prepared using the funds flow measurement focus and modified accrual method (see discussion at Section 34.4(j), Measurement Focus and Basis of Accounting). There will also be differences between the changes in net assets reported in the various activity statements.

A government should present a summary reconciliation to the government-wide financial statements at the bottom of the fund financial statements or in a schedule. Brief explanations

---

5.   It may sometimes be difficult or impractical to identify a specific function that generates a program revenue. For example, in many jurisdictions fines could be attributed to a public safety or a judicial function. If the source of a program revenue is not clear, the government should adopt a classification policy for assigning those revenues and apply it consistently.

CITY AND COUNTY OF SAN FRANCISCO
Statement of Activities
Year Ended June 30, 2006
(In Thousands)

| | | Program Revenues | | | Net (Expense) Revenue and Changes in Net Assets | | | | |
| | | | | | Primary Government | | | Component Units | |
Functions/Programs	Expenses	Charges for Services	Operating Grants and Contributions	Capital Grants and Contributions	Govern-mental Activities	Business-Type Activities	Total	San Francisco Redevelop-ment Agency	Treasure Island Development Authority
Primary government:									
Government activities:									
Public protection	$ 780,642	$ 51,874	$ 103,358	$ —	$ (625,410)	$ —	$ (625,410)	$ —	$ —
Public works, transportation and commerce	272,397	113,861	30,223	37,411	(90,902)	—	(90,902)	—	—
Human welfare and neighborhood development	858,396	29,181	437,381	150	(391,684)	—	(391,684)	—	—
Community health	478,844	52,183	278,218	—	(148,443)	—	(148,443)	—	—
Culture and recreation	244,423	64,720	3,144	210,768	34,209	—	34,209	—	—
General administration and finance	167,490	55,799	2,400	—	(109,291)	—	(109,291)	—	—
General City responsibilities	49,054	31,647	5,195	—	(12,212)	—	(12,212)	—	—
Unallocated interest on long-term debt	94,923	—	—	—	(94,923)	—	(94,923)	—	—
Total governmental activities	2,946,169	399,265	859,919	248,329	(1,438,656)	—	(1,438,656)	—	—
Business-type activities:									
Airport	633,102	455,342	—	48,544	—	(129,216)	(129,216)	—	—
Transportation	695,593	210,692	122,057	58,399	—	(304,445)	(304,445)	—	—
Port	55,329	58,588	—	3,460	—	6,719	6,719	—	—
Water	213,584	201,833	—	—	—	(11,751)	(11,751)	—	—
Power	119,146	149,500	—	—	—	30,354	30,354	—	—
Hospitals	646,149	472,327	66,585	—	—	(107,237)	(107,237)	—	—
Sewer	160,701	164,703	30	—	—	4,032	4,032	—	—
Market	1,035	1,503	—	—	—	468	468	—	—
Total Business-type activities	2,524,639	1,714,488	188,672	110,403	—	(511,076)	(511,076)	—	—
Total primary government	$5,470,808	$2,113,753	$1,048,591	$ 358,732	(1,438,656)	(511,076)	(1,949,732)	—	—
Component units									
San Francisco Redevelopment Agency	$142,493	$25,345	$13,912	$—				(103,236)	—
Treasure Island Development Authority	9,188	8,208	—	—				—	(980)
Total component units	$151,661	$33,553	$13,912	$—				(103,236)	(980)
General Revenues:									
Taxes:									
Property taxes					1,016,220	—	1,106,220	65,826	—
Business taxes					323,153	—	323,153	—	—
Other local taxes					595,664	—	595,664	5,549	—
Interest and investment income					71,129	53,161	124,290	10,751	56
Other					56,022	272,873	328,895	9,722	527
Transfers—internal activities of primary goverment					(329,996)	329,996	—	—	—
Total general revenues and transfers					1,732,192	656,030	2,388,222	91,848	583
Changes in net assets					293,536	144,954	438,490	(11,388)	(397)
Net assets (deficit)—beginning					1,501,082	4,267,479	5,768,561	(61,011)	(2,202)
Net assets (deficit)—ending					$1,794,618	$4,412,433	$6,207,051	$(72,399)	$(2,599)

EXHIBIT 34.7   CITY AND COUNTY OF SAN FRANCISCO STATEMENT OF ACTIVITIES (YEAR ENDED JUNE 30, 2006)

presented on the face of the statements often are sufficient. However, if aggregated information in the reconciliation obscures the nature of the individual elements of a particular reconciling item, a more detailed explanation should be provided in the notes to financial statements.

Exhibit 34.9 presents the reconciliation of the governmental funds balance sheet to the statement of net assets of the City and County of San Francisco. This reconciliation provides

CITY AND COUNTY OF SAN FRANCISCO
Balance Sheet
Governmental Funds
June 30, 2006
(with comparative financial information as of June 30, 2005)
(In Thousands)

	General Fund		Other Governmental Funds		Total Governmental Funds	
	2006	2005	2006	2005	2006	2005
ASSETS						
Deposits and investments with City Treasury	$ 443,102	$ 314,607	$ 1,060,891	$ 915,547	$ 1,503,993	$ 1,230,154
Deposits and investments outside City Treasury	1,465	355	22,287	45,745	23,752	46,100
Receivables:						
Property taxes and penalities	34,157	26,141	8,429	6,890	42,586	33,031
Other local taxes	154,505	148,744	13,952	12,788	168,457	161,532
Federal and state grants and subventions	63,843	61,412	90,243	89,559	154,086	150,971
Charges for services	17,117	7,416	5,077	6,832	22,194	14,248
Interest and other	6,184	4,406	9,035	3,726	15,219	8,132
Due from other funds	30,859	29,743	3,960	12,303	34,819	42,046
Due from component unit	3,848	2,416	958	959	4,806	3,375
Loans receivable (net of allowance for uncollectible amount of $383,869 in 2006; $165,336 in 2005)	—	1,174	74,041	241,728	74,041	242,902
Deferred charges and other Assets	7,243	6,797	1,729	1,570	8,972	8,367
Total assets	$762,323	$603,211	$1,290,602	$1,337,647	$2,052,925	$1,940,858
LIABILITIES AND FUND BALANCES						
Liabilities:						
Accounts payable	$ 84,710	$ 82,524	$ 88,151	$ 53,335	$ 172,861	$ 135,859
Accrued payroll	51,792	39,729	10,982	8,812	62,774	48,541
Deferred tax, grant, and subvention revenues	33,473	26,880	30,442	19,371	63,915	46,251
Due to other funds	821	1,857	61,964	77,614	62,785	79,471
Agency obligations	—	—	—	40	—	40
Deferred credits and other liabilities	130,251	144,541	94,755	267,899	225,006	412,440
Bonds, loans, capital leases, and other payables	—	—	150,000	150,000	150,000	150,000
Total liabilities	301,047	295,531	436,294	577,071	737,341	872,602
Fund balances:						
Reserved for rainy day	121,976	48,139	—	—	121,976	48,139
Reserved for assets not available for appropriation	10,710	9,031	20,202	17,683	30,912	26,714
Reserved for debt service	—	—	57,429	45,540	57,429	45,540
Reserved for encumbrances	38,159	57,762	423,120	97,920	461,279	155,682
Reserved for appropriation carryforward	124,009	36,198	294,340	549,571	418,349	585,769
Reserved for subsequent years' budgets	27,451	22,351	8,004	8,004	35,455	30,356
Unreserved (deficit), reported in:						
General fund	138,971	134,199	—	—	138,971	134,199
Special revenue funds	—	—	35,243	30,809	35,243	30,809
Capital project funds	—	—	13,662	7,193	13,662	7,193
Permanent fund	—	—	2,308	3,856	2,308	3,856
Total fund balances	461,276	307,680	854,308	760,576	1,315,584	1,068,256
Total liabilities and fund balances	$762,323	$603,211	$1,290,602	$1,337,647	$2,052,925	$1,940,858

EXHIBIT 34.8 CITY AND COUNTY OF SAN FRANCISCO BALANCE SHEET GOVERNMENTAL FUNDS

summarized explanations that do not describe the nature of the individual elements of these reconciling items. As a result, the City and County of San Francisco provides a more detailed explanation in the notes to financial statements.

Reconciling items between the Governmental Funds Balance Sheets and the Government-Wide Statement of Net Assets include the effects of

- Reporting capital assets at their acquisition cost and depreciating them instead of reporting capital acquisitions as expenditures when incurred.
- Adding general long-term liabilities not due and payable in the current period.
- Reducing deferred revenue for amounts not available to pay current-period expenditures.
- Adding internal service fund net asset balances.

CITY AND COUNTY OF SAN FRANCISCO
Reconciliation of the Governmental Funds Balance Sheet
to the Statement of Net Assets
June 30, 2006

(In Thousands)

Fund balances—total governmental funds	$ 1,315,584
Amounts reported for governmental activities in the statement of net assets are different because:	
Capital assets used in governmental activities are not financial resources and, therefore, are not reported in the funds.	2,670,387
Bond issue costs are not financial resources and, therefore, are not reported in the funds.	14,338
Long-term liabilities, including bonds payable, are not due and payable in the current period and therefore are not reported in the funds.	(2,161,461)
Interest on long-term debt is not accrued in the funds, but rather is recognized as an expenditure when due.	(6,459)
Because the focus of governmental funds is on short-term financing, some assets will not be available to pay for current period expenditures. Those assets are offset by deferred revenue in the funds.	164.015
Internal service funds are used by management to charge the costs of capital lease financing, fleet management, printing and mailing services, and information systems to individual funds. The assets and liabilities of internal service funds are included in governmental activities in the statement of net assets.	(201,786)
Net assets of governmental activities	$1,794,618

Exhibit 34.9   City and County of San Francisco Reconciliation of the Governmental Funds Balance Sheet to the Statement of Net Assets (June 30, 2006)

Reconciling items between the Governmental Funds Statement of Revenues, Expenditures and Changes in Fund Balances and the Government-Wide Statement of Activities include the effects of

- Reporting revenues on the accrual basis.
- Reporting annual depreciation expense instead of expenditures for capital outlays.
- Reporting long-term debt proceeds in the statement of net assets as liabilities instead of other financing sources.
- Reporting debt principal payments in the statement of net assets as reductions of liabilities instead of expenditures.
- Reporting other expenses on the accrual basis.
- Adding the net revenue or subtracting the expense of internal service funds.

For enterprise funds, (1) total enterprise fund net assets should be reconciled to the net assets of business-type activities (however, since both are on the accrual basis, there often are no differences) and (2) the total change in enterprise fund net assets should be reconciled to the change in net assets of business-type activities, provided there are differences that require reconciliation.

(E) Reporting Internal Service Fund Balances
Internal service funds are reported as proprietary funds. Nevertheless, their activities, financing goods and services for other funds, are usually more governmental than business type.

Therefore, internal service fund asset and liability balances not eliminated should normally be reported in the governmental activities column of the statement of net assets. However, if enterprise funds are the predominant or only participants in an internal service fund, that fund's residual assets and liabilities should be reported in the business-type activities column.

(F) DISCLOSURE REQUIREMENTS

Information essential to fair presentation in the financial statements that cannot be displayed on the faces of the statements should be presented in the notes to the financial statements, which should focus on the PG—its governmental activities, business-type activities, major funds, and non-major funds in the aggregate. Information about the government's discretely presented component units should be presented as discussed in GASB Statement No. 14, paragraph 63.

General Disclosure Requirements.   Governments should provide the following added disclosures to the extent applicable in their summaries of significant accounting policies:

- A description of the government-wide financial statements, indicating that fiduciary funds and component units that are fiduciary in nature are not included
- The measurement focus and basis of accounting used in the government-wide statements
- The policy for eliminating internal activity in the statement of activities
- The policy for applying FASB pronouncements issued after November 30, 1989, to business-type activities and to enterprise funds of the PG
- The policy for capitalizing assets and for estimating their useful lives (A government that uses the modified approach for reporting eligible infrastructure assets should describe the approach.)
- A description of the kinds of transactions included in program revenues
- A description of the policy for allocating indirect expenses to functions in the statement of activities
- The government's policy for defining operating and nonoperating revenues of proprietary funds
- The government's policy on whether to first use restricted or unrestricted resources when an expense is incurred for purposes for which both restricted and unrestricted net assets are available

Required Note Disclosures about Cash and Investments.   A government is subject to numerous GASB disclosures about cash and investments. The following are among the required disclosures:

- Description of how investments are valued, including the methods and significant assumptions used to estimate the fair value of investments
- The types of investments authorized by legal or contractual provisions
- The types of investments made during the period but not owned as of the balance-sheet date
- By type of investment, the investments' carrying amounts and fair values at year-end
- The custodial credit risk for uncollateralized deposits with financial institutions and investment securities that are uninsured and unregistered
- The credit and interest rate risks related to investments in debt instruments

- Terms of investments with fair values that are highly sensitive to changes in interest rates
- The concentration of credit risk for amount invested in a separate issuer (except investments held in or guaranteed by the U.S. government) when that amount is at least 5 percent of total investments
- The foreign currency risk of its investments denominated in a foreign currency
- Details about derivative instruments that are not reported at fair value
- The assignment of investment income between funds
- Specific information related to investment appreciation and income available for spending on donor-restricted endowments

Required Note Disclosures about Capital Assets and Long-Term Liabilities.   Details should be disclosed in the notes about capital assets and long-term liabilities of the PG, divided into their major classes and between those associated with governmental activities and those associated with business-type activities. Capital assets not being depreciated should be disclosed separately. The following information should be disclosed about major classes of capital assets:

- Beginning- and end-of-year balances, with accumulated depreciation presented separately from acquisition cost
- Capital acquisitions
- Sales or other dispositions
- Current depreciation expense, including the amounts charged to each of the functions in the statement of activities

Collections of works of art, historical treasures, and similar assets not capitalized should be described, and the reasons they are not capitalized should be given. Disclosures, as previously stated, should be given for collections capitalized.

The following information should be disclosed about long-term debt and other long-term liabilities, such as compensated absences, claims, and judgments:

- Beginning- and end-of-year balances
- Increases and decreases, presented separately
- The portions of each due within one year
- The governmental funds that typically have been used to liquidate other long-term liabilities

Debt service to maturity separated by principal and interest for each of the succeeding five fiscal years and in at least five-year increments thereafter for all outstanding debt should be disclosed. Interest on variable-rate debt should be calculated using the rate in effect at the financial statement date, and the terms that the interest rates change for variable-rate debt should also be disclosed.

Whether to make similar disclosures about capital assets and long-term liabilities of discretely presented component units is a matter of professional judgment, depending on each individual component unit's significance to the total of all discretely presented component units and the component unit's relationship with the PG.

(G) REQUIRED SUPPLEMENTARY INFORMATION

Management Discussion and Analysis.   A management discussion and analysis (MD&A) is an overview and analysis of the government's financial statements. It should provide an objective and easily readable analysis of the government's financial activities based on facts, decisions, or conditions of which management is aware as of the date of the auditor's report. It should discuss the current-year results and compare them with the results of the prior year, including positive and negative aspects.

MD&A requirements are general to encourage effective reporting of only the most relevant information and to avoid boilerplate discussion. The information presented should be confined to the following eight items, including additional details pertaining to those items:

1. A brief discussion of the basic financial statements, including the relationships of the statements to each other and the significant differences in the information they provide. Analyses should be provided that help users understand why measurements and results reported in fund financial statements either reinforce information in government-wide statements or provide additional information.

2. Condensed financial information derived from government-wide financial statements comparing the current year to the prior year. Governments should present the information needed to support their analysis of financial position and results of operations.

3. An analysis of the government's overall financial position and results of operations, addressing both governmental and business-type activities as reported in the government-wide financial statements, to help users assess whether the financial position has improved or deteriorated as a result of the year's operations.

4. An analysis of balances and transactions of the individual funds, including the reasons for significant changes in fund balances or fund net assets and whether restrictions, commitments, or other limitations significantly affect the availability of fund resources for future use.

5. An analysis of significant variations between original and final budget amounts and between final budget amounts and actual budget results for the general fund or its equivalent, including any known reasons for such of those variations that are expected to have a significant effect on future services or liquidity.

6. A description of significant capital-asset and long-term debt activity during the year, including a discussion of commitments for capital expenditures, changes in credit ratings, and debt limitations that may affect financing of planned facilities or services.

7. A discussion by governments that use the modified approach to report some or all of their infrastructure assets.

8. A description of facts, decisions, or conditions of which management is aware at the date of the independent auditor's report that are expected to significantly affect financial position or results of operations—revenues, expenses, and other changes in net assets.

In addition to the information required to be presented as Required Supplementary Information (RSI) by GASB Statement Nos. 10, 25, 27, 43, 45, and other RSI required to be presented by GASB Statement No. 34 includes MD&A, budgetary comparison schedules for governmental funds, and information about infrastructure assets reported using the modified approach.

Budgetary Comparison Information.   Under GASB Statement No. 34, budgetary comparison schedules should present (1) the original appropriated budgets; (2) the final appropriated budgets; and (3) actual inflows, outflows, and balances, stated on the governmental budgetary basis as discussed in NCGA Statement No. 1, paragraph 154.

Information in a separate schedule or in notes to RSI should be provided that reconciles budgetary information to GAAP information. Notes to RSI should disclose excesses of expenditures over appropriations in individual funds presented in the budgetary comparison, as discussed in NCGA Interpretation No. 6, paragraph 4, as amended by GASB Statement No. 37. (If the budgetary comparison information is included in the basic statements, these disclosures should be in the notes to the financial statements rather than as notes to RSI.)

Modified Approach for Reporting Infrastructure.   A government with eligible infrastructure assets (for subsystems, if any) reported using the modified approach should present as RSI these schedules derived from the asset management systems:

- The assessed condition, based on assessments performed at least every three years, for at least the three most recent complete condition assessments, indicating the dates of the assessments
- The estimated annual amount calculated at the beginning of the year to maintain and preserve the assets at or above the condition level established and disclosed by the government compared with the amounts actually reported as expense for each of the past five reporting periods

The following should be disclosed with the schedules:

- The basis for the condition measurement and the measurement scale used to assess and report condition. For example, a basis could be distresses in pavement surfaces. A scale could range from zero for a failed pavement to 100 for pavement in perfect condition.
- The condition level at which the government intends to preserve its eligible infrastructure assets reported using the modified approach.
- Factors that significantly affect trends in the information reported in the schedules, including any changes in the basis for the condition measurement, the measurement scale, or the condition measurement methods used. Also to be disclosed is an estimate of the effect of a change in the condition level at which the government intends to preserve eligible infrastructure assets of the estimated annual amount to maintain and preserve the assets for the current period.

A government that has asset management systems for infrastructure assets that gather the information required under this subsection but do not use the modified approach is encouraged to disclose it as supplement information.

(iii) Comprehensive Annual Financial Report (CAFR)   Even though the GASB encourages each governmental entity to prepare a CAFR, the basic financial statement constitutes fair presentation of financial position and the respective changes in financial position and cash flows, where applicable in accordance with GAAP and could be opined on as such by an independent auditor. The statements would be suitable for inclusion in an official statement for a securities offering and for widespread distribution to users requiring less detailed information about the governmental unit's finances than is contained in the CAFR.

The CAFR differs from the BFS in the level of detail and the quantity of data presented. The additional data are *not* necessary for fair presentation of financial position or results of operation in accordance with GAAP, but they are useful and informative for certain readers of a government's financial report. Furthermore, the CAFR may be the vehicle for providing the necessary information for fulfilling the legal and other disclosure requirements of higher levels of government, bondholders, and similar groups. It is also useful in demonstrating management's stewardship responsibilities, since alongside the comparative budgets it presents in more detail the use of the available resources.

The recommended contents of the general-purpose government's CAFR include the following:

- *Introductory section:*
  - Title page. Contains the title "Comprehensive Annual Financial Report," the name of the governmental unit, the period of time covered, and the names of the principal government officials. Component units that issue separate statements should indicate the PG of which it is a component.
  - A title such as "City Hospital, a Component Unit of City, Any State" is recommended.
  - Table of contents. Identifies the presence and location of each item included in the report.
  - Transmittal letter. From the government's chief finance officer (or CEO), other information that is not included in the management's discussion and analysis that provides basic information about the government and how it operates along with other information useful in assessing the government's economic condition. The letter may include, for example, changes in financial policies; discussion of internal controls; significant elements of financial management; budget procedures and current budget; and a preview of the significant developments or changes contemplated in the coming year including economic conditions, outlook, and major initiatives.
- *Financial section:*
  - Independent auditor's report.
  - Basic financial statements. Includes all required financial statements and related notes as previously described.
  - Required supplementary information. Included when disclosure is required by the GASB.
  - Combining financial statements. Used when a governmental unit has more than one fund of a given type.
  - Individual fund financial statements and schedules. Used when this information is not provided in a separate column in a combining statement or it is desirable to present a level of detail that would be excessive for the BFS or the combining statements. Examples are detail comparisons to budgets that cannot be reflected on the combining statements, comparative data for prior years, or a demonstration of an individual fund's compliance with legal provisions.
  - Schedules necessary to demonstrate compliance. Included when such are required by state law or by a bond covenant.
  - Other schedules desired by the government. Used for reporting particular kinds of information that are spread throughout the numerous financial statements and that can be brought together and presented in greater detail than in the individual

statements, or that show the details of a specific amount or amounts presented in the BFS, the combining statements, or the individual fund financial statements.

- *Statistical section*:
  - Statistical tables cover a period of several years and contain data drawn from more than just the accounting records. Their purpose is to present social, economic, and financial trends, and the fiscal capacity of the governmental unit. The following titles indicate recommended statistical tables for a local general-purpose government's CAFR:
    - ◇ Net Assets by Components—Last Ten Fiscal Years
    - ◇ Changes in Net Assets—Last Ten Fiscal Years
    - ◇ Governmental Activities Tax Revenue by Source—Last Ten Fiscal Years
    - ◇ Changes in Fund Balances of Governmental Funds—Last Ten Fiscal Years
    - ◇ General Governmental Tax Revenues by Source—Last Ten Fiscal Years
    - ◇ Assessed Value and Estimated Actual Value of Taxable Property—Last Ten Fiscal Years
    - ◇ Property Tax Rates—Direct and Overlapping Governments—Last Ten Fiscal Years
    - ◇ Principal Taxpayers—Current Fiscal Year and Nine Years Ago
    - ◇ Property Tax Levies and Collections—Last Ten Fiscal Years
    - ◇ Ratios of Outstanding Debt by Type—Last Ten Fiscal Years
    - ◇ Direct and Overlapping Governmental Activities Debt
    - ◇ Legal Debt Margin Information Last Ten Fiscal Years
    - ◇ Pledged-Revenue Coverage Last Ten Fiscal Years
    - ◇ Demographic and Economic Statistics—Last Ten Fiscal Years
    - ◇ Principal Employers—Current Fiscal Year and Nine Years Ago
    - ◇ Full-time Equivalent City Government Employees by Function—Last Ten Fiscal Years
    - ◇ Operating Indicators by Function—Last Ten Fiscal Years
    - ◇ Capital Asset Statistics by Function—Last Ten Fiscal Years
- *Single Audit section*:
    Although it is not a required part of a CAFR, some governments include in a separate section the information, including auditor's reports, required by the Single Audit Act Amendments of 1996.

(iv) Certificate of Achievement Program   Governmental units may submit their CAFRs to the GFOA (180 North Michigan Avenue, Chicago, IL 60601) for evaluation in accordance with the standards of financial reporting established by the GASB and the GFOA. If the report substantially adheres to these standards, the government is awarded a Certificate of Achievement for Excellence in Financial Reporting. The certificate is valid for only one year. It may be reproduced in the government's annual report and should be included in the subsequent year's CAFR. Annually, the GFOA publishes a list of the governments that hold valid certificates.

Many governments endeavor to obtain the certificate. They realize that credit rating agencies and others familiar with governmental accounting and financial reporting recognize that governments holding a certificate typically maintain complete financial records and effectively report their financial information to permit detailed analyses to be performed. This characteristic can improve the government's bond rating.

(v) Popular Reports   Governments also prepare popular reports to communicate with persons who are neither interested in a complete set of financial statements nor able to review them. Popular reports are also called *condensed summary data.*

There are three types of popular reports. The first is an aggregation of the data from the financial statements that disregards the distinction among fund types and the different bases of accounting and presents the data as if all the assets, liabilities, equities, revenues, and expenditures (expenses) pertained not to the fund types but to the government as a whole. This results in a presentation similar to that made by corporations and their subsidiaries. In such cases, the government usually eliminates significant interfund transactions before arriving at totals.

The second approach is to visually present the entity's financial information—for example, by using pie charts or bar graphs. A common presentation is to present one pie to show the composition of revenue by cutting the pie into slices with each slice representing a major revenue source. The size of the slice would reflect the magnitude of the respective revenue source. Similar pie charts can be used to show the major categories of expenditures, the major categories of assets, and the major categories of liabilities.

The third approach is to issue consolidated government-wide financial statements. Such a consolidated approach replaces the funds and government-wide financial statements by a single "fund" that is used to report the financial position and results of operations of the entire oversight unit or reporting entity. Intragovernmental transactions are eliminated in the consolidation process, and a single basis of accounting (normally accrual) is used for all transactions.

Consolidated financial statements typically include a balance sheet and an operating statement. Because the accrual basis of accounting is normally used, capital assets are reported and depreciated. In addition, long-term obligations are reported.

34.5 BASIC FINANCIAL STATEMENTS REQUIRED FOR SPECIAL-PURPOSE GOVERNMENTS

Special-purpose governments are legally separate entities that are component units or other stand-alone governments, which are legally separate government organizations that (1) do not have separately elected governing bodies and (2) are not component units, plus joint ventures, jointly governed organizations, and pools.

A special-purpose government that is engaged in more than one governmental program or that has both governmental and business-type activities should meet the reporting requirements for governments that are not special-purpose governments. A special-purpose government is engaged in more than one governmental program if it budgets, manages, or accounts for its activities as multiple programs, such as a school district that provides regular instruction, special instruction, vocational education, and adult education.

(a) REPORTING BY SPECIAL-PURPOSE GOVERNMENTS ENGAGED IN GOVERNMENTAL ACTIVITIES   A special-purpose government engaged in a single governmental activity, such as some cemetery districts, levee districts, assessment districts, and drainage districts, may combine its government-wide financial statements and its fund financial statements in a columnar format that reconciles line items of fund financial information to government-wide information in a separate column on the face of the financial statements rather than at the bottom of the statements or in an accompanying schedule. Otherwise, the special-purpose government may present separate government-wide and fund financial statements and may present its government-wide statement of activities in a different format. For example, it may be

presented in a single column that reports expenses first followed by revenues by major sources. The difference, net revenue or expense, should be followed by contributions to permanent and term endowments, special and extraordinary items, transfers, and beginning and ending net assets.

(b) REPORTING BY SPECIAL-PURPOSE GOVERNMENTS ENGAGED ONLY IN BUSINESS-TYPE ACTIVITIES   A government engaged in only business-type activities should present only the financial statement required for enterprise funds, as follows:

- MD&A
- Enterprise fund financial statements:
  - ○ Statement of net assets or balance sheet
  - ○ Statement of revenues, expenses, and changes in fund net assets
  - ○ Statement of cash flows
  - ○ Notes to financial statements
- Applicable RSI other than MD&A

(c) REPORTING BY SPECIAL-PURPOSE GOVERNMENTS ENGAGED ONLY IN FIDUCIARY ACTIVITIES   A special-purpose government engaged in only fiduciary activities should present only the financial statement required for fiduciary funds, as follows:

- MD&A
- Statement of fiduciary net assets
- Statement of changes in fiduciary net assets
- Notes to financial statements

A Public Employees Retirement System (PERS) is a special-purpose government that administers one or more defined benefit pension plans and may also administer other kinds of employee benefit plans, such as defined contribution, deferred compensation, and postemployment health care plans. One that administers more than one defined benefit pension plan or postemployment health care plan should present combining financial statements for all such plans and, if applicable, required schedules for each plan. (A PERS that administers one or more agent multiple-employer plans applies these requirement at the aggregate plan level.) It should (1) present a separate column for each plan on the statement of fiduciary net assets and the statement of changes in fiduciary net assets or (2) present combining statements for the plans as part of the basic financial statements.

34.6   ACCOUNTING PRINCIPLES AND PRACTICES—PUBLIC COLLEGES AND UNIVERSITIES

Public colleges and universities should apply the principles discussed in this chapter. The primary guidance for public colleges and universities is GASB Statement No. 35, "Basic Financial Statements—and Management's Discussion and Analysis—for Public Colleges and Universities."

34.7   AUDITS OF GOVERNMENTAL UNITS

Audits of governmental units with financial statements can be performed in accordance with

- Generally accepted auditing standards (GAAS)
- *Government Auditing Standards* (the Yellow Book)

- The Single Audit Act Amendments of 1996 and Office of Management and Budget (OMB) Circular A-133

When performing an audit in accordance with GAAS, the guidance contained in the *AICPA Professional Standards* is followed. This is the same guidance followed by auditors when auditing the financial statement of commercial entities and typically results in the issuance of an opinion of the financial statements and perhaps a management letter. *Government Auditing Standards,* also known as the *Yellow Book* (U.S. Comptroller General, rev. 2007), establishes the concept of an expanded scope audit that includes both financial and compliance features. According to the Yellow Book, a financial audit can help determine whether

- The financial statements of an audited entity present fairly the financial position and the results of financial operations in accordance with GAAP.
- The entity has complied with laws and regulations that may have a material effect on the financial statements.

The Yellow Book incorporates the AICPA Professional Standards previously mentioned and sets forth additional standards and requirements, including the following six:

1. A review is to be made of compliance with applicable laws and regulations, as set forth in federal audit guides and other applicable reference sources.
2. The auditor reports on the entity's compliance with laws, regulations, contracts, and grant agreements and shall also include material instances of noncompliance and instances or indications of noncompliance or fraud found during or in connection with the audit.
3. The auditors shall report on their consideration of the entity's internal control over financial reporting as part of the financial audit.
   They shall identify as a minimum:
   a. Scope of auditor's work in obtaining an understanding of the internal control over financial reporting.
   b. The significant deficiencies including separate identification of material weaknesses identified as a result of the auditor's work.
4. Auditors performing government audits are required to obtain 80 hours of continuing education that directly enhance the auditor's professional proficiency to perform audits and/or attestation engagements every two years, of which 24 hours should be directly related to government. At least 20 of the 80 hours should be completed in each year of the two-year period.
5. Audit organizations performing government audits are required to establish an internal quality control system and participate in an external quality control review program.
6. The auditor communicates certain information related to the conduct of the audit to the audit committee or to the individuals with whom they have contracted for the audit.

(a) THE SINGLE AUDIT ACT AMENDMENTS OF 1996   Many state and local governments are required to obtain a periodic audit of the federal funds they receive, usually once a year. The audits are normally performed by an independent certified public accountant (CPA) or public accountant, or, in some states, by the government's internal audit personnel. A few jurisdictions have an independently elected or appointed auditor who conducts the audit. Single audits are conducted in accordance with GAAS, *Government Auditing Standards,* and the Single Audit Amendments Act of 1996 and its implementing regulation OMB Circular A-133, including its Compliance Supplement. These requirements have been updated for fiscal years beginning on or after July 1, 1997, by the Single Audit Amendments Act of 1996 (the Act).

The objectives of the Act are

- To improve the financial management of state and local governments with respect to federal financial assistance programs through improved auditing
- To establish uniform requirements for audits of federal financial assistance provided to state and local governments
- To promote the efficient and effective use of audit resources
- To ensure that federal departments and agencies, to the maximum extent practicable, rely on and use audit work performed pursuant to the requirements of the Single Audit Act

Though the single audit builds on the annual financial statement audit currently required by most state and larger local governments, it places substantial additional emphasis on the consideration and testing of internal controls and the testing of compliance with laws and regulations.

The Single Audit Act and OMB Circular A-133 require the auditor to determine whether

- The financial statements of the government, department, agency, or establishment present fairly its financial position and the results of operations in conformity with GAAP.
- The organization has internal and other control structures to provide reasonable assurance that it is managing federal financial assistance programs in compliance with applicable laws and regulations.
- The organization has complied with laws and regulations that may have a material effect on its financial statements and on each major federal financial assistance program.

Nonfederal entities that expend $500,000 or more in a year in federal awards are subject to a single audit unless they elect (if qualified) to have a program-specific audit conducted. If less than $500,000 is expended, the entity is exempt from federal audit requirements for that year, but records must be retained for review or audit by, for example, the General Accountability Office (GAO).

The Single Audit Act provides auditors with guidance on the focus of the audit by defining a level of audit work based on the concept of "major" federal programs. OMB Circular A-133 §___.520 provides specific guidance on how to determine what are major federal programs and outlines the three steps required in identifying "major" federal programs. These three steps are as follows:

1. Identify "Type A" and "Type B" programs. For most small and medium-sized governments, a Type A program is defined as the larger of $300,000 or 3 percent of the total federal *expenditures* for all federal programs. For larger governments whose total federal expenditures exceed $100 million, a major federal financial assistance program is based on a sliding scale. All programs that are not categorized as a Type A program are "Type B" programs.
2. Identify "Low Risk Type A" programs by assessing all Type A programs. Typically, a Low Risk Type A program must have been audited as a "major" program within the last two years and must have no audit findings as defined in §___.510(a). All

Type A programs which are not low risk are high risk and must be audited as a major program.

3. Identify "High Risk Type B" programs if there are one or more Low Risk Type A programs identified. Auditors have two options in assessing risks in Type B programs:

   o *Option one.* Complete a risk assessment for *all* Type B programs that are greater than the Type B floor amount, then classify as major programs one-half of the Type B programs greater than the floor amount identified as high risk with a cap in the number of major programs at the number of Low Risk Type A programs.

   o *Option two.* Complete a risk assessment for *some* of the Type B programs that are greater than the Type B floor amount until the same number high-risk Type B programs are greater than or equal to the number of Low Risk Type A programs.

If a federal grantor agency formally designates a program to be major, this program must also be audited in addition to the major programs identified in previous steps.

The Single Audit Act and OMB Circular A-133 require the auditor to issue the following reports:

- A report on the audit of the basic financial statements of the entity as a whole, or the department, agency, or establishment covered by the audit
- A report on compliance and internal control based on an audit of the basic financial statements
- A report on compliance and internal control over compliance applicable to each major federal award program

In a single audit, the report on the audit of the basic financial statements is typically expanded to include an opinion on the fair presentation of the supplementary schedule of expenditures of federal awards in relation to the audited financial statements.

(b) OTHER CONSIDERATIONS Most government officials and auditors of governmental units realize that a good audit should furnish more than an opinion on the financial statements. Other services a governmental auditor can provide are pinpointing the key information upon which decisions should be based and contributing to the presentation of this information in a manner that facilitates decision making; uncovering deficiencies in the accounting system and providing suggestions for improving the efficiency and effectiveness of the system; and obtaining and presenting information useful for marketing securities.

Obtaining a qualified auditor, particularly one who can provide the additional services described above, requires that the selection be based on qualifications and experience, and not solely cost. The National Intergovernmental Audit Forum, in its handbook *How to Avoid a Substandard Audit: Suggestions for Procuring an Audit*, indicates that

> Public entities should never select auditors without considering five basic elements of an effective audit procurement process:
>
> planning (determining what needs to be done and when),
> fostering competition by soliciting proposals (writing a clear and direct solicitation document and disseminating it widely),

technically evaluating proposals and qualifications (authorizing a committee of knowledgeable persons to evaluate the ability of prospective auditors to effectively carry out the audit),

preparing a written agreement (documenting the expectations of both the entity and the auditor), and

monitoring the auditor's performance (periodically reviewing the progress of that performance).

This handbook provides detailed information about the five elements of procurement previously listed as well as the use of audit committees in a government environment, along with other useful information about the auditor procurement process.

(i) Governmental Rotation of Auditors   The automatic rotation of auditors after a given number of years is a common practice in many governments; however, it is not always beneficial. Many governments have followed this policy, believing that they will (1) receive a fresh outlook from the audit, (2) spread the work among several firms, and (3) encourage lower fees. What the Government Accountability Office (GAO) found in its November 2003 *Required Study on the Potential Effects of Mandatory Audit Firm Rotation* is that mandatory audit firm rotation may not be the most efficient way to strengthen auditor independence and improve auditing quality, considering the additional financial costs and the loss of institutional knowledge. Automatic rotation may be harmful in that it could deprive the government of the extensive knowledge of the entity developed by the current auditor. It may also impair auditing effectiveness, given that a new auditor may need to spend considerable time learning the government's system. The government may actually incur more cost since its personnel will need to spend time explaining the organization, systems, and data to the new auditors, and the new auditors will need to spend valuable time reviewing information that is already part of the previous auditor's workpapers. Although a government should continuously monitor its auditor's performance to ensure that the service obtained is commensurate with the cost, the entity should normally change auditors only because of dissatisfaction with services and not for the sake of receiving a lower fee.

(ii) Audit Committees   In recent years, governments have started establishing audit committees similar to those in the private sector. Some appropriate tasks for a local government's audit committee include the following:

- Reviewing significant financial information for reliability, timeliness, clarity, appropriateness of disclosure, and compliance with GAAP and legal requirements
- Ascertaining that internal controls are appropriately designed and functioning effectively
- Evaluating independent audit firms and selecting one for approval by the appropriate body
- Overseeing the scope and performance of the independent audit function
- Ensuring that the auditors' recommendations for improvements in internal controls and operating methods receive management's attention and are implemented on a timely basis
- Providing an effective communications link between the auditors and the full governing board

The primary benefit of an audit committee is in assisting the full governing board to fulfill its responsibilities for the presentation of financial information about the governmental unit. There are also secondary benefits: The other parties involved in the issuance of financial information—management and independent and internal auditors—can perform their roles more effectively if an audit committee is involved in the process. Finally, there are advantages for the government's constituencies—in particular, the taxpayers and bondholders.

34.8 CONCLUDING REMARKS

Governmental accounting and reporting is changing and expanding at an increasing rapid rate. Coupling this with public accountability issues, the federal government's pressure for increased audit quality, and the penalties for substandard audit performance results in increasing levels of audit risk. Government audits, often considered low-risk engagements by many, are quickly becoming areas of extremely high risk. Auditing professionals need to recognize the risk associated with government engagements now and in the future before incurring severe penalties or embarrassment. The technical issues involved in government auditing are on a par with those in the commercial environment, but auditors have much less experience and less technical guidance to fall back on.

Dealing with these technical issues requires well-trained, highly motivated individuals and can no longer be left to less experienced members of the audit team. Dealing with the *real* issues governments are facing (e.g., infrastructure, terrorism, prison overcrowding, drugs, etc.) requires even more from the individuals in the profession. Like it or not, government accounting and reporting is being thrust into the spotlight and will be scrutinized by a multitude of individuals and groups. It is imperative that individuals in the industry realize this fact and begin now to prepare for the future.

34.9 SOURCES AND SUGGESTED REFERENCES

American Institute of Certified Public Accountants, "AICPA Audit and Accounting Guide: State and Local Governments." AICPA, New York, 2007.

_____, "AICPA Audit and Accounting Guide: Government Auditing Standards and Circular A-133 Audits." AICPA, New York, 2007.

_____, "AICPA Professional Standards." AICPA, New York, 2007.

City and County of San Francisco, California, "Comprehensive Annual Financial Report For the Year Ended June 30, 2006," 2006.

Financial Accounting Standards Board, "Classification of Short-Term Obligations Expected to Be Refinanced," Statement of Financial Accounting Standards No. 6. FASB, Stamford, CT, 1975.

_____, "Accounting for Leases," Statement of Financial Accounting Standards Board No. 13. FASB, Stamford, CT, 1975.

_____, "Objectives of Financial Reporting by Nonbusiness Organizations," Statement of Financial Accounting Concepts No. 4. FASB, Stamford, CT, 1980.

General Accounting Office, "Government Auditing Standards, July 2007 Revision." GAO, Washington, DC, 2003.

_____, "Required Study on the Potential Effects of Mandatory Audit Firm Rotation." GAO, Washington, DC, 2003.

Governmental Accounting Standards Board, "Basic Financial Statements—and Management's Discussion and Analysis—for State and Local Governments." GASB Statement No. 34. GASB, Norwalk, CT, 1999.

_____, "Codification of Governmental Accounting and Financial Reporting Standards." GASB, Norwalk, CT, 2007.

Government Finance Officers Association, "Governmental Accounting, Auditing and Financial Reporting." GFOA, Chicago, IL, 2005. (Study guide available)

Ives, Martin, "The Governmental Accounting Standards Board: Factors Influencing Its Operation and Initial Technical Agenda," *Government Accounting Journal*, Spring 2002, vol. 49 (1), pp. 22–27.

Mead, Dean Michael, "What You Should Know About Your Local Government's Finances." GASB, Norwalk, CT, 2007.

Office of Management and Budget, "Circular No. A-133, Audits of States, Local Governments, and Non-Profit Organizations, June 27, 2003 Revision." Office of Management and Budget, Washington, DC, 2003.

APPENDIX 34A PRONOUNCEMENTS ON STATE AND LOCAL GOVERNMENT ACCOUNTING

	Government Accounting Standard Board	Effective Date
Statement No. 1	Authoritative Status of NCGA Pronouncements and AICPA Industry Audit Guide	On issuance (7/84)
Statement No. 2	Financial Reporting of Deferred Compensation Plans Adopted under the Provisions of Internal Revenue Code Section 457	Superseded by GASB Statement No. 32
Statement No. 3	Deposits with Financial Institutions, Investments (including Repurchase Agreements), and Reverse Repurchase Agreements	Financial statements for periods ending after 2/15/86
Statement No. 4	Applicability of FASB Statement No. 87, "Employers' Accounting for Pensions," to State and Local Governmental Employers	Superseded by GASB Statement No. 27
Statement No. 5	Disclosure of Pension Information by Public Employee Retirement Systems and State and Local Governmental Employers	Financial reports issued for fiscal years beginning after 12/15/86
Statement No. 6	Accounting and Financial Reporting for Special Assessments	Financial statements for periods beginning after 6/15/87
Statement No. 7	Advance Refundings Resulting in Defeasance of Debt	Fiscal periods beginning after 12/15/86
Statement No. 8	Applicability of FASB Statement No. 93, "Recognition of Depreciation by Not-for-Profit Organizations," to Certain State and Local Governmental Entities	Superseded by GASB Statement No. 35
Statement No. 9	Reporting Cash Flows of Proprietary and Nonexpendable Trust Funds and Governmental Entries that Use Proprietary Fund Accounting	Fiscal periods beginning after 12/15/89
Statement No. 10	Accounting and Financial Reporting for Risk Financing and Related Insurance Issues	Pools—Fiscal periods beginning after 6/15/90
		Other—Fiscal periods beginning after 6/15/93

(Continued)

APPENDIX 34A *(Continued)*

	Government Accounting Standard Board	Effective Date
Statement No. 11	Measurement Focus and Basis of Accounting—Governmental Fund Operating Statements	Fiscal periods beginning after 6/15/94
Statement No. 12	Disclosure of Information on Postemployment Benefits Other than Pension Benefits by State and Local Governmental Employers	Fiscal periods beginning after 6/15/90
Statement No. 13	Accounting for Operating Leases with Scheduled Rent Increases	Leases with terms beginning after 6/30/90
Statement No. 14	The Financial Reporting Entity	Fiscal periods beginning after 12/15/92
Statement No. 15	Governmental College and University Accounting and Financial Reporting Models	Superseded by GASB Statement No. 35
Statement No. 16	Accounting for Compensated Absences	Fiscal periods beginning after 6/15/93
Statement No. 17	Measurement Focus and Basis of Accounting—Governmental Fund Operating Statements: Amendment of Effective Dates of GASB Statement No. 11 and Related Statements	Immediately
Statement No. 18	Accounting for Municipal Solid Waste Landfill Closure and Post-closure Care Costs	Fiscal periods beginning after 6/15/93
Statement No. 19	Governmental College and University Omnibus Statement–an Amendment of GASB Statements No. 10 and 15	Superseded by GASB Statement No. 35
Statement No. 20	Accounting and Financial Reporting for Proprietary Funds and Other Governmental Entities That Use Proprietary Fund Accounting	Fiscal periods beginning after 12/15/93
Statement No. 21	Accounting for Escheat Property	Fiscal periods beginning after 12/15/94
Statement No. 22	Accounting for Taxpayer-Assessed Tax Revenues in Governmental Funds	Superseded by GASB Statement No. 33
Statement No. 23	Accounting and Financial Reporting for Refundings of Debt Reported by Proprietary Activities	Fiscal periods beginning after 6/15/94

	Government Accounting Standard Board	**Effective Date**
Statement No. 24	Accounting and Financial Reporting for Certain Grants and Other Financial Assistance	Fiscal periods beginning after 6/15/95
Statement No. 25	Financial Reporting for Defined Benefit Pension Plans and Note Disclosures for Defined Contribution Plans	Fiscal periods beginning after 6/15/96, Statement No. 26 must be implemented simultaneously
Statement No. 26	Financial Reporting for Postemployment Healthcare Plans Administered by Defined Benefit Pension Plans	Fiscal periods beginning after 6/15/96, Statement No. 25 must be implemented simultaneously
Statement No. 27	Accounting for Pensions by State and Local Governmental Employers	Fiscal periods beginning after 6/15/97
Statement No. 28	Accounting and Financial Reporting for Securities Lending Transactions	Fiscal periods beginning after 12/15/95
Statement No. 29	The Use of Not-for-Profit Accounting and Financial Reporting Principles by Governmental Entities	Fiscal periods beginning after 12/15/95
Statement No. 30	Risk Financing Omnibus	Fiscal periods beginning after 6/15/96
Statement No. 31	Accounting and Financial Reporting for Certain Investments and for External Investment Pools	Fiscal periods beginning after 6/15/96
Statement No. 32	Accounting and Financial Reporting for Internal Revenue Code Section 457 Deferred Compensation Plans	Earlier of fiscal periods beginning after 12/31/98, or amendment of the IRC Section 457 Plan
Statement No. 33	Accounting and Financial Reporting for Nonexchange Transactions	Periods beginning after 6/15/00
Statement No. 34	Basic Financial Statements—and Management's Discussion and Analysis—for State and Local Governments	[6]

(Continued)

6. In three phases, based on total annual revenue in the first fiscal year ending after June 15, 1999; Phase 1—governments with total annual revenues of $100 million or more, fiscal periods beginning after June 15, 2001; Phase 2—governments with total annual revenues of $10 or more but less than $100 million, fiscal periods beginning after June 15, 2002; Phase 3—governments with total annual revenues of less than $10 million, fiscal periods beginning after June 15, 2003.

APPENDIX 34A *(Continued)*

	Government Accounting Standard Board	Effective Date
Statement No. 35	Basic Financial Statements—and Management's Discussion and Analysis— for Public Colleges and Universities: Amendment of GASB Statement No. 34 [7]	
Statement No. 36	Recipient Reporting for Certain Shared Nonexchange Revenues: Amendment of GASB Statement No. 33	Simultaneously with Statement No. 33
Statement No. 37	Basic Financial Statements—and Management's Discussion and Analysis— for State and Local Governments: Omnibus [8]	
Statement No. 38	Certain Financial Statement Note Disclosures and Discussion and Analysis— for State and Local Governments [9]	
Statement No. 39	Determining Whether Certain Organizations Are Component Units	Periods beginning after 6/15/03
Statement No. 40	Deposit and Investment Risk Disclosures— An Amendment of GASB Statement No. 3	Periods beginning after 6/15/04
Statement No. 41	Budgetary Comparison Schedules— Perspective Differences—An Amendment of GASB Statement No. 34	Simultaneously with Statement 34
Statement No. 42	Accounting and Financial Reporting for Impairment of Capital Assets and for Insurance Recoveries	Periods beginning after 12/15/04

7. Public institutions that are components of another reporting entity should implement the Statement no later than the same year as their primary government. For public institutions that are not components of another reporting entity, this Statement is effective in the three phases indicated in the preceding footnote.
8. Simultaneously with Statement No. 34. For governments that implemented Statement No. 34 before Statement No. 37 was issued, Statement No. 37 is effective for periods beginning after June 15, 2000.
9. In three phases, based on total annual revenue in the first fiscal year ending after June 15, 1999: Phase 1—governments with total annual revenues of $100 million or more, fiscal periods beginning after June 15, 2001; Phase 2—governments with total annual revenues of $10 million or more but less than $100 million, fiscal periods beginning after June 15, 2002; Phase 3—governments with total annual revenues of less than $10 million, fiscal periods beginning after June 15, 2003.

	Government Accounting Standard Board	Effective Date
Statement No. 43	Financial Reporting for Postemployment Benefit Plans Other Than Pension Plans	Effective in three phases based on a government's total annual revenues in the first fiscal year ending after 6/15/99: for periods beginning after 12/15/05, 2006, and 2007
Statement No. 44	Economic Condition Reporting—The Statistical Section—An Amendment of NCGA Statement 1	Statistical sections prepared for periods beginning after 6/15/05
Statement No. 45	Accounting and Financial Reporting by Employers for Postemployment Benefits Other Than Pensions	Effective in three phases based on a government's total annual revenues in the first fiscal year ending after 6/15/99: for periods beginning after 12/15/06, 2007, and 2008
Statement No. 46	Net Assets Restricted by Enabling Legislation—An Amendment of GASB Statement No. 34	Periods beginning after 6/15/05
Statement No. 47	Accounting for Termination Benefits	For termination benefits provided through an existing defined benefit OPEB plan, the provisions of this Statement should be implemented simultaneously with the requirements of Statement 45. For all other termination benefits, this Statement is effective for financial statements for periods beginning after 6/15/05.
Statement No. 48	Sales and Pledges of Receivables and Future Revenues and Intra-Entity Transfers of Assets and Future Revenues	Periods beginning after 12/15/06
Statement No. 49	Accounting and Financial Reporting for Pollution Remediation Obligations	Periods beginning after 12/15/07

(Continued)

APPENDIX 34A *(Continued)*

Government Accounting Standard Board		Effective Date
Statement No. 50	Pension Disclosures—an amendment of GASB Statements No. 25 and No. 27	Periods beginning after 6/15/07, except for requirements related to the use of the entry age actuarial cost method for the purpose of reporting a surrogate funded status and funding progress of plans that use the aggregate actuarial cost method, which are effective for periods for which the financial statements and RSI contain information resulting from actuarial valuations as of 6/15/07, or later.
Statement No. 51	Accounting and Financial Reporting for Intangible Assets	Periods beginning after 6/15/09
Statement No. 52	Land and Other Real Estate Held as Investments by Endowments	Periods beginning after 6/15/08
Interpretation No. 1	Demand Bonds Issued by State and Local Governmental Entities	Fiscal periods ending after 6/15/85
Interpretation No. 2	Disclosure of Conduit Debt Obligations	Fiscal periods beginning after 12/15/95
Interpretation No. 3	Financial Reporting for Reverse Repurchase Agreements	Fiscal periods beginning after 12/15/95
Interpretation No. 4	Accounting and Financial Reporting for Capitalization Contributions to Public Entity Risk Pools	Fiscal periods beginning after 6/15/96
Interpretation No. 5	Property Tax Revenue Recognition in Governmental Funds	Fiscal periods beginning after 6/15/00
Interpretation No. 6	Recognition and Measurement of Certain Liabilities and Expenditures in Governmental Fund Financial Statements: an Interpretation of NCGA Statements 1, 4, and 5, NCGA Interpretation 8, and GASB Statement Nos. 10, 16, and 18	Simultaneously with Statement No. 34
Technical Bulletin No. 84–1	Purpose and Scope of GASB Technical Bulletins and Procedures for Issuance	None

	Government Accounting Standard Board	Effective Date
Technical Bulletin No. 2003–1	Disclosure Requirements for Derivatives Not Reported at Fair Value on the Statement of Net Assets	Financial statements issued after 6/15/03
Technical Bulletin No. 2004–1	Tobacco Settlement Recognition and Financial Reporting Entity Issues	6/15/04
Technical Bulletin No. 2004–2	Recognition of Pension and Other Postemployment Benefit Expenditures/ Expense and Liabilities by Cost-Sharing Employers	Pension transactions: for financial statements for periods ending after 12/15/04. OPEB transactions: applied simultaneously with the requirements of Statement 45
Technical Bulletin No. 2006–1	Accounting and Financial Reporting by Employers and OPEB Plans for Payments from the Federal Government Pursuant to the Retiree Drug Subsidy Provisions of Medicare Part D	On issuance (6/06) except for the portions of answers pertaining specifically to measurement, recognition, or required supplementary information requirements of Statement No. 43 or Statement No. 45. Those provisions should be applied simultaneously with the implementation of Statement 43 or Statement 45.
Concepts Statement No. 1	Objectives of Financial Reporting	None
Concepts Statement No. 2	Reporting Service Efforts and Accomplishments	None
Concepts Statement No. 3	Communication Methods in General Purpose External Financial Reports That Contain Basic Financial Statements	None
Concepts Statement No. 4	Elements of Financial Statements	None

	National Council on Government Accounting	Effective Date
Statement 1	Governmental Accounting and Financial Reporting Principles	Fiscal years ending after 6/30/80
Statement 2	Grant, Entitlement, and Shared Revenue Accounting by State and Local Governments	Fiscal years ending after 6/30/80
Statement 3	Defining the Governmental Reporting Entity	Issued 12/81; superseded by GASB Statement No. 14
Statement 4	Accounting and Financial Reporting Principles for Claims and Judgments and Compensated Absences	Fiscal years beginning after 12/31/82; 20 extended indefinitely by NCGAS 11
Statement 5	Accounting and Financial Reporting Principles for Lease Agreements of State and Local Governments	Fiscal years beginning after 6/30/83
Interpretation 1	GAAFR and the AICPA Audit Guide (Superseded)	Issued 4/86; superseded by NCGAS 1
Interpretation 2	Segment Information for Enterprise Funds	Issued 6/80; superseded by GASB Statement No. 34
Interpretation 3	Revenue Recognition—Property Taxes	Fiscal years beginning after 9/30/81
Interpretation 4	Accounting and Financial Reporting for Public Employee Retirement Systems and Pension Trust Funds (Superseded)	Fiscal years beginning after 6/15/82; superseded by NCGAS 6 and repealed by NCGAI 8
Interpretation 5	Authoritative Status of Governmental Accounting, Auditing, and Financial Reporting	Issued 3/82; superseded by GASB Statement No. 34
Interpretation 6	Notes to the Financial Statements Disclosure	Prospectively for fiscal years beginning after 12/31/82
Interpretation 7	Clarification as to the Application of the Criteria in NCGA Statement, "Defining the Governmental Reporting Entity"	Issued 9/83; superseded by GASB Statement No. 14
Interpretation 8	Certain Pension Matters	Fiscal years ending after 12/31/83
Interpretation 9	Certain Fund Classifications and Balance Sheet Accounts	Fiscal years ending after 6/30/84
Interpretation 10	State and Local Government Budgetary Reporting	Fiscal years ending after 6/30/84
Interpretation 11	Claim and Judgment Transactions for Governmental Funds	Issued 4/84; superseded by GASB Statement No. 10

CHAPTER 44

VALUATION OF ASSETS, LIABILITIES, AND NONPUBLIC COMPANIES (REVISED)

NEIL J. BEATON, CPA/ABV, CFA, ASA
Grant Thornton LLP†

---

†   The information contained in this chapter does not necessarily represent the views of Grant Thornton LLP.

44.1   INTRODUCTION

The current accounting environment is unprecedented in its need for accountants to be familiar with, and have a rudimentary understanding of, business valuation theory and implementation. The Financial Accounting Standards Board (FASB) has issued a number of pronouncements relating to business and asset valuation for financial reporting, including the latest comprehensive statement, FAS (Statement of Financial Accounting Standard) No. 157. This chapter focuses on the valuation of assets, liabilities, and nonpublic companies and must be viewed only as a primer since there are whole books, not just a chapter, devoted to the art and science of asset and business valuation.

(a) **DEFINITION OF *NONPUBLIC COMPANIES***   Unlike public companies whose common stock is actively traded and has readily ascertainable value, the common stock of a nonpublic company is typically concentrated in only a few individuals with infrequent trades (if any). As such, there is no objective means to quantify the value of such shares. Fortunately, a number of professional valuation organizations exist, including the AICPA, that provide training, education, and guidance for business valuation professionals. In addition, a number of excellent books have been written on the subject, allowing the curious accountant a means to dig deeper into valuation theory and practice.[1]

(b) **REASONS FOR A BUSINESS VALUATION**   The need for valuing the stock of a nonpublic or closely held company is triggered by a number of circumstances. Among the more important situations requiring the valuation of nonpublic stock are estate planning, employee stock ownership plan transactions, granting employee stock options, buy/sell agreements, marital and corporate dissolutions, restructurings, sales, mergers, and divestitures, and litigation. In addition, financial reporting requires that valuations be performed to identify specific tangible and intangible assets in an acquisition (FAS 141R), for the testing of goodwill impairment (FAS 142), and for other listed assets and liabilities (FAS 144 and 157).

44.2   STANDARDS OF VALUE

The *International Glossary of Business Valuation Terms*[2] defines *standard of value* as the identification of the type of value being utilized in a specific engagement (e.g., fair market value, fair value, investment value). The common standards of value include the following:

- Fair market value
- Fair value, including *statutory* and *financial reporting* definitions
- Investment value
- Intrinsic value
- Book value
- Liquidation value
- Fair value in alternative contexts

Of the foregoing, fair market value and fair value are the most prevalent as these standards are promulgated primarily by the Internal Revenue Service and FASB, respectively.

---

1.   See Appendix 44B.
2.   *International Glossary of Business Valuation Terms.*

(a) FAIR MARKET VALUE DEFINED   *Fair market value* is defined as the price, expressed in terms of cash equivalents, at which property would change hands between a hypothetical willing and able buyer and a hypothetical willing and able seller, acting at arm's length in an open and unrestricted market, when neither is under compulsion to buy or sell and when both have reasonable knowledge of the relevant facts.[3]

(b) FAIR VALUE DEFINED   FAS 157 defines *fair value* as the price that would be received to sell an asset or paid to transfer a liability in an orderly transaction between market participants at the measurement date.[4] The definition of fair value is quite close to that of fair market value except for one key difference. The universe of potential buyers and sellers under fair value consists of "market participants," whereas under fair market value there is no limitation to the hypothetical buyer or seller. To increase consistency and comparability in fair value measurements and related disclosures, the fair value hierarchy prioritizes the inputs to valuation techniques used to measure fair value into three broad levels. The fair value hierarchy gives the highest priority to quoted prices (unadjusted) in active markets for identical assets or liabilities (Level 1) and the lowest priority to developing fair values from unobservable inputs (Level 3).[5] Quoted market prices in active markets are considered the best evidence of fair value of a security and should be used as the basis the measurement, if available. If quoted market prices are not available, the estimate of fair value should be based on the best information available, including prices for similar securities and the results of using other valuation techniques.

44.3 AUDITING GUIDANCE

Fair values are estimates, and are frequently used in assessing the realizable value of assets and liabilities and indicating whether an allowance or write-down of the asset or liability might be required. SAS (Statement of Auditing Standards) No. 57, *Auditing Accounting Estimates*, defines the general responsibilities of management and the auditor with respect to accounting estimates and provides guidance to auditors in obtaining and evaluating sufficient competent evidential matter to support most significant accounting estimates in an audit of financial statements. For audits beginning after June 15, 2003, SAS No. 101, *Auditing Fair Value Estimates and Disclosures*, is effective, setting a higher standard for auditing fair value estimates than for other estimates. In broad terms it states:

- *Management* is responsible for making accounting estimates (including estimates related to a business combination or valuation of company stock).
- The *auditor* is responsible for evaluating the reasonableness of accounting estimates made by management in the context of the financial statements as a whole. In that context, the auditor should:
  - Obtain an understanding of the *events and circumstances* that result in an asset being valued.
  - Evaluate that the *methodology used* to estimate value is appropriate.
  - Evaluate that the *assumptions underlying* the methodology used are not unreasonable in the circumstances.

---

3.   Id.
4.   Statement of Financial Accounting Standards No. 157.
5.   Id.

The AICPA Toolkit, *Auditing Fair Value Measurements and Disclosures,* contains substantial guidance to auditors on fair value issues in financial reporting, but predates the issuance of FAS 157. As such, although it provides excellent guidance on auditing fair value, its guidance is not as comprehensive as current accounting pronouncements.

44.4   BUSINESS VALUATION BASICS

A business valuation begins with an understanding of the business at the *micro* level (operations and finances) and then expands into more *macro* levels for context (industry, economy, competition). A thorough understanding of the company is required before any meaningful valuation analysis takes place. This knowledge is used to assess the "riskiness" of the company, which will impact implied discount rates and the selection of valuation multiples. Revenue Ruling 59-60, an oft-cited treatise on business valuation from the IRS, outlines the specific business areas an appraiser should consider in a valuation.[6] These include:

- The nature of the business and the history of the enterprise from its inception
- The economic outlook in general and the condition and outlook of the specific industry in particular
- The book value of the stock and the financial condition of the business
- The earnings capacity of the company
- The dividend-paying capacity
- Whether the enterprise has goodwill or other intangible value
- Sales of the stock and the size of the block of stock to be valued
- The market price of stocks of corporations engaged in the same or a similar line of business having their stocks actively traded in a free and open market, either on an exchange or over-the-counter

Analyzing a company's history can help identify past stability or instability, growth trends, operational diversity, and other facts needed to form an opinion of the degree of risk involved in the business. A historical analysis should include the nature of the business, its products or services, its operating and investment assets, capital structure, plant facilities, sales records, and management. Similarly, the economic and industry conditions in which a company operates can have a positive or negative impact on value. A historical financial analysis can provide insight into future growth potential, as well as place the company's current performance in context. Finally, an analysis of "comparable" or guideline companies is important to gage the success of the company vis-à-vis its peers.

44.5   WHAT A VALUATION REPORT SHOULD CONTAIN

In general, a valuation report should articulate a clear understanding of the company, its industry, and the transaction(s) giving rise to the valuation assignment, and that understanding should be consistent with the circumstances. For example, the valuation of a 10 percent equity interest in a software development company for shareholder buyout purposes should indicate

---

6.   IRS Revenue Ruling 59-60.

the standard of value and premise of value under which the valuation is to be performed. The report should also set forth the methods and conclusions in a manner sufficiently comprehensive and clear to allow the reader to gain a clear understanding of the:

- Methods used and rationale for those methods
- Significant assumptions used and basis for selected assumption inputs

44.6 BUSINESS VALUATION METHODS

In its most fundamental form, the theory surrounding the value of an asset or an interest in a business depends on the future benefits that will accrue to the particular owner. The value of the asset or business interest, in short, depends on an estimate of the future benefits and the required rate of return at which those future benefits are discounted back to the valuation date.

The governing bodies of the major valuation credentialing organizations recognize three fundamental valuation approaches that prevail in the valuation industry and literature:

1. Income approach
2. Market approach
3. Asset-based, or cost, approach

Depending on the circumstance, any of the three approaches or some combination of the three approaches may be appropriate.

(a) INCOME APPROACH This is a general way of determining a value indication of a business, business ownership interest, security, or intangible asset using one or more methods that convert anticipated economic benefits into a present single amount.[7]

The income approach is at the very heart of valuation theory. It involves either capitalizing a single estimate of a company's future expected cash flows or discounting a stream of periodic future cash flows. In either case, events and circumstances internal and external to the company must be considered. *Economic income* can mean different things. In a valuation context, economic income is most frequently measured as *free cash flows* that ultimately inure to the benefit of the business owner. Another term sometimes used (particularly in a valuation prepared for gift and estate tax purposes) is *dividend-paying capacity*. Once economic income is forecast, it is then discounted using an expected rate of return that the market requires in order to attract funds to that unique investment opportunity. The result, in general terms, is the value of the enterprise.

So, valuation of an enterprise using the income approach requires two fundamental steps:

1. Measure the expected future free cash flows that inure to the benefit of the equity owners.
2. Convert those free cash flows to a present value using the appropriate cost of capital.

Exhibit 44.1 will help illustrate these concepts.

---

7. *International Glossary of Business Valuation Terms.*

Tech Co.
Valuation Analysis
Discounted Future Cash Flows

Inputs:
  Discount Rate   25.00%
  Sustainable Growth Rate 3.00%

	YEAR 1	YEAR 2	YEAR 3	YEAR 4	YEAR 5
Discounted Future Earnings:					
Forecasted After Tax Earnings	200	350	400	450	500
Add Back Depreciation	35	40	45	45	45
Deduct Capital Additions	(50)	(45)	(45)	(45)	(45)
Add (Deduct) Working Capital Change	(55)	(75)	(75)	(75)	(75)
Add (Deduct) LTD borrowings/ repayments	100	(25)	(25)	(25)	0
Net Forecasted Future Cash Flow	130	270	325	375	425
Discounted	123	204	197	182	165
Five-Year Sum					870
Terminal Value	1,990				771
Implied Value of Equity Capital					1,641

Exhibit 44.1   Illustration of a Discounted Cash Flow Analysis

In this case, management is forecasting that Tech Co. will experience earnings increases for the next five years and then is expected to stabilize at a constant growth rate of 3 percent. Certain adjustments have been made to convert reported earnings to anticipated free cash flows to the equity owner. Typical adjustments include adding back noncash items (like depreciation), deducting capital expenditures, and adding or deducting changes in working capital during the growth years. The amount of cash forecast to be received by the enterprise from borrowings on long-term debt to sustain operations, or used to pay back borrowed amounts, are added or subtracted as they are part of free cash flows available to the equity holder.

Each year's cash flow is then discounted at the selected cost of equity, in this case 25 percent, back to the valuation date. Since a going-concern business does not have a defined life, a *terminal value* is computed at the end of year 5. This terminal value may be viewed as the hypothetical sale price of the business in the future based on a perpetual level of cash flow. The terminal value is also discounted back to the valuation date using the 25 percent discount rate and added to the sum of the discounted values of years 1–5 to arrive at the implied value of equity capital. Exhibit 44.2 shows a detail of how the terminal value is computed.

Tech Co.
Valution Analysis
Computation of Terminal Value

Inputs:	
Discount Rate	25.00%
Sustainable Growth Rate	3.00%

	YEAR 5
Discounted Future Earnings:	
Forecasted After Tax Earnings	500
Add Back Depreciation	45
Deduct Capital Additions	(45)
Add (Deduct) Working Capital Change	(75)
Add (Deduct) LTD borrowings/repayments	0
Net Forecasted Future Cash Flow	425
Growth of Year 5 Cash Flow (at sustainable rate)	438
Terminal Value ($438/Cap Rate of 22%)	1,990
Discounted Terminal Value (to Valuation Date)	**771**

EXHIBIT 44.2   ILLUSTRATION OF TERMINAL VALUE CALCULATION

(i) Discount Rates   The term *discount rate* is used in this application interchangeably with *cost of capital* as they are similar in concept, and its derivation here is done to specifically reflect the appraiser's assessment of risk specific to this company. Under other circumstances, apart from the valuation of a company, a discount rate reflects the risk specific to a particular expected future cashflow such as interest on a loan or other debt instrument. In a business valuation, however, the cost of capital is the expected rate of return that the market requires in order to attract investment into a specific business. The fundamental building blocks for "building up" a discount rate in a business valuation are derived from a modified form of the Capital Asset Pricing Model (CAPM):

- *Safe rate of interest.* Valuators typically select U.S. Treasury obligations as these rates line up with the equity risk premium (discussed below) derived from studies performed by Ibbotson Associates, Inc. ("Ibbotson"). U.S. Treasury data can be found at www.federalreserve.gov under the "Economic Research and Data" link and then going to "Statistical Releases and Historical Data." Ibbotson is a commonly relied-upon source for empirical information that is used in building a discount rate. Ibbotson provides equity risk premium data in short-term, intermediate-term, and long-term forms based on data corresponding to the aforementioned Treasury maturities. The safe rate of interest provides for inflation and maturity risk. For most valuations, the consensus in the industry is to use the 20-year U.S. Treasury rate, which matches the Ibbotson data calculated in the annually published book, *Stocks, Bonds, Bills and Inflation.*

- *Equity risk premium.* Ibbotson data is also used to measure the increased risk of holding an equity security over a debt security. To accept this higher risk, an investor demands higher expected returns for investing in equities than for investing in U.S. Treasury obligations. Ibbotson tracks the historical average excess return of equities (broad stock market) over U.S. Treasuries as a measure of this risk. This premium is added to the safe rate of interest.
- *Small stock premium.* In addition, Ibbotson data is available that measures the increased risk of investing in a smaller company. Studies show that there is an additional return demanded by investors who invest in small-capitalization companies. This premium is added to the safe rate of interest and the equity risk premium.
- *Specific company risk premium.* Finally, many business valuation professionals add an additional premium for attributes present or lacking in a subject company. Examples include:

  o   Size smaller than the smallest size premium group
  o   Industry risk
  o   Volatility of returns
  o   Leverage
  o   Other company-specific factors

This premium is added to the safe rate of interest, the equity risk premium, and the small stock premium.

Exhibit 44.3 shows the cost of equity measured for the Tech Co. example.

Tech Co.
Valuation Analysis
Discount Rate Buildup

Long-term U.S. Treasury Bond	4.00%
Equity risk premium (*Ibbotson Associates*)	7.50%
Equity size premium (*Ibbotson Associates*)	6.00%
Company-specific premium, including industry risk (judgmental)	7.50%
Discount Rate	25.00%
Sustainable Growth Rate	3%
Capitalization Rate	22.00%

EXHIBIT 44.3   ILLUSTRATION OF A DISCOUNT RATE BUILDUP

Many valuation analysts have refined the equity risk premium with current academic studies and other industry studies, such as the Duff & Phelps Cost of Capital Study, but the Ibbotson data is still widely used. Some professionals opt for the "pure" Capital Asset Pricing Model to estimate the cost of equity capital rather than the buildup method described earlier. Despite many criticisms, CAPM is still the most widely used model for estimating the cost of equity capital, especially for larger companies.

A third alternative discount rate methodology often used by valuation analysts is the *weighted-average cost of capital* (WACC). Here, the subject company's capital structure (equity and long-term debt) is taken into account. WACC is used to measure the value of the company's invested capital (equity and long-term debt), so the market value of long-term debt is subtracted from the implied value of invested capital to arrive at the equity value. This method is particularly useful when the subject's capital structure is different from other companies in that company's industry (more or less highly leveraged) or the valuation is being done on a control basis (from the perspective of a control owner who can change the capital structure to optimize the company's return).

(b) MARKET APPROACH The market approach is a general way of determining a value indication of a business, business ownership interest, security, or intangible asset by using one or more methods that compare the subject to similar businesses, business ownership interests, securities, or intangible assets that have been sold.[8] Underlying the market approach to valuation is the economic principle of substitution: A prudent investor would not pay more for an investment opportunity than he or she would have to pay for an equally desirable alternative.

The market approach is commonly implemented by (1) selecting a group of peer or "guideline" public companies, (2) analyzing those companies, and (3) selecting one or more multiples from the guidelines to apply to the subject company's fundamentals. Using the example we started with under the income approach, through discussions with company management at Tech Co. and a review of several analysts' reports, five "guideline" companies were selected. Of course, these companies typically are not identical to Tech Co. because they may be many times its size or may have diversified operations. It is often difficult to find companies that are truly *comparable* companies, because most private company valuations involve companies that are relatively undiversified and small compared to companies that trade on public exchanges. This fact does not render the market method useless, but rather less compelling as the differences become larger.

Once guideline companies are selected, they are evaluated for comparability with the subject company. There are six common financial comparisons that are made:

1. *Size* (generally measured by revenues or assets)
2. *Growth* (generally measured as compound growth of sales, cash flow, or some other income statement measure)
3. *Leverage* (generally debt to equity)
4. *Profitability* (generally measured by gross margin, operating margin, or other intermediate income statement steps depending on the industry)
5. *Turnover* (generally measured as a percentage of sales to assets or sales to book equity; which also varies by industry)
6. *Liquidity* (generally measured by current, quick, or similar ratios)

---

8. *International Glossary of Business Valuation Terms.*

This comparison assists in narrowing the group of selected guidelines and/or selecting an appropriate multiplier, or multipliers, from among them. A simple example of what this may look like is shown in Exhibit 44.4.

Tech Co.
Business Valuation Analysis
Guideline Public Company Analysis

($,000 except per share data)	Valuation Ratios Based on Peer Group							
	AGIL	CIMK.OB	ITWH	MANU	NCLM	Mean	Median
Market Capitalization of Equity (MCE)							
Price per Share	$ 7.31	$ 0.50	$ 13.75	$ 2.14	$ 13.77		
Shares Outstanding (000)	22,990	7,294	7,550	83,600	34,500		
Market Cap. of Equity	$ 168,057	$ 3,647	$ 103,813	$ 178,904	$ 475,065	$ 185,897	$ 168,057
Financial Statistics							
Revenues—trailing 12 months	$ 48,431	$ 2,184	$ 157,292	$ 205,637	$ 71,762	$ 97,061	$ 71,762
Gross Margin—trailing 12 months	32,257	1,861	97,021	95,671	47,697	54,901	47,697
Net Income—trailing 12 months	Loss	Loss	Loss	Loss	19,462		
Implied Ratios							
MCE/Revenues	3.47	1.67	0.66	0.87	6.62	2.66	1.67
MCE/Gross Margin	5.21	1.96	1.07	1.87	9.96	4.01	1.96
MCE/Net Income	NA	NA	NA	NA	24.41	24.41	24.41

Exhibit 44.4   Illustration of Market Multiples

In this instance, one might use the *MCE* (market capitalization of equity)/*gross profit* as a multiplier. A revenue multiplier would likely not be selected because revenue multipliers, while still prevalent in some industries, generally become less relevant as companies grow in size or have different cost structures from the guideline companies. The net income multiplier would likely not be selected because, in this case, four of the five companies reported a loss. Often, industries have specific multipliers that are commonly used, so try to be familiar with them and consider their application.

Selecting an MCE/gross profit multiplier from the range of observed multipliers to apply to Tech Co. requires judgment. In exercising this judgment, some of the selected companies may be weighted much more heavily than others, or some of the selected companies may be eliminated altogether because they are not very compelling once the financial and nonfinancial comparisons are made.

Assume an MCE/gross profit multiplier of 2.5 is selected based on an analysis of the guideline companies. Application of this multiplier to Tech Co.'s gross profit of $800 results in an implied value for Tech Co.'s equity of $2,000. The result from the application of the market approach is compared with the results of the income or other approaches used and conclusions about the value of Tech Co. can be reached.

(c) ASSET-BASED OR COST APPROACH   This is a general way of determining a value indication of an individual asset or business by quantifying the amount of capital required to replace the future service capability of that asset or business. On one hand, the theoretical underpinning of this method is simple: The value of the business enterprise is the value of the business assets (both tangible and intangible) less the value of the business liabilities (both recorded and contingent). On the other hand, the arduous task of valuing the separate intangibles in a business where the value is not contained in the hard assets makes this approach more costly and cumbersome to apply than the income or market approaches.

An example where the cost approach is used is in the valuation of a real estate holding company. In such a company, there may be very little value in the intangible assets, and the value of real properties can generally be ascertained with reasonable accuracy and cost.

The cost approach provides a systematic framework of estimating the value of an intangible asset also based on the economic principle of substitution. Accordingly, this approach does have its place in some of the analyses that take place in the valuation of separate intangibles under FAS 141R. For example, the determination of the value of an assembled workforce is typically done through the evaluation of the costs required to hire and train qualified people to do the task necessary in the company being acquired.

44.7 DISCOUNTS AND PREMIUMS

Depending on the purpose of the valuation and the source of information used to derive value, it may be necessary to adjust the concluded value. Most commonly, these adjustments would comprise a *discount for lack of marketability* (DLOM) (e.g., when public company guidelines are used to derive a value for a private company) or a *discount for lack of control* (e.g., when a group of acquired companies is used to derive a value for a minority interest in a private company). Under FAS 157, the concepts of discounts are rare since most valuations under FAS 157 are performed assuming control attributes. More commonly, a premium for control is encountered under FAS 157 whenever a minority interest valuation methodology is utilized, such as the public guideline company approach described earlier.

The concept underlying the DLOM is straightforward: The marketplace will pay more for an asset that can be liquidated quickly (such as a public company stock) than one that has limited near-term liquidity (such as a private company stock). Here, the differences in value are generally measured by empirical evidence that demonstrates discounts for lack of marketability between 0 and 90 percent but generally comes in between 35 and 45 percent.

Buyers will also pay more for an asset that is controlled by them than for an asset where they have little or no control. This can be readily observed in the marketplace when there is a buyout of a public company by an outside acquirer. Here, the whole is typically valued at greater than the sum of its parts (the individual holdings of the common shareholders). Here, too, the differences can be quantified by empirical evidence through reference to Morningstar's MergerStat Review or other data sources, such as Pratt's Stats.

44.8 INTANGIBLE ASSETS

(a) FAS 141R/142 ANALYSES Intangible assets have become an important part of the economy in general, and for specific companies in particular. Intangible assets can be developed internally, acquired, or licensed. Each method of attaining those rights has a different approach to accounting associated with it. However, the economics underlying these assets are the same, and thus the valuation of these assets follows those principles that have already been discussed in this chapter. Identifying the intangible assets of a company begins with understanding the company itself. Intangible assets can be found in every area of a company, including operations, marketing, research, administration, distribution, and information technologies. Wherever a competitive advantage exists or rights have been established, you will most likely find intangible assets.

COMMONLY IDENTIFIED INTANGIBLE ASSETS

- Airport gates and slots
- Architectural drawings
- Assembled workforce
- Backlogs
- Blueprints
- Brand names
- Broadcast rights/licenses
- Certificates of need
- Contracts
- Cooperative ventures
- Copyrights
- Core bank deposits
- Customer contracts
- Customer lists
- Customer relationships
- Databases
- Designs
- Development rights
- Distribution networks
- Distribution rights
- Drawings
- Drilling rights
- Electronic media
- Employment agreements
- Exploration rights
- FCC licenses
- Film libraries
- Formulas
- Franchise agreements
- In-process research and development
- Insurance contracts
- Joint ventures
- Laboratory notebooks
- Landing rights
- Leasehold interests
- Licensing agreements
- Lyrics
- Management contracts
- Manuscripts
- Mask works
- Medical charts and records
- Mineral rights
- Musical compositions
- Noncompetition covenants and contracts
- Patent applications
- Patents
- Patterns
- Permits
- Processes
- Product designs
- Property rights
- Proprietary processes
- Proprietary products
- Proprietary technology
- Publications
- Retail shelf space
- Royalty agreements
- Service marks
- Schematics and diagrams
- Shareholder agreements
- Slogans
- Software
- Subscription lists
- Supplier relationships
- Technical documentation
- Technology rights
- Trade secrets
- Trademarks
- Trade names
- Trade dress

EXHIBIT 44.5   COMMONLY IDENTIFIED INTANGIBLE ASSETS

Generally, intangible assets are considered to exist as a separate asset of the company when they either stem from contractual rights or legally defined rights, or can be separated from the business in some form. If they do not have these attributes, they are generally grouped into an amorphous category commonly referred to as *goodwill*. Advances in the use of real option techniques now assist in the quantification of broader conceptual goodwill, including first-mover advantage, abandonment options, and expansion options.

(b) DETERMINE WHICH INTANGIBLE ASSETS ARE PRESENT   Intangible assets can be categorized according to their characteristics. This can be useful in the valuation process. For example, the category of *brand names* typically would include trademarks, trade names, trade dress (e.g., the shape of a container or color of the packaging), and slogans. A fundamental categorization of intangible assets is based on whether they have a limited life or an indefinite life. *Limited-life* intangible assets deteriorate due to some form of obsolescence brought on by either environmental changes or legally determined limits. *Indefinite-life* intangible assets can be renewed indefinitely or can last for an indeterminate period, depending on market factors or upkeep. Intangible assets can either indirectly support the business or directly generate revenue. *Supporting* intangible assets, such as an assembled and trained workforce or manufacturing processes, are necessary for sales to occur but do not drive sales. *Revenue-generating* intangible assets are directly associated with dollars in the door, such as customer contracts, production software, or charging a fee for using a franchised name. Exhibit 44.5 lists some of the most common forms of intangible assets.

(c) DETERMINE THE ACCOUNTING GUIDANCE   Whereas a number of GAAP pronouncements deal with intangible assets, there are three main pronouncements that give rise to intangible asset valuations, Statements of Financial Accounting Standards (FAS) Nos. 141R, 142, and 144. Application of these standards requires that both the appraiser and the auditor be familiar with the specifics in these pronouncements as well as the other relevant accounting pronouncements.

(d) DETERMINE THE APPROPRIATE METHODOLOGY TO ESTIMATE FAIR VALUE
Once a company's specific intangible assets have been identified (and the applicable GAAP and tax implications are understood), the next step is to value each one. The first step in that process is to determine the most appropriate methodology (or methodologies) to value a specific intangible. As was discussed in the foregoing section, there are generally three approaches to valuing intangible assets: the cost approach, the market approach, and the income approach. We will not go over those methodologies again, but instead we will focus on their application under FAS 141R and 142. The *cost approach* considers the cost to re-create a particular asset. It is typically used for intangible assets where there is no direct cash flow generation, such as an assembled workforce. The market approach considers information from sales of similar assets in the open marketplace. The market approach is difficult to utilize, because it is almost impossible to identify individual sales of intangible assets that are similar enough to the particular intangible asset to be relevant. The income approach is the most robust approach for valuing income-producing intangibles as it focuses on cash flow directly attributable to the intangible asset being valued. The following paragraphs discuss the general methodologies related to valuing intangible assets under FAS 141R.

Under the cost (or asset-based) approach, there are two general methodologies to valuing an intangible asset:

1. Directly estimate current cost to replace the asset at its current stage of obsolescence.
2. Adjust historical expenses to reflect current costs to create the asset.

When determining the current value of an asset under the cost approach, all historical costs must be reviewed and compared against the current state of technology. In addition, the effects of inflation and the time value of money need to be appropriately reflected.

Quantifying the impact of functional and technological obsolescence is challenging, but it can often be estimated after an understanding is obtained concerning the facts and circumstances surrounding the intangible asset and its environment. This often begins with discussions with the company's technical staff. For example, the cost approach might be used for valuing software code that is useful only in older computers. Another factor in the consideration of functional and technical obsolescence is quantifying the reduction in value attributable to historical benefits that are no longer available for the particular intangible asset. For example, a chemical plant that relied upon a state-of-the-art, two-step chemical process at the time of construction is now disadvantaged since current technology requires only a one-step process. The new, one-step process takes 10 percent less energy, thereby creating a cost savings over the older technology. This cost benefit, of course, reduces the value of the older facility by the present value of such anticipated benefits and can be quantified using a discounted cash flow model.

Finally, economic obsolescence must always be considered. Simply stated, an asset has become economically obsolete when no one will buy it because there are better alternatives. Whenever the cost of continued use exceeds the benefits, a downward adjustment in the value of the asset should be considered.

Although the cost approach is well recognized among valuation analysts, it does have shortcomings when used in the valuation of intangible assets. While the value of most intangible asset values is measured based on a future benefit that will be derived by that asset, the cost approach is rearward looking and, therefore, ignores future benefits. Furthermore, the duration of future economic benefits specific to the intangible asset is ignored by the cost approach. For example, a patent has a specific contractual life, but under the cost approach, value is not impacted whether it has only one year or five years left of protection. In addition, the expected trend of future potential economic benefits is lost under the cost approach. As with a photograph compared to a movie, under the cost approach one cannot tell whether the asset's past performance was up or down or which direction future performance will take. This is often critical when valuing intangible assets that are based on rapidly changing technology.

Given these shortcomings, the use of the cost approach is limited in valuing intangible assets. As is discussed below, the income approach is considerably more robust in capturing the value of intangible assets for purposes of FAS 141R.

The *market approach* has its own set of hurdles to overcome in valuing intangible assets. When applied to intangible assets, the market approach requires the valuation analyst to identify "guideline" transactions (similar to the identification of guideline public companies illustrated earlier). Although there are a number of sources where one can obtain market research, identifying relevant transactions is challenging, to say the least. Online databases such as www.royaltysource.com and publications such as *Licensing Economics Review* provide general data on various market transactions, but their relevance to a particular intangible asset may be difficult to establish. Careful analysis of each potential transaction must be made for relevance, for arm's-length determination, and for determination of relevant units for comparison.

Application of the market approach also requires that the valuation analyst identify the specific rights that attach to the asset that was transferred in the guideline transaction. These rights could include specified geographic territories, product or market exclusivity, sales channel access, or other unique attributes. Once the rights have been identified and analyzed, the valuation analyst will need to identify the full consideration paid in the transaction, including special financing terms that may mask the "real" price paid. If the transaction is dated, say over a year old, the analyst must also consider environmental changes from the time of the transaction, including economic conditions, industry trends, regulatory changes, and the possible existence of new substitute products. Another consideration that often muddles market transactions is the sale of a group of intangible assets rather than a single asset. If a group of assets is sold, adjustments will need to be considered if the subject asset is a single intangible asset. Unfortunately, adequate information to make such adjustments is often missing.

An example of bundled intangibles under the market approach may be helpful. In an engagement to value a manufacturing plant that utilized proprietary processes, licensed technology and publicly available components were combined in a unique way to produce some "widgets." We were able to identify a number of sales of similar plants within the prior two years of the valuation date, so we got excited. However, upon further inspection, key components of the sales were lacking, including the technology that was included in the sale, whether licenses for proprietary technology were obtained and when licenses were obtained, and the amount and duration of the licenses. Ultimately, we were unable to satisfy ourselves that we had adequate data points to apply the valuation metrics gleaned from these sales to our specific facility.

After discussing the cost and market approaches, it is no wonder the income approach is the most widely used valuation technique in the FAS 141R arsenal. Because most identified intangible assets can be individually addressed through application of the income approach, it is by far the most prevalent of the three approaches in valuing intangible assets.

Look at the *income approach* as it is applied to intangible assets. Unlike valuing an entire business using the income approach, as we saw previously, application of the income approach to a single intangible asset or a bundle of intangible assets requires that the economic benefit generated by each individually identified intangible asset be separately quantified. At the same time, in order to isolate the value of each intangible asset and to avoid double counting asset values, adjustments need to be made for *supporting assets*. Supporting assets include such things as working capital, plant, and equipment as well as the other separately identified intangible assets. The economic benefit streams so identified should be tested against the market whenever possible as long as the cost to do so is reasonable. Market forces also come into play in considering the duration of the income stream and the economic life of the asset. For example, the economic life of a current version of software will be limited if the company plans to issue new software versions on a periodic basis. In addition to the duration and economic life of the asset, the valuation analyst must identify the specific risks related to that asset's economic benefit stream and determine the appropriate rate of return for the risks associated with that benefit stream.

When assessing the useful life of an asset, determinants, when present, should include:

- Legal life
- Contractual life

- Judicial life
- Functional life
- Economic life
- Analytical life (based on analysis of available data)

These determinants allow for the specific measurement of the duration of cash flows generated by an identifiable intangible asset. Once duration is determined, the economic benefit can be modeled over its useful life and avoid overvaluing the asset by including future benefits that are contractually or otherwise limited.

Specific applications of the income approach that are commonly used in determining the value of intangible assets include:

- *Residual cash flow method*—focuses on the present value of cash flows after the consideration of returns for supporting assets (discussed above). This method includes both the excess earnings and multiperiod excess earnings methods.
- *Differential cash flow method*—ascertains the difference between the value of the income stream with the asset in place and the value of the income stream without the asset in place.
- *Relief from royalty method*—quantifies the value of owning an asset as based on what it would cost to pay a royalty for use of the asset over the estimated benefit period (sometimes considered a market approach since royalty rates may be estimated from market data).
- *Options methodology*—focuses on contingent aspects of future value and ability to achieve those values.

Another unique factor that comes into play when applying the income approach to the valuation of intangible assets is commonly referred to as the *amortization benefit*. An amortization benefit arises as a result of the deductibility, over a 15-year term, of the intangible asset on the company's income tax return. Since most valuations are in consideration of the value if sold, the tax benefit of the 15-year amortization must be added back to capture the full economic benefit of ownership.

There are a number of ways to compute the amortization benefit, but we have found the following formula to be a simple and straightforward means to do so:

$$TAB = VBA * n/[n - ((AF * t * (1 + r)^{0.5}) - 1)]$$

where:

TAB = Tax amortization benefit
VBA = Value before amortization
n = Number of amortization periods in years
(15 years in U.S., see IRC 197)
AF = Annuity factor ($AF = 1/r - 1/r(1 + r)^n$)
t = Tax rate
r = discount rate

As if the foregoing procedures were not enough, one must also assess the useful life of the asset in building a valuation model for specific intangible assets under the income approach. The useful life of an intangible asset to an entity is the period over which the asset is expected to contribute directly or indirectly to the future cash flows of the entity. Some factors set forth in FAS 142 that should be considered in such an analysis include:

- The expected use of the asset by the entity
- The expected useful life of another asset or a group of assets related to the intangible asset
- Any legal, regulatory, or contractual provisions that may limit the useful life
- Any legal, regulatory, or contractual provisions that enable the renewal or extension of the asset's legal or contractual life without substantial costs
- The effects of obsolescence, demand, competition, and other economic factors
- The level of maintenance expenditures required to obtain the expected future cash flows from the asset

Survivor curves are often employed to assist in determining the remaining useful life of an asset. Although a complete discussion of survivor curves is beyond the scope of this chapter, there are a number of books that discuss these techniques in depth, including *Financial Valuation: Applications and Models*, edited by James R. Hitchener, and *Valuing Intangible Assets*, by Robert F. Reilly and Robert P. Schweihs. Exhibit 44.6 captures the essence of such an analysis in valuing intangible assets.

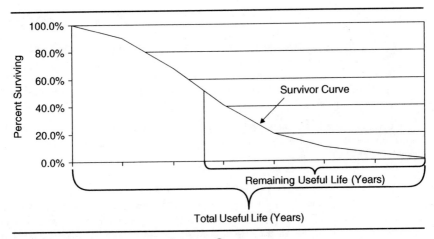

EXHIBIT 44.6 ILLUSTRATION OF A SURVIVOR CURVE

Once all of the foregoing steps have been completed and the identifiable intangible assets have been valued, those values, along with any associated goodwill, need to be allocated to specific reporting units. The allocation process is prescribed by the FASB; however, it is anything but clear-cut in many instances. Although there have been a number of EITF bulletins addressing specific circumstances related to the attribution of intangible assets to reporting units, the following guidelines help in the allocation process:

- The asset will be employed in, or the liability relates to, the reporting unit's operations.
- The asset or liability will be considered in determining the reporting unit's fair value.

- All goodwill will be assigned to reporting units in a manner that is reasonable and supportable and consistent.

EITF Abstracts, Topic D-101, *Clarification of Reporting Unit Guidance in Paragraph 30 of FASB Statement No. 142,* provides additional guidance in the identification of reporting units. According to the abstract, a business segment must constitute a business, have discrete financial information, be reviewed by segment management, and have similar economic characteristics in order to be characterized as a separate reporting unit.

44.9   DOES IT ALL ADD UP?

Upon completion of the engagement, it is prudent to perform a reasonableness check of the underlying assumptions and valuation outputs. This also applies when reviewing the valuation analyst's work under an audit engagement for your particular firm. Some questions to ask are:

- Does the forecast correspond to internal budgets or external forecasts by stock analysts?
- Is the current forecast consistent with previous forecasts?
- Do the assumptions in the forecast appear reasonable in relation to historical performance?
- Do the assumptions in the forecast appear reasonable in relation to performance and structure of guideline companies?
- Do expectations for the industry and economy generally support management's assumptions?
- Does a discounted cash flow of the forecast reasonably tie out to the value of the reporting unit?
- Does the weighted average of the discount rates of the separate tangible and intangible assets (net of non-interest-bearing liabilities) aggregate to the discount rate for the entire business?

These questions should be addressed by the valuation analyst. They are also questions the reviewing party (auditor or their valuation resource) should ask in assessing the valuation analyst's work product.

44.10   CREDENTIALS OF A VALUATION ANALYST

In assessing the credentials of a valuation analyst, professional certifications are a starting point, but not a panacea. The AICPA has established the Accredited in Business Valuation (ABV) credential, whereas the American Society of Appraisers confers the Accredited Senior Appraiser (ASA) and Accredited Member (AM) designations. Other certifying organizations include the National Association of Certified Valuation Analysts, which confers a plethora of designations, and the Institute of Business Appraisers, which confers the Certified Business Appraiser (CBA) designation. A less specific, but highly respected, credential is the Chartered Financial Analyst (CFA) designation sanctioned by the CFA Institute. These credentials are a starting point; there is no substitute for experience. When assessing the expertise of any valuation analyst, always inquire as to the experience of the individuals performing the work.

In addition to professional certifications, it is important that any valuation be performed in accordance with applicable professional standards. The primary standards governing the valuation industry are the Uniform Standards of Professional Appraisal Practice (USPAP) and the newly issued Statement on Standards for Valuation Services (SSVS1) promulgated by the AICPA. A compliant valuation report will contain a list of "Contingent and Limiting Conditions" as well as an appraisal certification expressing compliance with USPAP, SSVS1, or both. These standards can be found under the respective Web sites of the issuing organizations, www.appraisers.org for USPAP or www.aicpa.org for SSVS1.

44.11 SOURCES AND SUGGESTED REFERENCES

The following reference materials have been reprinted with permission and are included as an aid to the participant.

Appendix 44A—International Glossary of Business Valuation Terms—a reprint from the *ABV Credential Candidates Handbook*

Appendix 44B—Additional Sources of Study—a reprint from the *ABV Credential Candidates Handbook*

INTERNATIONAL GLOSSARY OF BUSINESS VALUATION TERMS

To enhance and sustain the quality of business valuations for the benefit of the business valuation profession and the users of the services of its practitioners, the below-identified societies and organizations whose members provide business valuation services have adopted the definitions for the terms included in this glossary.

The performance of business valuation services requires a high degree of skill, and imposes upon the valuation professional a duty to communicate the valuation process and conclusion, as appropriate to the scope of the engagement, in a manner that is clear and not misleading. This duty is advanced through the use of terms whose meanings are clearly established and consistently applied throughout the profession.

If, in the opinion of the business valuation professional, one or more of these terms needs to be used in a manner which materially departs from the enclosed definitions, it is recommended that the term be defined as used within that valuation engagement.

This glossary has been developed to provide guidance to the business valuation practitioners who are members of the listed societies, organizations, and others performing valuations of business interests or securities by further memorializing the body of knowledge which constitutes the competent and careful determination of value and, more particularly, the communication of how that value was determined.

Departure from this glossary is not intended to provide a basis for civil liability and should not be presumed to create evidence that any duty has been breached.

Adjusted Book Value—the value that results after one or more asset or liability amounts are added, deleted, or changed from their respective financial statement amounts.

Appraisal—See **Valuation**.

Appraisal Approach—See **Valuation Approach**.

Appraisal Date—See **Valuation Date**.

Appraisal Method—See **Valuation Method**.

Appraisal Procedure—See **Valuation Procedure**.

Asset (Asset-Based) Approach—a general way of determining a value indication of a business, business ownership interest, or security by using one or more methods based on the value of the assets of that business net of liabilities.

Benefit Stream—any level of income, cash flow, or earnings generated by an asset, group of assets, or business enterprise. When the term is used, it should be supplemented by a definition of exactly what it means in the given valuation context.

Beta—a measure of systematic risk of a security; the tendency of a security's returns to correlate with swings in the broad market.

Blockage Discount—an amount or percentage deducted from the current market price of a publicly traded security to reflect the decrease in the per share value of a block of those securities that is of a size that could not be sold in a reasonable period of time given normal trading volume.

Business—See **Business Enterprise**.

Business Enterprise—a commercial, industrial, service, or investment entity, or a combination thereof, pursuing an economic activity.

Business Valuation—the act or process of determining the value of a business enterprise or ownership interest therein.

Capital Asset Pricing Model (CAPM)—a model in which the cost of capital for any security or portfolio of securities equals a risk-free rate plus a risk premium that is proportionate to the systematic risk of the security or portfolio.

Capital Structure—the composition of the invested capital of a business enterprise; the mix of debt and equity financing.

Capitalization—a conversion of a single period stream of benefits into value.

Capitalization Factor—any multiple or divisor used to convert anticipated benefits into value.

Capitalization Rate—any divisor (usually expressed as a percentage) used to convert anticipated benefits into value.

Cash Flow—cash that is generated over a period of time by an asset, group of assets, or business enterprise. It may be used in a general sense to encompass various levels of specifically defined cash flows. When the term is used, it should be supplemented by a qualifier (for example, *discretionary* or *operating*) and a definition of exactly what it means in the given valuation context.

Control—the power to direct the management and policies of a business enterprise.

Control Premium—an amount (expressed in either dollar or percentage form) by which the pro rata value of a controlling interest exceeds the pro rata value of a noncontrolling interest in a business enterprise that reflects the power of control.

Cost Approach—a general way of estimating a value indication of an individual asset by quantifying the amount of money that would be required to replace the future service capability of that asset.

Cost of Capital—the expected rate of return (discount rate) that the market requires in order to attract funds to a particular investment.

Discount—a reduction in value or the act of reducing value.

Discount for Lack of Control—an amount or percentage deducted from the pro rata share of value of one hundred percent (100%) of an equity interest in a business to reflect the absence of some or all of the powers of control.

Discount for Lack of Marketability—an amount or percentage deducted from the value of an ownership interest to reflect the relative absence of marketability.

Discount Rate—a rate of return (cost of capital) used to convert a monetary sum, payable or receivable in the future, into present value.

Economic Life—the period of time over which property may generate economic benefits.

Effective Date—See **Valuation Date**.

Enterprise—See **Business Enterprise**.

Equity Net Cash Flows—those cash flows available to pay out to equity holders (in the form of dividends) after funding operations of the business enterprise, making necessary capital investments, and reflecting increases or decreases in debt financing.

Equity Risk Premium—a rate of return in addition to a risk-free rate to compensate for investing in equity instruments because they have a higher degree of probable risk than risk-free instruments (a component of the cost of equity capital or equity discount rate).

Excess Earnings—that amount of anticipated benefits that exceeds a fair rate of return on the value of a selected asset base (often net tangible assets) used to generate those anticipated benefits.

Excess Earnings Method—a specific way of determining a value indication of a business, business ownership interest, or security determined as the sum of (a) the value of the assets obtained by capitalizing excess earnings and (b) the value of the selected asset base. Also frequently used to value intangible assets. See **Excess Earnings**.

Fair Market Value—the price, expressed in terms of cash equivalents, at which property would change hands between a hypothetical willing and able buyer and a hypothetical willing and able seller, acting at arm's length in an open and unrestricted market, when neither is under compulsion to buy or sell and when both have reasonable knowledge of the relevant facts. **(NOTE: In Canada, the term *price* should be replaced with the term *highest price*.)**

Forced Liquidation Value—liquidation value at which the asset or assets are sold as quickly as possible, such as at an auction.

Going Concern—an ongoing operating business enterprise.

Going Concern Value—the value of a business enterprise that is expected to continue to operate into the future. The intangible elements of Going Concern Value result from factors such as having a trained workforce, an operational plant, and the necessary licenses, systems, and procedures in place.

Goodwill—that intangible asset arising as a result of name, reputation, customer loyalty, location, products, and similar factors not separately identified.

Goodwill Value—the value attributable to goodwill.

Income (Income-Based) Approach—a general way of determining a value indication of a business, business ownership interest, security, or intangible asset using one or more methods that convert anticipated benefits into a present single amount.

Intangible Assets—nonphysical assets (such as franchises, trademarks, patents, copyrights, goodwill, equities, mineral rights, securities, and contracts as distinguished from physical assets) that grant rights, privileges, and have economic benefits for the owner.

Invested Capital—the sum of equity and debt in a business enterprise. Debt is typically (a) long-term liabilities or (b) the sum of short-term interest-bearing debt and long-term liabilities. When the term is used, it should be supplemented by a definition of exactly what it means in the given valuation context.

Invested Capital Net Cash Flows—those cash flows available to pay out to equity holders (in the form of dividends) and debt investors (in the form of principal and interest) after funding operations of the business enterprise and making necessary capital investments.

Investment Risk—the degree of uncertainty as to the realization of expected returns.

Investment Value—the value to a particular investor based on individual investment requirements and expectations. (**NOTE: in Canada, the term used is** *Value to the Owner*.)

Key Person Discount—an amount or percentage deducted from the value of an ownership interest to reflect the reduction in value resulting from the actual or potential loss of a key person in a business enterprise.

Levered Beta—the beta reflecting a capital structure that includes debt.

Liquidation Value—the net amount that can be realized if the business is terminated and the assets are sold piecemeal. Liquidation can be either "orderly" or "forced."

Liquidity—the ability to quickly convert property to cash or pay a liability.

Majority Control—the degree of control provided by a majority position.

Majority Interest—an ownership interest greater than fifty percent (50%) of the voting interest in a business enterprise.

Market (Market-Based) Approach—a general way of determining a value indication of a business, business ownership interest, security, or intangible asset by using one or more methods that compare the subject to similar businesses, business ownership interests, securities, or intangible assets that have been sold.

Marketability—the ability to quickly convert property to cash at minimal cost.

Marketability Discount—See **Discount for Lack of Marketability**.

Minority Discount—a discount for lack of control applicable to a minority interest.

Minority Interest—an ownership interest less than fifty percent (50%) of the voting interest in a business enterprise.

Net Book Value—with respect to a business enterprise, the difference between total assets (net of accumulated depreciation, depletion, and amortization) and total liabilities of a business enterprise as they appear on the balance sheet (synonymous with Shareholder's Equity); with respect to an intangible asset, the capitalized cost of an intangible asset less accumulated amortization as it appears on the books of account of the business enterprise.

Net Cash Flow—a form of cash flow. When the term is used, it should be supplemented by a qualifier (for example, *equity* or *invested capital*) and a definition of exactly what it means in the given valuation context.

Net Tangible Asset Value—the value of the business enterprise's tangible assets (excluding excess assets and non-operating assets) minus the value of its liabilities. (**NOTE: in Canada, tangible assets also include identifiable intangible assets.**)

Non-Operating Assets—assets not necessary to ongoing operations of the business enterprise. (**NOTE: In Canada, the term used is** *Redundant Assets*.)

Orderly Liquidation Value—liquidation value at which the asset or assets are sold over a reasonable period of time to maximize proceeds received.

Portfolio Discount—an amount or percentage that may be deducted from the value of a business enterprise to reflect the fact that it owns dissimilar operations or assets that may not fit well together.

Premise of Value—an assumption regarding the most likely set of transactional circumstances that may be applicable to the subject valuation; e.g., going concern, liquidation.

Rate of Return—an amount of income (loss) and/or change in value realized or anticipated on an investment, expressed as a percentage of that investment.

Redundant Assets (NOTE: In Canada, see Non-Operating Assets.)

Replacement Cost New—the current cost of a similar new property having the nearest equivalent utility to the property being valued.

Report Date—the date conclusions are transmitted to the client.

Reproduction Cost New—the current cost of an identical new property.

Residual Value—the prospective value as of the end of the discrete projection period in a discounted benefit streams model.

Risk-Free Rate—the rate of return available in the market on an investment free of default risk.

Risk Premium—a rate of return in addition to a risk-free rate to compensate the investor for accepting risk.

Rule of Thumb—a mathematical relationship between or among variables based on experience, observation, hearsay, or a combination of these, usually applicable to a specific industry.

Special Interest Purchasers—acquirers who believe they can enjoy post-acquisition economies of scale, synergies, or strategic advantages by combining the acquired business interest with their own.

Standard of Value—the identification of the type of value being utilized in a specific engagement; e.g., fair market value, fair value, investment value.

Sustaining Capital Reinvestment—the periodic capital outlay required to maintain operations at existing levels, net of the tax shield available from such outlays.

Systematic Risk—the risk that is common to all risky securities and cannot be eliminated through diversification. When using the capital asset pricing model, systematic risk is measured by beta.

Terminal Value—See **Residual Value.**

APPENDIX **44B**

ADDITIONAL SOURCES
OF STUDY BOOKS

- *Understanding Business Valuation: A Practical Guide to Valuing Small to Medium Sized Businesses*, by G. Trugman; 2nd Edition.
- *Valuing a Business*, by S. Pratt, R. Reilly, and R. Schweihs; 4th Edition.
- *Financial Valuation: Application and Models*, edited by J. Hitchner; 1st Edition.
- *CCH Business Valuation Guide*, by G. Hawkins and M. Pashall; updated annually.
- *Business Valuation Body of Knowledge: Exam Review and Professional Reference*, by S. Pratt; 2002.
- *Cost of Capital: Estimation and Applications*, by S. Pratt; 2002.
- *The Market Approach to Valuing Businesses*, by S. Pratt; 2001.
- *Competitive Strategy: Techniques for Analyzing Industries and Competitors*, by M. Porter; 1998.
- *Statistical Techniques in Business and Economics*, by R. Mason, D. Lind, and W. Marchal; 2005.
- *Fannon's Guide to the Valuation of Subchapter S Corporations*, by N. Fannon; 2007.

AICPA Publications and Pronouncements Related to Business Valuation

- Consulting Services Division, "AICPA Consulting Services Practice Aid—Valuing Private Equity Securities in Other Than a Business Combination," 2003.
- Consulting Services Division, "AICPA Consulting Services Practice Aid 96-3—Communicating in Litigation Services: Reports." New York: AICPA, 1996. Product No. 055000.
- Consulting Services Division, "AICPA Consulting Services Special Report 93-2—Conflicts of Interest in Litigation Services Engagements." New York: AICPA, 1993. Product No. 048563.
- Frank, Peter B., and Michael J. Wagner, "AICPA Consulting Services Practice Aid 93-4—Providing Litigation Services." New York: AICPA, 1993. Product No. 055145.
- Menelaides, Susan, Lynford Graham, and Gretchen Fischbach, "The Auditor's Approach to Fair Value," *Journal of Accountancy* (June 2003), pp. 73–76.

- Miller, Warren D., "Assessing Unsystematic Risk: Part I," *CPA Expert*, Vol. 5, No. 3 (Summer 1999), pp. 1–5.
- Miller, Warren D., "Assessing Unsystematic Risk: Part II—The Macroenvironment," *CPA Expert*, Vol. 6, No. 1 (Winter 2000), pp. 1–5.
- Miller, Warren D., "Assessing Unsystematic Risk: Part III—Market Structure," *CPA Expert*, Vol. 6, No. 3 (Summer 2000), pp. 1–5.
- Miller, Warren D., "Assessing Unsystematic Risk: Part IV—Industry Dynamics," *CPA Expert*, Vol. 8, No. 1 (Winter 2002), pp. 1–5.
- Trugman, Gary R., "AICPA Consulting Services Practice Aid 93-3—Conducting a Valuation of a Closely Held Business." New York: AICPA. Product No. 055148.

*CHAPTER **46**

FORENSIC ACCOUNTING IN LITIGATION CONSULTING SERVICES, INVESTIGATIONS, AND COMPLIANCE MATTERS (REVISED)

YOGESH BAHL, CPA, MBA
Deloitte Financial Advisory Services LLP[†]
FRANK HYDOSKI, PH.D.
Deloitte Financial Advisory Services LLP

[†] The information contained in this chapter does not necessarily represent the views of Deloitte Financial Advisory Services LLP.

46.1 INTRODUCTION

Forensic accounting can be defined as the application of accounting principles, theories, and discipline to facts and hypotheses at issue in a legal or investigatory context. This legal context is generally litigation, but any dispute resolution proceeding (e.g., arbitration or mediation) is a candidate for the application of forensic accounting, as are a number of other contexts, including investigations involving accounting issues, information, or systems, and regulatory and corporate compliance matters.

Litigation consulting services can include forensic accounting, but also involve any professional assistance nonlawyers provide to lawyers in the litigation process in connection with pending or potential formal legal or regulatory proceedings before a trier of fact in connection with the resolution of a dispute between two or more parties. A trier of fact can be a court, regulatory body, or government authority; its agents; a grand jury; or an arbitrator of a dispute. Litigation consulting services also include the application of specialized disciplines to the issues involved in a matter in order to express an expert opinion that would help the trier of fact reach an informed conclusion.

Forensic accounting and litigation consulting services apply to both civil and criminal litigation. The principal focus of this chapter will be civil litigation because it is by far the most frequent dispute resolution proceeding in which the professional accountant will be involved. However, this chapter will also focus on corporate investigations, compliance, and other contexts in which forensic accountants are increasingly involved.

Although some may want to use the terms *forensic accounting, dispute analysis, litigation support,* and *litigation consulting* as synonyms, a distinction should be made. For purposes of this chapter, *forensic accounting* involves the exploration of accounting issues, information, or systems and refers to the disciplined process used in gathering facts and understanding issues prior to a dispute resolution proceeding, or in the course of an investigation, or in relation to the compliance matters this chapter describes. In addition, *litigation consulting services* refers to the assistance provided during a dispute resolution proceeding in the case, for example, of expert jury consulting.

(a) COMPARING LITIGATION CONSULTING SERVICES TO ATTEST SERVICES The role of the practitioner in a litigation consulting engagement is different from that in an attestation engagement, where the certified public accountant (CPA) can express different levels of opinion about the reliability of a written assertion of another party. In a litigation consulting engagement, the practitioner provides his or her individual opinion around the facts at issue in the case, usually to opine on liability or damage amounts.

In an attestation engagement, the audience is composed of all persons relying on the accountant's report, whereas in a litigation consulting engagement, the audience for the litigation consulting practitioner's opinion and work product is generally limited to the trier of fact and the parties to the dispute who have the opportunity to evaluate and question the practitioner's conclusions, support for the conclusions, and methodology.

This chapter provides a brief description of litigation consulting matters relevant to accountants and explains their role in them. It also describes the role of accountants in a number of other contexts, including investigations, compliance, and technology. In this chapter, although the terms *accountant, practitioner, CPA,* and *litigation consultant* are used in various ways to describe an accountant who is providing forensic accounting and litigation consulting services, it should be noted that distinctions between service providers are often made, particularly with those who are licensed as CPAs and those who are not. The chapter includes a description of the types of cases in which accountants typically get involved, the types of services accountants usually provide, and a discussion of the professional standards relevant to litigation consulting services. Section 46.3(d)(iii) gives a brief overview of bankruptcy, while Chapter 45 discusses bankruptcy in detail. Section 46.2(g), "Testimony," provides examples of how to prepare and deliver deposition and trial testimony. Discussions of some of the issues related to expert testimony in this chapter are extended in Chapter 47, "Financial Expert Witness Challenges and Exclusions: Results and Trends in Federal and State Cases since Kumho Tire." Additionally, Chapter 48, "Introduction to E-Discovery," provides insight into the tools and techniques of modern forensic analysis. Finally, Chapter 49, "Detecting Fraud," provides an overview of the subject of fraud.

46.2 THE ACCOUNTANT'S ROLE IN DISPUTE RESOLUTION PROCEEDINGS

(a) U.S. LEGAL SYSTEM: GENERAL INFORMATION

(i) The Adversarial Process In civil disputes, it is generally up to the parties (i.e., the plaintiff and defendant), not the court, to initiate and prosecute litigation, to investigate the pertinent facts, and to present proof and legal argument to the adjudicative body. The court's function, in general, is limited to adjudicating the issues that the parties submit to the court, based on the proofs presented by the parties.

(ii) Stages in a Civil Suit Civil suits have four basic stages, barring appeal, which are the same for virtually all adversarial proceedings, whether in a federal, state, or administrative court:

1. *Pleadings.* A lawsuit is started by a complaint that is filed with the clerk of the trial court and served on the defendants. The complaint lays out the facts and causes of action alleged by the plaintiff. The defendants may file a motion to dismis s (arguing that the defendant is not legally liable even if the alleged facts are true) or an answer to the complaint. The answer may contain a denial of the allegations or an

affirmative defense (e.g., statute of limitations has expired). The defendant also may file a counterclaim that presents a claim by the defendant (counterplaintiff) against the plaintiff (counterdefendant).

2. *Pretrial discovery.* The purpose of pretrial discovery is to narrow the issues that need to be decided at trial and to obtain evidence to support legal and factual arguments. It is essentially an information-gathering process. Evidence is obtained in advance to facilitate presentation of an organized, concise case as well as to prevent any surprises at trial. This sharing of information often will result in the settlement of the case before trial.

   ○ The first step in discovery typically involves the use of interrogatories and document requests. Interrogatories are sets of formal written questions directed by one party in the lawsuit to the other. They are usually broad in nature and are used to fill in and amplify the fact situation set out in the pleadings. Interrogatories are also used to identify individuals who may possess unique knowledge or information about the issues in the case. Requests for production of documents identify specific documents and records that the requesting party believes are relevant to its case and that are in the possession of and controlled by the opposing party. The opposing party is required to produce only the specific documents requested. Accordingly, when drafting these requests, care must be taken to be as broad as possible so as to include all relevant documents but narrow enough to be descriptive. It is not unusual for more than one set of interrogatories and document requests to be issued during the course of a lawsuit. The accountant is often involved in developing interrogatories and document requests on financial and business issues.

   ○ Depositions are the second step in the discovery process. They are the sworn testimony of a witness recorded by a court reporter. During the deposition, the witness may be asked questions by the attorneys for each party to the suit. The questions and answers are transcribed, sworn to, and signed. The testimony will allow the party taking the deposition to better understand the facts of the case and may be used as evidence in the trial. The accountant may be heavily involved at this stage, both in being deposed and in developing questions for the deposition of opposing witnesses.

3. *Trial.* The third stage of the litigation/adversarial process is the trial. It is the judicial examination and determination of issues between the parties to the action. In a jury trial, the trial begins with the selection of a jury. The attorneys for each party then make opening statements concerning the facts they expect to prove during the trial. Then the plaintiff puts forth its case, calling all of the witnesses it believes are required to prove its case. Each witness will be subject to direct examination and then cross-examination by the opposing party's attorney. After the plaintiff has called all of its witnesses and presented all of its evidence, the defendant will then present its case in the same manner. The plaintiff then has an opportunity to present additional evidence to refute the defendant's case in a rebuttal. The defendant can respond in a surrebuttal. Finally, each party has the opportunity to make a closing statement before the court.

4. *Settlement.* At any time in the litigation process, the parties can attempt to settle the dispute without the intervention of the court. This can be accomplished by participating in settlement discussions or by using alternative methods of dispute resolution.

(iii) Alternative Dispute Resolution   Alternative dispute resolution can encompass mediation, arbitration, facilitation, and other ways of resolving disputes focused on effective communication and negotiation, rather than using adversarial processes such as the courtroom. Two basic types of alternative dispute resolution exist. There are nonbinding methods, such as mediation, negotiation, or facilitation, which assist in reaching, but do not impose, a resolution of the dispute. There are also more binding methods, such as arbitration or adjudication, in which a neutral decision maker rules on the issues presented. Combinations of these methods also exist. Alternative dispute resolution is often used because it is the vehicle prescribed in an agreement or contract for the resolution of a dispute.

The U.S. Constitution and most state constitutions provide for the right of trial by jury in most cases. This right does not have to be exercised, and many cases are tried without a jury (i.e., a bench trial where the judge is the trier of fact). In most states and in federal courts, one of the parties must request a jury or the right is presumed to be waived.

(iv) Required Proofs   In order for a plaintiff to succeed in a claim for damages, it must satisfy three different but related proofs: liability, causation, and amount of damages if applicable. If the burden of proof is not met on any one of these, the claim will fail:

1. *Liability.* The plaintiff must prove that one of its legal rights has been transgressed by the defendant. The plaintiff will present evidence attempting to prove that the actions of the defendant were in violation of the plaintiff's legal rights. Similarly, the defendant will present evidence in an effort to prove that the plaintiff's rights were not violated, or at least were not violated by the defendant.
2. *Causation.* If the plaintiff proves that the defendant has violated one of its legal rights, it must be shown that this violation resulted in some harm to the plaintiff. Here, attorneys for the plaintiff and defendant will try to prove or disprove the nexus between the defendant's actions and some harm to the plaintiff.
3. *Damages.* After presenting the evidence relating to the liability and causation issues, the parties' next step in most cases is to prove damages. Damages are one of a number of remedies that may be available to a prevailing plaintiff. Other types of remedies include specific performance (performance of the act that was promised), injunctions (an order by the court forbidding or restraining a party from doing an act), and restitution (the return of goods, property, or money previously conveyed). Damages are the only type of remedy discussed in this chapter. The general principle in awarding damages is to put the plaintiff in the same position it would have been in if its legal rights had not been transgressed. There are three main categories of damages: compensatory, consequential, and punitive. Compensatory damages compensate the injured party only for injuries or losses actually sustained and proved to have arisen directly from the violation of the plaintiff's rights. Consequential damages are foreseeable damages that are caused by special circumstances beyond the action itself; they flow only from the consequences or results of an action. Punitive damages are intended to penalize the guilty party and to make an example of the party to deter similar conduct in the future; they are awarded only in certain types of cases (e.g., fraud). The quantification of damages is primarily a question of fact. The burden of proving the damage amount normally falls on the plaintiff. Although accountants can be used in cases in which damages are not an issue, accountants are most frequently used in cases in which damages are an issue.

(b) THE ACCOUNTANT'S ROLE IN THE LITIGATION PROCESS   Typically the account-ant is hired by attorneys representing either the plaintiff or the defendant. In some cases, how-ever, an accountant may be engaged directly by one of the parties to the action. No matter who engages the accountant, a number of possible roles might be played. A litigation consulting practitioner can work as a testifying expert, a consultant, a trier of fact (e.g., an arbitrator), a special master (working for the court), or a court-appointed neutral party (an expert, not for the parties to the dispute, but to the court as a neutral party). A detailed discussion of the role of the testifying expert and the consultant follows.

(i) The Testifying Expert   Frequently, the accountant's purpose in the case will be to develop and render an opinion regarding financial or accounting issues. Ordinarily, only facts and firsthand knowledge can be presented by witnesses at trial. The only exception to this rule is the testimony of experts, which can include an expression of the expert's opinions.

According to the courts and the law, experts are those who are qualified to testify authori-tatively because of their education, special training, and experience. A professional accountant can qualify as an expert in issues relating to accounting and financial data.

The accountant as expert may be asked to develop and present evidence in support of any or all of the required proofs. For example, the accountant can review and offer an opinion as to the adequacy of the work performed by another accountant in a professional liability suit (proof of liability).The accountant might review the financial records and the business environment of a company to determine whether a bank's withdrawal of credit caused the company to go out of business (proof of causation). Most commonly, the accountant will be asked to provide an opinion regarding the economic loss suffered by the plaintiff in the case or to rebut the damages alleged by the plaintiff on behalf of the defendant (proof of damages).

(ii) Nontestifying Consultant   In certain situations, the accountant will be asked to be a consultant rather than a testifying expert. The accountant will take on more of an advisory role and will not provide testimony. The work the accountant performs for the attorney as a consultant is generally protected by the attorney's work product privilege and as such is not discoverable by the opposing party. For this reason, accountants are often engaged initially as consultants. This enables the attorney to explore avenues and conduct analyses from which he might want to shield his testifying expert. However, once the accountant has been designated as an expert, all work products may be subject to discovery. It is critical for any account-ant to work closely with the attorney to understand the processes that must be maintained to safeguard the consulting, as opposed to the expert, role. In certain circumstances, courts have pierced through the veil of the consulting role to suggest that the consultant's work, particularly in circumstances where the consultant has worked closely with the expert, should be made available.

(iii) Case Analysis and Planning   Whether in the role as testifying expert or nontestifying consultant, the litigation consulting practitioner can provide valuable assistance throughout the litigation process.

In many circumstances, the accountant can be of use to the attorney before the complaint is even filed. The accountant can help the attorney understand the accounting, financial, and economic issues involved in the case and can also help assess the potential value of the claim by providing an estimate of the amount of damages. In certain cases, the accountant may actu-ally help to identify causes of action to be included in the complaint.

Once a case has been filed, the accountant can help the attorney understand and evaluate critical accounting, financial, and economic issues and assist with the formulation of an appropriate strategy. Strategy formulation is a continual process; as new information is received and additional issues uncovered, the overall strategy is revised. During the planning phase, the accountant will help evaluate alternative approaches and help the attorney determine the most reasonable approach to take based on all available information. At the same time, the accountant will assess the strengths and weaknesses of the opponent's case. The accountant's involvement in this phase will help the attorney to focus on those issues that have the greatest impact on proving the case.

(iv) Discovery Discovery is the information-gathering stage of the litigation process. During discovery, each party attempts to identify and obtain all the information and documents necessary to prove its case. The accountant's initial assistance may be in formulating specific accounting and financially oriented questions to be included in interrogatories. The accountant will also assist in drafting document requests by identifying in a very specific manner the types of documents (particularly accounting records and reports) that would be of interest and that the opposing party is likely to have retained. The more specific the requests are, the more likely the response will be useful. The accountant will also be able to assist the attorney with the preparation of responses to the opposing party's interrogatories and document requests.

A significant role that the litigation consulting practitioner can play during the discovery phase is in the review and analysis of the documents. During this review, the litigation consulting practitioner can identify key documents that are helpful or harmful to the parties that have retained him. It is also during this phase that the litigation consulting practitioner identifies documents requiring further explanation that can be provided during deposition. Depending on the legal forum in which the case is being tried, expert reports are usually drafted, issued, and exchanged with the opposing party during or just after the discovery phase.

Depositions provide each side with an opportunity to elicit relevant facts and to identify weaknesses in an opponent's argument. The accountant can be helpful in this area by assisting the attorney in identifying subjects to be explored and in developing specific deposition questions, especially when financial executives or experts are being deposed. Frequently, an attorney will request the accountant to be present at these key depositions. Here, the accountant can help the attorney understand and interpret the deponent's responses and help formulate follow-up questions to probe more deeply into the subject area. Having the accountant present at the deposition will enable the attorney to better understand and consider the financial issues.

The accountant who will be a testifying expert may be subject to deposition by the opposing attorney. The opposition will attempt to gain a thorough understanding of the accountant's analysis and conclusions and, when possible, identify weaknesses and lay the groundwork for attack at trial. Section 46.2(g)(i) presents a description of the deposition process.

(v) Settlement Analysis Settlement negotiations can occur at any point during the litigation process. They can be greatly facilitated by the use of an accountant. The accountant can be instrumental in helping evaluate existing alternatives and terms as well as in proposing other strategic approaches. The accountant's evaluation may involve analyses of (1) the economic value and feasibility of various strategies or (2) the strengths and weaknesses of the two sides' positions.

When assisting with the determination of value and evaluation of feasibility, the accountant can estimate potential damages under various scenarios and help assess the probability of occurrence for each, thereby giving the attorney a better understanding of the risks involved.

Just as important, the accountant can help evaluate the true economic value of various settlement alternatives and assist in determining possible tax effects of each. This will enable the attorney and client to make a more informed decision regarding settlement options and perhaps offer alternatives that benefit both parties. The accountant can also assist with an analysis of the relative strengths and weaknesses of both the plaintiff's and the defendant's positions, thereby helping the attorney strengthen his bargaining position and anticipate potential problems.

(vi) *Pretrial*   When preparing for trial, the accountant can assist the attorney with: (1) preparation of courtroom graphics, presentations, and exhibits; (2) preparation of witnesses for trial testimony; (3) preparation for the cross examination of opposing witnesses; and (4) fine-tuning the overall case strategy.

(vii) *Trial*   If the case does not settle, the final role of the accountant will be to assist during the trial itself. The accountant's testimony in court is a key part of this role. In testimony, the accountant, as expert, presents the opinions developed as a result of his or her information gathering, review, and analysis. It is imperative that the accountant present opinions in a straightforward, cogent, and concise manner. Section 46.2(g)(ii) describes the course of direct testimony and suggests ways that could enhance the effectiveness of the testimony.

Although opinion testimony is of paramount importance at the trial stage, the accountant can play other valuable roles. For example, the accountant can be of tremendous value to attorneys during the cross-examination of opposing experts and financial witnesses. The accountant can work with the attorney to prepare cross-examination questions in an effort to challenge the statements made during testimony or the credibility of the witness. The accountant will be important in this phase because of his or her ability to help formulate accounting and financially oriented questions designed to be difficult for the witness to evade or deflect. More important, the accountant will be able to assess the responses and provide follow-up questions to close the loop on important issues.

(viii) *Credentials and Certifications*   Experts or consultants in a litigation case bring their skills and past experience to the table. Increasingly, individuals are obtaining professional certifications to reflect those attributes. Along with increased societal and regulatory attention to fraud, as evidenced in the passage of the Sarbanes-Oxley Act of 2002 (SOX), various professional organizations are increasingly offering professional certifications in forensic and fraud-related subject matters. Fraud-specific specialty certifications, in most instances, are obtained as a supplement to the widely recognized designation of CPA, but holding a CPA designation may not be a prerequisite to holding other certifications.

One of the better-recognized certifications is the Certified Fraud Examiner (CFE) designation of the 40,000-member Association of Certified Fraud Examiners (ACFEs). The American Institute of Certified Public Accountants (AICPA) and ACFE have been working together for some years to leverage expertise and develop joint training programs. The American College of Forensic Examiners Institute (ACFEI) offers certifications such as the Certified Forensic Consultant (CFC) and Certified Forensic Accountant (Cr.FA), as well as specialized certifications in homeland security and certain aspects of forensic medical practice. The National Association of Certified Valuation Analysts (NACVA) supports the business valuation, litigation consulting, and fraud deterrence disciplines. It offers the Certified Forensic Financial Analyst (CFFA) and Certified Fraud Deterrence Analyst (CFD) credentials. The Forensic CPA

Society was founded in 2005, and offers a Forensic Certified Public Accountant certification to those CPAs passing an examination who also demonstrate relevant practical experience. There are other certification organizations other than those mentioned here.

Most certifications require candidates to pass a written examination and have prerequisite experience requirements and annual continuing education requirements as well as requiring adherence to a code of professional ethics.

(c) FEDERAL RULES OF EVIDENCE

(i) Federal Rule of Evidence 702

Many witnesses who testify during litigation are fact witnesses. A fact witness can provide testimony based on what she has seen, heard, or otherwise observed. A fact witness may not offer opinions. By contrast, an expert witness by reason of education or specialized experience possesses superior knowledge about a subject and as such may offer opinions at trial. An accountant may testify as an expert witness if his opinion will assist the trier of fact in understanding the evidence or determining the issues in a case.

Federal Rule of Evidence 702 governs the admissibility of expert opinion testimony. Rule 702 states that "if scientific, technical, or other specialized knowledge will assist the trier of fact to understand the evidence or to determine a fact in issue, a witness qualified as an expert by knowledge, skill, experience, training, or education, may testify thereto in the form of an opinion or otherwise."

(ii) Effect of Daubert v. Merrell Dow Pharmaceuticals

In *Daubert v. Merrell Dow Pharmaceuticals*, 113 S. Ct. 2796 (1993) (*Daubert*), the Supreme Court addressed the rules pertaining to the admission of expert testimony.

Since 1923, based on *Frye v. United States*, 293 F.1013 (D.C. Cir 1923), the federal courts applied a test (the general acceptance test) by which scientific expert opinions should be admitted into evidence. Under this standard, an opinion was admitted only if it was based on generally accepted methodology within the industry.

In the *Daubert* decision, the Supreme Court determined that in order for expert witness opinions to be admitted under Rule 702, they did not have to meet the *Frye* general acceptance test and clarified that Rule 702 does not establish general acceptance as a criteria for admissibility. The *Daubert* decision clarified the trial court's role in determining the admissibility of expert testimony. In doing so, the court need not determine whether the methodology meets the general acceptance test; instead the court must assess the validity of the methodology used and the applicability of that methodology to the specific facts of the case. Discussions of issues of expert testimony are extended in Chapter 47, "Financial Expert Witness Challenges and Exclusions: Results and Trends in Federal and State Cases since Kumho Tire."

(iii) Federal Rule of Civil Procedure 26

If the accountant has been engaged to serve as a testifying expert witness, he must become aware of the effect of Rule 26 of the Federal Rules of Civil Procedure, which deals with the procedure for written disclosure of expert testimony.

Pursuant to Rule 26, the identity of one side's potential testifying experts, as well as information about the expected testimony, must be voluntarily disclosed at the outset of a case, without receipt of a formal discovery request.

In addition, Rule 26 provides that the expert prepare and sign a written report. This report must be disclosed to the other parties before the expert will be allowed to testify at trial. Unless the date by which disclosure of the written report must be made is decided by the trial judge, rules of the local court, or agreement of the parties, the report must be disclosed at least 90 days before the date of trial. If an expert is retained solely to rebut the testimony of an opposing expert, the report of the rebuttal witness must be disclosed within 30 days of the disclosure of the other expert's report.

Generally, the expert witness will not be permitted to testify at trial to his opinions unless the opinions are contained in the expert witness's written report. Therefore, the content of the expert's report should contain all of his opinions and the bases for the opinions. In addition, once the expert's report is disclosed to the other side, any changes to the report must be disclosed before the commencement of trial.

Rule 26 requires that the expert's report contain:

- A complete statement of the opinion to be expressed and the bases and reasons therefore
- The data or other information the witness considered in forming the opinions
- Any exhibits to be used as a summary of or as support for the opinions
- Qualifications of the witness, including a list of publications the witness authored within the preceding 10 years
- The compensation to be paid to the witness for the study and testimony
- A list of all other cases in which the witness has testified as an expert at trial or in deposition within the preceding four years
- Signature of the expert

Pursuant to Rule 26, once the expert's written report required by Rule 26 has been disclosed, the opposing side has the right to take the deposition of any person who has been identified as an expert whose opinions may be presented at trial.

The accountant who is engaged as an expert witness in a matter to be tried in a federal court should ascertain the current status of Rule 26 in the applicable federal district and discuss compliance with Rule 26 with the counsel retaining him.

It is important to point out that the Federal Rules of Civil Procedure give local courts the option of not complying with certain provisions, including the provisions of Rule 26 discussed above. The accountant should consult with the retaining attorney to ascertain whether the case is to be tried in federal or local court and the local rules that apply to the case.

(d) TYPES OF SERVICES
(i) Damage Calculations

- *Patent infringement.* These cases typically involve unauthorized or unreported use or sale of licensed intellectual property, transfer pricing errors, inaccurate allocation of sales value to the patented components, and other erroneous deductions. Damages are in the form of lost royalties. Determining revenue loss may involve steps such as conducting interviews, examining sales records, pricing, freight, parts, and other types of deductions, and testing sales, production, and inventory for underreporting.
- *Breach of contract.* Typically, the plaintiff has a contract with the defendant that the defendant is accused of breaching. For example, the contract may call for the defendant to buy a certain quantity of product for a certain price. The defendant, however, fails to make the required purchases. Or the defendant may be accused of breaching a warranty on its goods or services. The accountant may be asked to quantify the damages suffered by the plaintiff as a result of the breach. Usually the damages are measured by lost profits, that is, the additional profits the plaintiff would have earned

but for the defendant's breach. Among the issues the accountant may address are lost revenues, avoided costs, available capacity, and possible mitigating actions, including sale of the product to others.

• *Business interruption.* A business interruption claim may arise from an accident, fire, flood, strike, or other unexpected event. It may even arise from a contract or warranty claim where the defendant's breach has caused the plaintiff to suspend operations. Typically, these claims are filed by a business against its insurance carrier, though a claim against the entity causing the event is possible. In a business interruption case, the plaintiff claims the event caused the business to suffer losses. Often the accountant is asked to quantify the loss. Elements to be considered may include lost profits, loss of tangible assets, loss of intangible assets (including goodwill), loss of an entire business or business line, cost to repair or reestablish the business, cost of downtime, or cost of wasted effort (time spent fixing the problem instead of generating operating profits).

• *Antitrust.* The plaintiff in antitrust litigation may be either the government or a private party. The government usually brings suit to oppose a merger or to break up a monopoly. Government suits are usually not for monetary damages. Experts in these suits, particularly in liability issues involving monopolistic practices, relevant market share, and the like, are often economists, not accountants. In a private suit, the plaintiff accuses the defendant of violating antitrust laws, resulting in injury to competition, including (or especially) injury to the plaintiff. The accountant's role again may be the computation of lost profits. A company may be accused of violating antitrust laws by selling the same goods at different prices to different parties in the same channel of distribution. This ostensibly discriminatory pricing may be refuted if the defendant can show that the price differences are justified by differences in cost of production, service, freight, and so on. An accountant may conduct these cost justification studies. Accusations of predatory pricing also fall under the antitrust laws. The defendant in a predatory pricing case is accused of pricing so low that competitors lose money and are driven out of business. Once the competition is eliminated, the defendant presumably raises prices and enjoys monopoly profits. One legal standard for predatory pricing is pricing below cost of production. Depending on the law, the standard may be either incremental costs or fully allocated costs. An accountant may help establish or refute this claim by studying product pricing and production costs and measuring the resulting profit margins.

• *Personal injury.* Personal injury cases stem from automobile accidents, slip-and-falls, and the like. Typically, damage components include medical expenses, pain and suffering, lost earnings, and loss of consortium to the injured party's spouse. The accountant is usually involved in the calculation of lost earnings and in calculations regarding the interest components of the judgment. For identification of the issues involved, see Section 46.2(e).

(ii) Arbitration Arbitration is a form of alternative dispute resolution that is binding upon the parties involved. An impartial arbitrator listens to the evidence presented and renders a decision. Disputes in connection with a purchase and sale agreement are common candidates for arbitration. These can arise for a variety of reasons, such as disagreements related to purchase price adjustments based on a closing date balance sheet or some other financial measure; representation and warranty provisions involving financial information; transition services and related cost-sharing provisions; and earnout provisions or other deferred payment mechanisms that generally depend on future operations or earnings results. Many of these issues involve questions of fact and how those facts should be reflected in financial statements prepared in accordance with generally accepted accounting principles (GAAP) or another basis of accounting.

Buy–sell agreements may also contain a component of compensation to the seller in the form of an earnout that is typically based on future performance and attaining certain mutually agreed-on financial metrics. Disputes frequently result over the contractual wording and earnout measurement mechanisms when the company, according to the buyer's calculation, does not meet earnout targets and, therefore, the seller does not receive any or all of the potential earnout compensation that was anticipated. An accountant may be helpful in assisting both buyers and sellers in offering strategic advice during the drafting of earnout provisions as well as evaluating the relevant financial results to establish whether any or all of the earnout has been attained.

Because certain accounting issues disputed in a post-closing purchase price dispute may also be at issue in an earlier balance sheet that is subject to representations and warranties of the seller, these same issues might be disputed in a different forum under a breach of representation or warranty claim. While these disputes are often decided in a litigation context as opposed to private arbitration, the skills and experience of professionals are also highly applicable in these matters. The accounting issues in a dispute may or may not include some of the same issues involved in a post-closing purchase price adjustment. However, in addition to accounting and financial reporting, there are numerous other issues that can arise in a breach case, including:

- The manner in which the purchase price was established by the buyer
- The nature and extent of due diligence by the buyer
- The reliance and causation issues that may stem from any alleged accounting errors
- The damages alleged by the buyer

Addressing such issues may involve analyzing the underlying records, researching complex accounting questions, or interpreting contractual modifications of GAAP. The accountant may provide consultation to the buyer, seller, or the arbitrator himself, or may render expert opinions in breach of representation litigation matters. The accountant may be asked to assist with:

- Evaluating the accounting transactions and policies and practices that underlie a balance sheet transaction and assisting in identifying relevant and appropriate GAAP or other applicable accounting standards, including any contractual adjustments required by the buy–sell agreement.
- Identifying potential issues that a party may choose to pursue in an objection to a closing statement forming the basis of a purchase price adjustment.
- Helping guide the arbitration process in terms of the quantity and quality of documents to be shared, the extent of interviews of witnesses, or the number of submissions by the parties.
- Assisting the buyer or the seller in documenting their positions regarding the disputed issues and preparing one or more rebuttals. Although there is no standard format for these written submissions, professionals experienced with such disputes can help to convey the underlying issues and facts with clarity and express a party's view

with persuasiveness. Crafting submissions that are articulate, well organized, and responsive to the facts and circumstances is critical to success.

• Providing expert testimony as needed. Because many buy–sell agreement disputes are resolved in ad hoc arbitration where the arbitrator is also an expert in accounting, formal expert testimony is not always necessary to explain a party's position. However, expert testimony may be necessary in some disputes, particularly where parties have brought the issues before a court of law. The accountant may be called in to explain the nature of certain provisions, such as typical purchase price adjustment provisions, to distinguish unusual financial features of the contract, or to explain the nature of underlying evidence and related facts and help judges and juries understand complex accounting and industry issues.

(iii) Bankruptcy   Bankruptcy matters may require an accountant's services for many different tasks. The role of the accountant and scope of services to be performed are influenced by the size of the company and by whether the accountant is working for the trustee, debtor in possession, secured creditors, or the creditors' committee(s).

Accountants for the debtor in possession may be asked to prepare analyses supporting the solvency or insolvency of the debtor, which may affect creditors' claims, recoveries, or security interests. Such accountants may also be involved in preparing prospective financial information filed with the U.S. Trustee's Office or used in negotiating plans of reorganization with the parties of interest. Another important role may require making analyses to support a debtor's use of cash collateral and analyses showing that adequate protection is available to the secured creditor.

An accountant for the creditors' committee, in addition to reviewing any analyses prepared for the debtor, will have additional responsibilities. The accountant may initially be asked to determine the cause for the business failure and may need to determine quickly whether the debtor's operation may be further depleting the assets available for creditors. The creditors' accountants may also need to investigate the conduct of the debtor. The scope and depth may vary significantly based on the relationship and confidence the creditors have with existing management. At a minimum, an analysis to determine possible preferential payments, fraudulent conveyances, and insider transactions is usually performed. The roles, definitions, and exceptions to preferences and fraudulent conveyances are detailed in the Bankruptcy Code as well as in Newton.[1]

The work required to establish liability in bankruptcy cases revolves around the question of whether the debtor is liable for debts and/or claims expressed by various parties and classes of claimants. However, liability issues in bankruptcy have the benefit of explicit rules in the Bankruptcy Code (Title 11 USC, more specifically, Subsections 543–549). These sections of the Bankruptcy Code detail the powers of a trustee to avoid transfers that defraud, hinder, or delay creditors, give preferential treatment to certain creditors, or do not give the bankrupt person or entity fair value for the transfer. Since these Code sections define the scope of the trustee's power, an accountant engaged by the trustee should first read and understand the relevant provisions before planning the work. In addition, an accountant should obtain an understanding of certain sections of the Uniform Commercial Code and in particular the Uniform Fraudulent

---

1.   Grant W. Newton, *Bankruptcy and Insolvency Accounting* (New York: John Wiley & Sons, 1994).

Transfer Act of the state where the business is situated. The location of the business may influence the scope of the work since the time period under the bankruptcy statute only allows for recovery one year prior to the bankruptcy, whereas state laws vary from 3 to 10 years.

Once the appropriate time period and scope have been determined, the accountant needs to review all material transactions to gain an understanding of the economic benefit of the exchange to the bankrupt party, including all monetary and nonmonetary exchanges. In addition, the accountant needs to determine the timing and explanation for any liens or other security interest granted or recorded during the time period. This review should include any asset sales, purchases, foreclosures, and tax assessments. Transactions between related entities or commonly controlled entities or their affiliates must be reviewed. In a bankruptcy case, the accountant is trying to develop any evidence that might show fraud or fraudulent intent.

A preferential payment analysis covers a review of transactions within 90 days for non-insiders and one year for insiders prior to filing for bankruptcy protection wherein a creditor is paid for an antecedent debt at a time the debtor is insolvent and such payment is not in the ordinary course of business. The definition of insolvency for this purpose is the fair value of assets compared with the fair value of liabilities—a balance sheet approach. *Ordinary course of business* is not defined except by reference to case precedents. For example, if creditors are routinely paid in 90 days but certain creditors get paid just before bankruptcy within 30 days, such payments are probably not in the ordinary course of business.

Certain leveraged buyouts (LBOs) have encountered financial difficulty shortly after consummation, and some creditors have used various security law and bankruptcy law theories to unwind these transactions and seek recoveries from selling shareholders, secured creditors, and others.

The accountant's work in helping establish or defend liability is critical. Analyses that show the cash flow of the entity before and after the LBO help establish whether sufficient capital or working capital was available to the company. Changes in a company's borrowing, especially where a significant amount of assets have been recently pledged, also illustrate the potential damage to unsecured creditors. The accountant's ability to distinguish operating losses caused by the form and structure of the buyout from losses due to the economy or other competing companies will also assist counsel in determining whether the LBO can be attacked as a fraudulent transfer. For a more detailed discussion on bankruptcy matters and issues, please refer to Chapter 45 of this handbook.

(e) CALCULATING DAMAGES

(i) General Concepts   In proving liability, the plaintiff must demonstrate that the defendant's actions were in violation of the plaintiff's legal rights. In moving from liability to causation, the plaintiff must demonstrate that the illegal actions caused injury to the defendant; only then can damages be calculated. In discussing damages, we rely on the concept of the *but-for world*. The but-for world is the economic and physical environment that would have existed *but for* the actions of the defendant. In other words, it is the *undamaged* world, in contrast to the *actual*, damaged world that did occur and in which the defendant performed the alleged illegal acts.

(ii) Measuring Damages   Depending on the case, there are many different standards by which damages are measured, including the following four:

1. Lost profits (past profits, prospective profits, or both, including increased costs)
2. Lost asset value (the appraised value of identified assets, including goodwill, or other intangibles)

3. Lost personal earnings (wages, salary, etc.)
4. Lost royalties or licensing fees (amounts due for use of the plaintiff's assets or rights) or share of profits pursuant to participation agreements

In most cases, these approaches are all attempts to compute the difference between the but-for world and the actual world. That is, they attempt to measure the difference between what should have happened and what actually did happen.

Lost profits are the most common standard for business cases. Valuations are used in both business disputes and marital dissolution proceedings. Personal earnings are the damages standard for the economic component of personal injury suits. Other components are medical costs and pain and suffering. Reasonable royalty is used in intellectual property disputes, especially patent cases.

(iii) Mitigation   A plaintiff has the obligation to mitigate damages. This means that the plaintiff must take reasonable steps to minimize the damages suffered. More specifically, the courts (and damages experts or consultants) will compute damages as if the plaintiff mitigated, whether the mitigation really occurred or not.

In many cases, reasonable mitigation occurred, and the expert or consultant may look at the difference between what should have occurred and what did occur as the measure of damages. After all, the plaintiff's recovery through litigation is uncertain, and plaintiff has every incentive to reduce their damages. However, if reasonable mitigation did not occur, the accountant should consider what adjustments may be necessary.

(iv) Present Value and Inflation   Time is a factor in most damage claims. A violation typically occurs sometime prior to the loss suffered by the plaintiff; the loss can continue into the future (e.g., lost earnings in a personal injury case); the trial can occur either after the entire loss has been suffered or prior to the full recovery from the effects of the violation; and the award may not be paid until sometime after the trial. Thus, a damage award must compensate the plaintiff for both past and future losses, but it must be made in full at the present time. This requires that the accountant accumulate both past and future lost profits to the present. This accumulation is accomplished by discounting the projected lost profits to the date of violation using a rate of interest and compounding the resulting amount to the present at some prejudgment interest rate. The choice of discount rate depends on the circumstances. A nominal discount rate (such as the Treasury bill rate, the prime rate, or any other market rate) includes both a real rate of interest and an inflation premium. If the damages into the future are computed in constant (uninflated) dollars, then discounting at a real rate (net of inflation) may be appropriate. If inflation has been built into the projected damage figures, a nominal interest rate is correct. In either case, the appropriate discount rate should include an adjustment for risk.

For more on determining the present value of a damage award, see Kabe and Blonder.[2]

(v) Income Taxes   Under the law, some damage awards are taxable to the recipient, whereas others are tax-free. In computing damages, the goal is to properly account for taxes so the plaintiff is in the same position as it would have been if the liability act had never occurred.

---

2.   Elo R. Kabe and Brian L. Blonder, "Discounting Concepts and Damages," in *Litigation Services Handbook,* 1996 Suppl., ed. Roman L. Weil, Michael J. Wagner, and Peter B. Frank (New York: John Wiley & Sons, 1986).

If the award is taxable, then the damages should be computed on a before-tax basis. The plaintiff then receives the damage award, pays taxes, and is in the proper after-tax position. If the amount is tax-free, only the after-tax amount should be assessed as damages.

Complications arise in the two areas: (1) if prejudgment interest is due, and (2) if tax rates have changed from the damage date to the payment date. As discussed above, prejudgment interest is computed on the after-tax amount, since that is the amount the plaintiff would have had to invest. However, if the award is taxable, the damages must be expressed in pretax dollars. A reasonable approach is to compute the entire award, including damages and interest, in after-tax dollars. Then gross up the award by the tax rate in the year of payment. When the plaintiff receives this amount and pays tax on it, plaintiff will be in the proper after-tax position. This approach, although accurate, has been relatively untested in court.

A similar situation arises if tax rates have changed. If pretax damages are used, the change in tax rates will result in an incorrect after-tax award. A reasonable approach is again to compute the after-tax amounts, then gross up the award for the current tax rate.

(f) SUPPORT FOR OPINIONS

(i) Sources of Information   The accountant acting as expert witness should have adequate data to authoritatively support opinions or conclusions The data should be of high reliability since the accountant is subject to cross-examination.

There are two primary sources for data: the litigating parties (either the plaintiff or the defendant) and external sources, such as industry publications, economic statistics, and so on. The former is obtained through the discovery phase discussed previously. The latter is discussed here.

Many reference books list sources of business information. Also, computer databases are widely available and eliminate the need for data entry as the information can be downloaded into a computer file.

Often an accountant may need to call on other specialists or persons knowledgeable in the particular industry. These specialists may be found within a different practice area of the accountant's firm, or the accountant may need to obtain assistance from specialists outside his or her firm.

(ii) Reliance on Others   The accountant as an expert witness may rely on the work of employees as well as personal research or sources in forming his or her opinion. Federal Rule of Evidence No. 703 describes permissible bases on which expert testimony may be founded: (1) information acquired through firsthand observation, (2) facts observed by, or presented to, the expert witness at the trial or at the hearing, and (3) data considered by the expert witness outside of court. Rule 703 permits an expert to rely on facts that are not normally admissible in evidence if they are of a type reasonably relied on by experts in the field. *Reasonably relied on* means *trustworthy*. *Type relied on* is left to the discretion of the trial judge. In turn, the judge may question the accountant-witness as to the appropriate degree of reliance.

(iii) Documentation   All materials prepared, accumulated, or referred to by the accountant acting as an expert witness in a case may have to be made available to the opposing side. At the outset, the attorney and accountant should develop a clear understanding of exactly what the accountant will be preparing and retaining for the engagement. Then the accountant should carefully control the content of supporting documentation and collect relevant materials or avoid collecting materials that are irrelevant to forming an opinion. This should be an ongoing

process, as the accountant may not be able to remove anything after receiving a subpoena. All work products of an expert may be discoverable and could be thoroughly scrutinized by the opposing party. Any errors, inconsistencies, and irrelevant materials may form the basis for an effective challenge to the testimony of the accountant.

(g) TESTIMONY

(i) Giving Deposition Testimony   A deposition of an expert witness is part of the discovery process in which counsel seeks to fulfill several major objectives. The most obvious objective is to find out what opinions the expert is going to offer at trial, and why. A deposition is also an opportunity to commit the expert to sworn testimony that can be later used for impeachment purposes, should the expert try to change his or her opinion. Additionally, counsel will use the deposition to assess the expert's effectiveness as a witness and the strength of the case for purposes of settlement negotiation and development of trial strategy. Consequently, expert depositions may be more important than the trial testimony and should be regarded with due respect.

Adequate preparation is crucial to giving an effective deposition. Naturally, a thorough review of the expert's opinions and underlying support is in order. The expert should also review any prior writings and testimony for previous positions that may be construed as contradictory. Being caught unaware in an apparent contradiction can have a debilitating effect on the credibility of a deponent's testimony. The expert should know the information and sources relied on, the various analyses performed, the opinions reached, and the strengths as well as the weaknesses of the case. Above all, the expert should tell the truth.

Finally, the expert witness insist on a detailed predeposition briefing with counsel. This briefing should include a conclusion regarding disclosure strategy. If the objective is to cause a settlement to occur, a complete disclosure of all the strengths of the case should be made. If the case is likely to proceed to trial, then a restrictive approach may be called for. For example, counsel may instruct the expert to be careful to answer the questions asked by opposing counsel very directly and to avoid volunteering any related issues.

(ii) Giving Trial Testimony

- *Direct testimony.* The objective of direct testimony is to present an opinion in a manner such that it will be understood and believed by the judge and jury or other trier of fact. The testimony will begin by reviewing the witness's qualifications, which provide the prerequisite skill and training enabling the witness to provide the court with expert testimony. Opposing counsel will then have the opportunity to *voir dire* the expert and to challenge his qualifications as an expert. The judge will then decide whether the court will qualify the accountant as an expert. The expert's opinions then will be solicited. It is imperative that the expert not appear to be an advocate for the plaintiff or defendant but rather appear fair and unbiased. The job of advocacy should be reserved for the attorney. Violation of this precept will tend to undermine the expert's credibility. Finally, the basis for the expert's opinion will be presented. The engagement scope is reviewed, including who retained the expert and why, documents reviewed, interviews conducted, the engagement team, manner of supervision and time spent, compensation, and any engagement scope limitations imposed. Next, the methodology employed is explained, which leads to the conclusions and opinions reached. Typically, any weaknesses are acknowledged and explained in a preemptive fashion to reduce potential damage on cross-examination. The key to persuasive and effective testimony is communication. The expert's position may be a technical marvel, but it is worthless if the jury does not understand the testimony or is not convinced. Therefore, the expert should speak plain English and avoid technical accounting and financial jargon. Concepts should be explained by way of common, everyday occurrences. Condescending or patronizing speech is usually deemed inappropriate. The expert's job is to educate the jury and the court in an interesting fashion. This job can be facilitated by the use of and reference to trial exhibits. Trial exhibits are used to lead the jury, court, and the expert himself through the basis of the opinion, as well as to keep everyone's attention focused. As with the language used in testimony, the exhibits should be kept clear and simple so the point is clear and memorable. In many jurisdictions, the jury cannot take notes, and visual exhibits can be an effective way to impress the point or conclusion upon the jurors' memories.

- *Cross-examination.* The purpose of cross-examination is to cast doubt on or, if possible, undermine the expert witness's credibility and testimony. One of the simpler ways to accomplish this objective is through impeachment. Consequently, a thorough review of prior testimony, writings, and the deposition transcript is required. The expert must make sure not to be on record as holding a view that is or appears to be contrary to the one he is now presenting, or he must be able to provide an explanation.
- *Redirect examination.* The purpose of redirect examination is to rehabilitate points made by the witness and clarify responses and mischaracterizations. It is generally counterproductive to a witness's credibility to argue with opposing counsel or to resist answering questions that, to the jury, appear reasonable and straightforward. An evasive witness generally is a less credible witness. The expert is back in friendly hands during redirect, and this is the time to mitigate any real or perceived damage. During the redirect examination, the attorney will typically select two or three areas where additional explanation is necessary to counter the points made on cross-examination. This is the witness' opportunity to clearly explain why the points made during cross-examination are irrelevant and have no bearing on the expert's opinion.

46.3 THE ACCOUNTANT'S ROLE IN INVESTIGATIONS AND COMPLIANCE MATTERS

Forensic accountants are increasingly involved in a wide variety of client issues and projects that go far beyond litigation and litigation consulting. Most prominently, accountants have a key role in conducting corporate investigations and in using many of the tools developed in the litigation support context to do so. However, accountants are also involved in compliance investigations and compliance consulting. For example, forensic accountants are often involved in antibribery investigations, anti–money laundering investigations and consulting, and antifraud consulting. They are also deeply involved in other corporate issues, such as the protection of intellectual property. Finally, due to the penetration of technology in the corporate world, accountants have helped lead the way in developing the field of forensic technology. Today, forensic accounting and forensic technology are intertwined.

(a) CORPORATE INVESTIGATIONS
(i) General/White Collar   This is a growing field within the area of forensic accounting and covers a wide range of cases. Examples of fraud and white-collar crime cases are schemes by executives, employees, and customers to siphon funds from financial institutions for their

personal use, check kiting, lapping, computer fraud, embezzlement, defense procurement fraud, costing fraud, schemes involving kickbacks, income tax frauds, charity and religious frauds, money laundering, insider trading cases, and fraudulent bankruptcy actions. Additional examples include investigations of *boiler-room* operations that solicit funds from investors based on promises of high investment return and Ponzi arrangements in which there are no real profits; instead, funds from new investors are used to pay investment returns to existing investors, giving the impression of profits.

The accountant's work in this area centers on investigating what happened and helping companies and their attorneys evaluate potential liability. After the investigation is completed, the accountant may be asked to quantify the amount of the loss attributable to the allegation.

The accountant will typically review and analyze many types of data, including correspondence, e-mail, journal entries, financial statements, and financial schedules. Many times, the accountant commences his or her investigation with little or no detail as to the extent of the situation and must put the pieces of a puzzle together. This involves developing and testing hypotheses throughout the investigation. Therefore, when reviewing documents and other data, it is important to keep an open mind and not dismiss any reasonable possibilities. Very often, an investigation in one area will lead to other problem areas.

Most corporate investigations take place in an adversarial environment. This is especially true in cases involving white-collar crime or fraud. The forensic accountant may conduct or assist the attorney in conducting interviews of relevant parties. Often the forensic accountant or attorney is attempting to obtain information from the persons who are the subject of the investigation and who may be attempting to conceal their activities. As such, the forensic accountant should maintain a high level of professional skepticism throughout the investigation.

Since the forensic accountant's investigation, work product, and findings may form the basis of evidence in a litigation case or prosecution, it is critical to understand the importance of obtaining and preserving evidence and seek guidance from the retaining attorney about such matters whenever necessary. In addition, the forensic accountant may have to coordinate his or her efforts with those of law enforcement officials who may have an interest in the matter.

The circumstances of each engagement are unique, and the forensic accountant or retaining attorney may need to engage other specialists or experts. Computer forensic specialists are frequently used in these types of cases to extract data from computer drives or to search the contents of computer disks using keyword searches. Private investigators can also be of great assistance in performing detailed background checks or surveillance of potential suspects.

In white-collar crime cases where Ponzi schemes are suspected, the accountant will want to document how the enterprise was structured and to develop organizational charts and flowcharts. Tracing transactions from the receipt of investor funds to their ultimate investment or disposition will be required. Analyses that illustrate the lack of any positive cash flow other than by raising additional investor funds can be useful to the attorney in proving liability. Documenting the flow of all cash transactions or custodial arrangements is within the accountant's scope.

The accountant should also analyze cash disbursements to see whether any patterns indicating self-dealing emerge and to help identify possible related entities or personal use or benefit of company assets. Unusual expenses should be vouched, and particular attention should be devoted to traditionally sensitive areas, such as travel and entertainment expenses. While some suspicious transactions are easily detected, such as employee fraud schemes involving payments to fake vendors, many illegal activities involve disguised transactions. Still, it is likely that things like paid bills and supporting evidence will be fairly self-explanatory.

In the case of a penny stock fraud scheme, the accountant may shift greater attention to the financial results and reports to shareholders, press releases, and the like to determine whether there is evidence that such public information is incorrect or inaccurate. Income recognition abuses or improper capitalization of expenses are typical categories of abuses used by penny stock promoters to misstate the operating results and mislead investors. In addition, the accountant should analyze key contracts, employment agreements, and other consulting arrangements. A timeline analysis that reflects all key "publicized events" should be developed and used to help determine whether such events did occur. The timeline can be used to analyze whether, in the same time frame, all acquisitions or dispositions of assets and other financial transactions were accounted for properly.

In recent years, forensic accountants have played a significant role in stock option investigations. Option-related issues arose principally with companies that were compensating their employees through stock—mainly companies in the high-tech industry and other start-up ventures. Stock option investigations generally involve looking into how companies have awarded, accounted for, and disclosed employee stock option grants. Improper *backdating*, in particular, carries substantial risk. An example of backdating is when the purported grant date of an award or the purported approval date is a date prior to the actual grant date or approval date. In addition to the investigation of whether potential problems with backdating existed, there was often a disconnect between those granting the options and how the options were being accounted for.

A company may choose to begin looking at its options activity with statistical analyses to see whether there are any indications of potential issues.

The accountant may be called in during this process to assist with one or more of the following:

- Performing preliminary analysis of historical data to see whether there is any indication that the company's stock price tends to rise following nonroutine grant dates or performing the now commonly used test of options backdating
- Quantifying grantee gains, often associated with backdating damages, to estimate the extent to which executives and the board may have actually benefited from any alleged backdating
- Analyzing alleged damages to understand alternative damage models
- Investigating liability by examining corporate communications and other records

In addition, a 2006 letter from the Chief Accountant of the SEC[3] is intended to provide guidance to assist companies in the determination of the appropriate measurement date in situations where indications of intentional backdating are not present. The letter addresses items such as:

- Administrative delays
- Validity of prior grants
- Uncertainty as to individual award recipients
- Documentation of option-granting activities incomplete or unable to be located
- Springloading

(ii) Securities Violations Lawsuits in this area usually involve alleged violations of the federal acts, specifically Sections 11 and 12(2) of the Securities Act of 1933 and Section 10(b) of the Securities Exchange Act of 1934. These sections are concerned with making false or

---

3.   www.sec.gov/info/accountants/staffletters/fei_aicpa091906.htm.

misleading public statements about a company or omitting a material fact (either in a prospectus or in public statements, including financial statements), resulting in an alleged overvaluing of the company's stock. Plaintiffs claim that, but for the misleading statements, they would not have bought the stock or they would have bought the stock at a lower price. These lawsuits are often brought against officers, directors, investment bankers, lawyers, accountants, and others who may have been party to the misstatements.

Accountants may be accused of being involved in the liability, causation, and damages portions of securities cases. Involvement with liability issues is most common when there are allegations that the alleged fraud on the market was caused by the issuance of financial statements that were materially misstated or by the absence of important disclosures in the financial statements. On other occasions, an accounting firm may be a defendant accused of violating Section 10(b)5 by failing to perform an audit in accordance with generally accepted auditing standards (GAAS) and/or by giving a clean opinion to financial statements that do not conform to GAAP. Cases involving public company audits dated after the effective date of PCAOB[4] Auditing Standard No. 1, *References in Auditor's Reports to Standards of the Public Company Auditing Oversight Board*, will reference the standards of the PCAOB in lieu of GAAS. In these types of cases and investigations, the forensic accountant will review the auditor's workpapers and other relevant materials to analyze the adequacy of the audit of the financial statements within the context of the applicable professional standards.

The causation and damages phases of securities cases are closely linked. They consist of determining whether the information had any impact on the stock price and quantifying the losses suffered by the plaintiff investors as a result. Typically, the type of analysis performed by a forensic accountant involves determining what the stock price would have been if the proper information had been released at the proper time. The methods for doing this are beyond the scope of this chapter; see de Silva et al. for a treatment of this subject.[5]

(b) ANTI–MONEY LAUNDERING Money laundering is the criminal practice of illegally filtering money (or lawfully derived money intended to be used for illicit purposes) through a series of transactions to break the trail of ownership. Money laundering is a diverse and often complex process and most often plays a fundamental role in facilitating the ambitions of drug traffickers, terrorists, organized criminals, insider traders, and tax evaders as well as many others who need to avoid the kind of attention that "sudden" wealth brings. A professional money launderer is typically limited only by the breadth of his or her imagination. No business, whether it takes cash or operates under a strict no-cash policy, is immune from becoming the unwitting accomplice of the money launderer.

Accountants' anti–money laundering (AML) and Bank Secrecy Act (BSA) responsibilities vary depending on the clients they serve and the services they perform. In general, accountants and auditors who serve the financial services industry are the most affected by the AML/BSA

---

4.   PCAOB is the Public Company Accounting Oversight Board (www.pcaobus.org), a non-profit organization created by the Sarbanes-Oxley Act of 2002 to oversee the auditors of public companies.

5.   Harinda de Silva, Nancy N. Low, and Tara N. Nells, "Securities Act Violations: Estimation of Damages," in *Litigation Services Handbook: The Role of the Accountant as Expert,* ed. Roman L. Weil, Michael J. Wagner, and Peter B. Frank (New York: John Wiley & Sons, 1995).

requirements of their respective clients. Accountants providing services for clients—acting in a fiduciary capacity, for example—also need to be concerned about not running afoul of the money laundering criminal statutes by unknowingly participating in a money laundering scheme. The *willful blindness* theory of criminal liability could apply as well, as noted below, but an attorney should always be consulted on these issues.

Financial institutions, and certain other businesses such as casinos, broker-dealers, and others, are required under the BSA and USA Patriot Act to implement and maintain a program of controls to deter and detect money laundering and terrorist financing. These programs can typically include:

- *Policies and procedures* to establish how an organization's AML controls are implemented, assigning responsibility for monitoring and maintaining controls, and helping ensure timely reporting of suspicious activity.
- *Know Your Customer (KYC) procedures and Customer Information Program (CIP) requirements* that establish the process for understanding who the organization's customers are, what information is required to adequately identify the customer, as well as assessing the customer's risk profile and risk to the organization.
- *Transaction monitoring*, a key component of an effective AML program. Transaction monitoring is typically automated, either on a real-time (i.e., as transactions are occurring), or batched (e.g., daily, weekly, monthly, etc.) basis. Transaction monitoring seeks to identify unusual and/or potentially suspicious activity by applying a set of defined AML scenarios or rules against the transaction activity for each customer.
- *Suspicious activity reporting (SAR)*. Once identified, suspicious activity must be reported within a specified number of days following identification. The Financial Crimes Enforcement Network (FinCEN), a department of the U.S. Treasury, is responsible for receiving and analyzing all SAR filings for all U.S. financial institutions.

In the course of providing accounting services to clients or in conducting an audit for a financial institution or a client, an accountant may find it necessary to:

- Exercise due diligence when performing client acceptance activities. Launderers may seek assistance from accounting professionals without the accountants fully realizing it. A client may ask an accountant to wire funds to and from various bank accounts without giving any reasonable explanation, to make cash deposits in different financial institutions with amounts just under the $10,000 reporting requirement, or issue checks to clients or their vendors in return for cash.
- Perform audit procedures pursuant to SAS 54, *Illegal Acts by Clients*, to determine whether money laundering has taken place and to obtain a more detailed understanding of the questionable transactions, the business reasons behind the transactions, and the parties involved.
- Analyze findings in previous examination reports, in areas other than BSA compliance, for adequacy of internal controls and audit procedures. If prior internal control audits have significant or a large number of findings, this may be indicative of deficiencies in the AML compliance program.
- Report money laundering activities to the client's Board of Directors (Board) if the accountant believes that money laundering has occurred under the Private Securities Litigation Reform Act of 1995. The Board is required to notify the Securities and Exchange Commission (SEC) within one day of being notified by the accountant. The Act further requires accountants to notify the SEC if the Board does not do so.

- Express a qualified or adverse opinion on the financial statements if the accountant believes the consequences of money laundering have not been properly accounted for or disclosed in the company's financial statements in accordance with SAS 54.
- Resign if a client refuses to accept the auditor's modified report.
- Advise clients who become subject to asset forfeiture.
- Provide remediation advice to clients regarding Internal Revenue Service (IRS) Form W-8, acceptance of and reliance upon which has been disallowed by the IRS due to incompleteness or lack of appropriate treaty status claimed. Additionally, accountants may be called on to advise clients who may have incorrectly filed or failed to appropriately file IRS Form 8300 (Currency Transactions). Such advice might involve counseling or consulting with the client's legal counsel (for internal auditors) or other specialists.
- Estimate increased contingent liabilities for clients who become subject to AML-related litigation, particularly criminal actions.
- Advise on accrual methods for presumptive legal and regulatory penalties and fines.
- Seek professional advice whenever appropriate and consult with the client's legal counsel (for internal auditors) or other specialists.

Accountants may become inadvertently exposed to potential money laundering activities through the processing and evaluating of their clients' financial records and activities. Accountants are often viewed as "gatekeepers" for their clients' financial transactions and need to conduct appropriate risk-based due diligence. Accountants should consider attending periodic training on money laundering–related issues, including preventive techniques, and courses of action in cases where the clients are suspected to be involved in money laundering. One of the most effective steps an accountant can take to understand how the accounting profession can work with clients to help prevent money laundering is to become familiar with the Bank Secrecy Act and the USA Patriot Act. Additionally, accountants and auditors who focus on the financial services industry should have an awareness of the AML self-regulatory mechanisms proposed by industry organizations,[6] previous enforcement actions, and regulatory penalties.

Accountants should also be aware of the *willful blindness* concept and should always consult an attorney on this issue. *Willful blindness* means attempting to avoid criminal or civil liability for a wrongful act by intentionally putting oneself in a position to be unaware of facts that would render one otherwise liable.[7] The government may charge accountants as accomplices to a money laundering crime. If the government is not able to prove the accountants' actual knowledge of criminal activities, the government may use the willful blindness argument sometimes employed by prosecuting attorneys.

(i) AML Technology   AML technology should be leveraged to support an organization's money laundering risk management undertaking. Such technology includes account behavior and transaction-monitoring software, systems that capture suspicious data, provide for analysis, investigation, and resolution, and produce SAR and currency transaction reports as well as monitor Office of Foreign Assets Control (OFAC) obligations and compliance with other sanctions programs.

---

6. The New York Stock Exchange and the National Association of Securities Dealers, now collectively FINRA.
7. http://en.wikipedia.org/wiki/Willful_blindness.

These technologies can provide organizations with the capability to effectively monitor the behavior of millions of client accounts and complex financial real-time and transactional activity, to identify potential unusual activity that may need further investigation, and to ensure the subsequent and timely reporting of suspicious activity to FinCEN or other jurisdictional regulatory authorities. In addition, these systems can provide an organization with the ability to define various types of potential suspicious activities based on customers' type of business, country of incorporation, transaction type, product, channel, time, and other dimensions that may be applicable to the business.

Because of the nature of the technologies in use, consultation with forensic technology specialists is generally required.

(c) FOREIGN CORRUPT PRACTICES ACT VIOLATIONS In recent years, with the increasing globalization of business, U.S. regulators have focused on the conduct of businesses. Although an act dating back from the post-Watergate era, the Foreign Corrupt Practices Act of 1977 (FCPA) has been the focal point for investigations of companies and for actions being taken by the U.S. Department of Justice (DOJ) and the SEC. The increasing number of FCPA investigations has been considerable over the past several years, resulting in potentially high civil penalties. Official corruption investigations have also been spurred, during the latter part of 2007 and in 2008, by some foreign governments taking actions in antibribery matters that parallel the types of investigations coming from the United States.

The FCPA's most critical parts include the following:

- The *antibribery provision* covers a wide array of prohibited actions by any U.S. individual or organization, as well as non-U.S. persons and entities within U.S. jurisdiction, including paying, offering to pay, or authorizing payments to foreign officials in order to secure an improper business advantage. In other words, companies, their employees, and their agents are prohibited from offering or authorizing anything of value, directly or through third parties, to foreign officials for the purpose of obtaining or retaining business. The Act is both a criminal statute enforced by the DOJ and a civil statute enforced by the SEC.

- The *accounting requirements*—also known as the *books and records* provisions— apply to public companies that are "issuers" of securities under the Exchange Act of 1934. The accounting provisions require that issuers (including foreign issuers) accurately record payments in their books and records detailing their financial transactions. The accounting provisions apply to U.S. issuers' domestic and foreign majority-owned subsidiaries.

- The *internal controls provision* requires companies to establish and maintain a system of internal controls that provide reasonable assurances that transactions are properly authorized and recorded, and that companies do not make inappropriate payments to foreign officials. Companies must also make a *good-faith* effort to use their influence to cause entities (domestic and foreign) in which they hold a minority interest to devise and maintain an adequate system of controls.

Because the individuals involved with transactions that violate the FCPA often know the transaction is illegal, they will likely take precautions to hide the transaction, misrecord it, or move it off the financial records completely. Typical controls and processes rely on the accurate disclosure of the nature of a transaction, the truth of the underlying document, or primary approval. These assumptions may not be appropriate, and may not catch what is purposely hidden. A different focus from normal internal audit or investigatory procedures may be called for as a result. Sifting through transactions looking for bribes has a needle-in-a-haystack aspect and makes sampling less effective than it is in an audit context. Not only do transactions need to be reviewed more comprehensively, but the investigator also needs to be aware of the way in which bribes are often masked.

The forensic accountant's role in the course of an investigation into potential FCPA violations often includes analyzing electronic and hardcopy financial records and assisting counsel in conducting interviews of relevant personnel to help identify whether schemes exist and to understand how the schemes work, assess the scope of the violations, and report on findings. Accountants might also be called in to help their clients respond to specific allegations or requests that might not relate to wrongdoing on their part.

To review company records for the presence of schemes, accountants must inspect payable records, and especially journal entries regarding payables, including the text for such entries and words that mask the true purpose of the transaction (referring to a bribe as a *tuition payment*, for example), employee expense records and reimbursements, and e-mails and other forms of corporate communication. Forensic accountants who typically do this work have at their disposal a wealth of knowledge about how schemes work and therefore a number of specific tests they employ to determine whether instances of schemes are present in transactions. Because the records of most companies are electronic these days, the forensic accountant usually works closely with forensic technologists who have developed deep knowledge of the major accounting systems and techniques for exploring the data in these systems.

(d) ANTIFRAUD PROGRAMS AND CONTROLS With the advent of Auditing Standard No. 2 (AS 2), Auditing Standard No. 5 (AS 5), and the related SOX Section 404 (404) guidance, the need for companies to implement an effective Antifraud Programs and Controls Framework (AFPC) has been reemphasized, particularly for public companies. For example, it is now clear that management has a responsibility to assess fraud risks for their organization utilizing "sound and thoughtful judgments that reflect a company's individual facts and circumstances."[8] An overall risk assessment that does not appropriately consider specific fraud risks to the organization is not compliant with current legislation and regulation. Further, current legislation and regulations emphasize the use of a top-down risk-based approach in the design and implementation of entity-level controls, the intent being that appropriately designed entity-level controls can reduce process-level testing.

A focus of the accountant as AFPC consultant is to understand whether corporate management is fulfilling their responsibilities and duties in a manner that reflects the underlying spirit, guidance, and requirements under AS 2, AS 5, the Financial Accounting Standards Board Statement of Auditing Standards No. 99 (SAS 99), and SOX 404. Delivery of AFPC consulting services requires specialized training and experience. The practitioner must develop a thorough understanding of the client's antifraud program and make determinations as to the effectiveness of the program in terms of preventing and detecting fraud.

---

8. Securities and Exchange Commission, 17 CFR Part 241, *Commission Guidance Regarding Management's Report on Internal Control over Financial Reporting under Section 13(a) or 15(d) of the Securities Exchange Act of 1934*; Final Rule, page 15.

(i) AFPC Service Types   AFPC services generally fall into three broad categories that can be tailored to meet the needs of the engagement:

1. Assisting management with its design and implementation of an AFPC program or its components
2. Assessing the design and operating effectiveness of an organization's existing AFPC framework in order to aid management in meeting their responsibilities under 404
3. Assisting the audit engagement team in assessing the design and operating effectiveness of an audit client's AFPC framework, in connection with assurance services, as required under SAS 99 and AS 5

The accountant can add value to the AFPC process by assisting clients in several specific ways, including:

- Assessing the client's antifraud programs and controls in each of the five main COSO (Committee of Sponsoring Organizations of the Treadway Commission) areas, including:
  ○ *Control environment*—assessing the effectiveness of oversight provided by the Audit Committee and the Board, evaluating the Code of Conduct/Ethics, assessing the effectiveness of the whistleblower hotline and incident reporting within the entity, assessing the effectiveness of the entity's investigation and remediation processes, assessing the client's hiring and promotion procedures in terms of fraud risk, and other control environment considerations
  ○ *Risk assessment*—evaluating the client's approach and fraud risk assessment, assisting in the client's fraud risk assessment implementation, and providing training in the fraud risk assessment process
  ○ *Control activities*—considering the linkage of control activities the entity has identified as being antifraud in nature and assessing the effectiveness of those controls.
  ○ *Information and communication*—assessing the client's approach to fraud training, assessing knowledge and records management around fraud, evaluating data and system security and antifraud measures
  ○ *Monitoring*—evaluating the effectiveness and extent of monitoring activities by management and internal audit
- Assisting in the company's fraud risk assessment
- Providing fraud awareness training to client personnel

For non-404 attest clients, especially those considering a future initial public offering, the AFPC team can also add value by conducting a formal assessment of the client's antifraud programs and controls with the goal of providing a road map of their required steps toward SOX readiness.

(e) LICENSING AND CONTRACT INVESTIGATIONS   Protecting company assets, particularly intellectual property, and securing the global supply chain has become a strategic initiative for companies entering into contracts with other entities through joint ventures, profit sharing, patent, trademark and copyright licensing, or distribution transactions. Corporations may have entered into production/distribution agreements with an international partner or into licensing contracts with global manufacturers of consumer products. In these situations, effective management of revenues and costs involving other entities can help protect a company's return on investment and bottom-line profits. In addition, specific industry knowledge is particularly important with respect to investigations involving contracts among the parties.

An accountant may be called in to assist in these matters by providing services, including:

- Conducting investigations to help clients evaluate whether they have been paid properly pursuant to their agreements, and if not, providing analyses to help quantify potential discrepancies
- Providing forensic services aimed at detecting and quantifying:
  - Unpaid royalties, understated joint venture profits, and unreported revenue streams
  - Inaccurate calculations of royalties payable
  - Overstatements of joint venture costs
- Helping clients understand financial implications related to licensing, co-promotion, and joint venture partners and the interpretations of financial calculations in the relevant agreements
- Assisting in evaluating business transactions, helping to identify potential transaction partners, and assessing the relative merits of various forms of compensation, including upfront payments, ongoing royalties, cross-licenses, and strategic partnerships
- Assisting in developing processes that could help reduce the risk of revenue loss and identify unauthorized use of licensed intellectual property
- Facilitating or assisting settlement negotiations regarding financial aspects of the agreements and damage calculations
- Helping develop the financial, accounting, and auditing provisions in licensing/profit sharing/distribution agreements
- Helping clients establish royalty rates for various technologies

(f) FORENSIC TECHNOLOGY   Business records today are largely kept in electronic form. Corporate correspondence, corporate policies and procedures, compliance and governance records, records of transactions, manufacturing records, accounting ledgers, employee records, records of services, and so on, are generated and maintained in computerized format for most companies. The information forensic accountants need to do their work, whether the context is dispute resolution or investigations, is therefore increasingly electronic. An entire business dispute or multimillion-dollar litigation may hinge on identifying when a single piece of data was generated—or altered or deleted—by whom, and under what circumstances, or on a demonstration that no data was altered or deleted. Similarly, anti–money laundering investigations and investigations based on corruption allegations require the ability to sift through huge numbers of transactions to confi rm or disconfi rm the presence of money laundering transactions or bribes—the proverbial needle-in-a-haystack problem. Not only must various forms of computer technology be available to the forensic accountant to perform tests and development opinions, but forensic accountants must be skilled in how they can most effectively be used as well. Simply put, the accountant must have the ability to acquire the information in a forensically sound manner and to analyze it. Lastly, forensic accountants and data management professionals need to take into account local and regional data security and privacy regulations at all times.

(i) Computer Forensics   Computer forensics is the science of retrieving and chronicling evidence located on computers, disks, tapes, thumb drives, voicemail systems—any form of electronically stored information (ESI) for use as evidence in a court of law, or in an investigation, or in a compliance context. The practice of computer forensics includes the use of formal, accepted techniques for collecting, analyzing, and presenting suspect data in court, concentrating on rules of evidence, the legal processes, the integrity and perpetuity of evidence, reporting of facts, and the preparation and presentation of expert testimony. The same disciplined collection techniques are used in investigations where the key issues are the same—demonstrating that there was no bias in the collection of information, that the information was not altered in the collection process, and that the chain of custody was maintained.

A wealth of information may be recoverable from computer hard drives and backup tapes, including active, deleted, hidden, lost, or encrypted files, or file fragments. Even files that were created but never saved may be recovered. In addition to collecting information for litigation consulting and investigations, computer forensic specialists are also called on to analyze information technology (IT) systems for evidence of potential malfeasance, such as information deletion, policy violations, or unauthorized access. The process used by a computer forensic specialist often involves taking an image or exact replica of the hard drive, which is preserved in a locked, fireproof safe for evidentiary and chain-of-custody purposes. Diagnostic software tools are then run against copies of the image to search for the existence of relevant files. Paper documents still play a significant role in many litigation matters. Computer forensics may also be used to compare paper documents with their electronic counterparts to help determine whether the document has been altered.

After collecting information, computer forensics professionals can then look for e-mails, documents, spreadsheet files, Web downloads, and other electronic data that may have been deleted or encrypted, or may exist only in fragments. Such bits and pieces of data can have tremendous value in an investigation.

An accountant may be tasked with leading cases or investigations involving computer forensics or may assist counsel in the investigatory process of preserving, collecting, processing, and reviewing data. The accountant's role may include providing assistance with:

- Identifying the "trigger" that initiated the investigation (e.g., a document, an e-mail, a spreadsheet) and ensuring that the computer or IT systems involved are secured to prevent tampering or deleting evidence.
- Defining the scope and timeline of the investigation, considering complexities such as locations involved, global regions, type of accounting systems in use, language barriers, and the like. Because the very act of investigating can often reveal more layers of data and avenues to explore, *scope creep* is a common problem. Tightly defining the project parameters and specific tasks to be accomplished can help control "creep."
- Identifying and prioritizing individuals involved, particularly the custodians (i.e., owners or creators) of data in question, and interviewing them as needed.
- Engaging and consulting with computer forensics specialists to collect data and verify that the collection was done correctly and that a defensible chain of custody was maintained.
- Providing micro or macro financial analyses as needed, such as analyzing recovered files or assessing the situation in the context of the organization's broader financial picture.

(ii) Data Analysis   After data is collected, computer technology is also required to analyze it. Data analysis takes two principal forms: (1) Textual information is put into discovery databases so it can be explored by the forensic accountant and other members of the litigation or investigation team. The process and role of such databases is discussed fully in Chapter 48; (2) numeric information, such as accounting transaction data, is usually put into relational database management systems so that it can be ordered into patterns. Various analyses can be performed on the data, such as date analysis or analysis by type of transaction, or the database can be searched for particular types of transactions, such as those that may be in violation of the FCPA requirements. The data analysis component of litigation and investigations can often help put together pieces of the litigation puzzle by searching, analyzing, and modeling data obtained as part of the discovery process. Data can be obtained from various sources including accounting systems (such as SAP, Oracle Financials, etc.), manufacturing systems, human resource and payroll systems, billing systems, customer relationship management (CRM) systems, spreadsheets, and more. Individuals' personal files and folders are also open to scrutiny.

Leveraging data analysis to support the accounting investigation can yield several advantages, including the ability to:

- Extract and restore data from the original (native) format, which reduces the risk of working with potentially manipulated data.
- Maintain and process data in a secure environment.
- Summarize data for reconciliation to financial or system reports to check for completeness.
- Search and analyze the entire population of data for anomalies to identify a smaller set of exceptions for detailed review.
- Piece together data from different sources to create a coherent understanding of past transactions (e.g., bringing contract, payment, shipping, and banking records together to identify the full history of transactions).
- Obtain faster access to information by electronically processing large volumes of data, given that speed and accuracy are essential in a litigation case.
- Perform advanced keyword and pattern searches, including handling foreign languages.
- Compare data from various systems potentially in different formats (e.g., matching vendor names, addresses, bank accounts, etc. from the payables ledger to the employee master and payroll system).
- Reperform the analysis efficiently by changing the parameters.

The forensic accountant plays an active role in the data analysis process, particularly in defining tests, various forms of data reconciliation (such as reconciling general ledger data to the financial statements), assisting with the development of keywords for searching, developing anomaly detection tests in AML and FCPA contexts, and reviewing and interpreting analysis results for potentially responsive or hot transactions.

Given the specialized skills required to manipulate various database systems, understand the client's business processes, load the data into a platform for analysis, and develop and generate programs for analysis, it is advisable for the forensic accountant to work closely with a practitioner who specializes in data analysis. The background of such professionals typically includes an understanding of relational database systems, knowledge of financial information, and appropriate computer programming skills.

46.4 GLOBALIZATION IMPACT—IFRS

Increasingly, forensic accountants must focus on globalization, including in regard to accounting principles. IFRS is a single set of accounting principles that is more focused on objectives and principles and less reliant on detailed rules than U.S. GAAP. With more than 100 countries and approximately 40 percent of the Global Fortune 500 companies already using IFRS, and with the SEC expected to push for allowing U.S. multinationals to use IFRS by 2011, this will be an important challenge for the accounting profession. In addition, U.S. public companies will likely have the option of using either IFRS or U.S. GAAP. IFRS requires more use of professional judgment and provides less detailed, principles-based guidance. It focuses on reflecting "economic reality." Many U.S. public companies will face the challenge of converting their books and records and financial reporting obligations to IFRS and may face future litigation issues as a result. In addition, any other litigation issues currently accounted for under U.S. GAAP will translate into IFRS issues.

CHAPTER 50

COST-VOLUME-REVENUE ANALYSIS FOR NONPROFIT ORGANIZATIONS† (NEW)

JAE K. SHIM, PHD
California State University, Long Beach

---

† This entire chapter also appeared in the 2006 Cumulative Supplement to the *Accountants' Handbook*, Tenth Edition.

Managers of nonprofit organizations generally are not skilled in financial matters. They often are preoccupied with welfare objectives and ignore operations efficiency and operating cost controls. There are nine questions that nonprofit financial managers should address in connection with an organization's financial condition and activity:

1. Do we have a profit or a loss?
2. Do we have sufficient reserves?
3. Are we liquid?
4. Do we have strong internal controls?
5. Are we operating efficiently?
6. Are we meeting our budget goals?
7. Are our programs financially healthy?
8. Are we competing successfully?
9. Is our prioritizing of programs and activities reasonable?

By definition, the goal of a nonprofit entity is *not* to earn a profit. Its objective is to render as much suitable service as possible while using the least amount of human and physical services as possible. Ideally, breaking even should be the goal of a nonprofit organization. Breaking even occurs when revenues equal costs. If the nonprofit generates a surplus, it may not receive the same amount from the funding agency as last year. On the other hand, by operating at a deficit, the nonprofit may become insolvent or unable to perform the maximum amount of services. Chances are the nonprofit may not be able to borrow money from the bank as not-for-profit entities often have a weak financial stance. However, one thing is clear—over the long run, nonprofit entities cannot sustain persistent deficits unless they have large reserves. Even with large reserves, a nonprofit may have to operate below potential. This means the benefit of the nonprofit will not be maximized.

This chapter deals with many planning issues surrounding nonprofit organizations. Cost-volume-revenue (CVR) analysis, together with cost behavior information, helps nonprofit managers perform many useful planning analyses. CVR analysis deals with how revenue and costs change with a change in the service level. More specifically, it looks at the effects on revenues from changes in such factors as variable costs, fixed costs, prices, service level, and mix of services offered. By studying the relationships of costs, service volume, and revenue, nonprofit management is better able to cope with many planning decisions.

Break-even analysis, a branch of CVR analysis, determines the break-even service level. The break-even point (the financial crossover point at which revenues exactly match costs) does not show up in financial reports, but nonprofit financial managers find it an extremely useful measurement in numerous ways. It reveals which programs are self-supporting and which are subsidized.

50.1   QUESTIONS ANSWERED BY CVR ANALYSIS

CVR analysis tries to answer four questions:

1. What service level (or which units of service) is required to break even?
2. How would changes in price, variable costs, fixed costs, and service volume affect a surplus?
3. How do changes in program levels and mix affect aggregate surplus/deficit?
4. What alternative break-even strategies are available?

50.2 ANALYSIS OF REVENUES

Revenues for nonprofit entities are typically classified into the following categories:

- Grants from governments
- Grants from private sources
- Cost reimbursements and sales
- Membership dues
- Public contributions received directly or indirectly
- Donations and pledges
- Legacies, bequests, and memorials
- Program fees
- Other revenue, such as investment income (e.g., interest, dividends)

For managerial purposes, however, each type of revenue is grouped into its fixed and variable parts. Fixed revenues are those that remain unchanged regardless of the level of service. Examples are gifts, grants, and contracts. As an example, in a university setting, donations, gifts, and grants have no relationship to the number of students enrolled. In contrast to fixed revenues, variable revenues are the ones that vary in proportion to the volume of activity. Examples include cost reimbursements and membership fees. Continuing the example of a university setting, the total amount of tuition and fees received varies as the number of students enrolled increases or decreases. Different nonprofit entities may have different sources of revenue: variable revenue only, fixed revenue only, or a combination of both. In this chapter, we discuss all three cases in analyzing break-even and CVR applications.

50.3 ANALYSIS OF COST BEHAVIOR

For external reporting purposes, costs are classified by managerial function such as payroll, occupancy, office, and so on, as well as by programs and supporting services. See Exhibit 50.1 for a model functional classification.

For managerial purposes (i.e., planning, control, and decision making), further classification of costs is desirable. One classification is by behavior. Depending on how they react or respond to changes in the level of activity, costs may be viewed as variable or fixed. This classification assumes a known high and low volume of service activity called the *relative range of activity*. The relevant range is the volume zone within which the behavior of variable costs, fixed costs, and prices can be predicted with reasonable accuracy. The relevant range falls between the planned highest and lowest service level for the nonprofit. Within this level of normal activity the behavior of variable costs, fixed costs, and prices can be predicted with reasonable accuracy. Typical activity measures are summarized in Exhibit 50.2.

(a) VARIABLE COSTS   Total variable costs change as the volume or level of activity changes. Examples of variable costs include supplies, hourly wages, printing and publications, and postage and shipping.

(b) FIXED COSTS   Total fixed costs do not change regardless of the volume or level of activity. Examples include property tax, yearly salaries, accounting and consulting fees, and depreciation. Exhibit 50.3 shows the fixed-variable breakdown of IRS Form 990 functional expenses.

IRS Form 990 Line #	Functional Expense Category
26	Salaries and wages
27	Pension plan contributions
28	Other employee benefits
29	Payroll taxes
30	Professional fundraising fees
31	Accounting fees
32	Legal fees
33	Supplies
34	Telephone
35	Postage and shipping
36	Occupancy
37	Equipment rental and maintenance
38	Printing and publications
39	Travel
40	Conferences, conventions, meetings
41	Interest
42	Depreciation, depletion, etc.
43	Other expenses (itemize)

Exhibit 50.1   IRS Form 990 Part II—Statement of Functional Expenses

Nonprofit Types	Units of Service
Hospital or Healthcare	Bed days, patient contact hours, patient days, service hours
Educational	Number of student enrollments, class size, FTE (full-time equivalent) hours
Social Clubs	Number of members served

Exhibit 50.2   Measures of the Service Level

(c) TYPES OF FIXED COSTS: PROGRAM-SPECIFIC OR COMMON   Fixed costs of nonprofit entities are subdivided into two groups: (1) direct or program-specific fixed costs and (2) common costs. Direct or program-specific fixed costs are those that can be directly identified with individual programs. These costs are avoidable or escapable if the program is dropped. Examples include the salaries of those staff members whose services can be used only in a given program and depreciation of equipment used exclusively for the program. Common fixed costs continue even if an individual program has been discontinued. Examples include depreciation of the building and property taxes.

IRS FORM 990 LINE	EXPENSE CATEGORY
Fixed Costs	
26	Salaries and wages (not hourly employees)
27	Pension plan
28	Other benefits
29	Payroll taxes
30	Fund-raising fees
31	Accounting fees
32	Legal fees
36	Occupancy
37	Equipment rental/maintenance
41	Interest
42	Depreciation
43	Other
Variable Costs	
33	Supplies
34	Telephone
35	Postage and shipping
38	Printing and publications
39	Travel
40	Conferences, meetings
43	Other

EXHIBIT 50.3 FIXED-VARIABLE BREAKDOWN OF IRS FORM 990, FUNCTIONAL EXPENSES

50.4 CVR ANALYSIS WITH VARIABLE REVENUE ONLY

For accurate CVR analysis, a distinction must be made between variable costs and fixed costs. In order to compute the break-even point and perform various CVR analyses, the following concepts are important.

(a) CONTRIBUTION MARGIN (CM) The contribution margin is the amount by which total revenue (R) exceeds the variable costs (VC) of the service. It is the amount of money available to cover fixed costs (FC) and to generate surplus. This is symbolically expressed as:

$$CM = R - VC \tag{1}$$

(b) UNIT CM The unit CM is the amount by which the unit price (p) exceeds the unit variable cost (v). This is symbolically expressed as:

$$unit\ CM = p - v$$

(c) CM RATIO The CM ratio is the contribution margin as a percentage of revenue:

$$CM\ ratio = CM/R = (R - VC)/R = 1 - (VC/R) \tag{2}$$

or

$$\text{Unit CM} = (p - v)/p = 1 - (v/p) \tag{3}$$

Note: Once you know the contribution margin ratio, then the variable cost ratio is 1–CM ratio. Similarly, if you know the variable cost ratio (VC/R), the contribution margin ratio is (1–VC ratio).

EXAMPLE 50.1

The Los Altos Community Hospital has the following data. This information will be used to illustrate the various concepts of contribution margin and contribution margin ratio:

Average revenue per day	=	$ 250
Variable costs per patient day	=	$ 50
Total fixed costs	=	$650,000
Expected number of patient days	=	4,000

	Total	Per unit	Percentage
Revenue (4,000 days)	$1,000,000	$250	100%
Less: Variable costs (4,000 days)	200,000	50	20
Contribution margin	$ 800,000	$200	80%
Less: Fixed costs (annual)	650,000		
Net income	$ 150,000		

Note that unit CM = p − v = $250 − $50 = $200 and CM ratio = unit CM/p = $200/$250 = .8 = 80%

50.5   BREAK-EVEN ANALYSIS

The break-even point represents the level of revenue that equals the total of the variable and fixed costs for a given volume of output service at a particular capacity use rate. Other things being equal, the lower the break-even point, the higher the surplus and the less the operating risk. The break-even point also provides nonprofit managers with insights into surplus/deficit planning. To develop the formula for the break-even units of service, we set:

$$R = TC \text{ (total costs)} \tag{4}$$

$$R = VC + FC \tag{5}$$

$$px = vx + FC \tag{6}$$

Solving for x yields the following formula for break-even sales volume:

$$x = \frac{FC}{(p - v)} = \frac{\text{Fixed Costs}}{\text{Unit CM}}$$

or

$$\text{Break-even point in dollars (R)} = \frac{\text{Fixed Costs}}{\text{CM Ratio}}$$

EXAMPLE 50.2

Using the same data given in Example 50.1, the number of break-even patient days and break-even dollars are computed as follows:

Break-even point in units = FC/unit CM = \$650,000/\$200 = 3,250 patient days

Break-even point in dollars = FC/CM Ratio = \$650,000/0.8 = \$812,500

Or, alternatively,

Break-even point in dollars = 3,250 patient days × \$250 revenue per patient
= 3,250 × \$250 = \$812,500

The hospital therefore needs 3,250 patient days or \$812,500 dollars of revenue to break even.

(a) GRAPHICAL APPROACH IN A SPREADSHEET FORMAT The graphical approach to obtaining the break-even point is based on the so-called break-even (B-E) chart as shown in Exhibit 50.4. Revenue, variable costs, and fixed costs are plotted on the vertical axis while service volume, x, is plotted on the horizontal axis. The break-even point is the point where the total revenue line intersects the total cost line. The chart can report surplus potentials over a wide range of activity and therefore can be used as a tool for discussion and presentation.

The surplus-volume (S-V) chart, as shown in Exhibit 50.5, focuses on how surplus varies with changes in volume. Surplus is plotted on the vertical axis while units of output are shown on the horizontal axis. The S-V chart provides a quick condensed comparison of how alternatives related to pricing, variable costs, or fixed costs may affect surplus (or deficit) as volume changes. The S-V chart can be easily constructed from the B-E chart. Note that the slope of the chart is the unit CM.

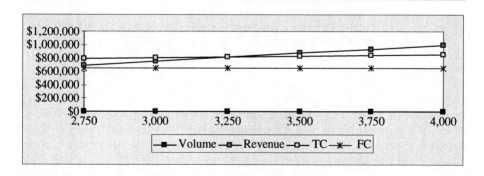

EXHIBIT 50.4 BREAK-EVEN (B-E) CHART—VARIABLE REVENUE

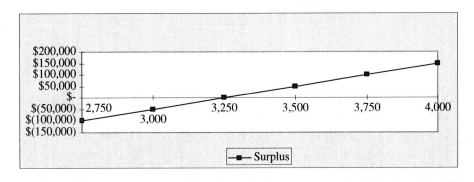

EXHIBIT 50.5 SURPLUS-VOLUME (S-V) CHART—VARIABLE REVENUE

(b) DETERMINATION OF TARGET SURPLUS VOLUME Cost-Volume-Revenue (CVR) analysis can be used to determine the activity levels necessary to attain a target surplus (TS). Once the break-even level of activity has been computed, it is useful to determine the level of activity necessary to create a desired surplus. At the break-even point, all fixed costs have been covered.

Therefore, any additional revenue above the break-even level increases the surplus. To calculate the level of service needed to obtain our target surplus, we only need to expand our break-even formula—that is, expand the numerator of the break-even formula to include the amount of desired surplus in addition to fixed costs. In other words, to achieve our desired increase in surplus, not only fixed costs must be recovered but also the desired increase in surplus.

By expanding the break-even formula to obtain the level of activity for a desired target surplus, the formula becomes:

$$\text{Target income surplus level} = \frac{\text{Fixed Costs} + \text{Target Surplus}}{\text{Unit CM}} \qquad (7)$$

EXAMPLE 50.3
Using the same data given in Example 50.1, assume the hospital wishes to accumulate a surplus of $250,000 per year. Then the target surplus service level would be:

$$\frac{\text{Fixed Costs} + \text{Target Surplus}}{\text{Unit CM}} = \frac{\$650,000 + \$250,000}{\$200} = 4,500 \text{ patient days}$$

(c) MARGIN OF SAFETY The margin of safety is a measure of difference between the actual level of service and the break-even level of service. It is expressed as a percentage of expected service level. The margin of safety determines how far the estimated or expected level of service can decline and have the nonprofit still be profitable.

$$\text{Margin of safety} = \frac{\text{Expected Level} - \text{Break-Even Level}}{\text{Expected Level}}$$

The margin of safety is used as a measure of operating risk. The larger the ratio, the safer the situation since there is less risk of reaching the break-even point.

EXAMPLE 50.4

Assume Los Altos Hospital projects 4,000 patient days with a break-even level of 3,250. The projected margin of safety is:

$$\frac{4,000 - 3,250}{4,000} = 18.75\%$$

This means that the hospital's revenue can drop 18.75% before it suffers a deficit.

EXAMPLE 50.5

A nonprofit college offers a program in management for executives. The program has been experiencing financial difficulties. The dean of the school wants to know how many participants are needed to break even. Operating data for the most recent year are shown as follows.

Tuition per participant	= $ 7,000	
Variable expense per participant	= $ 4,000	
Total fixed expenses	= $150,000	
Tuition revenue (40 participants @$7,000)		$280,000
Less variable expenses (@$4,000)		160,000
Contribution margin		$120,000
Less: Fixed expenses		150,000
Operating deficit		$ (30,000)

The break-even calculation is:

$$\$150,000/(\$7,000 - \$4,000) = 50 \text{ participants}$$

EXAMPLE 50.6

In Example 50.5, the dean of the school is convinced that the class size can be increased to more economic levels without lowering the quality. He is prepared to spend $15,000 per year in additional promotional and other support expenses. The promotional and other support expenses are additional fixed costs. If he spends the $15,000 on promotional expenses, the dean wants to know the new break-even number of participants and how many participants are needed to generate a surplus of $30,000.

If that is the case, the formula to calculate the new break-even point is

$$(\$150,000 + \$15,000)/\$3,000 = 55 \text{ participants to break even}$$

The formula to calculate the number of participants necessary to generate a target surplus of $30,000 is

$$[(\$150,000 + \$15,000) + \$30,000]/\$3,000 = 65 \text{ participants}$$

(d) SOME APPLICATIONS OF CVR ANALYSIS AND WHAT-IF ANALYSIS   The concepts of contribution margin and the contribution income statement have many applications in surplus/deficit planning and short-term decision making. Many "what-if" scenarios can be evaluated using these concepts as planning tools, especially utilizing a spreadsheet program. Some applications are illustrated in Example 50.7 using the same data as in Example 50.1.

EXAMPLE 50.7

Assume that the Los Altos Community Hospital in Example 50.1 expects revenues to go up by $250,000 for the next period. How much will surplus increase?

Using the CM concepts, we can quickly compute the impact of a change in the service level on surplus or deficit. The formula for computing the impact is

Change in surplus = Dollar change in revenue × CM ratio

Thus:

$$\text{Increase in surplus} = \$250,000 \times 80\% = \$200,000$$

Therefore, the income will go up by $200,000, assuming there is no change in fixed costs. If we are given a change in service units (e.g., patient days) instead of dollars, then the formula becomes:

$$\text{Change in surplus} = \text{Change in units} \times \text{Unit CM.}$$

EXAMPLE 50.8

Assume the Los Altos Community Hospital in Example 50.1 expects patient days to go up by 500 units. How much will surplus increase? From Example 50.1, the hospital's unit CM is $200. Again, assuming there is no change in fixed costs, the surplus will increase by $100,000, computed as follows:

$$500 \text{ additional patient days} \times \$200 \text{ CM per day} = \$100,000$$

EXAMPLE 50.9

Referring back to Example 50.5, another alternative under consideration is to hold the present program without any change in the regular campus facilities instead of in rented outside facilities that are better located. If adopted, this proposal will reduce fixed costs by $60,000. The variable costs will decrease by $100 per participant. Is the move to campus facilities advisable if it leads to a decline in the number of participants by 5?

	Present		Proposed
S(40 × $7,000)	$280,000	(35 × $7,000)	245,000
VC(40 × $4,000)	160,000	(35 × $3,900)	136,500
CM	$120,000		$108,500
FC	150,000		90,000
Surplus	$(30,000)		$18,500

The answer is yes, since the move will turn into a surplus.

50.6   CVR ANALYSIS WITH FIXED REVENUE ONLY

In many nonprofit activities, the objectives are not as clear-cut as the objective of profit in commercial business. Furthermore, the relationship between revenue and volume for a nonprofit organization (NPO) is not nearly as well established as is the revenue–volume relationship in business. For example, some NPOs may have only one source of revenue, which is a lump-sum appropriation. This source does not change with changes in volume. Let FR be fixed revenue, or lump-sum appropriation. At break-even,

$$FR = VC + FC$$

$$FR = vx + FC$$

$$x = (FR-FC)\,v$$

$$\text{or break-even units} = \frac{\text{Fixed revenue } - \text{ Fixed costs}}{\text{Unit variable cost}}$$

EXAMPLE 50.10

A social service agency has a government budget appropriation of $750,000. The agency's main mission is to assist handicapped people who are unable to seek or hold jobs. On average, the agency supplements each individual's income by $6,000 annually. The agency's fixed costs are $150,000. The agency CEO wants to know how many people could be served in a given year. The break-even point can be computed as follows:

$$\text{Break-even units} = \frac{\text{Fixed revenue } - \text{ Fixed costs}}{\text{Unit variable cost}} = \frac{750,000 - \$150,000}{\$6,000} = 100$$

The number of people that could be served in a given year is 100.

Exhibits 50.6 and 50.7 display the B-E and S-V charts for this situation.

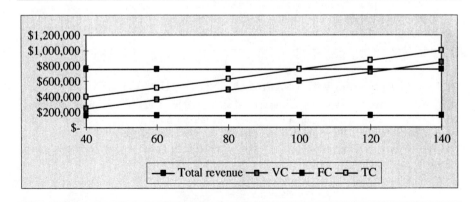

EXHIBIT 50.6   BREAK-EVEN (B-E) CHART—FIXED REVENUE

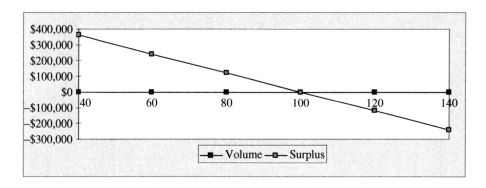

EXHIBIT 50.7   SURPLUS-VOLUME (S-V) CHART—FIXED REVENUE

Nonprofits with a lump-sum appropriation have little incentive to increase their level of service. Doing so would either increase a deficit or reduce a surplus (see Exhibit 50.7). Either of these alternatives more than likely would result in a poorer performance evaluation for the program.

EXAMPLE 50.11

In Example 50.10, assume that the CEO is concerned that the total budget for the year will be reduced by 10 percent to a new amount of 90 percent ($750,000) = $675,000.
The new break-even point is:

$$\text{Break-even units} = \frac{\text{Fixed revenue} - \text{Fixed costs}}{\text{Unit variable cost}} = \frac{\$675,000 - \$150,000}{\$6,000} = 88 \text{ (rounded)}$$

The CEO's options facing budget cuts can be any one or a combination of three ways: (1) cut the service level as computed previously, (2) reduce the variable cost (the supplement per person), and (3) seek to cut down on the total fixed costs.

50.7   CVR ANALYSIS WITH VARIABLE AND FIXED REVENUES

Many NPOs derive two types of revenue: fixed and variable. A lump-sum appropriation may exist to subsidize the activity, and a fee for services may also exist (e.g., state-supported colleges and universities). There are two cases in this situation, however.

Case 1: Lump-sum appropriation is less than total fixed costs; fee for service is greater than unit variable cost of service.

Note that $R = FR + px$

At break-even, $FR + px = vx + FC$, where $FR < FC$ and $p > v$

$$x = \frac{FC - FR}{pv}$$

or break-even units $= \dfrac{\text{Fixed costs} - \text{Fixed revenue}}{\text{Unit CM}}$

Case 2: Lump-sum appropriation is higher than total fixed costs; fee is lower than unit variable cost (subsidized activity) resulting in negative unit CM.

Note that $R = FR + px$

At break-even, $FR + px = vx + FC$, where $FR > FC$ and $p < v$

$$x = \frac{FR - FC}{vp}$$

or break-even units $= \dfrac{\text{Fixed revenue} - \text{Fixed costs}}{-\text{Unit CM}}$

In this situation, the fixed revenue covers more than the actual fixed costs. However, the variable costs for service are already more than the nonprofit can charge. In this scenario the number of units that can be served is limited. There is a heavily subsidized unit with a small fee for service to discourage unnecessary use but still making the service available at low cost. This type of appropriate and unit pricing can be used for essential services such as community health services or mass transit.

EXAMPLE 50.12

ACM, Inc., a mental rehabilitation provider, has the following:

- $1,200,000 lump-sum annual budget appropriation to help rehabilitate mentally ill clients
- Monthly charge per patient for board and care = $600
- Monthly variable cost for rehabilitation activity per patient = $700
- Yearly fixed cost = $800,000

The agency manager wants to know how many clients can be served.

Break-even number of patients $= \dfrac{\text{Fixed revenue} - \text{Fixed costs}}{-\text{Unit CM}} = \dfrac{1,200,000 - \$800,000}{-(\$600 - \$700)}$

$$= \frac{\$400,000}{-(-\$10)} = \frac{\$400,000}{\$100} = 4,000 \text{ per year}$$

The number of patients that can be served is 4,000 per year.

Exhibits 50.8 and 50.9 display the B-E and S-V charts for variable and fixed revenue.

Note that at the level of service greater than B-E service (i.e., 4,000 units), the service is overused or underpriced (or both) (see Exhibit 50.9). We will investigate two "what-if" scenarios.

EXAMPLE 50.13

Using the same data as in Example 50.12, suppose the manager of the agency is concerned that the total budget for the coming year will be cut by 10 percent to a new amount of $1,080,000. All other things remain unchanged. The manager wants to know how this budget cut affects the next year's service level. Using the formula yields

$$\text{Break-even number of patients} = \frac{\text{Fixed revenue} - \text{Fixed costs}}{-\text{Unit CM}} = \frac{\$1,080,000 - \$800,000}{-(\$600 - \$700)}$$

$$= \frac{\$280,000}{-(-\$10)} = 2,800 \text{ Clients per year}$$

The service level will be cut from 4,000 clients to 2,800 clients.

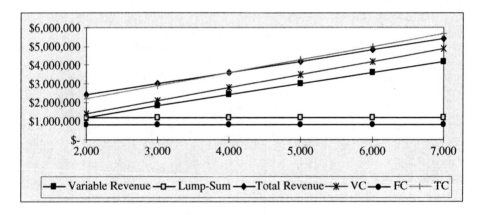

EXHIBIT 50.8 BREAK-EVEN (B-E) CHART—VARIABLE AND FIXED REVENUE (CASE 2)

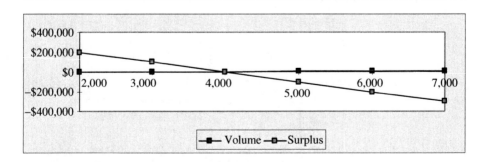

EXHIBIT 50.9 SURPLUS-VOLUME (S-V) CHART—VARIABLE AND FIXED REVENUE (CASE 2)

EXAMPLE 50.14

In Example 50.13, suppose that the manager does not reduce the number of clients served despite a budget cut of 10 percent. All other things remain unchanged. How much more does the manager have to charge clients for board and care?

Let v = board and care charge per year and x = 4,000 = number of clients served.

The following formula can be used to make this determination:

$$R = \$1,080,000 + 4,000p$$

$$VC + FC = \$700(4,000) + \$800,000$$

$$R + VC + FC$$

$$\$1,080,000 + 4,000p = \$700(4,000) + \$800,000$$

$$4,000p = \$2,800,000 + \$800,000 - 1,080,000$$

$$4,000p = \$2,520,000$$

$$p = \$630$$

Thus, the monthly board and care charge must be increased to $630.

50.8 PROGRAM MIX ANALYSIS

Previously, our main concern was to determine program-specific break-even volume. However, most nonprofit organizations are involved in multiservice, multiprogram activities. One major concern is how to plan aggregate break-even volume, surplus, and deficits. Break-even and Cost-Volume-Revenue analysis requires additional computations and assumptions when an organization offers more than one program. In multiprogram organizations, program mix is an important factor in calculating an overall break-even point. Different rates and different variable costs result in different unit CMs. As a result, break-even points and Cost-Volume-Revenue relationships vary with the relative proportions of the programs offered.

By defining the product as a package, the multiprogram problem is converted into a single-program problem. The first step is to determine the number of packages that need to be served to break even. The following example illustrates a multiprogram, multiservice situation.

EXAMPLE 50.15 (SHEET 1 OF 2)

The Cypress Counseling Services is a nonprofit agency offering two programs: psychological counseling (PC) and alcohol addiction control (AAC). The agency charges individual clients an average of $10 per hour of counseling provided under the PC program. The local Chamber of Commerce reimburses the nonprofit organizations at the rate of $20 per hour of direct service provided under the AAC. The nonprofit organization believes that this billing variable rate is low enough to be affordable for most clients and also high enough to derive clients' commitment to the program objectives. Costs of administering the two programs are given as follows:

	PC	AAC
Variable costs	$ 4.6	$ 11.5
Direct fixed costs	$120,000	$180,000

EXAMPLE 50.15 (SHEET 2 OF 2)

Other fixed costs are common to the two programs, including general, administrative, and fundraising costs of $255,100 per year. The projected surplus for the coming year, segmented by programs, follows.

	PC	AAC	TOTAL
Revenue	$500,000	$800,000	$1,300,000
Program mix in hours	(50,000)	(40,000)	
Less: VC	(230,000)	(460,000)	(690,000)
Contribution margin	$270,000	$340,000	$ 610,000
Less: Direct FC	(120,000)	(180,000)	(300,000)
Program margin	$150,000	$160,000	$ 310,000
Less: Common FC			(255,100)
Surplus			$ 54,900

First, based on program-specific data on the rates, the variable costs, and the program mix, we can compute the package (aggregate) value as follows:

PROGRAM	P	V	UNIT CM	MIX*	PACKAGE CM
PC	$10`	$4.6	$5.4	5	$27
AAC	20	11.5	8.5	4	34
Package total					$61

*The mix ratio is 5:4 (50,000 hours for PC and 40,000 hours for AAC).

We know that the total fixed costs for the agency are $555,100. Thus, the package (aggregate) break-even point is:

$$\$555,100/\$61 = 9,100 \text{ packages}$$

The company must provide 45,500 hours of PC (5 × 9,100) and 36,400 hours of AAC (4 × 9,100) to avoid a deficit. To prove,

	PC	AAC	TOTAL
Revenue	$ 455,000(a)	$ 728,000(b)	$1,183,000
Program mix in hours	(45,500)	(36,400)	
Less: VC	(209,300)(c)	(418,600)(d)	(627,900)
Contribution margin	$ 245,700	$ 309,400	$ 555,100
Less: Direct FC	(120,000)	(180,000)	(300,000)
Program margin	$ 125,700	$ 129,400	$ 255,100
Less: Common FC			(255,100)
Surplus			$ 0

(a) 45,500 × $10   (c) 45,500 × $4.60
(b) 36,400 × $20   (d) 36,400 × $11.50

EXAMPLE 50.16

Assume in Example 50.15 that 56,000 hours of PC services are budgeted for the next period. The nonprofit organization wants to know how many hours of AAC services are necessary during that period to avoid an overall deficit. The answer is 29,729 hours, shown as follows:

INPUT DATA	PC	AAC
Rates	$ 10	$ 20
Units of service (Hours)	56,000	29,729
Variable cost per unit	$ 4.6	$ 11.5

CONTRIBUTION STATEMENT OF SURPLUS OR DEFICIT

	PC	AAC	TOTAL
Revenue	$560,000	$594,588	$1,154,588
Less: Variable costs	257,600	341,888	599,488
Contribution margin	$302,400	$252,700	$ 555,100
Less: Direct fixed costs	120,000	180,000	300,000
Program margin	$182,400	$72,700	$ 255,100
Less: Common fixed costs			255,100
Surplus			$ (0)

50.9 MANAGEMENT OPTIONS

Cost-Volume-Revenue analysis is useful as a frame of reference, as a vehicle for expressing overall managerial performance, and as a planning device via break-even techniques and what-if scenarios. Using CVR, many planning decisions, such as adding or dropping a service, outsourcing, answering special requests, and changing budget limits, can be made on a sounder basis.

In many practical situations, management will have to resort to a combination of approaches to reverse a deficit, including

- Selected changes in volume of activity
- Planned savings in fixed costs at all levels
- Some savings in variable costs
- Additional fund drives or grant seeking
- Upward adjustments in pricing
- Cost reimbursement contracts

All of these must be mixed to form a feasible planning package. Many nonprofit managers fail to develop such analytical approaches to the economics of their operations. Further, the accounting system is not designed to provide the information needed to investigate Cost-Volume-Revenue relations.

50.10 REFERENCES AND SUGGESTED READINGS

Shim, Jae K., *Cost Accounting for Managers: A Managerial Emphasis,* 6th ed. (Buena Park, CA: Delta Publishing, 2006).

Siegel, Joel, and Shim, Jae K., *Barron's Accounting Handbook* (New York: Barron's, 2005).

INDEX